American Red Cross

lifeguarding today

Courtney middleton

Important certification information

American Red Cross certificates may be issued upon successful completion of a training program, which uses this textbook as an integral part of the course. By itself, the text material does not constitute comprehensive Red Cross training. In order to issue ARC certificates, your instructor must be authorized by the American Red Cross, and must follow prescribed policies and procedures. Make certain that you have attended a course authorized by the Red Cross. Ask your instructor about receiving American Red Cross certification, or contact your local chapter for more information.

American
Red Cross

lifeguarding today

StayWell

A Times Mirror Company

This participant's manual is an integral part of American Red Cross training. By itself, it does not constitute complete and comprehensive training.

The emergency care procedures outlined in this book reflect the standard of knowledge and accepted emergency practices in the United States at the time this book was published. It is the reader's responsibility to stay informed of changes in the emergency care procedures.

Printed in the United States of America.

Composition by Graphic World, Inc.
Printing/binding by Danner Press

StayWell
263 Summer Street
Boston, MA 02210

Library of Congress Cataloging-in-Publication Data

Lifeguarding today   /   American Red Cross.
     p.   cm.
    Includes bibliographical reference and index.
    ISBN 0-8016-7555-3
    1. Life-saving. 2. Lifeguards—Training of. I. American Red Cross.
GV838.7.L54   1994
797.2'00289—dc20

94-19885
CIP

00   01/12   11   10

ACKNOWLEDGMENTS

This manual was developed and produced through the combined effort of the American Red Cross and the Mosby-Year Book Publishing Company. Without the commitment to excellence of both paid and volunteer staff, this manual could not have been created.

The Health and Safety Program Development team at American Red Cross national headquarters responsible for designing and writing this book included: Lawrence D. Newell, Ed.D. NREMT-P, Manager; Rhonda Starr, Senior Associate; Martha F. Beshers, Bruce Carney, M.A.Ed., Thomas J. S. Edwards, Ph.D., Michael Espino, Marian F.H. Kirk, and Paul Stearns, Associates; Mary F. Baudo, Lori Compton, Michael Giles, Jr., and Patricia Appleford Terrell, Analysts. Administrative support was provided by Erika Miller and Elizabeth A. Taylor.

The following American Red Cross national headquarters Health and Safety paid and volunteer staff provided guidance and review: Ray Cranston, Program Development Volunteer Chairman; Karen D. White, Associate, Operations; and Cathy Brennan, Marketing Specialist.

The Mosby-Year Book Editorial and Production team included: Richard Weimer and Claire Merrick, Executive Editors; Jennifer Roe, John Probst, and Ross Goldberg, Assistant Editors; Colleen Foley, Editorial Assistant; Carol Sullivan Wiseman, Project Manager; Shannon Canty, Senior Production Editor; Kay Kramer, Director of Art & Design; Sheilah Barrett, Designer; Jerry Wood, Director of Manufacturing; Theresa Fuchs, Manufacturing Supervisor; and Patricia Stinecipher, Special Product Manager.

Special thanks go to Tom Lochhaas, ABD, Developmental Editor; Carol Fuchs, M.A., M.P.W., Joseph Matthews, Daniel Cima, Vincent Knaus, Jeanette Ortiz Osorio, Mark Wieland, Nick Caloyianis, and Clarita Berger, Photographers; and Harriet Kastarsis and Associates and Rolin Graphics, Illustrators.

Guidance, writing, and review were also provided by members of the American Red Cross Lifeguard Advisory Group:

Michael C. Giles, Sr.
Advisory Group Chair and Aquatics Director and
    Risk Manager, Recreation Sports
The University of Southern Mississippi
Hattiesburg, Mississippi

Charles Bittenbring
Division Manager, Fairfax County Park Authority
Fairfax, Virginia

Robert L. Burhans, R.S.
Chief Sanitarian, Bureau of Community Sanitation and
    Food Protection
New York State Department of Health
Albany, New York

Molly A. Casey, M.S.
Director, Safety Services
American Red Cross
Metropolitan Atlanta Chapter
Atlanta, Georgia

Gerald DeMers, Ph.D.
Associate Professor and Director, Aquatic Program
Physical Education and Kinesiology Department
California Polytechnic State University
San Luis Obispo, California

Julie J. Good
Leisure Service Department
University of New Mexico
Albuquerque, New Mexico

Jerry Huey
Field Representative, Health and Safety Services
American Red Cross
Southeastern Michigan Chapter
Detroit, Michigan

Charles Kunsman, M.S.Ed.
Aquatic Manager, Ocasek Natatorium
University of Akron
Akron, Ohio

James P. Morgan
Director of Parks and Recreation
City of Lincoln
Lincoln, Nebraska

Frank Pia
Former Chief Lifeguard
Orchard Beach
Bronx, New York
Former Supervising Chief Lifeguard
Bronx, New York

Judith Sperling
Manager and Aquatics Director
Department of Cultural and Recreational Affairs
University of California Los Angeles
Los Angeles, California

Margaret Sweeney-Fedders
Assistant Director of Safety
American Red Cross
Dayton Area Chapter
Dayton, Ohio

Kim Tyson
Aquatic Safety Lecturer
Department of Kinesiology
University of Texas
Austin, Texas

Thomas C. Werts
Recreation Specialist
Walt Disney World, Co.
Orlando, Florida

External review was provided by the following individuals:

Reginald W. Clarke
Professor of Human Services
Northern Virginia Community College
Alexandria, Virginia

Susan T. Dempf, Ph.D.
Assistant Professor of Physical Education
Canisius College
Buffalo, New York

Tom Griffiths, Ed.D.
Director of Aquatics
The Pennsylvania State University
University Park, Pennsylvania

Susan J. Grosse, M.S.
Teacher, Milwaukee Public Schools and
    Chair, Aquatic Council AAHPERD
Milwaukee, Wisconsin

Kevin Hannigan
Deputy Sheriff
Los Angeles County
    Sheriff's Department
Los Angeles, California

Harriet J. Helmer
Aquatic Consultant
Sun Mountain Enterprises
Golden, Colorado

John E. Hendrickson
Director, Safety and Health
American Red Cross Mid-America Chapter
Chicago, Illinois

Mike Higginbotham
Camp Counselors USA
Palo Alto, California

Shannon Hokkanen
Recreation Specialist
Oklahoma City Department of Parks and Recreation
Oklahoma City, Oklahoma

Newton Jackson
Department of Physical Education
Howard University
Washington, DC

Ron Morrow
Director of Physical Education
Davidson College
Davidson, North Carolina

James S. O'Connor, M.S.
Aquatics Coordinator
Dade County Parks and Recreation Department
Miami, Florida

Fontaine Piper, Ph.D.
Director and Associate Professor
Biomechanics/Motor Learning Laboratory
Northeast Missouri State University
Kirksville, Missouri

Larry Pizzi
Operations Supervisor
City of Miami Beach Lifeguards
Miami Beach, Florida

William A. Rich
Aquatics Director
Milander Pool
City of Hialeah, Florida

Daniel R. Ruth
Associate Director
Boy Scouts of America
Irving, Texas

Ann Hood Weiser, M.S., M.F.A.
Coordinator of Aquatics Instruction
University of North Carolina
Greensboro, North Carolina

SPECIAL ACKNOWLEDGMENTS

The American Red Cross would like to thank the following individuals and facilities who provided talent and locations for much of the photography in this book:

Gary Adelhardt
Sandy Point State Park
Annapolis, MD

Ashburn Village Sports Pavillion
Ashburn, Virginia

Thomas A. Bates
Prince William County Park Authority
Prince William, Virginia

Melissa Johnson and Jean Skinner
Fairfax County Park Authority
South Run Recreation Center
Fairfax, Virginia

Janis Carley
Cape Coral Yacht Club
Sun Splash Family Waterpark
Cape Coral, Florida

Dean Cerdan
Lee County Public Parks and Recreation
Cypress Lakes
Fort Myers, Florida

Dale and Barbara Dohner
Camp Oneka
Wayne, Pennsylvania

Gerry Dworkin
Lifesaving Resources, Inc.

Pat Harrison Waterway District
Flint Creek
Wiggins, Mississippi

Scot Hunsaker
Councilman, Hunsaker & Associates
St. Louis, Missouri

Gary Peterson
Belle Isle Beach
Detroit Park and Recreation
Detroit, Michigan

Yvonne Schoonover
Osbourn Park High School
Manassas, Virginia

Sterling Volunteer Rescue Squad
Sterling, Virginia

Acknowledgments

Steve Wyatt
Rolling Hills Water Park
Ypsilanti, Michigan

AAA Ambulance Service
Hattiesburg, Mississippi

Baltimore County Parks and Recreation
Oregan Ridge Lake
Baltimore, Maryland

Fritz Cheek
Camp Copneconic
Fenton, Michigan

Concord Mews Pool
Arlington, Virginia

Greenbrier State Park
Greenbrier Lake
Boonsboro, Maryland

Gunpowder Falls State Park
Hammerman Area
Gunpowder River
Baltimore, Maryland

Hetherlea Pool
Arlington, Virginia

Metro Dade County Parks and Recreation
Miami, Florida

Peps Point
Hattiesburg, Mississippi

Reston Association and Park Recreation
Reston, Virgina

The University of Southern Mississippi
M.C. Johnson Natatorium, Recreational Sports, a Division of
    Student Affairs
Hattiesburg, Mississippi

Virginia Department of Conservation and Recreation
Lake Anna State Park
Spotsylvania, Virginia

Walt Disney World
Orlando, Florida

Washington DC Department of Recreation
Washington, DC

American Red Cross chapters that participated in the
pilot test of skills include:

San Luis Obispo County Chapter
San Luis Obispo, California

American Red Cross of Massachusetts Bay
Somerville, Massachusetts

Southeastern Michigan Chapter
Bloomfield Hills, Michigan

Mid-Rio Grande Chapter
Albuquerque, New Mexico

Prince William County Chapter
Manassas, Virginia

PREFACE

"A moment of truth provides one with the only true test of human character. It is associated with a life-threatening event when the line between life and death becomes blurred and the outcome is unknown."

Fifty-four percent of the population across the nation enjoys swimming as a leisure activity, and total participation exceeds all other popular activities such as walking for pleasure, cycling, golf, tennis, and boating. Since swimming is one of the top participation sports across the country and because there is an ever-increasing number of aquatic facilities being built to meet the demand, lifeguarding responsibilities have undergone extensive changes.

In spite of the efforts made by the many American Red Cross instructors, lifeguards, volunteers, and sponsors of water safety programs, drownings and near-drownings do occur. Aquatic injuries can happen at any time or place for a number of reasons. Because situations like these occur, it is essential that lifeguards receive proper training.

Lifeguards must be able to recognize hazardous situations to prevent injury. They must be able to supervise swimmers, minimize dangers, educate facility users about safety, enforce rules and regulations, give assistance, and prepare records and reports. The position of the lifeguard today has become one of greater responsibility than in the past.

In the 1990s, lifeguards have a host of new challenges: infectious diseases, medical waste, increased skin cancer risk, crowd control, and environmental issues. Increased levels of education, training, and preventive measures are all used by today's professionals to meet these problems. This evolution is indicative of the increasingly important role lifeguards play in their communities. Rather than remaining static, lifeguards have expanded their horizons to successfully meet these challenges. The lifeguard's interaction with many other elements of society has elevated the prestige of the profession while allowing lifeguards to use their training and skills to prevent drownings and lessen the frequency and severity of injuries.

CONTENTS

Contents

HEALTH PRECAUTIONS AND GUIDELINES DURING TRAINING

The American Red Cross has trained millions of people in first aid and CPR (cardiopulmonary resuscitation) using manikins as training aids. According to the Centers for Disease Control (CDC), there has never been a documented case of any disease caused by bacteria, a fungus, or a virus transmitted through the use of training aids such as manikins used for CPR.

The Red Cross follows widely accepted guidelines for cleaning and decontaminating training manikins. **If these guidelines are adhered to, the risk of any kind of disease transmission during training is extremely low.**

To help minimize the risk of disease transmission, you should follow some basic health precautions and guidelines while participating in training. You should take precautions if you have a condition that would increase your risk or other participants' risk of exposure to infections. Request a separate training manikin if you—

• Have an acute condition, such as a cold a sore throat, or cuts or sores on the hands or around your mouth.

• Know you are seropositive (have had a positive blood test) for hepatitis B surface antigen (HBsAg), indicating that you are currently infected with the hepatitis B virus.*

• Know you have a chronic infection indicated by long-term seropositivity (long-term positive blood tests) for the hepatitis B surface antigen (HBsAg)* or a positive blood test for anti-HIV (that is, a positive test for antibodies to HIV, the virus that causes many severe infections including AIDS).

  *A person with hepatitis B infection will test positive for the hepatitis B surface antigen (HBsAg). Most persons infected with hepatitis B will get better within a period of time. However, some hepatitis B infections will become chronic and will linger for much longer. These persons will continue to test positive for HBsAg. Their decision to participate in CPR training should be guided by their physician.

  After a person has had an acute hepatitis B infection, he or she will no longer test positive for the surface antigen but will test positive for the hepatitis B antibody (anti-HBs). Persons who have been vaccinated for hepatitis B will also test positive for the hepatitis antibody. A positive test for the hepatitis B antibody (anti-HBs) should not be confused with a positive test for the hepatitis B surface antigen (HBsAg).

• Have a type of condition that makes you unusually likely to get an infection.

If you decide you should have your own manikin, ask your instructor if he or she can provide one for you to use. You will not be asked to explain why in your request. The manikin will not be used by anyone else until it has been cleaned according to the recommended end-of-class decontamination procedures. Because the number of manikins available for class use is limited, the more advance notice you give, the more likely it is that you can be provided a separate manikin.

You can further protect yourself and other participants from infection during CPR training by following these guidelines:

• Wash your hands thoroughly before participating in class activities.

• Do not eat, drink, use tobacco products, or chew gum during class when manikins are used.

• Clean the manikin properly before use. For some manikins, this means vigorously wiping the manikin's face and the inside of its mouth with a clean gauze pad soaked with either a solution of liquid chlorine bleach and water (sodium hypochlorite and water) or rubbing alcohol. For other manikins, it means changing the rubber face. Your instructor will provide you with instructions for cleaning the type of manikin used in your class.

• Follow the guidelines provided by your instructor when practicing skills such as clearing a blocked airway with your finger.

PHYSICAL STRESS AND INJURY

Training in lifeguarding requires physical activity. If you have a medical condition or disability that will prevent you from taking part in the practice sessions, please let your instructor know. Certain rescue skills pose the possibility of physical stress or injury. Always follow your instructor's directions and take the following precautions when performing rescue skills:

- When performing skills that require you to lift, lift with your legs, not with your back.
- Some rescue skills require you to hold your breath during a rescue. If you run out of air during a simulated underwater rescue, return to the surface. During simulated rescues, you and your partner will use predetermined signals to advise each other of any problems.
- Whether you are acting as the victim or the rescuer, do not hyperventilate before submerging. Doing so could cause you to lose consciousness.
- If you are acting as a rescuer, be especially careful to support the victim's head when the victim is being removed from the water.

HOW TO USE THIS TEXTBOOK

TEXTBOOK

This textbook has been designed to help you learn and understand the material it presents. It includes the following features:

Objectives

At the beginning of each chapter is a list of objectives. Read these objectives carefully and refer back to them from time to time as you read the chapter. The objectives describe what you should know and be able to do after reading the chapter and participating in class activities.

Key terms

At the beginning of each chapter is a list of defined key terms that you need to know to understand chapter content. Some key terms are listed in more than one chapter because they are essential to your understanding of the material presented in each. In the chapter, key terms are printed in bold italics the first time they are defined or explained.

Sidebars

Feature articles called sidebars enhance the information in the main body of the text. They appear in most chapters. They present a variety of material ranging from historical information and accounts of actual events to everyday application of the information presented in the main body of the text. You will not be tested on any information presented in these sidebars as part of the American Red Cross course completion requirements.

Skill summaries

Skill summaries in certain chapters provide you with step-by-step directions for performing specific skills described in the chapter. The major steps of each skill are illustrated.

Study questions

Study questions appear at the end of each chapter. They are designed to help you understand and remember the material you have read in the chapter. Answering these questions will help you evaluate your progress and prepare for the final written examination. Answer them after you have read the chapter. Many of the multiple choice questions have more than one correct answer. Discuss any questions with which you have difficulty with your instructor.

Appendixes

Appendixes, located at the end of this textbook, provide additional information on topics lifeguards will find useful.

Glossary

The glossary includes definitions of all the key terms and of other words in the text that may be unfamiliar. All glossary terms appear in the textbook in bold type the first time they are used or explained.

HOW TO USE THIS TEXTBOOK

You should complete the following three steps for each chapter to gain the most from this course:

1. Read the chapter objectives before reading the chapter.
2. As you read the chapter, keep the objectives in mind. When you finish, go back and review the objectives. Check to see that you can meet them without difficulty.
3. Answer the study questions after you have read the chapter.

1 THE PROFESSIONAL LIFEGUARD

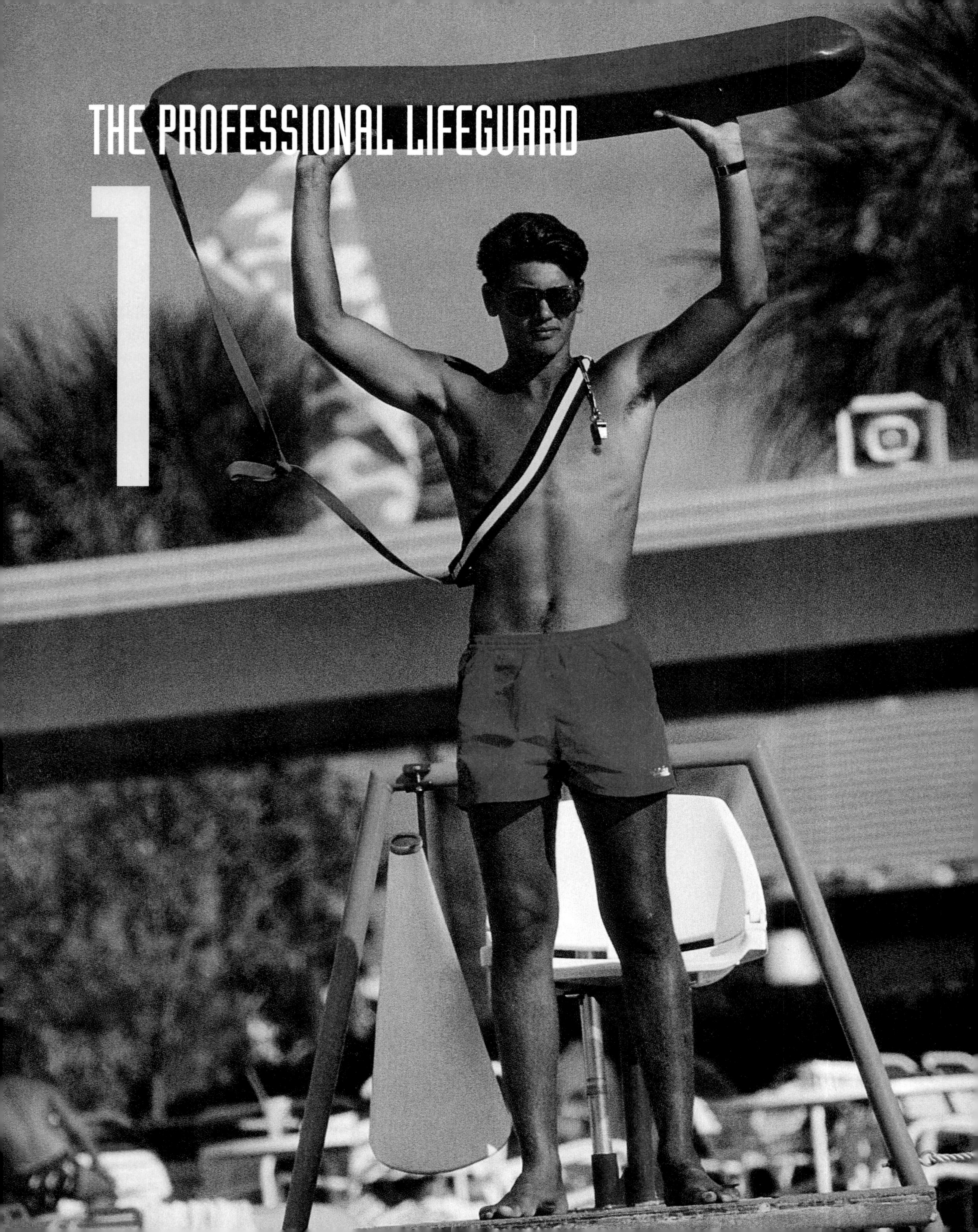

Objectives

After reading this chapter, you should be able to—

1. List six characteristics of a professional lifeguard.
2. List six benefits of regular exercise.
3. List three reasons why a professional lifeguard's appearance and behavior are important.
4. List five primary responsibilities of a professional lifeguard.
5. List four secondary responsibilities of a professional lifeguard.
6. Describe six legal considerations that shape the role of the professional lifeguard.
7. Explain the importance of ongoing professional development for lifeguards.
8. Describe five benefits of being a professional lifeguard.
9. Define the key terms for this chapter.

Key Terms

Incident: An occurrence or event that interrupts normal procedure or brings about a crisis.

In-service training: Regularly scheduled staff meetings and practice sessions that cover lifeguarding information and skills.

Lifeguard competitions: Events and contests designed to evaluate the skills and knowledge of individual lifeguards and teams of lifeguards.

Professional rescuers: Paid or volunteer personnel, including lifeguards, who have a legal duty to act in an emergency.

Surveillance: A close watch kept over someone or something, such as a patron or a facility.

INTRODUCTION

You are beginning your training for one of today's best jobs (Fig. 1-1). Being a lifeguard is—

- Dynamic—Each day on the job may present new situations.
- Challenging—Doing your job well requires split-second judgment.
- Exciting—You may respond at any moment to an emergency.
- Important—Your knowledge, skills, and attitude can save a life.

This chapter discusses how to *be, look,* and *stay* professional as a lifeguard. It highlights the characteristics of a lifeguard and the importance of staying fit and healthy. It also describes the responsibilities of a lifeguard and the importance of keeping your knowledge and skills sharp. Finally, this chapter discusses the rewards of being a professional lifeguard.

figure 1-1 *Lifeguard training begins with class time.*

History of Lifesaving and Lifeguarding

The American Red Cross became involved in lifeguarding largely due to the work of one person, Commodore Wilbert E. Longfellow. At the turn of the century, the Commodore was one of the first people to see that the rapidly mounting death toll from drowning, unless curbed, would assume the proportions of a national tragedy. He saw the need for a nationwide program of swimming and lifesaving instruction.

In 1914, the Commodore established the volunteer-based Life Saving Service of the American Red Cross. At that time, his primary objective involved "waterproofing America" by establishing local volunteer lifesaving corps to teach swimming, supervise bathing areas, and raise awareness of the need for water safety education. Longfellow's dedication and charisma led to an increase in the popularity of aquatic activities and a significant decline in the national drowning rate.

Historically, lifesaving courses emphasized personal safety: how to prevent accidents and protect oneself in emergencies. Nonswimming rescues were the rule; the rescuer was taught to make a swimming rescue only as a last resort. However, the development of the American Red Cross Lifeguard Training program in 1983 represented a philosophical departure from lifesaving programs of the past. The emphasis of the program moved beyond the realm of personal safety, requiring the lifeguard to place primary concern on the safety of others.

The American Red Cross Lifeguard Training program was developed in response to the growing need for professional lifeguards. Today, the American Red Cross trains more than 140,000 lifeguards annually and sets the standards that lead the field of lifeguarding.

History of Lifesaving and Lifeguarding—cont'd

Here are some highlights from the history of lifesaving and lifeguarding:

1785   Massachusetts Human Society founded the Lifesaving Service

1878   Secretary of Treasury formed the United States Lifesaving Service

1897   First rescue float equipment developed by Captain Harry Sheffield

1908   British Lifesaving Service established in Ontario, Canada

1911   Boy Scouts of America (BSA) established Swimming and Lifesaving Merit Badges

1912   George E. Goss completed the first systematic study of lifesaving in the United States

1912   Young Men's Christian Association (YMCA) developed the National Lifesaving Service

1914   Commodore Longfellow established the Life Saving Service of the American Red Cross

1914   American Red Cross developed the Senior Life Saving program

1919   American Red Cross developed the Junior Life Saving program

1938   BSA developed the Safe Swim Defense Plan

1938   BSA established the National Aquatic School Lifeguard program

1951   Council for National Cooperation in Aquatics formed

1966   National Surf Lifesaving Association formed

1973   American Alliance for Health, Physical Education, Recreation and Dance established the Aquatics Council

1974   American Red Cross developed the Advanced Lifesaving program

1979   United States Lifesaving Association formed

1979   YMCA developed the Aquatic Safety and Lifesaving program

1980   World Waterpark Association formed

1983   American Red Cross established the Lifeguard Training program

1983   Ellis & Associates established the National Pool & Waterpark Lifeguard Training program

1988   American Red Cross developed the Lifeguarding course

1988   National Recreation and Park Association established the National Aquatic Section

1990 and 1994   American Red Cross revised the Lifeguard Training program

Since the days of Commodore Longfellow, statistics indicate a dramatic decrease in the number of deaths caused by drowning.* This can be traced to the efforts of many individuals, agencies, and organizations.

Over the decades, lifeguarding roles, responsibilities, and environments have become more demanding and complex. As a result, organizations like the American Red Cross have trained lifeguards to an ever-increasing level of preparedness and professionalism. With ongoing cooperation, the field of lifeguarding can continue to evolve and more injuries and deaths can be prevented.

* Number of drownings per 100,000 in the United States (National Safety Council)

1914—10.4

1947—5.2

1991—1.8

Continued.

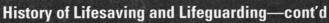

History of Lifesaving and Lifeguarding—cont'd

Commodore Wilbert E. Longfellow demonstrates rescue techniques.

First Red Cross Life Saving Corps station, built in 1914 in Pablo Beach, Florida.

Olympic swimming great Duke Kahanamoku and Commodore Longfellow (second and third from right) are shown when the Commodore introduced Red Cross lifesaving methods to the Hawaiian islands in 1920.

Red Cross Women's Lifesaving Corps, Jacksonville, Florida, 1920.

CHARACTERISTICS OF A PROFESSIONAL LIFEGUARD

Being a professional lifeguard means more than just getting a paycheck. Professionalism means being mentally and physically prepared to do your very best at all times. It means you bring commitment and competence to your job every day.

Lifeguard professionalism begins with training and certification. Your knowledge and skills are probably the most obvious requirements for any lifeguarding job. Being an effective lifeguard also involves certain physical, mental, and emotional characteristics (Fig. 1-2). These characteristics follow in Figure 1-2 and on page 6.

Commodore Longfellow teaching swimming and lifesaving techniques.

Navy's flying swimmers learn Red Cross lifesaving techniques at Pensacola Station, Florida, 1936.

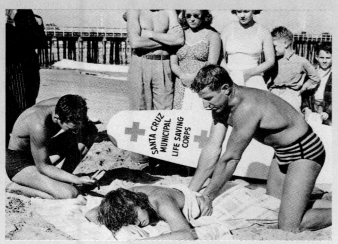

Members of the Lifesaving Corps in Santa Cruz, California make a rescue, 1941.

figure 1-2 Characteristics of a professional lifeguard.

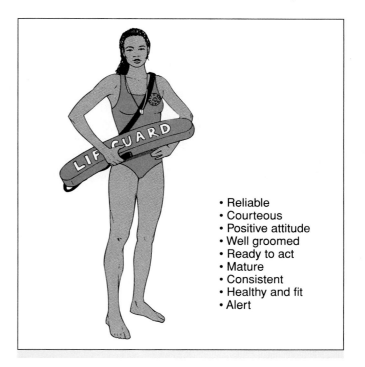

- Reliable
- Courteous
- Positive attitude
- Well groomed
- Ready to act
- Mature
- Consistent
- Healthy and fit
- Alert

Sample Job Description for a Lifeguard

Job Title: Lifeguard (entry level)

Job Description:
Responsible for ensuring the safety of the facility patrons by preventing and responding to emergencies

Minimum Qualifications:
Current certification in the following:
- American Red Cross Lifeguard Training
- American Red Cross Community First Aid and Safety
- American Red Cross CPR for the Professional Rescuer

Knowledge and Skills:
- Thorough knowledge and application of lifeguarding surveillance and rescue techniques
- An understanding of facility policies, procedures, and rules
- Leadership qualities and public relations skills

Responsibilities:
- Enforces all aquatic facility policies, rules, and regulations
- Recognizes and responds effectively to emergencies
- Inspects the aquatic facility on a daily schedule and reports unsafe conditions and equipment to supervisor
- Completes records and reports
- Participates in in-service training
- Completes additional duties as assigned by supervisor

Responsible To:
Head lifeguard, pool manager, or aquatics director

Reliability

When you are reliable, others know they can depend on you for assistance and care. Both your co-workers and the public need to feel they can trust and depend on you. You show that you are reliable by arriving to work on time, accepting assignments willingly, and responding to all *incidents* promptly and effectively. (An incident is an occurrence or event that interrupts normal procedure or brings about a crisis.)

Maturity

As a lifeguard, you have an important leadership role. You need maturity to take initiative, be resourceful, and take your job seriously. The mature lifeguard stays calm and makes good decisions—in both everyday tasks and emergencies.

Courtesy and consistency

Courtesy means being kind and polite to everyone. Consistency means that you enforce rules firmly and uniformly. Courtesy and consistency help you gain the respect and cooperation of patrons and staff.

Positive attitude

Your attitude significantly affects your job. With a positive attitude, you can enjoy your job more and be more successful in the facility. You can let others see your positive attitude through everyday actions, such as cooperating with co-workers and treating patrons with respect. The best thing about a positive attitude is that it is contagious!

Health and fitness

In an emergency, a lifeguard often responds with a burst of strenuous activity. Staying healthy and physically fit is part of being a professional because it helps ensure that you have the attentiveness, strength, and stamina to prevent and respond to emergencies. The flexibility and endurance that come with being in good physical condition can help you perform rescues with minimal personal danger. Being healthy and fit also improves your overall well being. You simply feel better. Here are some guidelines on staying healthy and fit.

Exercise. Regular exercise improves your ability to—

- Respond quickly to any situation.
- Perform even the most strenuous rescues.
- Stay alert.
- Cope with stress and fatigue.
- Stay healthy.
- Feel good.

There are many ways to stay fit (Figs. 1-3 and 1-4). Your supervisor may require fitness training as part of your job. If your facility does not have a fitness program, you can help develop one that is right for you. Talk to a health professional before you start a fitness program so that he or she can work with you to create a plan based on your current fitness level. The Cooper 12-Minute Swimming Test (see page 8) is a good way to evaluate your present fitness level.

The American Red Cross offers two resources to help you develop a personal fitness program: *Aqua Fitness* and *Swimming and Diving*. Both resources provide basic health and fitness information, as well as guidelines to help you design personalized workouts.

Rest. Being rested when you come to work helps you stay focused and alert. This usually means sleeping 6 to 8 hours every night, depending on the individual. Caffeine can give you a temporary lift, but it can't take the place of sleep.

Nutrition. A **balanced diet** helps provide the energy a lifeguard needs to stay alert and active. Check with a health professional to make sure you are getting all the **nutrients** you need to stay healthy and fit.

Drinking plenty of water or other fluids also helps you stay at a level for peak performance. Try to drink at least eight glasses of non-alcoholic, non-caffeinated beverages each day (Fig. 1-5). You need this much fluid to prevent **dehydration,** which can be caused by exposure to sun, wind, and high temperatures. Even indoors, temperatures higher than normal can drain your body of fluid and nutrients.

Sun protection. Lifeguards at outdoor facilities risk health problems caused by too much exposure to the sun. You must understand the effects of sun exposure and how to protect yourself from them.

figure 1-3 *Dry-land training may be part of a fitness program.*

figure 1-4 *In-water training may be part of a fitness program.*

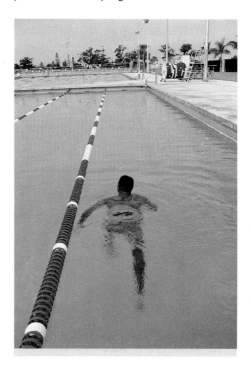

Cooper 12-Minute Swimming Test

The 12-minute swimming test, devised by Kenneth Cooper, M.D., is an easy, inexpensive way for men and women of all ages to test their aerobic capacity (oxygen consumption) and to chart their fitness program.

The test encourages the swimmer to cover the greatest distance possible in 12 minutes, using whatever stroke is preferred, resting as necessary, but doing the best he or she can. For instance, a woman between the ages of 30 and 39 is in excellent condition if she can swim 550 yards or more in the 12 minutes allowed for the test. However, a woman of the same age would be considered in very poor condition if she could not swim at least 250 yards in the same amount of time.

The easiest way to take the test is to swim in a pool with known dimensions, and it helps to have someone there to record the number of laps and the time.

Care must be taken with the 12-minute test, however. It is not recommended for anyone over 35 years of age, unless he or she has already developed good aerobic capacity. The best way to determine this, of course, is to see a physician.

Fitness Category		(Age years)					
		13-19	20-29	30-39	40-49	50-59	<60
I. Very Poor	(men)	<500[1]	<400	<350	<300	<250	<250
	(women)	<400	<300	<250	<200	<150	<150
II. Poor	(men)	500-599	400-499	350-449	300-399	250-349	250-299
	(women)	400-499	300-399	250-349	200-299	150-249	150-199
III. Fair	(men)	600-699	500-599	450-549	400-449	350-449	300-399
	(women)	500-599	400-499	350-449	300-399	250-349	200-299
IV. Good	(men)	700-799	600-699	550-649	500-599	450-549	400-499
	(women)	600-699	500-599	450-549	400-499	350-449	300-399
V. Excellent	(men)	>800	>700	>650	>600	>550	>500
	(women)	>700	>600	>550	>500	>450	>400

[1] < Means less than; > means more than.

From Cooper KH: *The Aerobics Program for Total Well-being,* New York, 1982, Bantam Books.

figure 1-5 *Drink plenty of water to prevent dehydration*

figure 1-6 *Protect yourself from the sun.*

Overexposure to the sun can cause many problems—from sunburns to **sun poisoning**, **heat stroke, heat exhaustion**, and even skin cancer. Your tolerance to the sun depends on many factors, such as length of exposure, skin type, family health history, and the use of certain medications. Always ask your doctor about the effects of any medications he or she may prescribe for you. Even your facility's **geographic location** and altitude can affect your tolerance to the sun.

Lifeguards must limit their exposure to the sun to stay healthy and do their job well (Fig. 1-6). You may reduce the harmful effects of the sun by using a sunscreen with a **sun protection factor (SPF)** of at least 15 or by wearing protective clothing, such as a t-shirt and hat. Some facilities have sun umbrellas on the lifeguard stands. Remember also to wear sunglasses that reduce glare and protect your eyes from **ultraviolet light.** You can be a more effective, healthy, and comfortable lifeguard if you protect yourself from sun overexposure.

Alcohol and other drugs. Using alcohol or other drugs on the job is a serious offense and can affect your job performance. Using them off duty also can affect your job performance. Even a small amount of alcohol consumed can remain in your body for hours, making you sluggish and keeping you from doing your best.

Alcohol and other depressants slow down your body and your mind in many ways. They dull your senses and your skills. They affect your mental abilities such as perception and judgment, making it difficult for you to recognize that someone needs help and decide how to respond appropriately. They affect your **motor function,** making it hard to react to situations quickly and effectively. They even affect your mood and your **metabolism.** As your mind and body slow down, your mood drops and it is more difficult to get the proper nutrients from the food you eat. This puts you at greater risk for **burnout** and illness.

Being professional means being willing and able to do your best while on the job. On- and off-duty use of alcohol or other drugs can prevent you from giving 100 percent.

Appearance and behavior

It is important to show your professionalism to others through your appearance and behavior. Looking professional and behaving professionally promote a safe atmosphere at your facility by—

- Helping patrons, co-workers, and facility managers have confidence in you and thus feel safe.
- Reinforcing rules and setting the tone for proper behavior.
- Reinforcing your attitude of professionalism.

As a lifeguard, you show your professionalism much more by how you look and act every day than by responding to emergencies. The image you project reflects your attitude and training. It also reflects on your facility. Looking the part of a true professional assures others, both patrons and supervisors, that you have what it takes to do your job (Fig. 1-7).

Because you are a professional lifeguard, people look up to you. Here are some guidelines to help you look the part:

- *Wear your uniform only during your lifeguarding shift*. While in uniform, you are a representative of the facility. As such, patrons and facility management hold you accountable for looking and acting professional. Your facility may have guidelines for wearing your uniform—if so, follow them. As a general rule, it is probably best not to wear your uniform if you visit the facility on your day off. If you stay at the facility beyond your shift, you may also want to change out of your uniform.
- *Keep yourself well groomed.* Report to work looking fresh and sharp. Make sure that your uniform is clean and neat; if it looks worn or faded, get a new one. Wear your hair in a style that does not obscure your vision in or out of the water. Do not wear any jewelry that could interfere when performing a rescue.

figure 1-7 *Maintain a professional image.*

- *Always keep your rescue equipment with you, positioned for an immediate response* (Fig. 1-8). Keep your tube strapped to you, and wear your whistle so that it is readily available.
- *Keep essential personal gear on or near you at all times.* This may include sunglasses, sunscreen, a water bottle, and a cap or visor.
- *Sit or stand erect at your lifeguarding station.* Sitting up straight and facing forward helps keep you alert and allows the best **surveillance**. Surveillance involves keeping a close watch over patrons and the facility.
- *Keep interactions with others short.* If you must talk to patrons or to other staff members during patron surveillance, be brief and direct. This applies whenever you are on duty.
- *Keep your eyes on your area of responsibility at all times.* Maintain constant surveillance of the patrons in your area. Conduct rotations efficiently without any break in surveillance. You may look away from your **area of responsibility** only if another lifeguard says he or she is scanning your area.
- *Transfer equipment carefully.* Make sure that tow ropes and straps from rescue tubes do not become tangled in stands or other equipment. Never toss equipment to another staff member. This can appear unprofessional and may also damage equipment or injure someone.
- *Observe all facility rules and policies.* This is important even when you are off duty. Since patrons look up to you, you must set a good example for them.

- *Eat only when on break or off duty.* Eating on duty is unprofessional because it may distract you from proper surveillance, hinder communication, or prevent you from responding quickly in an emergency. Eating on duty may also soil your uniform and equipment and violate health department regulations.

RESPONSIBILITIES OF A PROFESSIONAL LIFEGUARD

Being a professional lifeguard involves more than good health and a great attitude. You also need to fulfill your responsibilities. These responsibilities are summarized below and described in more detail in coming chapters.

Your primary responsibilities involve ensuring patrons' safety and protecting lives—including your own. These primary responsibilities include—

- Preventing injuries by minimizing or eliminating hazardous situations or behaviors (Fig. 1-9).
- Enforcing all facility rules and regulations (Fig. 1-10).
- Recognizing and responding effectively in all emergencies (Fig. 1-11).
- Administering first aid or CPR in an emergency (Fig. 1-12).
- Informing other lifeguards and facility staff when more help or equipment is needed.

figure 1-8 *Be ready to respond immediately.*

figure 1-9 *Be alert to hazardous situations or behaviors.*

figure 1-10 *Enforce all rules and regulations.*

figure 1-11 *Recognize and respond to emergencies.*

Your other responsibilities have to do with the everyday operations of the facility. They may involve patron relations or completing paperwork. These are called secondary responsibilities. Secondary responsibilities must never prevent you from meeting your primary responsibilities. For example, never let talking to a patron distract you from your surveillance responsibility. Secondary responsibilities include—

* Educating patrons about rules and regulations.
* Helping patrons locate a missing person.
* Completing required records and reports on schedule and submitting them to the proper person or office.
* Doing maintenance or other tasks assigned by your supervisor. (Note that some duties, such as overseeing pool chemistry, require training beyond this lifeguarding course.)

Remember: Perform secondary responsibilities only when you are not responsible for surveillance of patrons.

Legal considerations

As a lifeguard, you are considered a ***professional rescuer.*** This means that on the job you are legally obligated, within the bounds of your training, to respond to and provide care in an emergency. The legal considerations that shape your role and responsibilities as a professional rescuer follow on page 12.

figure 1-12 *Provide emergency care as needed.*

- **Duty to Act**—While on the job, a lifeguard has a legal responsibility to act in the event of an emergency. For example, you have a duty to rescue a patron who is drowning or in distress.

- **Standard of Care**—As a lifeguard, you are expected to meet a certain minimum standard of care, which may be set by state or local authorities. This standard requires you to provide proper warnings to patrons to help prevent injuries, recognize a person in an emergency situation, rescue that person, and give the care you have been trained to give.

- **Negligence**—If you do not follow the standard of care and someone is injured, you may be considered guilty of negligence. This includes failing to provide care, trying to give care beyond your training, or providing incorrect care. As a lifeguard, you may be found negligent if you are inattentive and fail to notice a person who is drowning or in distress, fail to rescue a person who is drowning or in distress, or fail to control horseplay or actions by patrons that cause an incident to occur.

- **Good Samaritan Laws**—Most states have enacted Good Samaritan Laws to protect people who provide emergency care. These laws, which differ from state to state, may protect you from legal liability as long as you act in good faith, are not negligent, and act within the scope of your training. Good Samaritan laws, however, may not protect people with a legal duty to respond.

- **Consent**—You have to obtain the consent of a conscious victim before you provide care. If the person is unable to give consent for some reason and is in obvious need of emergency care, the law assumes this person would grant consent if able to do so. For example, you do not need consent to rescue someone who is drowning. However, a conscious victim on the deck, who is able to speak, can refuse your offer of care.

- **Refusal of Care**—Some ill or injured people, even those who desperately need care, may refuse the care you offer. Even though the person may be seriously injured, you should honor his or her refusal of care. Try to convince the person of the need for care, but do not argue. If the person still refuses, have a witness hear the person's refusal and document it.

- **Abandonment**—Once you begin providing care, you should continue your care until Emergency Medical Services (EMS) personnel arrive and take over. You can be held legally responsible for the abandonment of a person in need if you leave the scene. You have a legal duty to continue care until someone with experience equal to or greater than yours takes over.

- **Confidentiality**—While making a rescue or providing care, you may learn things about the ill or injured person that are generally considered private and confidential. You must respect the person's privacy by maintaining confidentiality. Never discuss the person or the care you gave with anyone except law enforcement personnel or other personnel caring for the victim.

- **Record Keeping**—Documenting injuries and incidents is very important. Your record can help advanced health care professionals better assess the condition of an injured or ill person. If legal action occurs, a record can also provide legal documentation to support what you saw, heard, and did at the scene of the incident. It is important to complete the record as soon as possible after the incident, while all the facts are fresh in your memory. Many aquatic facilities have forms to record specific kinds of incidents.

STAYING PROFESSIONAL

Receiving your American Red Cross Lifeguarding certificate means that you have successfully completed the required course material and passed written and skill tests. This does not necessarily mean that you will retain your knowledge and skills for the certification period. In addition, it does not mean that you have learned everything there is to know about lifeguarding. Being a professional requires ongoing effort. You must stay dedicated to meet future challenges.

You can keep and improve your lifeguarding competency in many ways. Attend workshops, join aquatic associations, read literature and periodicals, and talk with other lifeguards about their ideas.

Lifeguard competitions provide another way to keep skills sharp and stay in shape (Fig. 1-13). *Lifeguard competitions* feature events and contests designed to evaluate the skills and knowledge of individual lifeguards and teams of lifeguards. Events may include relay races, rescue and resuscitation drills, and spinal injury management procedures. Lifeguard competitions are becoming increasingly popular because they are fun, exciting, and measure professional skills.

One of the best ways to stay current in your skills and knowledge and stay in peak physical form is in-service training (Fig. 1-14). *In-service training* involves regularly scheduled staff meetings and practice sessions that cover lifeguarding information and skills. Many facilities conduct in-service training. If your facility offers these sessions, take advantage of them. If your facility does not offer such training, ask the facility manager about other options. For example, if you work at a single-guard facility, you may be able to participate in this type of training at another facility. (See Chapter 3 for more information about in-service training.)

You can also enhance your professionalism by taking additional courses. The American Red Cross offers options such as the Head Lifeguard course and the Lifeguarding Instructor course. Such training enhances your skills and knowledge, improves your self-confidence, and increases your opportunities for employment.

BENEFITS OF BEING A PROFESSIONAL LIFEGUARD

As a professional lifeguard, you shoulder much responsibility. But you experience many benefits as well, including—

- Knowing your actions can save a life.
- Earning the respect and appreciation of peers, patrons, and the public.
- Gaining a sense of pride by accepting challenges and meeting your goals and the facility's standards.
- Gaining discipline and decision-making skills that will help prepare you for your future.

Effective lifeguarding requires commitment and constant effort, but the benefits you receive will exceed the efforts you expend.

figure 1-13 *Lifeguard competitions are becoming increasingly popular.*

Chris Moler/White Water Bay

figure 1-14 *In-service training helps you do your best.*

SUMMARY

Being a professional lifeguard means being fully prepared for this challenging and important work. *Looking* professional lets others know that you are prepared to do the job. *Staying* professional requires practice and commitment.

Preparing for lifeguarding responsibilities is what this course is all about. Throughout your training, remember that no one is born a lifeguard; it takes hard work. With practice and dedication, you can meet the challenges and gain the rewards of being a professional lifeguard.

STUDY QUESTIONS

Circle the letter of the best answer or answers.

1. The most important function of a professional lifeguard is to—
   a) Perform as many tasks as possible.
   b) Engage in public relations for the facility.
   c) Keep the facility clean.
   d) Protect lives.
2. A lifeguard's primary responsibilities include—
   a) Preventing injuries by minimizing or eliminating hazardous situations or behaviors.
   b) Administering first aid and CPR in an emergency.
   c) Recognizing and responding quickly and effectively to all emergency situations.
   d) Helping patrons locate a missing person.
   e) Enforcing all rules and regulations of the facility.
   f) Informing other lifeguards and facility staff when more help and/or equipment is needed.
3. A lifeguard's secondary responsibilities include—
   a) Completing all required records and reports on schedule and submitting them to the proper person or office.
   b) Educating patrons about rules and regulations.
   c) Conducting surveillance.
   d) Doing maintenance and recreational duties assigned by the supervisor.
4. The characteristics of a professional lifeguard include—
   a) Reliability.
   b) Maturity.
   c) A sense of humor.
   d) Courtesy and consistency.
   e) Positive attitude.
5. Some of the benefits of maintaining your own health and physical fitness include—
   a) Improving your job performance.
   b) Being happier and more relaxed.
   c) Being able to stay up late at night yet still be rested in the morning.
   d) Increased strength and stamina.
6. Regular exercise helps keep you and your lifeguarding skills sharp by providing—
   a) Enhanced flexibility and endurance.
   b) Reduced resistance to illness.
   c) Greater ability to cope with stress and fatigue.
   d) Improved alertness and response time.
7. Getting plenty of rest each night before work helps keep you focused, alert, and prepared. The suggested range of hours of sleep per night is ___.
   a) 5 to 6.
   b) 6 to 7.
   c) 6 to 8.
   d) 8 to 9.
8. To perform at your peak, it is best to drink at least _____ glasses of non-alcoholic, non-caffeinated beverages per day.
   a) 3
   b) 4
   c) 8
   d) 10
9. Overexposure to the sun can cause—
   a) Heat stroke.
   b) High blood pressure.
   c) Heat exhaustion.
   d) Dehydration.
10. You can reduce the harmful effects of the sun's ultraviolet rays by—
    a) Using a sunscreen with an SPF of at least 30.
    b) Wearing a t-shirt or hat.
    c) Using a detachable umbrella at the lifeguard stand.
    d) Wearing sunglasses.
    e) Using a sunscreen with an SPF of at least 15.
11. The side effects of drinking alcohol or using other depressants include—
    a) Slowed reaction time.
    b) Improved decision-making ability.
    c) Improved mood.
    d) Reduced perception.
    e) Improved ability to obtain nutrients from food.

12. Looking professional helps promote an atmosphere of safety at your facility by—
    a) Instilling confidence in patrons, co-workers, and facility manager.
    b) Reinforcing facility rules by setting the tone for proper behavior.
    c) Reinforcing your attitude of professionalism.
    d) Impressing others with your flair.

13. You can maintain and upgrade your competency in lifeguarding by—
    a) Attending workshops, joining an aquatic association, or reading related literature and periodicals.
    b) Participating in in-service training.
    c) Participating in lifeguard competitions.
    d) Discussing successful techniques with other lifeguards while conducting surveillance.
    e) Taking additional courses or modules.

14. If a lifeguard fails to provide care, tries to provide care beyond the scope of his or her training, or provides incorrect care, he or she may be—
    a) Breaking confidentiality.
    b) Breaking Good Samaritan laws.
    c) Abandoning.
    d) Negligent.
    e) Failing to obtain consent.

Circle *True* or *False*.

15. Drinking alcohol while on the job is a serious offense, but drinking while off duty will not affect your job performance. True or False?

16. Once you have received your American Red Cross Lifeguarding certificate, you will retain your knowledge and skills for the duration of your certification and will have learned everything there is to know about lifeguarding. True or False?

See answers to study questions on p. 286.

2

Objectives

After reading this chapter, you should be able to—

1. Describe four steps for responding to patrons' inquiries.
2. Describe seven steps for handling patrons' suggestions or concerns.
3. Describe what to do when a patron is uncooperative.
4. Describe four ways to help prevent or prepare for a violent situation.
5. List two aspects of cultural behavior relevant to lifeguarding situations.
6. List three general categories of disabilities.
7. Describe four ways to accommodate patrons with disabilities.
8. Define the key terms for this chapter.

Key Terms

Accommodations: Arrangements to help people with disabilities participate in programs and activities.

Cultural diversity: Differences among groups of people related to cultural background and exemplified through customs, beliefs, and practices.

Disability: The loss, absence, or impairment of motor, sensory, or mental function.

Hearing impairment: Partial or total loss of hearing.

Mainstreaming: Including people with disabilities in the same programs and activities as the non-disabled.

Tactile impairment: Partial or total loss of the sense of touch.

Vandalism: An act of violence used to damage an object or a place.

Violence: Physical force used to harm a person or damage an object.

Vision impairment: Partial or total loss of sight.

INTRODUCTION

P eople visit aquatic facilities for many reasons. They may come to take swimming lessons, to stay fit, to compete in aquatics, or just to have fun (Fig. 2-1). They may come with family members or an organized group like a swim team. They may come alone or with friends. They may be of different ages, races, and cultures. They will have a wide range of abilities. Regardless of these differences, every patron has the right to expect safety at the facility—that is your first goal. You can also help their experience to be enjoyable.

As discussed in Chapter 1, your primary task as a professional lifeguard is to ensure the safety of patrons at your facility. In the course of a day, you supervise patrons, enforce rules, and check the facility to reduce the possibility of injury. You may also answer questions, listen to complaints and suggestions, and assist someone who needs help. Remember that courtesy and consistency help make your efforts more effective. In an emergency, patrons are more likely to follow your directions and help out if you have established an atmosphere of cooperation and mutual respect.

This chapter contains general guidelines for interacting with patrons in different situations. Facility management probably has expectations about how you should treat patrons, as well as specific policies and procedures you should follow as a representative of the facility. You can learn about these guidelines during orientation training (see Chapter 3). Although this chapter emphasizes being kind and courteous to patrons, remember your first concern must always be their safety (Fig. 2-2).

RESPONDING TO INQUIRIES

B e careful to never be distracted from your surveillance by talking to patrons. Sometimes, a patron will ask you a question or need a rule explained. You do need to be responsive to these patrons. How you respond, however, depends on your duties at the time.

If you are not conducting surveillance, give the patron your full attention. Listen carefully. Be polite and make eye contact while speaking, removing your sunglasses if you are wearing them (Fig. 2-3). Speak clearly and directly. Before finishing, ask if there is anything else you can do for him or her. This kind of courtesy shows your professionalism.

figure 2-1 *Many facilities host multiple activities.*

figure 2-2 *Safety is always a lifeguard's first priority.*

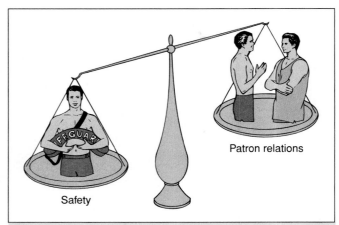

Patron relations

Safety

When you are involved in direct surveillance, you interact with patrons differently (Fig. 2-4). Nothing should prevent you from scanning your area of responsibility (see Chapter 5). Here are some tips to help you respond to patrons without interrupting your surveillance:

1 Continue to scan your area of responsibility.

2 Acknowledge the patron. Explain quickly that you cannot look at him or her while talking but that you are listening to the question.

3 Politely answer the patron, keeping the response brief. In most cases, this means only a few seconds.

4 If the patron needs more help, direct him or her to the facility manager, the head lifeguard, or a staff member on break.

As a lifeguard, you must know your facility's rules and regulations and be able to explain them to patrons (Fig. 2-5). For example, a patron says, "I lost my watch. Is there a lost-and-found area?" You answer, "Yes. Please enter the room behind me. Someone there can help you." Always be patient. By answering promptly and politely, you help create and maintain a safe, orderly, and respectful atmosphere.

figure 2-4 *While involved in surveillance, continue scanning while speaking to a patron.*

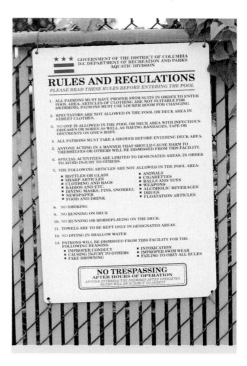

figure 2-5 *Know the rules and regulations that apply to the facility.*

figure 2-3 *Make eye contact with patrons when not involved in surveillance.*

HANDLING SUGGESTIONS AND CONCERNS

In addition to questions, patrons may also have criticisms, suggestions, or concerns. Your facility may have a specific system for accepting them, such as a "suggestion box." If this type of system is not in place at your facility, you can accept suggestions, criticisms, and concerns in person. Accept them in a positive and appreciative manner. A patron might give you an idea for preventing a possible incident or injury or improving the facility or its services. Handle it this way *if you are not involved in surveillance:*

1 **Listen attentively, without interrupting.**

2 **Repeat the patron's suggestion or concern back to him or her to let the person know you understand.**

3 **Thank the patron for bringing the matter to your attention.**

4 **If the concern alerts you to a dangerous situation, such as a broken ladder, try to remedy it or keep patrons from that area until a repair is made.**

5 **If you cannot remedy the situation, notify the head lifeguard or facility manager.**

6 **Document the suggestion or concern as soon as possible, using your facility's procedures (some facilities have a log book for this purpose).**

7 **If necessary, ask someone on staff to follow up with the patron to let him or her know what is being done.**

If you are on surveillance duty and the patron's concern does not involve a dangerous situation, direct the person to the facility manager or to a staff member not on surveillance.

ADDRESSING UNCOOPERATIVE PATRONS

You interact often with patrons when enforcing rules. (Chapter 4 discusses how to enforce rules effectively and courteously.) No matter how fair and consistent you are when enforcing rules, you may occasionally encounter an uncooperative patron. Before you assume a patron is uncooperative, ensure that he or she can hear and understand you. Communication may fail because of a disability or difference in language. If so, be patient and try to ease the situation. Ways to improve communication are discussed later in this chapter.

Uncooperative behavior may occur for a variety of reasons and can take many forms: patrons may allow their fun to get out of hand, they may be under the influence of alcohol or other drugs, or a conflict between two or more patrons may prevent them from paying attention to the rules. Regardless of the cause or form of the uncooperative behavior, you must take action right away, because patrons who break rules endanger themselves and other patrons.

Your facility may have specific procedures for addressing uncooperative patrons. If so, follow them. If not, it is best to contact the head lifeguard or facility manager for help as soon as possible. In many facilities, you get the attention of other staff members by blowing two short blasts on your whistle.

DEALING WITH VIOLENCE

Violent acts have become more prevalent at aquatic facilities in recent years. *Violence* occurs when physical force is used to harm a person or damage an object or a place. Violence used to damage an object or a place is commonly known as *vandalism.* If you find that your facility has been vandalized, notify your supervisor immediately.

A violent act may be committed with a weapon, such as a knife or a gun; an object, such as a bottle or a stick; or a body part, such as a fist or a foot. Violence may never occur at your facility, but it is best to be prepared.

As with other kinds of emergencies, prevention is one of the best approaches toward the possibility of violence. If you establish an atmosphere of order and safety

Intervention Strategies

Sometimes a situation is not violent but involves a patron or patrons who are more agitated or argumentative than uncooperative. There is always a chance that such a situation could become violent. However, the way you handle it may help calm the people involved. Here are some general techniques for reducing a stressful situation—

- *Stay calm yourself.* This not only helps calm the person but also helps keep others present from becoming agitated or frightened.
- *Be mindful of your own nonverbal messages.* Avoid threatening stances or gestures. Keep your hands open, and don't make sudden moves. Give the person enough space. Stay close enough to communicate but far enough away to avoid danger (6 feet is a general suggestion). Be careful about your facial expressions. Avoid frowning or looking angry.
- *Be direct and reassuring toward the person.* Call the person by name if possible. To find out what he or she wants or needs, ask questions that require more than a "yes" or "no" answer. Tell the person you want to help. Be open minded about what he or she says. Answer in a calm, direct tone. Avoid raising your voice. Sometimes a soothing voice can stop or diffuse a situation.
- *Listen carefully.* Pay attention to every word. Try to help the person express what is bothering him or her. Express what the person is saying in your own words; don't just repeat the patron's words. Try to identify the "real problem," but don't give advice. Often a person can work through his or her emotions just by talking about the problem with someone who cares.
- *Pay attention to "feeling words,"* such as "I'm hurt" or "I'm angry." Listen for words that indicate what the person is feeling, then deal with the emotion.
- *Use these suggestions on how to communicate effectively:*
  1. Face the person.
  2. Maintain eye contact without staring.
  3. Hold conversation without physical barriers.
  4. Let the person talk.
  5. Provide verbal assurance that you're listening, but do not interrupt.
  6. Respect the person's need for occasional silence.

If, however, the patron seems beyond reason or becomes increasingly agitated, call for assistance. Never try to handle a situation that is beyond your control.

If two or more people are arguing, tell them to stop and, if necessary, ask them to move to different areas of the facility. Do not try to separate them physically. If your verbal warning does not stop the problem, call for assistance from the head lifeguard or facility manager immediately. Avoid becoming involved in the argument in any way. Do not attempt to resolve differences or find solutions.

Handling situations that involve a person's emotions can be puzzling, draining, and distressing. Part of the problem is that strong feelings are often stirred up in us during an interaction. However, if you remain on duty, you can't afford to let those feelings prevent you from doing your job. You may find it easier to handle your feelings if you try to put the situation in context. Don't take anything personally when you are working with patrons, because the person is talking to you the lifeguard, not you the individual.

at your facility, you can reduce chances that a violent incident will occur. Here are some tips to help prevent and be prepared for a violent situation:

- *Make sure everyone is aware of facility rules.* Rules should be posted where everyone can see them. Know why rules exist, and explain them to patrons if necessary.
- *Establish your authority at the facility.* Your behavior helps set a tone of safety. Look and act professional at all times. Be alert and enforce rules fairly and uniformly—particularly those concerning horseplay and disorderly behavior. If you put an end to dangerous behavior quickly and effectively, it tends not to escalate into violence.
- *Know your patrons.* It is easier to provide a safe facility if you have established a positive rapport with patrons. Patrons who follow the rules can help reinforce safe behavior in others.
- *Have a plan.* Your facility should have emergency procedures to deal with violent incidents. Be familiar with those procedures, and practice them regularly.

figure 2-6 *Violence is becoming more prevalent at aquatic facilities.*

Dealing with violence effectively is a complex issue. It takes training beyond this course to be able to assess the threat of violence and respond effectively. As a lifeguard, you must be realistic about what *you* can do in a violent or potentially violent situation. *If you suspect that a violent incident is about to happen,* notify the head lifeguard or facility manager immediately. *If a violent situation does erupt,* do not try to intervene. Avoid confronting a violent person physically or verbally. Above all, *NEVER* approach a patron who has a weapon. Retreat and follow your facility's emergency procedures for addressing violence.

When addressing violence, the most important point to remember is that safety must continue to be your main concern—the safety of patrons, as well as your own safety (Fig. 2-6).

WORKING WITH DIVERSE CULTURES

Our country began with people from different backgrounds and cultures. Today, most communities have a mixture of cultures. You will probably interact with people from a variety of cultures in your facility.

Cultural diversity refers to differences among groups of people relating to cultural background. Cultural differences may be seen or unseen. They may be exemplified through customs, beliefs, and practices. Cultural diversity can involve behaviors related to any of these characteristics:

- Age
- Gender
- Race
- Religion or spirituality
- Sexual orientation

As a representative of your facility, you should try to make every patron feel welcome. As a professional lifeguard, you have a duty to act fairly and effectively to maintain the safety of all patrons.

Although cultural diversity may lead to differences in patrons' appearance and behavior, culture does not come into play when a person is in distress or drowning. In these situations, the person shows instinctive, universal behaviors (see Chapter 5). During your surveillance, you should look for these specific behaviors rather than personal or cultural characteristics of patrons.

While cultural factors are not related to the risk of drowning, they may account for differences in dress or communication. Different cultures have different standards for what is appropriate to wear in various situations. Patrons may prefer to swim in more or less clothing. Some patrons may wear a turban or headpiece at all times. Most facilities have rules about acceptable swimming attire, but you must also be flexible and accepting of differences. Your supervisor can let you know what types of clothing are allowed in the pool.

Language use is another area affected by cultural background. Some patrons may not know enough English to read or understand facility rules posted only in English. If many patrons at your facility speak a language other than English, talk to your supervisor about posting rules in different languages or using signs with pictures or symbols. Some facilities employ lifeguards who speak languages besides English.

ACCOMMODATING PATRONS WITH DISABILITIES

Swimming is a popular recreation and exercise for many segments of the population. People with disabilities also enjoy and benefit from aquatic activities. Participation is becoming easier with the emphasis in recent years on *mainstreaming*—including people with disabilities in the same programs and activities as the non-disabled.

A loss, absence, or impairment of motor, sensory, or mental function is called a *disability.* The U.S. Department of Health and Human Services estimates that over 36 million people in the United States have disabilities. The law requires that people with disabilities have access to a wide variety of opportunities and services. For example, the **Americans With Disabilities Act (ADA)** guarantees people with disabilities access to all public facilities, including those for aquatic recreation and therapy.

Making aquatic facilities safer and more accessible for people with disabilities may require you and your facility to make special arrangements, or *accommodations.* Accommodations may include policies, procedures, and programs. The facility may have features to accommodate patrons with disabilities, such as ramps,

handrails, devices to get patrons in and out of the water, and more spacious locker rooms and rest rooms. Learning about these features and how to operate special equipment should be part of your orientation and in-service training.

In addition, you may accommodate patrons with disabilities by adapting your rescue skills, using special communication techniques, and adjusting patron surveillance as needed. For example, accommodation for a hearing-impaired person could include providing a sign language interpreter.

When interacting with patrons with disabilities, remember they are as diverse as other patrons. Their abilities in the water may be equal or superior to those of people without a disability. Some patrons with disabilities may need special accommodations; others may not. Do not base the supervision you give to disabled patrons on physical or mental characteristics alone.

The following discussion focuses on three general categories of disabilities: **sensory function, mental function,** and **motor function.** Patrons may be disabled in one or more of these areas. Consider what you need to do to ensure a safe aquatic experience for all patrons. With some adjustments and accommodations, you and fellow staff members can make your facility safe and enjoyable for everyone.

Sensory function

Sensory functions include hearing, sight, and touch, and any of these may be impaired. These impairments may cause communication difficulties, balance problems, or lack of the sensation of touch and pain. These differences can affect an individual's safety in and around the water, how he or she behaves in and around the water, and how the person communicates. A person with one sense impaired often tends to compensate by using other senses more.

Hearing impairment. *Hearing impairment* is a partial or total loss of hearing. People with hearing impairments rely more on visual communication (Fig. 2-7). They may wear hearing aids but cannot do so in the water. If the patron reads lips, you must speak clearly and look directly at him or her when speaking.

If a patron with a hearing impairment cannot hear emergency signals, you must alert him or her by signaling visually with hands, rescue equipment, lights, or flags. When enforcing rules, you may need the help of other lifeguards or patrons to get the attention of a hearing impaired patron who is some distance away from you. Some hearing impaired patrons may come to the pool with an interpreter or aide. Take advantage of this resource.

A person with a hearing impairment may also have trouble with balance or coordination. This may require the person to adapt how he or she swims and walks.

Vision impairment. *Vision impairment* is a partial or total loss of sight. A person with a vision impairment may have difficulty reading signs and markings, identifying lifeguards, and seeing changes in elevation, such as steps. He or she may compensate with greater use of hearing and touch.

Your facility might have tape-recorded rules for patrons with a vision impairment who cannot read a sign. Some facilities also use **sound targets,** directional devices that use sound to indicate water depth, exits, and location of emergency equipment.

A patron with partial vision may wish to wear glasses in the pool (Fig. 2-8). It is best to use glasses made of plastic with an elastic strap to keep them in place. Do not let anyone wearing glasses dive into the water.

If you must rescue a visually impaired patron, calling out that help is on the way may help reassure him or her.

Tactile impairment. *Tactile impairment* is a partial or total loss of the sense of touch. A lack of sensation should not keep anyone out of the water. However, since people with tactile impairment might not feel scratches, abrasions, or burns, they must take special care to avoid scraping their skin in the pool or on the deck and excessive exposure to the sun. If necessary, let these patrons wear footwear or additional protective clothing into the pool (Fig. 2-9).

figure 2-8 *Some patrons may have to wear glasses in the water.*

figure 2-7 *Some patrons rely on visual communication.*

Mental function

Mental functions include intelligence and the capacity to reason and process information. People with mental function impairments may learn more slowly than others. They may have trouble understanding and remembering rules. This does not mean they are being difficult or uncooperative. Be patient, and keep your explanations short and simple. Repeat yourself if necessary. Signs with pictures or symbols can be helpful for communicating with patrons with impaired mental function.

Most individuals with impairments in intelligence or information processing can participate in regular aquatic programs and environments. Some patrons may have difficulty following directions, following safety procedures, interacting with others, or dealing with reality. They may require close attention from instructors and aides. Let your supervisor know if you think additional lifeguard coverage is necessary.

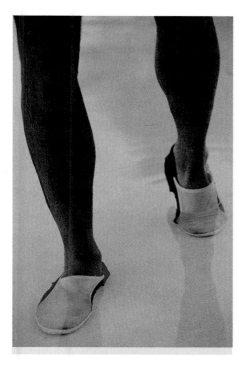

figure 2-9 *Some patrons may have to wear protective footwear in the water.*

Finally, individuals with impaired mental function may also have limited motor function and balance.

Motor function

Motor function depends on the brain's ability to direct physical activity. If a person cannot use a body part because of impaired or lost function, motor function is impaired.

Motor function can be impaired as a result of **paralysis, cerebral palsy, muscular dystrophy, multiple sclerosis,** or loss of a limb. Although individuals with these conditions may have problems with balance and have a restricted range of joint motion, they can often move well in the water. Swimming can be an important recreational and therapeutic activity.

Individuals with missing or non-functioning limbs adapt their swimming strokes to compensate. To the untrained eye, a patron with an adapted stroke may seem to be having difficulty in the water. As a lifeguard, you must distinguish swimming **adaptations** from signs of distress or drowning. As you become familiar with disabled patrons who come to your facility, you will recognize the swimming strokes they use and better recognize signs of difficulty in the water.

You may have to modify your rescue techniques for patrons with motor function impairment. If, for example, a patron has missing or non-functioning arms, you would not extend the rescue tube to him or her to grasp. Instead, grasp the victim with the tube between you.

SUMMARY

Patrons come to your facility primarily for enjoyment. Your main concern, however, is always their safety, which is necessary for their enjoyment. In your interactions with patrons, always be positive and courteous to everyone. As well, be sensitive to cultural diversity, and treat people with disabilities like non-disabled patrons, providing accommodations as needed. By treating everyone with respect, you support your primary goal of providing for their safety.

STUDY QUESTIONS

Circle the letter of the best answer or answers.

1. Lifeguards are expected to maintain positive relations with patrons when—
   a) Enforcing the rules.
   b) Answering questions.
   c) Listening to their concerns.
   d) Accepting criticism and suggestions.

2. To ensure the safety of facility patrons, a lifeguard must—
   a) Communicate with and respond to patrons effectively.
   b) Work with, and anticipate the needs of, a wide variety of patrons.
   c) Speak the same languages the patrons speak.
   d) Base surveillance on cultural characteristics.

3. When a patron asks you a question or needs a rule clarified and you are not occupied with direct surveillance, you should—
   a) Make eye contact while speaking, even if you must remove your sunglasses temporarily.
   b) Begin scanning your area of responsibility.
   c) Be clear and thorough in responding to their needs.
   d) Ask if there is anything else you can do for them.

4. When a patron asks you a question or needs clarification of a rule and you are engaged in surveillance, you should—
   a) Devote your full attention to the patron.
   b) Explain quickly that you cannot look at him or her while talking.
   c) Continue to scan your area of responsibility.
   d) If necessary, refer the patron to a staff member who is not engaged in surveillance.

5. When dealing with an uncooperative patron, you should—
   a) Assume he or she can hear and understand you.
   b) Call for assistance from your supervisor, as necessary.
   c) Let the person know how irritated you are.
   d) Follow your facility's procedures.

6. To help prevent or prepare for a violent situation, you should—
   a) Make sure everyone is aware of facility rules.
   b) Establish your own authority at the facility.
   c) Know your patrons.
   d) Feel confident that you can handle the situation without help.
   e) Have a plan.

7. The loss, absence, or impairment of motor, sensory, or mental function is called a—
   a) Limitation.
   b) Disability.
   c) Challenge.

8. People with sensory function impairments include individuals with _____ limitations.
   a) Physical
   b) Hearing
   c) Mental
   d) Tactile
   e) Vision

9. It may be necessary to allow patrons with a _____ impairment to wear clothing or footwear into the pool.
   a) Mental
   b) Hearing
   c) Tactile

10. Number the following tips for handling a patron's suggestions or concerns in the correct order:

_____ Try to remedy the situation or, if necessary, keep patrons away from a dangerous area.

_____ Listen attentively, without interruption.

_____ If necessary, follow up with the patron to let him or her know the status of the issue.

_____ Thank the patron for bringing the concern to your attention.

_____ Document the suggestion or concern as soon as possible.

_____ Repeat the patron's suggestion or concern back to him or her to make sure you understand.

_____ If you cannot remedy the situation, notify the head lifeguard or facility manager.

Circle *True* or *False*.

11. You must enforce rules fairly and consistently, although you can give special treatment to friends and family members. True or False?

12. To conduct effective surveillance of patrons from diverse cultures, it is important that you pay attention to their swim wear. True or False?

See answers to study questions on p. 286.

3

YOUR PLACE IN FACILITY OPERATIONS

Objectives

After reading this chapter, you should be able to—

1. Describe the people who may be on a safety team.
2. List two ways in which a bystander can help in an emergency.
3. List two benefits of being part of a safety team.
4. Describe five responsibilities of management for ensuring the safety of everyone at a facility.
5. Explain the importance of three regulations that affect facility operations.
6. List three ways in which management can support lifeguards' professional development.
7. Define the key terms for this chapter.

Key Terms

Bloodborne Pathogens Standard: A federal regulation designed to protect employees from exposure to bodily fluids that might contain a disease-causing agent.

Bystanders: People at the scene of an emergency who do not have a duty to provide care.

Chain of command: The structure of employee and management positions in a facility or organization.

Civil rights: Rights that belong to a person simply because he or she is a member of the general public.

Emergency medical services (EMS) system: A network of community resources and medical personnel that provides emergency care to victims of injury or sudden illness.

Hazard Communication Standard: A federal regulation designed to protect employees from exposure to hazardous substances in the workplace.

Head lifeguard: A lifeguard who has a supervisory position in a facility's chain of command.

In-service training: Regularly scheduled staff meetings and practice sessions that cover lifeguarding information and skills.

Pathogen: A disease-causing agent; also called a microorganism or germ.

Policies and procedures manual: A manual that provides detailed information about the daily and emergency operations of a facility.

Safety team: A network of people who can respond and assist in an emergency.

INTRODUCTION

While you are lifeguarding at a facility, you focus on patrons and their activities. During that time, you are not concerned with other tasks and responsibilities. For patrons, the lifeguard may be the only visible sign of the facility's protective system. Nonetheless, a much larger structure surrounds and supports you in your professional lifeguarding.

In this chapter, you will learn about this structure, beginning with the network of people who can assist you in an emergency. The chapter then describes management's responsibilities to ensure the safety of employees and patrons. Finally, you will learn the responsibilities of management to support your professional development as a lifeguard.

THE SAFETY TEAM

When you become a professional lifeguard, you become a member of a safety team. A *safety team* is a network of people who can assist you in an emergency (Fig. 3-1). You are never alone in a crisis. Even if you are the only lifeguard on duty, you can depend on others at your facility and beyond. Understanding the responsibilities of others on the safety team makes your job safer and more effective.

You and other lifeguards are the most visible members of this team. You and patrons may not see other members of the safety team unless an emergency occurs. Then these others take their assigned roles and perform their part of the team effort.

The safety team includes others at your facility, such as other lifeguards and facility management. In some facilities the team also includes staff, such as swimming instructors, security guards, and employees at concessions.

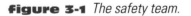 **figure 3-1** *The safety team.*

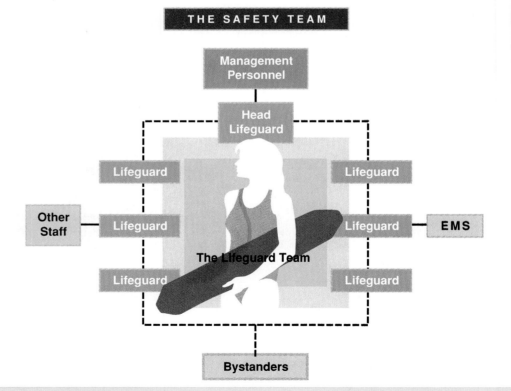

Staff responsibilities are usually defined by the facility's chain of command. The **chain of command** is the structure of employee and management positions in a facility or organization (Fig. 3-2). Be sure you know the names, titles, and responsibilities of all staff at your facility. Be familiar with how each position is related to the others. Then, in an emergency, you will know what help is available and whom to contact if your supervisor is not present. Be prepared with this information because in an emergency every second counts.

The facility's management is an important part of the safety team. The word *management* refers to all the persons responsible for the administration and supervision at your facility. Management may have several levels in the chain of command, such as a facility manager, pool manager, and head lifeguard.

figure 3-2 *Sample organizational chart showing the chain of command.*

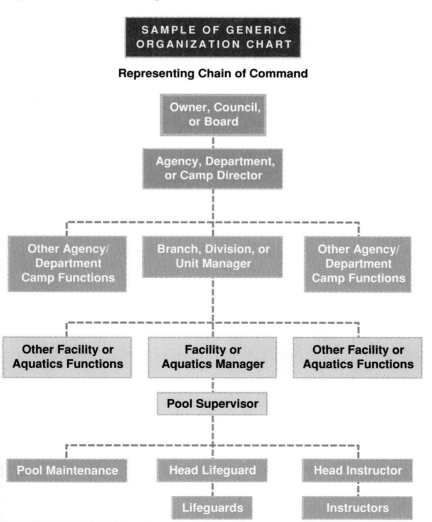

SAMPLE OF GENERIC
ORGANIZATION CHART

Representing Chain of Command

Owner, Council, or Board

Agency, Department, or Camp Director

Other Agency/ Department Camp Functions

Branch, Division, or Unit Manager

Other Agency/ Department Camp Functions

Other Facility or Aquatics Functions

Facility or Aquatics Manager

Other Facility or Aquatics Functions

Pool Supervisor

Pool Maintenance

Head Lifeguard

Head Instructor

Lifeguards

Instructors

Management has the primary responsibility to make sure the facility is safe and healthful for both patrons and staff. The specific responsibilities of managers are described later in this chapter.

Anyone who is available may help in an emergency. Thus, the safety team at your facility can include bystanders as well. *Bystanders* are people at the scene of an emergency who do not have the duty to provide care. Bystanders can help voluntarily in several ways (Fig. 3-3). Those bystanders with first aid or CPR skills can help give care until emergency personnel arrive. With guidance, even untrained bystanders can help out—by controlling a crowd, relaying a message to other team members, getting equipment or supplies, or calling for additional assistance.

The safety team also includes people outside the facility who may come there in an emergency, such as professionals in the *emergency medical services (EMS) system.* The EMS system is a network of community resources, including police, fire fighters, and medical personnel who give emergency care to victims of injury or sudden illness. As a lifeguard, you too are a key part of the EMS system, since it is part of your job to respond to emergencies.

As providers of emergency medical care, EMS personnel are an important part of a facility's safety team. They are especially significant for a single-lifeguard facility. If you work at such a facility, EMS personnel are your primary support in a medical emergency and should be contacted at once. Other staff members, even bystanders, can call EMS personnel. In many communi-

ties, you can reach EMS personnel, fire, or police by dialing 9-1-1. In some areas, you have to dial a local emergency telephone number or the operator. As long as you know the number to call, help is never more than a telephone call away (Fig. 3-4).

The lifeguard team

If you work at a facility where two or more lifeguards are on duty at a time, you are part of a lifeguard team that is part of the safety team. Your fellow lifeguards are your constant support on the job.

Lifeguards need to function well together because they alone share certain jobs and responsibilities (Fig. 3-5). The lifeguard team does not just happen, however. Teamwork and team spirit must be built and maintained. A team needs realistic, shared goals and effective communication. If your facility has a *head lifeguard*—a lifeguard in a supervisory position—he or she has a key role in developing the team and setting its goals.

Working as a team includes communication, safety checks of the facility, surveillance of patrons, rotation through lifeguarding positions, and response to emergencies (Fig. 3-6). As a team, you will have training to-

figure 3-4 *Calling EMS is often the most important action you can take in an emergency.*

figure 3-3 *Bystanders can provide help at the scene of an emergency.*

gether and may be inspected and evaluated as a team. As a lifeguard team, you may even represent your facility at special events or lifeguard competitions.

Team building and goal setting

An effective team does not just happen automatically. Like any structure, it has to be built. Creating a team whose members work together well takes time, commitment, shared expectations, and clear goals.

Team members need to practice together as a unit. Members of the safety team who work at the facility need to know what to do in an emergency and how and when to call for additional help. To become a team, the staff has to practice the facility's emergency action plans until everyone knows them well and can perform them correctly (Fig. 3-7). **Emergency action plans** are the written procedures that lifeguards and other staff follow in emergencies.

Teamwork also depends on the commitment of every team member. A team is effective when every member does the best he or she can to support every other member. This provides the needed foundation of trust. Others will trust you when you keep your lifeguarding skills and knowledge sharp and cooperate with every member of the team. This lets team members know you're willing and able to assist them.

Shared expectations also help build an effective team. This means all team members know what management expects from the team and what they can expect from each other. Management may state its expectations in writing, such as in an employee handbook. Learning what you and other team members expect from each other, however, often requires talking together. In-service training is an ideal time to talk this over with your teammates.

A team works to meet common safety goals, which are established by the team as a whole. The best goals are realistic, clearly defined, and consistent with the goals of the facility.

figure 3-6 *Lifeguards often work as a team in an emergency.*

figure 3-5 *Lifeguards cooperate on everyday tasks.*

figure 3-7 *Safety team members work together to practice emergency action plans.*

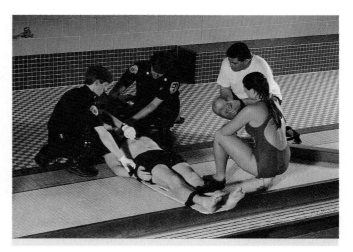

Your facility's overall mission is to provide certain services to patrons in specific ways. For example, a recreation department may have the mission to contribute to the health, well being, and development of the community through recreational activities. For the organization to meet this mission, these activities must be safe. That's where your duties start.

You and other members of the safety team assist management in meeting the facility's goal. Some parts of the team set their own goals to support this effort. For example, your lifeguard team might set the goal of having the best safety record of any comparable facility in your state, county, city, or town. This goal would help the facility continue to offer safe activities for your community.

The team also has to know how to reach its goals. For example, knowing the potential hazards at your facility is one way to help achieve a lifeguard team's safety goal. Other ways include educating patrons about facility rules, making sure all equipment is in good shape and easily accessible, staying aware of what is going on in your area of surveillance, knowing how to perform needed rescue skills, and working effectively as a team.

Communication

Effective communication means passing information to other members of your team in a clear and easily understandable way. Poor communication hinders effective teamwork. Speak directly and use terms that every team member knows and understands. Know the nonverbal ways your team communicates, such as with whistle signals and hand signals.

Most important, share your ideas and observations freely. Don't be afraid to speak up. Let management and other lifeguards know if you see a dangerous condition. If you are a new lifeguard, don't assume more experienced lifeguards have all the answers. If you are experienced, share your expertise with newer members of the team. In this way, everyone learns to perform his or her duties well.

Working relationships

As a lifeguard and safety team member, try to carry out your duties in a spirit of cooperation and satisfaction with your group. Team members do not have to like each other to work together well, although it would certainly help. If your co-workers are your friends, you can still act professionally and respectfully while on duty.

Each member of the safety team contributes to and gets support from other members. Make your contribution to the team by giving every team member your best effort.

The same principles apply in your relationship with management. Keep the lines of communication open and act respectfully, cooperatively, and professionally at all times. Use the chain of command to pass ideas and information along. If your facility has a head lifeguard, he or she is usually your contact for daily assignments or problems. If your facility does not have a head lifeguard, your supervisor is your contact.

Trust is also essential to your working well with management. You need to trust management to provide a safe environment for staff and patrons. Management needs to trust you and other members of the team to follow procedures and do your job well. Open two-way communication is one of the best ways to build trust.

Benefits of the safety team

Having others on your safety team has definite benefits. No matter how difficult a situation may be, you have backup. Even if you are the only lifeguard at a facility, you have the support of management, other staff members, EMS personnel, and even bystanders if necessary.

Being part of a team makes your job easier. Two or more people working together can get more done than by acting alone. Knowing that help is always at hand takes away some of the worry about what to do in an emergency. Being part of a team also makes your job more fun and rewarding. People who share a purpose and tasks can develop team spirit and friendship, as well as mutual support and respect.

RESPONSIBILITIES OF MANAGEMENT

Before you begin as a lifeguard, management has already done much to make and keep the facility safe. Management lays the groundwork for what you do as a lifeguard. Just as you have an obligation to ensure the safety of patrons, management has an obligation to protect *you,* as well as the patrons you are lifeguarding.

Different managers support lifeguarding efforts in different ways. A manager in an administrative position, such as a facility manager or an aquatics director, may support your safety team indirectly by creating policies and procedures to prevent injury and illness. A manager in a supervisory position, such as a pool manager or head lifeguard, more directly ensures a safe facility through daily interaction with patrons and staff (Fig. 3-8).

The responsibilities of management fall into two basic areas:

- Those that protect all people at the facility
- Those that enhance the professional development of the lifeguarding staff

Both of these responsibilities support the goal you share with management: safety.

Management has responsibilities to make the facility safe for every patron and staff member. These responsibilities include—

- Warning patrons and staff about actual and potential dangers.
- Addressing or fixing any known dangerous conditions.
- Complying with all federal, local, and state regulations.
- Keeping records on the facility and its employees.
- Assisting after an emergency.

These responsibilities are described in the following sections.

figure 3-8 *Management works with lifeguards to ensure safety at a facility.*

Warning patrons and staff

Safety is based on communication. One of the most obvious ways that management helps you as a lifeguard prevent injury is by posting signs and markings to inform patrons about actual and potential dangers. For example, "No diving" signs help patrons avoid spinal injury. Depth markings alert patrons to the potential dangers of deep and shallow water. Posted rules help patrons behave safely in and around the water.

Management must also protect you and other staff members from actual or potential dangers at the facility. Management can do this by providing you with specific written and verbal information, as well as protective equipment.

Addressing unsafe conditions

Management should respond to any unsafe conditions at the facility. Such conditions may include physical damage to the facility, such as a hole in a fence, a broken ladder, broken glass, or loose or missing tiles. These are often called **physical hazards**.

Unsafe conditions may also include **chemical hazards** (Fig. 3-9). Chemical hazards are harmful or poten-

figure 3-9 *Hazardous chemicals must be labeled.*

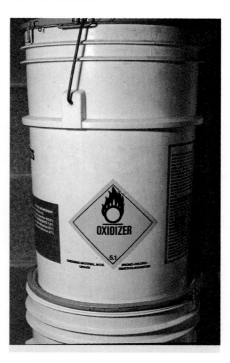

tially harmful substances in or around the facility (Fig. 3-10). These substances include chemicals used to disinfect and clarify pool water, pesticides, and office supplies, such as correction fluid.

You work in partnership with management to address dangerous conditions in your facility. Management gives you information about what to look for. Management then relies on you to detect and report dangers. Once you have detected and reported a dangerous situation, management has the responsibility to make sure the situation is corrected in a timely manner.

Complying with regulations

Regulations are created by federal, state, and local government agencies to protect people. Management must ensure that the facility as a whole, as well as all staff, comply with the regulations.

Some regulations protect your health by requiring managers to give you safety information and equipment. Others protect your civil rights and those of patrons who visit your facility. The following sections describe some federal regulations that impact you and patrons.

Hazard communication standard. Federal regulations protect people from chemical hazards in and around the facility. For example, the *Hazard Communication Standard* specifies the responsibilities of management to prevent illness and injury due to exposure to hazardous chemicals. Managers are required to give you

information about the chemicals in your workplace to which you may be exposed in your daily duties or during an emergency.

This standard also requires management to maintain a file of information on all chemicals at the facility. Each chemical has its own form, known as a **Material Safety Data Sheet (MSDS)**. The MSDS for each hazardous chemical must be readily accessible to employees. Make sure you know where MSDSs are kept and how to read them.

Before you start any work assignment, management must give you training and information on how the Hazard Communication Standard affects you and your facility. You must have the following specific information:

- Which hazardous chemicals are present in the facility
- Where those chemicals are located in the facility
- What specific dangers those chemicals pose
- How to identify chemical hazards in your facility
- How to protect yourself and others from being exposed to hazardous chemicals
- What to do if you or others are exposed to such hazards

The presence of hazardous chemicals at your facility is not cause for alarm *as long as they are handled and stored properly, as specified in the Hazard Communication Standard* (Fig. 3-11). All chemicals are potentially dangerous substances and must always be used with care.

figure 3-10 *Potentially harmful substances may exist in the pipes of a filter room.*

figure 3-11 *Chemical storage areas require warning signs.*

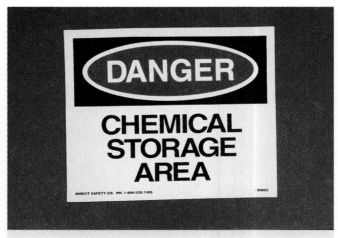

Bloodborne Pathogens Standard. The **Occupational Safety and Health Administration (OSHA),** a federal agency, developed the ***Bloodborne Pathogens Standard*** to reduce the risk of disease transmission. This standard helps protect you from contact with bodily fluids that might contain bloodborne pathogens. A ***pathogen*** is a disease-causing agent; it is also called a *microorganism* or *germ*. The management of your facility must help protect you from being exposed to pathogens in and around the facility and let you know what to do if exposure occurs. Help yourself and others avoid exposure by following the guidelines you will learn in *American Red Cross CPR for the Professional Rescuer* training.

Civil rights laws. *Civil rights* are those rights that a person has simply because he or she is a member of the general public. There are federal regulations that protect your civil rights, as well as those of your patrons. For example, the **Americans With Disabilities Act (ADA)** requires that people with disabilities have access to many kinds of opportunities and services. Management must comply with these requirements and let you know how the ADA affects the operation of your facility.

Civil rights laws also include **Equal Employment Opportunity Commission (EEOC)** policies. These require members of management to recruit, hire, and treat all employees fairly and impartially. EEOC policies protect all employees from being discriminated against or harassed on the basis of race, **ethnicity,** national origin, age, gender, religion, sexual orientation, disability, or military status. Your facility will have specific procedures to address EEOC violations. It is important to report violations and address them according to the guidelines of your facility.

State and local regulations. In addition to federal regulations, many state and local regulations also affect the operation of aquatic facilities. These regulations may cover the following:

- Lifeguard certification requirements
- Facility design and safety features
- Required chemical levels
- Staff training requirements
- Pool capacity
- Ratio of lifeguards to facility patrons
- Required first aid equipment and supplies
- Required lifeguarding equipment
- Required depths for diving

State and local regulations often vary greatly in different areas. It is important to learn about the ones that affect your facility. Ask your supervisor if you do not learn this information during orientation or in-service training.

Maintaining records and reports

Management at any facility uses a variety of records and reports. The larger the facility and its chain of command, often the more records and reports it uses.

As with other facility operations, you and management work together to make sure that records and reports are completed accurately. Management should provide you with blank forms, as well as with instructions and examples of how and when to complete them. On the job, you should complete forms promptly, accurately, and thoroughly. Once you have done your part in completing records and reports, management is responsible for maintaining them. Records and reports are used for the following reasons:

- To provide data about equipment, personnel, procedures, and improvements
- To provide data about the causes and prevention of injuries
- To comply with federal, state, and local laws requiring specific information about facility sanitation and maintenance
- To document incidents
- To protect the facility and its employees from possible legal actions

Records and reports are important to the facility's daily operation. Your facility's records and reports may include the following:

- Employee schedules
- Time sheets
- Health, sanitation, and maintenance records
- Daily attendance logs
- In-service training records
- Water conditions (pool temperature, clarity, chlorine and pH levels)
- Incident and injury reports

It is important to know your specific responsibilities for records and reports. These may be described to you during orientation or in-service training or detailed in your facility's policies and procedures manual.

Assisting after an emergency

Management also has responsibilities after an emergency occurs at the facility. Chapter 12 discusses these responsibilities and the support management can provide for lifeguards involved in the incident. After an emergency, management is generally responsible for—

- Closing and reopening the pool.
- Interacting with the media.
- Reporting procedures.
- Helping with stress-related problems.

Just as you work with management to prevent and respond to emergencies, you work together after an emergency occurs. Knowing that management is there to support you directly and indirectly can help you be more comfortable and confident on the job.

Supporting lifeguard professional development

Management has a role in supporting your professional development as a lifeguard. Management can support you by providing the following:

- A policies and procedures manual
- Orientation and in-service training at the facility
- Support after an emergency
- Opportunities for training in areas beyond your everyday duties
- Opportunities for recognition

Although all supports may not be present at every facility, these kinds of support promote safety and professionalism and may be a part of your facility's risk management plan. If your facility does not offer such support, talk to your supervisor. There may be ways he or she can develop this support or find other options outside your facility. These five types of professional support are described in the following sections.

Policies and procedures manual. Management should make sure that you receive the information you need to stay safe and perform your duties effectively. One of the best ways to provide this information is a *policies and procedures manual* (Fig. 3-12). This manual typically contains forms and information on topics such as the following:

- Administrative policies and procedures
- Rules and regulations
- Programming guidelines
- Guidelines for personnel (including hiring policies, conditions of employment, and standards of performance and conduct)
- An organizational chart (including chain of command and job descriptions)
- A floor plan of the facility that shows emergency evacuation routes
- Emergency action plans
- Samples of record and report forms
- Instructions for use of equipment
- Diagrams of areas of responsibility for patron surveillance

Although a manual may not be required by law, it can be the foundation for training staff and a reference guide for daily operations. If your facility has a policies and procedures manual, your supervisor should let you know where it is kept. Ideally, you would receive your own copy during orientation. As a lifeguard, you should know the information in the manual. This information may be reinforced during in-service training. Regardless of whether your facility has a policies and procedures manual, your supervisor is required to give you the information you need to perform your job safely and effectively.

figure 3-12 *A policies and procedures manual is an important part of facility operations.*

Orientation. An orientation session about facility operations and job requirements is helpful for both new and returning lifeguards. Orientation may include the following activities:

- Introduction of facility staff
- Completion of employment forms
- Distribution of uniforms
- Review of policies and procedures manual
- Overview of programs and services
- Overview of personnel policies and procedures
- Overview of operational policies and procedures
- Overview of management's expectations for lifeguards
- Tour of the facility, focusing on injury prevention strategies and the use of equipment
- Practice of emergency action plans

In a seasonal facility, orientation is an effective way to start each season. In a facility open year-round, orientation may be conducted as new staff are hired.

In-service training. In-service training is one of the best ways for management to help your knowledge and skills stay sharp. *In-service training* is training within the facility related to lifeguarding skills and information (Fig. 3-13). These sessions are "refresher" events. They may be conducted by a head lifeguard, the facility manager, or a member of the community, such as a public health official.

In-service training supplements the training you had before you were hired. While you practice what you have already learned, you gain more information related to your specific facility. In-service training bolsters your lifeguarding skills and knowledge. It helps you feel more a part of a team and boosts your attitude. It helps keep you fit and informed. Overall, you become and feel more professional. In-service training may include—

- Review of potential hazards at the facility
- Review and update of facility procedures, rules, and regulations
- Review and practice of emergency action plans
- Review and practice of rescue skills
- Review and practice of first aid, CPR, and spinal-injury management skills
- Physical conditioning
- Decision-making exercises
- Discussion of internal staff issues

As a professional lifeguard, you have an obligation to participate in all in-service activities.

Recognition and career development. Effective managers work to bring out the best in their employees, often helping motivate them with recognition and opportunities for career development. Management is not required to provide this type of support, however. You may be recognized through an achievement, an award, a promotion, or simply a "pat on the back" for a job well done. You may have career development opportunities through in-service training, special events like lifeguard competitions, or additional training or course work. The American Red Cross offers other courses or material to enhance your lifeguarding career.

figure 3-13 *In-service training helps keep lifeguards' skills sharp.*

Perhaps the most important thing to realize about your career is that you can actively shape it. Take advantage of opportunities that management offers for training and professional experience, and let your supervisor know what additional training you would like to have.

SUMMARY

Operating a safe and healthful facility is a team effort. Many other people can support you in your role as a lifeguard: professionals and bystanders, those within the facility and outside. If you work closely and communicate openly with both the lifeguard team and management, your lifeguarding experience will be rewarding and you will be part of an effective safety team.

STUDY QUESTIONS

Circle the letter of the best answer or answers.

1. Which of the following could be included on a safety team?
   a) Lifeguards
   b) Security guards
   c) Facility management
   d) Swimming instructors
   e) Bystanders

2. With guidance, untrained bystanders can help in which of the following ways during an emergency?
   a) Crowd control
   b) Calling for additional help
   c) Getting equipment and supplies
   d) Taking over surveillance for a lifeguard

3. As part of the safety team, lifeguards work together in which of the following ways?
   a) Safety checks of the facility
   b) Surveillance of patrons
   c) Response to emergencies
   d) Facility clean-up

4. Which of the following are necessary to create a team whose members work well together?
   a) Shared commitment
   b) Shared expectations
   c) Clear safety goals
   d) Effective communication
   e) Close friendship

5. Management's responsibilities include which of the following?
   a) Warning patrons and staff about actual and potential dangers within the facility
   b) Addressing or fixing any known dangerous conditions
   c) Complying with all local, state, and federal regulations
   d) Keeping records on the facility and its employees
   e) Assisting after an emergency
6. A material safety data sheet (MSDS) must be readily accessible to employees, according to—
   a) The Hazard Communication Standard
   b) The Bloodborne Pathogens Standard
   c) The Americans With Disabilities Act
   d) Equal Employment Opportunity Commission policies

7. Management can support lifeguard professional development in which of the following ways?
   a) By providing opportunities for recognition
   b) By providing a policies and procedures manual
   c) By offering orientation and in-service training
   d) By providing opportunites for training in areas beyond your everyday duties
   e) By monitoring records and reports

Circle *True* or *False*.
8. Only those bystanders with first aid or CPR skills can help in an emergency. True or False?
9. Two or more people working together can usually get more accomplished than by working alone. True or False?

See answers to study questions on p. 286.

PREVENTING AQUATIC INJURY

4

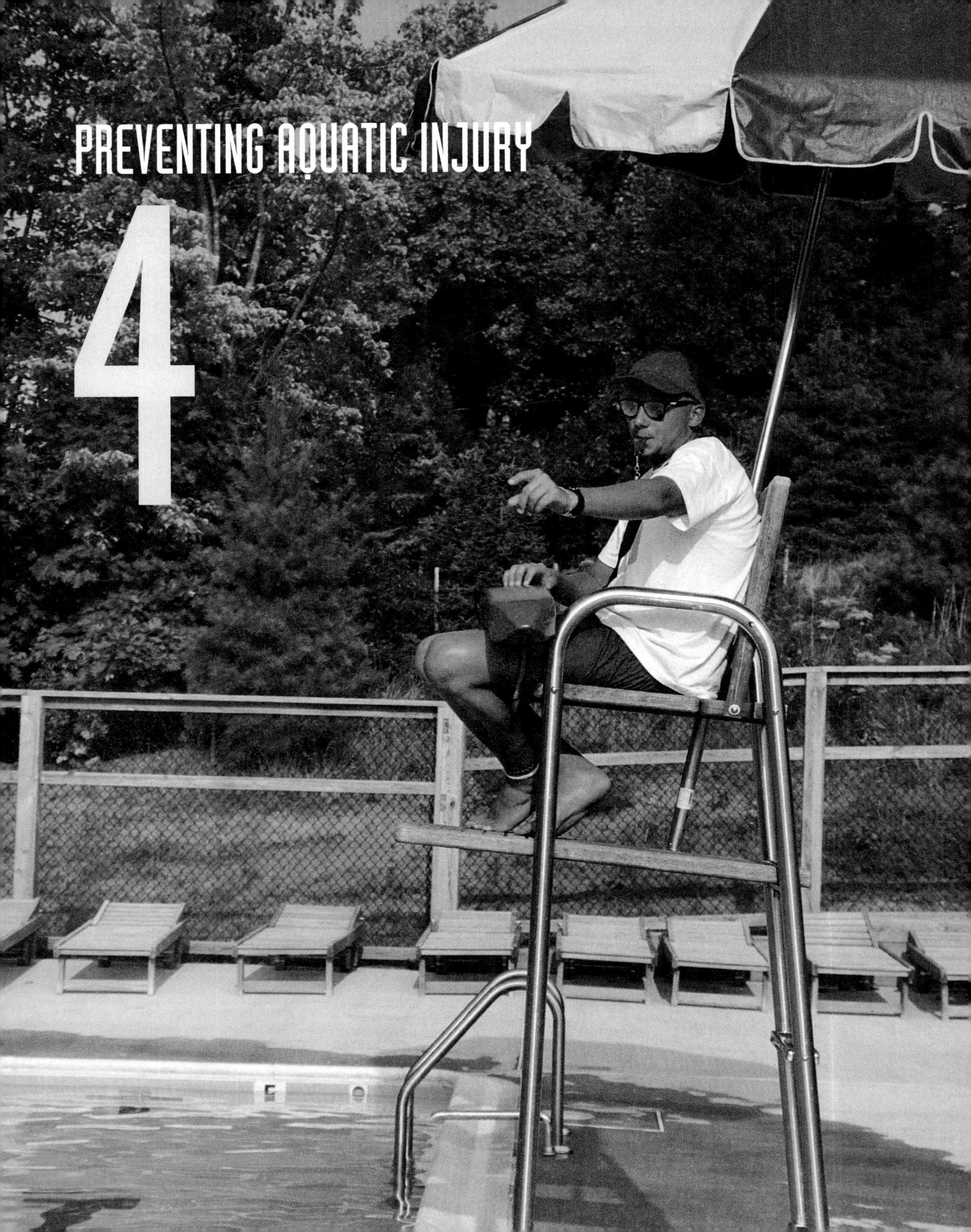

After reading this chapter, you should be able to—

1. Describe the three strategies a lifeguard uses for preventing injuries.
2. List the three parts of the communication strategy for injury control.
3. Explain the four-step process for verbally communicating with patrons about risky behavior.
4. List at least three unsafe practices you should watch for and prohibit.
5. Define the key terms for this chapter.

Aquatic injury prevention: Acting to prevent factors that may cause physical harm to patrons at an aquatic facility.

Injury: The physical harm from an external force on the body.

Preventive lifeguarding: The means of identifying and preventing potential life-threatening emergencies.

Risk management: Identifying, eliminating, or minimizing dangerous conditions that can cause injuries and financial loss.

Surveillance: A close watch kept over someone or something, such as patrons and the facility.

Victim: An injured or suddenly ill person; a drowning or near-drowning person.

INTRODUCTION

When people come to an aquatic facility, they expect it to be safe. The lifeguard is an essential element in providing that safety. Because of their training and responsibility to act in an emergency, lifeguards are considered professional rescuers. Unlike other professional rescuers, lifeguards are at the scene of potential injuries *before* they happen and can act to prevent them (Fig. 4-1).

You spend most of your time and attention as a lifeguard on injury prevention. *Aquatic injury prevention* is acting to prevent the factors that may cause physical harm to patrons. To do this well, you need to understand how injuries occur and how you can help prevent them.

PREVENTION OF AQUATIC INJURIES

Aquatic injury prevention is a part of your facility's risk management program. *Risk management* involves identifying and reducing dangerous conditions that can cause injuries and financial loss. As a lifeguard, you are an important part of your facility's risk management program. While emergency rescues are certainly a part of lifeguarding, you will spend far more time and energy in *preventive lifeguarding*—trying to make sure emergencies do not happen in the first place.

---

figure 4-1 *A lifeguard is on the scene to prevent or respond to any emergency.*

Many people believe that injuries just happen—that people who are injured are unfortunate victims of circumstance. However, the evidence shows that many injuries can be prevented. Although you cannot prevent all injuries at your facility, your knowledge of the factors that cause life-threatening aquatic injuries can help you prevent them. In this chapter, a *victim* is simply an injured person. In certain later chapters, victim refers to a person who needs help in the water.

The two most serious injuries you want to prevent are drowning and spinal injuries. Drowning occurs when a person suffocates while in the water. Most diving-related spinal injuries occur in shallow water—usually in 5 feet of water or less. If a diver's head hits the bottom or the side of the pool with enough force, the spinal cord could be injured and the person could become paralyzed or die.

An *injury* is physical harm resulting from the body being subjected to an external force. Injuries result from people and hazards interacting inappropriately in the environment, as seen in the following examples:

- A young girl is running along the deck. When she reaches a spot that is wet (a hazard), she slips and falls, bruising her leg (Fig. 4-2).
- A man ignores warning signs and dives into shallow water (a hazard). He hits his head on the bottom of the pool with enough force to permanently damage his spinal cord (Fig. 4-3).
- A child who cannot swim wades into water that is over her head and drowns. The water depth (which for her is a hazard) results in a death from drowning (Fig. 4-4).

Understanding how injuries are caused helps you know how to prevent them by—

- Increasing your awareness of risks and hazards.
- Helping patrons avoid risky behavior.
- Developing an attitude of safety at your facility.

In general, there are three injury prevention strategies that lifeguards use:

1 Communication with patrons

2 Patron *surveillance*

3 Facility surveillance

The first strategy is discussed in this chapter and the second and third in the following chapters.

figure 4-2 *Running on the deck of a pool can cause injuries.*

figure 4-3 *Diving into shallow water can permanently damage the spinal cord.*

figure 4-4 *Deep water can be hazardous for a nonswimmer.*

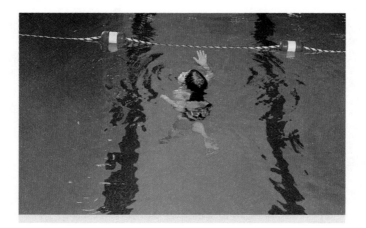

COMMUNICATION AS AN INJURY PREVENTION STRATEGY

ommunication as an injury prevention strategy has three aspects:

- Informing patrons about the potential for injury
- Educating patrons about the consequences of inappropriate behavior
- Enforcing rules and regulations that prevent injury

Informing patrons about the potential for injury

Patrons are informed about risks that could cause injury by signs that state warnings, tell how to use equipment, or list rules and regulations. For example, "No Diving" signs can help prevent spinal injuries, and depth markers can help prevent drownings. Rules and regulations inform patrons of behaviors that can lead to injury.

The facility manager or head lifeguard places safety signs and rules at appropriate places around the facility to warn patrons of potential hazards (Fig. 4-5). In some facilities, you may assist with the making and posting of signs. The signs should be easy to understand and should include pictures, when possible. You may need signs in more than one language. Signs should be visible to anyone entering the pool, approaching the water, or using equipment and play structures. Your job is to understand the information on the signs and make sure patrons understand and comply with it.

"No Diving" signs. In shallow-water areas, it is necessary to post "No Diving" signs (Fig. 4-6). Since spinal injuries are more common in people visiting an area for the first time, you must warn everyone of this hazard. Be sure signs are placed in key locations to help prevent injuries. The best locations are the deck near the edge of the pool and walls or fences by shallow water.

Depth markers. Drowning can often be prevented with proper warnings about water depth. Depth and distance markings may be posted in metric measure, as well as in feet and inches (Fig. 4-7). For the visually impaired, the head lifeguard or facility manager might make a tape recording of pool rules and develop sound coding to indicate depth, exits, and location of emergency equipment.

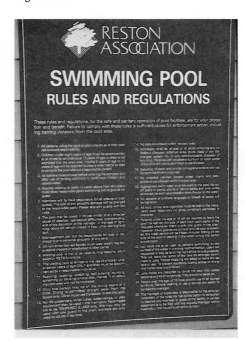

figure 4-5 *Signs indicate rules and regulations.*

figure 4-6 *"No diving" sign.*

Since many children cannot relate water depth to their height, some facilities paint cartoon characters on a nearby wall to show how tall a person has to be to stand safely in that part of the pool. If your facility has a way to illustrate water depth, show patrons how to use it.

Health department regulations. State, county, and local health department regulations help ensure safe facility operation. Health regulations can help prevent injuries and disease transmission by setting standards for pool design, construction, operation, maintenance, and management. Your facility manager should have a copy of these health regulations in the office (Fig. 4-8).

You do not need to know the technical information on pool design and construction or plumbing. However, knowing some parts of the health regulations can help you prevent drowning and spinal injuries. For example, to prevent toddlers from drowning, health regulations often require that a wading pool be separated by a fence or be an adequate distance away from the main pool. If the fence is damaged and does not help keep toddlers away from the main pool, ask your supervisor to have it repaired.

Health department regulations often require a lifeline with colored floats across the width of a pool. It should be placed at least 2 feet on the shallow end of a drop-off into deep water. This safety line helps prevent nonswimmers from accidently moving into water above their heads.

The following are other typical rules established by health departments or other local agencies:

- Patrons must shower before entering the water.
- Swimming caps are required.
- Spitting, spouting water, and blowing one's nose in the water are not allowed.
- Food, drinks, and smoking are allowed only in designated areas.
- Pets are not allowed in the facility.
- Street shoes are not allowed on the deck.
- No more than the maximum number of patrons are allowed in the facility at one time.
- Swimmers must wear appropriate swimming attire.
- First aid equipment can be used only by authorized personnel.

Facility rules and regulations. Rules are not designed to keep people from having fun. Rules are designed for the health and safety of patrons and facility staff. A facility may have its own rules for how to use the facility safely. Some rules may be based on the pattern of injuries at the facility, as shown in an incident and injury chart (see Chapter 6). The facility management can study the types, locations, and frequency of injuries at your facility and make a new rule to prevent certain injuries.

General rules of conduct give patrons guidelines for how to behave and can help them enjoy the facility without endangering themselves or others. These rules

---

figure 4-7 *Depth marking in metric measure and in feet.*

figure 4-8 *State or local health regulations.*

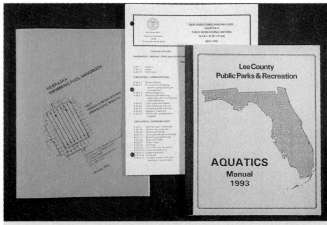

figure 4-9 *Place pool regulations at the facility entrance.*

figure 4-10 *Additional signs may be required to govern the use of equipment and structures.*

should be posted in plain view inside the facility and at its entrance so that you and the patrons can refer to them easily (Fig. 4-9). The following rules are typical:

- Swimming is allowed only when a lifeguard is on duty.
- Horseplay, such as running, splashing, shoving, or dunking, is not allowed.
- Swimming is allowed only in designated areas.
- Follow the schedule for different types of activities (such as lane swimming, free swims, use of play structures, and diving).
- Diving is allowed only in designated areas.
- Sunbathing is allowed only in designated areas.
- Glass containers are not allowed in the facility.
- Throwing objects, such as balls, is not allowed.
- Alcohol and other drugs are not allowed.
- Profanity, improper behavior, and intoxication are not allowed.
- Bicycles are not allowed in the facility.
- Changing clothes is allowed only in locker rooms.
- Swimming is not allowed in the diving area.
- Diving or jumping from the side of a pool into the diving area is not allowed.
- Instructions by the lifeguards must be obeyed at all times.

The facility may have other rules, such as—

- Only members and their guests may use the facility.
- Nonswimmers and children under a set age (or shorter than a set height) must be supervised by an adult.
- Patrons who wish to enter deep water may be required to demonstrate their swimming ability.

Your job is to understand and reinforce all facility rules and regulations.

You should watch for other unsafe practices that are not easily stated as rules, such as the following:

- "Wall walking"—weak swimmers traveling from shallow water to deep water by holding onto the wall or overflow trough
- Nonswimmers bouncing from shallow water toward deeper water
- Swimming under water alongside the wall (where a patron might be hit by someone who does not see him or her and jumps into the water)
- Placing legs or arms through the rungs of ladders

Equipment and structures. Additional rules govern the use of specific equipment and structures (Fig. 4-10). Typical rules include the following:

- One person at a time on a ladder.
- Do not gather at the top or at the bottom of ladders.
- Do not sit or hang on lifelines.
- Do not climb on lifeguard stands or towers.
- Do not gather around the base of lifeguard stands or towers.
- Flotation devices, toys, and balls are not allowed in the pool.
- For lap swimming, kickboards, hand paddles, **pull buoys,** masks, fins, and snorkels are allowed but only for their intended purpose and only in assigned lanes.
- **Starting blocks** may be used only during scheduled practices and competitions and only under direct supervision (Fig. 4-11).
- Emergency equipment is to be used by lifeguards only.

Diving boards and towers. Rules related to diving boards and towers should be displayed near them. The following rules are typical:

- The ladder must be used to climb to the diving board or tower.
- Only one person is allowed on the diving board at a time.
- Look before diving or jumping to make sure no one is in the diving area.
- Only one bounce is allowed on the diving board.
- Dive or jump only in a straight line from the end of the diving board or tower.
- Swim to the closest ladder or wall immediately after entering the water.
- Learn or practice difficult dives only under the supervision of a diving instructor.
- Use the diving board or tower only under the direct supervision of a lifeguard or coach.

Water slides. Typical rules for water slides include the following:

- You must be a certain height and able to swim to use the water slide.
- Enter, ride, and exit slide feetfirst.
- Standing, stopping, and sliding down headfirst are not allowed.

- Metal objects, locker keys, jewelry, metal snaps, watches, etc. are not allowed on the water slide.
- Keep hands inside the slide (Fig. 4-12).
- Only one person is allowed on the slide at a time.
- Do not wear glasses on the slide.
- Move away from the bottom of the slide quickly.

figure 4-11 *Starting block.*

figure 4-12 *Always ride feetfirst, and keep hands inside the slide.*

Educating patrons about the consequences of inappropriate behavior

Patrons arriving at a facility may at first be unfamiliar with some of its features or just excited to be there. They might not read signs or pay attention to the rules. You may have to let them know about the consequences of an unsafe act. Explaining the rules in a positive way encourages patrons to behave safely. The following is a quick four-step process to prevent a patron from engaging in risky behavior.

1 *Get the patron's attention by alerting him or her to the hazard.* You can say, "Excuse me, but what you are doing is very dangerous."

2 *Explain what the hazard or danger is.* Merely telling someone not to do something often does not work. People usually cooperate better when they know why something is dangerous. Explain the danger briefly. You can say, "The water in this area is too shallow for diving."

3 *Explain how the patron might be injured.* You can say, "Diving into shallow water can cause you to hit your head on the bottom and be injured."

4 *Say what to do to avoid being injured.* You can say, "If you wish to dive in the water, do it in the deep part of the pool, where it is safe."

This type of explanation in which you get the patron's attention, tell him or her what the danger is, emphasize the consequences of the risky behavior, and offer safe alternatives for what he or she wants to do should convince most patrons to follow pool rules. When you need to speak quickly, you can combine them in one quick comment to a patron. For example, say, "Excuse me, diving into shallow water is dangerous and can cause head injury. Please use the deep end."

Enforcing rules and regulations

Enforcing rules not only helps to prevent injuries but also leads to safer attitudes among patrons. In enforcing rules, you must always be consistent and fair. Different enforcement methods often work better for patrons of different ages. Be sure you use a method in accordance with facility policies.

You can deal with children who break rules repeatedly by having them sit out of the water for a set time. Another way is to have an off-duty lifeguard read the rules to them and explain them. If a parent or adult caregiver seems uncooperative, avoid getting into an argument but make your point clearly. You may have to call on the head lifeguard or the facility manager to help with the situation.

Since most teenagers and adults want to be treated with respect, a simple explanation of the rules is usually enough. If someone keeps breaking the rules, however, for the safety of all patrons, you may have to expel the person. Do this only as a last resort. If a patron continues to break the rules, the head lifeguard or facility manager may have to call police or security personnel.

Every facility needs a procedure to follow for removing someone from the facility. This procedure should have specific steps for lifeguards and management to follow and guidelines for calling police. Record any such action in the facility's daily log.

SUMMARY

The more you understand how injuries are caused, the better you can prevent them. Effective communication with patrons is critical to help prevent injuries. By informing patrons about the potential for injury, educating them about the consequences of risky behavior, and enforcing rules and regulations, you can help patrons have a safe and enjoyable time.

STUDY QUESTIONS

Circle the letter of the best answer or answers.

1. Risk management in preventive lifeguarding includes—
   a) Identifying all dangerous conditions or situations that can cause accidents and result in financial loss.
   b) Dramatic rescues.
   c) Eliminating or minimizing all dangerous conditions or situations that can cause accidents and result in financial loss.
   d) Trying to make sure dangerous conditions and situations do not happen in the first place.

2. The two injuries you are most concerned with preventing are—
   a) Internal bleeding and head injuries.
   b) Spinal injuries and broken arms.
   c) Drowning and internal bleeding.
   d) Spinal injuries and drowning.

3. Injury prevention strategies include—
   a) Increasing your awareness of risks and hazards.
   b) Keeping fit.
   c) Helping patrons avoid risky behavior.
   d) Strict adherence to rules.
   e) Developing an attitude of safety at the facility.

4. A lifeguard's injury control strategy involves proper communication, which includes—
   a) Informing patrons about the potential for injury.
   b) Talking with the other lifeguards.
   c) Educating patrons about the consequences of inappropriate behavior.
   d) Enforcing rules and regulations designed to prevent injury.
   e) Keeping an eye on trouble makers.

5. "No Diving" signs can help prevent ____, and depth markers can help prevent ____.
   a) Drownings.
   b) Spinal injuries.

6. Unsafe practices not easily stated as rules include—
   a) Wall walking.
   b) Swimming under water alongside a wall.
   c) Swimming in cut-offs.
   d) Nonswimmers bouncing from shallow to deep water.

7. Circle the correct answer. People receive injury prevention information at swimming pools only from lifeguards. True or False?

8. Sequence the four-step communication process to prevent a patron from engaging in risky behavior.
   ___ Tell the person how he or she might be injured.
   ___ Explain to the person what the hazard or danger is.
   ___ Tell the person how to avoid being injured.
   ___ Get the person's attention by alerting him or her to the hazard.

See answers to study questions on p. 286.

After reading this chapter, you should be able to—

1. Explain the four elements of effective surveillance.
2. Describe four behaviors to watch for that indicate a swimmer is in distress or is drowning.
3. Describe the characteristics of a distressed swimmer.
4. Describe the four characteristics of the instinctive drowning response.
5. Describe the characteristics of a passive drowning victim.
6. List at least four possible causes of passive drowning.
7. Explain how hyperventilation can affect the drowning process.
8. Explain how to prevent hyperthermia.
9. List the three elements of the RID factor as a cause of drowning.
10. Describe four factors that can influence effective scanning.
11. Describe how to relieve a lifeguard at a ground-level station and at an elevated station.
12. Explain total coverage and zone coverage.
13. Explain at least five ways for improving surveillence at competitive events and instructional/therapeutic activities.
14. Define the key terms for this chapter.

Active drowning victim: A person exhibiting universal behavior that includes struggling at the surface for 20 to 60 seconds before submerging.

Distressed swimmer: A person capable of staying afloat but likely to need assistance to get to safety.

Hyperthermia: A condition that occurs when a person's inner core temperature rises above its normal temperature of 98.6 degrees F.

Hyperventilation: Taking deep breaths in rapid succession and forcefully exhaling.

Hypothermia: A life-threatening condition in which the body is unable to maintain warmth and the entire body cools.

Instinctive drowning response: The four instinctive characteristics displayed by an active drowning victim. These involve breathing, arm and leg action, body position, and locomotion.

Intrusion: When lifeguards are assigned to perform nonsurveillance duties, thus leaving the pool without proper supervision.

Passive drowning victim: A face-down unconscious victim, submerged at or near the surface.

Patron surveillance: Maintaining a close watch over the people using your facility.

RID factor: Three elements: **r**ecognition, **i**ntrusion, and **d**istraction; related to drownings at guarded facilities.

Scanning: A visual technique used by lifeguards to properly observe and monitor patrons participating in water activities.

INTRODUCTION

Many fast-paced and dramatic events, like rescues and lifeguarding competitions, are part of being a lifeguard. Many ordinary tasks, like opening and closing the facility, may also be part of your job. There is no more important responsibility for a lifeguard than *patron surveillance*—maintaining a close watch over the people using your facility. Indeed, the greatest portion of a lifeguard's time is spent on patron surveillance.

To do this effectively, you must be alert and attentive at all times, supervising patrons continuously. Your surveillance is the key to recognizing conditions or situations that may lead to life-threatening emergencies, such as drowning and spinal injury. Effective surveillance has four elements:

1 Recognizing how distressed swimmers and drowning persons behave

2 Using appropriate scanning techniques to identify patrons in trouble in the water

3 Proper stationing of lifeguards

4 Knowing your area of responsibility

Effective surveillance is necessary for fast victim recognition and rescue. Drowning occurs when a person suffocates in the water. *Active drowning victims* remain at the surface for less than a minute; some struggle for as little as 20 seconds! A *passive drowning victim* does not struggle at all. Once a person submerges and breathing stops, brain cells are damaged within a few minutes (Fig. 5-1). To reduce the possibility of brain damage, you must quickly be able to recognize that a person needs help and provide that help promptly.

One key to patron surveillance is victim recognition—being able to identify those people who need help in the water. Drownings at guarded facilities often occur under three circumstances:

1 When lifeguards fail to recognize that someone is in trouble in the water

2 When lifeguards are removed from patron surveillance and assigned to perform other duties, leaving the pool without proper supervision

3 When lifeguards are distracted from their surveillance duties.

These circumstances, as well as other items that can affect the quality of your patron surveillance, are discussed in this chapter.

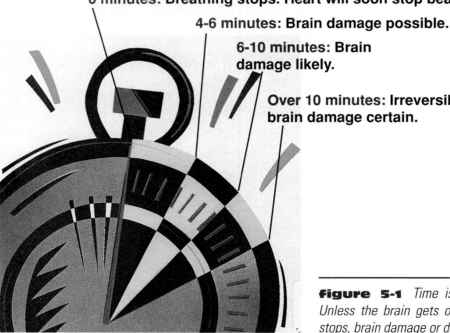

0 minutes: Breathing stops. Heart will soon stop beating.

4-6 minutes: Brain damage possible.

6-10 minutes: Brain damage likely.

Over 10 minutes: Irreversible brain damage certain.

figure 5-1 *Time is critical in life-threatening emergencies. Unless the brain gets oxygen within minutes of when breathing stops, brain damage or death will occur.*

VICTIM RECOGNITION: THE FIRST ELEMENT OF EFFECTIVE SURVEILLANCE

When you are conducting patron surveillance, you must *look for behavior that indicates a swimmer is in distress or a person is drowning*. Focusing on behavior can increase the effectiveness of your scanning because you are looking for a **universal response** indicating a patron is experiencing difficulty in the water.

It has been suggested that certain groups of people either drown or experience difficulty in the water at levels greater than other groups. Misuse of this information occurs when all members of these groups are labeled "high risk," in need of special attention.

Instead, every group and every individual must receive equal and fair treatment at your facility. You cannot single out a member of a group for special surveillance or swimming-ability testing based on anything other than observed swimming ability.

Besides drawing incorrect conclusions about an entire group of people, **criteria** that identify people as high risk are inappropriate when you work at a pool that is used primarily by members of a group labeled as high risk. Your determination of a person's difficulty must be based on his or her behavior, not on physical characteristics, such as age or ethnic or racial background.

The best way to maintain surveillance over patrons at your facility is to understand the behavior that indicates a person is in distress or drowning. Table 5-1 compares the behavior of a distressed swimmer and a drowning victim with the actions of a swimmer. For each description, there are behaviors to note in four areas: breathing, arm and leg action, body position, and **locomotion**—whether the patron is making progress through the water. Once you are familiar with these characteristics, you will be able to tell quickly whether a person in the water needs help.

In certain situations, such as being caught in an ocean current, a person might pass through all four sets of circumstances. As you scan a swimming pool, however, you are more likely to see a person in one category or another. By responding quickly to people who need help, you may help prevent their situations from becoming more serious.

Swimmer

Depending on his or her proficiency with the stroke, a swimmer's arms and legs work in a coordinated and effective way. The body position is nearly horizontal, and there is some breath control. The person is able to make recognizable progress through the water (Fig. 5-2). Note that a person with a physical disability (such as loss of a leg) may have to modify a stroke, but you can soon learn to recognize that person's unique swimming style.

table 5-1 *Characteristics of Distressed Swimmers and Drowning Victims Compared to Swimmers*

Behaviors	Swimmer	Distressed Swimmer	Active Drowning Victim	Passive Drowning Victim
Breathing	Rhythmic breathing	Can continue breathing and call for help	Struggles to breathe; cannot call out for help	Not breathing
Arm and Leg Action	Relatively coordinated movement	Floating, sculling, or treading water; can wave for help	Arms to sides, pressing down; no supporting kick	None
Body Position	Horizontal	Horizontal, vertical, or diagonal, depending on means of support	Vertical	Face-down submerged or near surface
Locomotion	Recognizable progress	Little or no forward progress; less and less able to support self	None; has only 20-60 seconds before submerging	None

figure 5-2 *A swimmer's arms and legs work in a coordinated manner.*

figure 5-3 *A distressed swimmer can stay afloat and usually call out for help.*

figure 5-4 *An active drowning victim struggles to stay afloat and is unable to call out for help.*

Distressed swimmer

For a variety of reasons, such as exhaustion, cramp, or sudden illness, a swimmer can become distressed. A *distressed swimmer* makes little or no forward progress and cannot reach safety without a lifeguard's help.

You can recognize distressed swimmers by the way they try to support themselves in the water. They may float or use swimming skills such as sculling or treading water. If a safety line or other floating object is nearby, a distressed swimmer may cling to it for support while waving or calling for help. Depending on the method used for support, the distressed swimmer's body may be horizontal, vertical, or diagonal.

The distressed swimmer usually has enough control of the arms and legs that he or she can keep the face out of the water to continue breathing and call for help. In most cases, a distressed swimmer is also able to wave for help. He or she can use the legs and one arm for support, while raising the other arm to wave for assistance (Fig. 5-3).

As conditions such as fatigue, cold, or sudden illness continue to affect the distressed swimmer, he or she is less and less able to support himself or herself in the water. As this occurs, the victim's mouth moves closer to the surface of the water, and anxiety increases. If a distressed swimmer is not rescued, he or she becomes an active drowning victim.

Active drowning victim

An active drowning victim struggles at the surface in a highly predictable fashion. Because the behavior that an active drowning person exhibits is universal, it has been called the *instinctive drowning response* (Pia, 1974). This instinctive action means that the victim's behavior is predictable. This gives you a distinct advantage in recognizing victims and tells you that the person is drowning and needs help. The instinctive drowning response has four characteristics. A drowning person—

1 Struggles to keep the face above water in an effort to breathe. Unable to do this, he or she begins to suffocate.

2 Has arms extended to the side, pressing down for support. There is no supporting kick.

3 Has a vertical body position in the water.

4 Struggles at the surface, unable to move forward, for approximately 20 to 60 seconds before submerging.

An active drowning victim is struggling to breathe. The mouth repeatedly sinks below the surface and reappears. While the mouth is below the surface, the drowning person keeps it closed to avoid swallowing water. When the mouth is above the surface, the drowning person quickly exhales and then attempts to inhale before the mouth starts to go below the surface again.

While the victim is gasping for air, he or she also may take water into the mouth. Some of this water can enter the windpipe (trachea) and produce a **spasm** of the vocal cords that will block the airway. This is the body's natural response to keep fluid or food out of the airway. Unfortunately, this may result in the victim suffocating and losing consciousness.

Many people believe that an active drowning person can call out for help, but this is not the case. He or she is barely able to take in enough air to breathe, so there is no air left over to call out for help (Fig. 5-4). Our bodies force us to breathe before we can speak.

The active drowning person uses an instinctive arm motion to stay at the surface. The arms are extended out to the side, where they are pressed down against the water to enable the person to raise the mouth out of the water. These arm movements are not under the drowning person's control. In contrast to the distressed swimmer, the active drowning person cannot wave for help. In addition, the active drowning person does not have an effective kick supporting him or her in the water (Fig. 5-5).

The active drowning victim's body is vertical in the water (Fig. 5-6). This allows the mouth to be at the highest point to provide the greatest chance for the person to breathe.

Finally, an active drowning victim does not make any forward progress in the water. All the person's energy is devoted to keeping the mouth above the surface of the water. The active drowning person usually stays at the surface for only 20 to 60 seconds. An adult may struggle for up to 60 seconds, whereas a child may submerge in as little as 20 seconds. The active drowning victim may continue to struggle under water but eventually loses consciousness and stops moving. This victim is now a passive drowning victim.

figure 5-5 *The active drowning victim's arms are extended at the side and pressing down. There is no supporting kick.*

figure 5-6 *An active drowning victim's body is vertical in the water.*

figure 5-7 *A passive drowning victim can be found* **A,** *floating near the surface or* **B,** *submerged on the bottom of a pool.*

A

B

figure 5-8 *Emergency care is best provided once the victim is removed from the water.*

Passive drowning victim

Besides knowing the progression from active to passive drowning, be aware that a person may suddenly slip under water without a struggle. The passive drowning victim may float face down at or near the surface, or the body may sink to the bottom (Fig. 5-7, *A* and *B*).

A passive drowning can stem from a variety of conditions resulting in a loss of consciousness including—

* A heart attack or stroke.
* A seizure.
* A head injury.
* *Hyperventilation* (taking deep breaths in rapid succession and forcefully exhaling).
* *Hyperthermia* (a condition that occurs when a person's core temperature becomes higher than normal).
* Use of alcohol or other drugs.
* *Hypothermia* (a life-threatening condition in which the body is unable to maintain warmth and the entire body cools (see Chapter 6)).

By using the scanning techniques described later in this chapter, you will be able to detect a passive drowning victim within seconds. When you make the rescue, remove the person from the water immediately so that emergency care can be provided (Fig. 5-8).

You should regard any person who is floating face down and motionless for about 30 seconds as an unconscious victim. Check the person's condition immediately. If the person is conscious and holding his or her breath, explain to the person why he or she should stop doing so. If the person persists in pretending to be a passive drowning victim, notify the head lifeguard or the facility manager.

Heart attack, stroke, seizure, and head injury. A person who has suffered a heart attack, seizure, stroke, or head injury may feel dizzy or faint or be temporarily paralyzed. These conditions cause great difficulty in swimming or even walking in the water. The person may also suddenly stop swimming and become a passive drowning victim.

Hyperventilation. Hyperventilating is a dangerous technique some swimmers have used to try to swim long distances under water. They mistakenly think that by taking a series of deep breaths in rapid succession and forcefully exhaling that they can increase the amount of oxygen they breathe in, allowing them to hold their breath longer under water. This is not true. Instead, it only lowers their carbon dioxide level.

The practice is risky because the level of **carbon dioxide** in the blood is what signals a person to breathe. As the level of carbon dioxide increases, a person normally takes a breath. However, with a decreased carbon dioxide level, the blood vessels in the brain become **constricted.** This constriction decreases blood flow to the brain, which will cause dizziness, unconsciousness, and occasionally seizures.

When a person hyperventilates and then swims under water, he or she can easily pass out before the body knows it is time to breathe. When the person finally does take a breath instinctively, water rushes in and the drowning process begins. In one study (Craig, 1982), a researcher interviewed experienced swimmers who lost consciousness after hyperventilating and swimming under water. All these swimmers reported suppressing the urge to breathe at the end of their first length of underwater swimming. For this reason, patrons should not attempt to hyperventilate and then swim under water.

Hyperthermia. Hyperthermia occurs when a person's inner core temperature rises above its normal temperature of 98.6 degrees F (37 degrees C) to 102.6 degrees F (39 degrees C). The victim becomes weak and dizzy, and may become confused or lose consciousness. The Consumer Product Safety Commission (1990) issued a warning about the hazards of drownings in spas where the water temperature is greater than 104 degrees F (40 degrees C) and alcohol consumption is involved.

If your facility has a spa, the warm water can make it difficult for a person to get out. It is important for you to monitor patrons as they use spas and hot tubs and to advise them not to stay in the water too long (Fig. 5-9). You should also advise pregnant women, adults with cardiac or circulatory problems, and parents or guardians of young children about the risk hot water can pose to their health. Since many health clubs and recreation departments with swimming pools now include spas, you should be aware that hot water can cause passive drownings.

ALCOHOL AS A CONTRIBUTING FACTOR TO DROWNING

Alcohol is the most popular drug in Western society. It is important to note, however, that only two drinks can cause a blood alcohol level of 0.05 percent in some people. This blood alcohol level impairs judgment and reflexes and makes certain activities unsafe. If a patron appears to be under the influence of alcohol, try to convince him or her not to go in the water.

Here are some of the ways alcohol can affect a person in the water and has caused drowning and spinal injuries.

- *Alcohol affects balance.* Some people with alcohol in their body have drowned in shallow water when they lost their balance and were unable to stand up. "Ordinary" actions on steps, ladders, diving boards, or play structures become hazardous for the intoxicated person.
- *Alcohol affects judgment.* A person might take risks, such as diving into shallow water, that he or she would not normally take.
- *Alcohol slows body movements.* It can greatly reduce swimming skills, even those of an excellent swimmer.

One of the biggest myths about alcohol in an aquatic setting is that an intoxicated person can sober up by going swimming. Splashing water on a person's face or immersing a person in water will *not* reduce the amount of alcohol in the bloodstream.

figure 5-9 *If you have a spa at your facility, you are responsible for the safety of the patrons who use it.*

An Incalculable Cost

The hospital morgue is full. There is a teenager who drowned while boating, an elderly man who died of a chronic liver disease, and a third victim who was shot by her boyfriend. The group seems to share no connection other than that they are lying in the same morgue.

But there is a connection—alcohol.

Public health officials are seeing a growing number of injuries, illnesses, and social problems in which alcohol plays a role. More than 100,000 people die each year from alcohol-related causes.[1] From the child abused by her alcoholic parent to the driver who drinks and causes a six-car pileup, our country feels the influence of alcohol abuse.

Because alcohol impairs judgment and coordination, even a first-time drinker who overindulges can become a death statistic. Nearly half of all deaths from motor vehicle crashes, one third of all drownings, and about half of all deaths caused by fire involve alcohol.[1] Researchers say strength, judgment, stamina, motor skills, speed, and intellect are all factors in injury prevention. Alcohol impairs many of these abilities. Subsequently, alcohol is a major risk factor for nearly every type of injury.

Tragically, it is a risk often taken by young people. Bruce Kimball was a 25-year-old Olympic diving champion when he drove into a group of teenagers at the end of a country road, killing two people and injuring four others. His blood alcohol concentration was 0.20 percent, twice the legal limit. In one night, both his life and the lives of many others were destroyed.[2]

Reckless and violent behavior has been linked to alcohol use in study after study. Nearly half of all homicides, a third of all suicides, and two thirds of all assaults involve alcohol.[3] One of the best predictors of violence is alcohol abuse, a study of violent men showed. In one 1986 survey of state prison populations, 18.5 percent of inmates reported that they were under the influence of alcohol at the time of the crime. Another 18 percent reported that they were under the influence of both alcohol and drugs. Other crimes and social problems are linked to alcohol. Social workers find alcohol use a factor in nearly 50 percent of their child abuse cases. Prevalence of alcohol abuse among the homeless ranges from 20 to 45 percent.

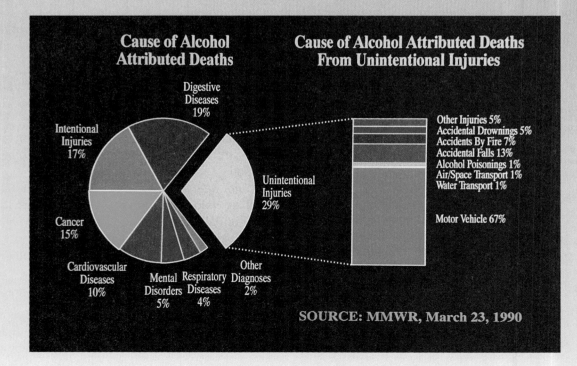

Cause of Alcohol Attributed Deaths

Cause of Alcohol Attributed Deaths From Unintentional Injuries

Digestive Diseases 19%

Intentional Injuries 17%

Cancer 15%

Cardiovascular Diseases 10%

Mental Disorders 5%

Respiratory Diseases 4%

Other Diagnoses 2%

Unintentional Injuries 29%

Other Injuries 5%
Accidental Drownings 5%
Accidents By Fire 7%
Accidental Falls 13%
Alcohol Poisonings 1%
Air/Space Transport 1%
Water Transport 1%

Motor Vehicle 67%

SOURCE: MMWR, March 23, 1990

An Incalculable Cost—cont'd

These personal and social consequences create a tremendous economic burden. A report to the U.S. Congress by the Secretary of Health and Human Services estimates that by 1995, the cost of alcohol abuse will reach $150 billion annually. The bulk of the cost comes in lost employment and reduced productivity.

Health care costs account for $15 to $20 billion of alcohol costs, and research documenting the detrimental health effects of alcohol is growing. Doctors now say that moderate drinking by pregnant women increases risks of high blood pressure, cirrhosis of the liver, and decreased motor development for their children. Heavy drinking—more than four drinks a day—causes more serious long-term effects on the health of the drinker, including risk of heart attack, many cancers, stroke, kidney failure, and problems of the nervous system such as shaking and dementia.

Our morgues are filling up with people ravaged by a drug whose use they could not or did not control. In terms of economic cost, lives, and productivity, alcohol abuse outdistances cocaine, heroin, and all other drugs. Avoid alcohol or drink moderately so you won't end up an unfortunate statistic.

1. Centers for Disease Control: Alcohol-related mortality and years of potential life lost—United States, 1987, MMWR 39(11):173, 1990.
2. Associated Press: The New York Times, p. 87, January 31, 1989.
3. National Clearinghouse for Alcohol and Drug Information: The fact is . . ., "OSAP responds to national crisis," Rockville, MD, Summer 1990.

THE RID FACTOR AS A CAUSE OF DROWNING

Most drownings at guarded aquatic facilities happen when neither the lifeguards nor patrons notice the drowning person slip below the surface. A research study of the published accounts of drownings in the United States from 1910 to 1980 (Pia, 1984), indicated that with the exception of passive drownings, swimming-related drownings in areas where lifeguards were on duty resulted from three causes, summarized as the *RID factor*:

- The failure of the lifeguard to *R*ecognize the instinctive drowning response
- The *I*ntrusion of secondary duties on the lifeguard's primary responsibility for patron surveillance
- *D*istraction from surveillance duties

Drowning may result because of any one element of the RID factor or a combination of them.

Recognition

The ability to recognize that a swimmer is in distress or a person is drowning is one of the most important lifeguarding skills. To recognize that someone is in distress or is drowning, you must be able to distinguish their behavior from that of people who are swimming or playing safely in the water. Remember, it is up to you to identify behavior that indicates a person needs to be rescued. Don't expect the drowning person or nearby patrons to call you to make a rescue.

Like most injuries, drowning can be prevented. Good scanning techniques can help you to quickly identify a person in trouble in the water. Even if a person slips under water without a struggle, good scanning techniques can help you see the person lying motionless within seconds.

Intrusion

Intrusion occurs when you are required to perform secondary duties, such as maintenance or recreational functions, when you should be engaged in patron surveillance. Lifeguards are often required to perform maintenance duties, such as sweeping the deck, emptying trash barrels, picking up towels, and checking locker rooms. Those with the proper training are often responsible for monitoring the chemistry of the pool water. Other facilities require lifeguards to give swimming lessons or rent recreational equipment.

While these duties are typically part of your job, you should not be removed from your primary role of maintaining patron safety unless another lifeguard relieves you (Fig. 5-10). If you are asked to perform other duties while you are watching patrons, ask that such duties be postponed until you are no longer responsible for patron surveillance.

Specific activities, such as instructional programs or swim meets, should have a direct supervisor, instructor, or coach for the participants. Since you cannot safely perform the duties of a lifeguard while coaching a team or teaching a lesson, the facility should arrange to have a separate lifeguard and a separate coach or instructor for these activities.

Distraction

Distraction is the third factor that can affect your supervision of patrons. Distractions may come from a variety of sources, such as observing the latest swimsuit styles, prolonged observation of troublemakers on the deck, or talking with other lifeguards or friends. During an "innocent" conversation, you may miss a 20-second struggle of a young child. That child may die because you were socializing! Social conversations should occur only when you are not on duty.

PROPER SCANNING: THE SECOND ELEMENT OF EFFECTIVE SURVEILLANCE

Now that you know how to recognize a person in trouble in the water, it is important to learn the techniques of effective scanning. *Scanning,* a visual technique for monitoring patrons in the water, is a very active process. When you scan a swimming pool, you are not just passively observing patrons in the water. You are actively monitoring their behavior and looking for signals that someone in the water needs help (Fig. 5-11).

figure 5-10 *If you are removed from your primary responsibility of patron surveillance, make certain that another lifeguard provides coverage.*

figure 5-11 *When scanning the pool, look for behavior that indicates a person needs help.*

Most of the time you are scanning, you use **peripheral vision,** what you see at the edges of your field of vision. Peripheral vision detects motion and changes of patterns more easily than frontal vision, what you see when you concentrate on the center of your field of vision. Use your peripheral vision to detect any of the characteristics described earlier of distressed swimmers and drowning victims and your **frontal vision** to closely examine the person's behavior (Fig. 5-12, *A* and *B*).

The following are some helpful suggestions for effective scanning:

- Limit your scanning to your defined area of responsibility.
- Scan thoroughly and repeatedly. You cannot afford to neglect any part of your zone. Scan those parts of the deck for which you are also responsible.
- Scan from point to point, rapidly glancing at all the movements of the people in your area.
- Spend slightly less time and attention on people who are good swimmers or who are playing safely in the water, but do not eliminate them from your scanning.
- Scan for potential problems. Body position, arm movements, and facial expressions are good indicators of weak swimmers and those in trouble in the water.
- Scan the bottom of the pool, as well as the surface.
- Scan crowded areas carefully. Partially hidden arm movements may indicate that a person is actively drowning.
- If someone is attempting to swim and his or her body is in a vertical position with the arms paddling in front, he or she is not a good swimmer and should not be in deep water.
- If a weak swimmer is slowly moving toward safety, watch him or her more frequently while you continue to scan your area.
- While you are scanning, do not be distracted by people or activities. Keep your attention focused on your area of responsibility.
- Don't rely on patrons or other lifeguards to tell you that someone might be drowning. A drowning person is often surrounded by people who are unaware a drowning is occurring right next to them. New lifeguards sometimes are unsure of themselves and mistakenly wait for patrons or more experienced lifeguards to tell them that someone is in trouble.
- Minimize areas that cannot be seen or are difficult to see. These blind spots may be caused when patrons cluster together or by water movement, such as fountains or bubbles. Adjust your body position as necessary to see into blind spots.
- Be aware of conditions that affect visibility, such as glare from the sun or from overhead lights, water clarity, or shadows cast on the water from surrounding objects at different times of the day.

The effectiveness of your scanning can be influenced by a variety of factors such as—

- The type and location of lifeguard stations.
- Your area of responsibility.
- Fatigue.
- The variety of patron activities that you must monitor.

figure 5-12 *A* and *B*, *Proper scanning techniques enable you to safely monitor the activity of your patrons.*

A

B

table 5-2 *A Day in the Life of a Pool*

SE, Shallow end of pool; *DE,* deep end of pool.

Time	Activity	Staff Needed	Surveillance Tips
5:30 AM	Open pool (turn on lights, perform safety check)	2 lifeguards	N/A
6:00-7:00 AM	Swim team practice	2 lifeguards; 1 on Chair A, 1 on break	Counting swimmers may help keep track of them. Scan up and down lap lanes. Watch for tired swimmers and collisions.
7:00 AM	Public lap swimming begins (continues until 1:00 PM)	2 lifeguards; 1 on Chair A, 1 on break	Counting swimmers may help keep track of them. Scan up and down lap lanes. Watch for tired swimmers and collisions.
7:30-8:30 AM	Lap swim; Senior water exercise (SE)	3 lifeguards; 2 on chairs, 1 on break	Extra lifeguard may need to assist patrons in or out of water. Watch for signs of fatigue, cramps, or injury in lanes.
9:00-10:00 AM	Lap swim; Swim lessons (SE) (DE)	4 lifeguards; 3 on chairs, 1 on break	Note the high number of children in the pool. Watch that children do not drift into water that is too deep. Prevent horseplay.
10:00-11:00 AM	Lap swim; SCUBA class (DE), Swim lessons (SE)	4 lifeguards; 3 on chairs, 1 on break	Bubbles at surface can temporarily obscure vision at the bottom—be sure SCUBA participants do not become motionless. Watch that children do not drift into water that is too deep.
11:00 AM-12:00 PM	Lap swim; Deep water exercise (DE); Adapted aquatics (SE)	4 lifeguards; 3 on chairs, 1 on break	Watch for signs of cramps. Be sure patrons are wearing equipment properly. Serve as extra pair of eyes during instruction. Watch for human waste accidents. Be sure participants do not drift into water that is too deep. Extra lifeguard may need to assist patrons in or out of water.
12:00-1:00 PM	Lap swim; Water aerobics (SE)	4 lifeguards; 2 on chairs (*A* and *B*), 1 on break, 1 roving	Counting swimmers may help keep track of them. Extra lifeguard may need to assist patrons in or out of water. Watch for signs of fatigue, cramps, and collisions at turns.
1:00-2:30 PM	Day camp (entire pool)	4 lifeguards; 3 on chairs, 1 on break	Watch that children do not drift into water that is too deep. Off-duty lifeguard occasionally acts as a roving lifeguard for extra surveillance.
2:30-5:30 PM	Swim team practice	2 lifeguards; 1 on Chair A, 1 on break	Same as morning practice.
5:30-7:30 PM	Lap swim continues; diving practice (DE); Open rec swim (SE)	4 lifeguards; 3 on chairs, 1 on break	Watch for divers striking the water in a manner that could result in injury. Watch for divers to return to surface after completing dive. Counting swimmers may help keep track of them. Watch for collisions at turns. Restrict deep end to diving team only.
7:30-9:30 PM	Lap swim; Water polo (DE); Open rec swim (SE)	4 lifeguards; 3 on chairs, 1 on break	Watch for signs of fatigue or cramps. Restrict horseplay. Watch that children do not drift into water that is too deep. Restrict deep end to water polo team only.
9:30-10:00 PM	Conduct closing safety check, store equipment, close facility	4 lifeguards	Be sure no one is still in facility, especially in the water.

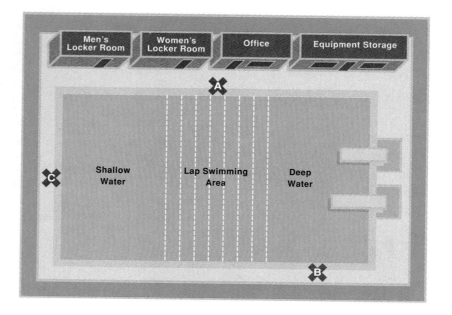

Depending on the types of patron activity at any given time, the number of people in the pool, and the number and location of lifeguards, you may have to adapt your scanning pattern to provide proper surveillance. Table 5-2 helps illustrate these issues and concerns.

LIFEGUARD STATIONS: THE THIRD ELEMENT OF EFFECTIVE SURVEILLANCE

You can supervise people from lifeguard stands or from the deck. When used together, both positions can help provide optimal coverage for the whole facility.

Elevated stations

The lifeguard stand is a very effective lifeguarding position for patron surveillance. Elevated stations provide you with an excellent position from which to scan your area of responsibility.

At a one-lifeguard facility, the elevated stand is the preferred position for surveillance. This view of patrons' activities is much better than the view you have from a ground-level lifeguard station (Fig. 5-13).

You should not interrupt the scanning of your area unless you are making a rescue or stopping someone from breaking a rule. If you are the only lifeguard on duty and must stop someone from breaking a safety rule, do it quickly. Get the person's attention, explain the danger, how he or she can become injured, and, if necessary, a way to avoid the injury. This process should take only a few seconds, and you can often do it while continuing to scan the pool. If the patron needs a detailed explanation, call for assistance or tell the patron that you can discuss it further with him or her when you take your break.

Lifeguard stands are designed to be used for surveillance. Do not store personal items on stands whether the items belong to you or to patrons. Keep food, radios, and jewelry off the lifeguard stand.

You should never dive from a lifeguard stand to make a rescue. Instead, use a feet-first entry or climb down to enter the water (Fig. 5-14).

You must also keep the area under the stand clear of people at all times. Having patrons in your way increases the amount of time it takes to reach a person who needs help. Be sure to scan the area of the water beneath

figure 5-13 *Elevated lifeguard stands provide you with an excellent position for scanning your zone.*

figure 5-14 *Enter the water feetfirst from a height, such as an elevated lifeguard station.*

your lifeguard station. This area can be a blind spot because you have to stop your normal scan and look straight down at the water below. Lifeguards on opposite sides of a pool can help remedy this problem by scanning below each other's lifeguard stands.

While on the lifeguard stand, keep the sling of the rescue tube across your shoulder and chest. If seated, place the rescue tube on your lap. When standing, position the tube across your stomach (Fig. 5-15, *A* and *B*). Make sure the towline is gathered so it will not get caught on part of the lifeguard stand. You can become seriously injured if this line becomes entangled on the lifeguard stand as you begin your rescue.

Ground-level stations

You may also be assigned to a walking patrol, a fixed location on the deck, or in the water near a play structure. In any of these positions, your view of the entire swimming area is limited and patrons are sometimes shielded from your surveillance (Fig. 5-16).

While you are walking, face the patrons in your area of responsibility. Do not turn your back on your area of

coverage. The primary purpose of the ground-level station is to have you close to patrons. From this position, you can easily enforce safety rules for patrons in the water and on the deck. While maintaining surveillance of patrons, you can also educate them about the reasons behind the rules. Never let yourself become distracted from surveillance duties by talking socially with patrons.

Lifeguard rotations

There are many causes of fatigue when you are lifeguarding. You may become fatigued if—

- You have not had enough sleep.
- You become **dehydrated.**
- You are involved in an unusually high number of rescues.
- You are exposed to too much sun or wind.
- You begin to experience **heat exhaustion.**

figure 5-15 *A* and *B*, Keep your rescue tube properly positioned at all times.

figure 5-16 *A ground-level station enables you to be closer to the patrons but sometimes limits your view of the entire area you are responsible for.*

figure 5-17 *By working as a team, lifeguards can rotate positions while still maintaining adequate patron surveillance.*

There are several measures to help prevent fatigue:

- Come to work well rested.
- Drink enough liquids.
- Use adequate protection against sun and wind.
- Rotate stations and take breaks.

Periodic rotations from one station to another, plus relief breaks, help keep you alert. Rotating from station to station also allows you to become familiar with the conditions and hazards in the total facility, rather than in just one location.

There should not be any interruption in patron surveillance while you are rotating from one station to another. To relieve a lifeguard at a ground-level station, walk to the side of that lifeguard and begin scanning. Once you have established your scanning pattern, you may signal the other lifeguard to proceed to his or her break or to the next assignment. Ask the lifeguard you are relieving whether there are any patrons in the zone who need closer than normal supervision.

To relieve a lifeguard at an elevated station—

1 Take a position next to the stand, and begin scanning the area of responsibility (Fig. 5-17). After a few moments of scanning, signal the lifeguard in the stand to climb down.

2 Once on the deck, this lifeguard takes a position next to the stand and resumes his or her surveillance of the area. You can then climb up in the stand and establish your scanning pattern. At that point, you signal the outgoing lifeguard that he or she can leave.

You should take a break at least once an hour. In one system of surveillance, you may spend 20 or 30 minutes at one station, rotate to another station for 20 or 30 minutes, and then take a 20- or 30-minute break. In another system, you may spend 45 minutes at one stand, take a break for 15 minutes, and then go to another stand.

You should not make changes or substitutions in the schedule of rotations and breaks without the consent of the head lifeguard or the facility manager. Nor should you leave the facility during a break without permission from the head lifeguard or the facility manager.

If you are the only lifeguard on duty, you must clear the water during your 15-minute rest period. You cannot leave swimmers in charge of the facility while you are on a break. Your facility manager or other staff member should monitor the pool while you are on a break to prevent adults and children from entering the water.

AREA OF RESPONSIBILITY: THE FOURTH ELEMENT OF EFFECTIVE SURVEILLANCE

The head lifeguard or the facility manager establishes each lifeguard's area of responsibility. This coverage may be either total coverage (responsible for an entire pool or waterfront area) or zone coverage (watching only part of a pool or waterfront area). Another type of coverage is backup coverage, in which you take over part or all of a zone for another lifeguard who is making a rescue. State or local regulations may determine the lifeguard-to-swimmer ratio that a facility must follow.

Total coverage

Total coverage is generally used at single-lifeguard facilities or when only one lifeguard is on duty with a small number of patrons and swimmers present. If you are the only lifeguard on duty, your responsibilities are considerable. You must scan the entire area, rescue distressed swimmers or drowning persons before they submerge, control the activities of patrons both in and out of the water, and recognize and respond to a variety of emergencies. If you find that you are unable to provide adequate coverage for the patrons in your area of responsibility, notify your supervisor that you need help.

Zone coverage

In **zone** coverage, the pool is divided into separate areas of responsibility for each lifeguard station. These areas can be designated by ladders, lane lines, lifelines, visual markers, or simply by the shape of the pool. Zone coverage is an effective way to provide surveillance for high-risk areas and to avoid blind spots in the surveillance system (Fig. 5-18).

The zones should overlap each other by several feet so that the boundaries between zones have double coverage. You should know the extent of the zone for each guarding position. You should also know your role in the emergency action plan for each lifeguarding position. This information is covered in Chapter 7.

figure 5-18 *Zone coverage enables lifeguards to overlap each other's areas of responsibility.*

SURVEILLANCE DURING SPECIAL ACTIVITIES

People may come to your facility to engage in a wide variety of activities: recreational swimming, lap swimming, water exercise, diving, and instruction in skills such as swimming, **SCUBA** diving, and snorkeling. The following sections contain ideas to help you provide better surveillance for people engaged in competitive events, those taking swimming or diving lessons, and those participating in exercise or therapy.

Competitive events

Participants in competitive events like swimming or diving meets, water polo games, and lifeguarding competitions usually have a high level of aquatic skill. However, they deserve your attention as much as anyone else at your facility. The following principles may help you **customize** your scanning technique to their specific needs.

- Be familiar with rules and regulations for the events you are guarding, as well as with the safety policies set forth by the governing body for the competitive program.
- Plan your rescues before an incident occurs. For instance, it is impossible to tow a victim across lane lines. Consult your emergency action plan for the appropriate place to remove a victim from the water when lane lines are in place. In addition, be sure you know how to remove lane lines (and where the appropriate tool is kept) in case lines must be removed during a rescue. The same is true for boundary lines in water polo.
- Have swimmers follow rules set for lane activity. For instance, designate lanes for warm-up, sprinting, or practicing starts.
- If your pool has **bulkheads,** position yourself so that you can see both sides or make sure there are enough lifeguards to scan both sides of the bulkhead. Do not allow swimmers under the bulkhead.
- If you are guarding at a **diving well,** be sure you know how to equalize pressure on your eardrums when you descend into very deep water. You can do this by pinching your nostrils together and gently trying to blow air out through your nose.

- In diving practice or competition, watch for each diver to return to the surface. Position yourself where your vision of the bottom is best.

Instructional or therapeutic activities

A swimming instructor should have a lifeguard available during swimming lessons. The same is true for those conducting water exercise classes or in-water therapy classes. The following points can help your surveillance during these activities:

- Different precautions may be necessary depending on the age and ability of participants in swimming instruction. Note the relation of the height of students to the water depth where they are practicing, and make sure nonswimmers do not enter water that is more than chest deep.
- Be sure infants and children in the water are accompanied by a parent or another responsible adult who actively watches them.
- During exercise programs, watch for signs of nausea or fatigue.
- During programs for therapy or **rehabilitation,** it is important to be familiar with the physical or medical conditions of the participants.

SUMMARY

Patron surveillance is one of three critical components of an injury prevention strategy. A lapse in coverage—even for just a few seconds—may lead to injury or even death. To guard a facility properly, you need the ability to recognize a distressed swimmer, an active drowning victim, and a passive drowning victim. Effective scanning techniques and proper positioning of lifeguard stations will help you to locate a person in trouble. Through zone coverage and regular lifeguard rotation, your surveillance efforts can be even more successful.

STUDY QUESTIONS

Circle the letter of the correct answer or answers.

1. The four elements of effective surveillance include—
   a) Victim recognition.
   b) Proper scanning.
   c) Proper stationing of lifeguards.
   d) Effective sunglasses.
   e) Knowledge of your area of responsibility.
   f) Adherence to facility rules and regulations.

2. To detect whether a swimmer is in distress, note the following areas of behavior:
   a) Breathing.
   b) Physical condition.
   c) Arm and leg action.
   d) Body position.
   e) Age.
   f) Locomotion.

3. You notice a person in the water whose body is diagonal and who is able to breathe and wave. The arms and legs are moving to keep the person's head above water, but there is no forward progress. This person is probably—
   a) An active drowning victim who needs help.
   b) A passive drowning victim who needs help.
   c) A distressed swimmer who needs help.
   d) A beginning swimmer who does not need help.

4. An active drowning person exhibits four universal characteristics. The instinctive drowning response includes—
   a) Struggles to keep the face above the water in an effort to breathe.
   b) Arms extended to the sides, pressing down for support. No supporting kick.
   c) Calling or waving for help.
   d) A vertical body position in the water.
   e) Struggles at the surface with no forward progress.
   f) A horizontal body position in the water.

5. Which of the following describes a passive drowning victim?
   a) Floating facedown and motionless.
   b) A horizontal body position but struggling to stay afloat.
   c) Body sinking to the bottom of the pool.
   d) Submerged and in a vertical body position.

6. Passive drowning can result from various conditions or situations, including—
   a) Hyperventilation.
   b) Hyperthermia.
   c) Alcohol use.
   d) Seizure.
   e) Heart attack or stroke.
   f) Head injury.

7. Hyperventilating can often cause the drowning process to begin. This is because the rapid breaths and forceful exhaling can result in—
    a) An increased amount of oxygen.
    b) A decreased level of carbon dioxide.
    c) A decreased level of oxygen.
    d) An increased amount of carbon dioxide.
8. To prevent hyperthermia, patrons should—
    a) Stay out of water that is too cold.
    b) Limit the amount of time spent in hot water.
    c) Not get into water over 98.6 degrees F.
    d) Not take rapid breaths before swimming under water.
9. The three causes of swimming-related drownings summarized as the RID factor include—
    a) Failure of the lifeguard to recognize the instinctive drowning response.
    b) Intrusion of secondary duties on the lifeguard, which leaves the pool inadequately supervised.
    c) Distraction from surveillance duties.
    d) Failure to reach the victim in time.

10. Effective scanning can be influenced by which of the following factors?
    a) The type and location of lifeguard stations.
    b) Improper diet.
    c) Knowing your area of responsibility.
    d) Fatigue.
    e) The variety of patron activities to be monitored.
    f) The age of the lifeguard.
    g) The age of the patrons.

Circle *True* or *False*.

11. Hyperthermia can be prevented by ensuring the water temperature stays above 104 degrees F. True or False?

See answers to study questions on p. 286.

FACILITY SURVEILLANCE

6

Objectives

After reading this chapter, you should be able to—

1. Explain the three-part safety check used for facility surveillance.
2. Describe the five areas of the facility that must be regularly inspected for safety.
3. List the types and causes of injuries that can occur in the four areas of the pool environment.
4. Explain the guideline for determining when to allow patrons to return to the water after a thunderstorm.
5. Define the key terms for this chapter.

Key Terms

Daily log: A written journal kept by lifeguards, the head lifeguard, and management with a daily account of safety precautions taken and meaningful events.

Facility surveillance: Checking the facility to help prevent injuries caused by avoidable hazards in the facility environment.

Safety check: An inspection of the facility to find and eliminate or minimize hazards.

Safety checklist form: A form on which lifeguards record safety inspections they make of the facility.

INTRODUCTION

Facility surveillance is checking the facility to help prevent injuries caused by avoidable hazards in the facility environment.

One way to help prevent injuries is to eliminate as many hazards at the facility as possible and to minimize any unavoidable hazards.

This chapter describes the following aspects of facility surveillance:

• Safety checks of the facility
• Tracking injuries at the facility using an incident and injury chart
• Weather as a potential hazard

SAFETY CHECKS

The *safety check* is your primary method of facility surveillance. You, the head lifeguard, or facility manager may do the safety check. At least three safety checks are done each day and should include all areas that are open to the public.

When you find an unsafe condition, if possible, correct it before the facility opens. If the hazard involves movable equipment, get help to move it to a safe place. If you cannot correct a problem yourself, contact the head lifeguard or facility manager immediately. If the condition is serious enough, the head lifeguard or facility manager may close the pool. Otherwise, you may have to keep patrons from the area. You can use signs, ropes, and **cones** (Fig. 6-1). In addition, you must alert other lifeguards about the hazard so that they can steer patrons away from the site. Record all such incidents in the *daily log*.

Opening safety check

The first safety check is made before the facility opens to the public. Walk around the entire area to make sure all safety equipment is properly placed and in working order. Be sure rescue tubes are in good condition and readily accessible. **Backboards** with **head immobilizers** and straps must be readily accessible. Check that the first aid station is clean and equipment and supplies are accessible and well stocked (Fig. 6-2). Check that telephones are working. Turn on lights, and test the **public address system** if there is one. Check the deck, pool, and locker rooms for any hazardous conditions. Unlock doors.

On-duty safety check

The head lifeguard or the facility manager determines the type and number of safety checks during the day. Safety checks during the day may involve some of the same items you check before the facility is opened and

figure 6-1 *Cones can be used to indicate or close off an unsafe condition.*

figure 6-2 *Make sure that the first aid equipment is complete and accessible.*

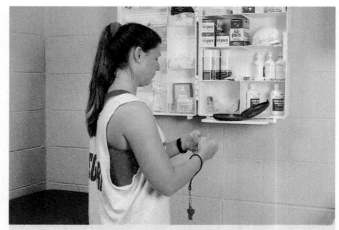

also things that could be affected by patrons. Check the weather. Make sure your surveillance area is covered whenever you make an on-duty safety check. Safety checks should never interfere with surveillance.

Closing safety check

At the end of each day, a lifeguard, the head lifeguard, or the facility manager completely inspects the facility before closing it. Make sure no one is in the pool or anywhere else in the facility. Check the pool, locker room, and shower area. The check may also include adjacent areas, such as playground and eating areas. At an outdoor facility, put away all equipment so that it is not stolen or damaged by weather.

After the closing inspection, write in the daily log that the water area is clear and you have made the safety check and taken any necessary steps to eliminate problems. Write your name and sign the log. Follow the facility procedure for turning off the lights and public address equipment and locking up.

Specific areas to inspect for safety

When you do a safety check, use a **safety checklist form** for your facility. Table 6-1 on pp. 80-82 is a sample safety checklist form. Your facility's form may be similar. The five facility parts that you are concerned with are the—

- Deck.
- Pool.
- Recreational equipment.
- Chemical storage areas.
- Showers, locker rooms, and restrooms.

Area 1: the deck. You can begin your safety check with the deck. The deck has three main potential hazards: entrance areas, flooring materials, and deck obstructions. Posting signs in these areas can help control injuries (Fig. 6-3).

Check that the deck does not have loose or broken flooring material, standing water, or slippery areas. Report such conditions immediately to the head lifeguard or the facility manager. Keep decks clear of equipment, personal belongings, and any other objects that may cause people to fall or to be injured.

figure 6-3 Post signs in areas with potential hazards.

Area 2: the pool. Check the pool next. Check the following five aspects of the pool: ladders and steps, drain covers, the lifeline between the shallow and deep end, water clarity, and water temperature.

Ladders and steps. Ladders must be secured properly. A bolt can come loose and cause injury when someone steps on the ladder. Chipped steps can cause puncture wounds. Report any such problems immediately to the head lifeguard or facility manager so that repairs can be made as soon as possible.

Drain covers. Drain covers should be firmly secured with noncorrosive screws (screws that will not wear away). A secure cover prevents a swimmer's hands or feet from becoming trapped in the holes (Fig. 6-4). Check drains to be sure the suction forces are not too strong by placing a cloth over the drain. You should be able to remove the cloth easily. Small children have been seriously injured by sitting on a drain cover with too much suction. Others have drowned by being trapped when their hair was pulled into the drain.

figure 6-4 *Covers should be placed over drains to prevent swimmers' hands or feet from becoming trapped.*

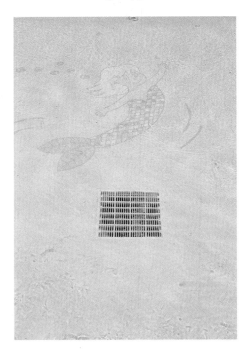

figure 6-5 *Buoyed lifelines should be used to show change in depth.*

Lifeline. Depth markers help make patrons aware of water depths and changes in water depths. A **buoyed lifeline** should mark the separation between shallow water and deep water (Fig. 6-5). The lifeline should be 2 feet on the shallow side of the drop-off to deep water. It should be tight enough to support an adult with his or her head above the water. The floats should be visible and separated from each other by only a few feet.

Water clarity. For effective patron surveillance, the water must be clear. You must be able to see the bottom, especially at the deep end, from anywhere on deck. To check water clarity, see if the main drain is clearly visible from the deck (Fig. 6-6). If the water is cloudy or if it has an unusual color, the chemical balance in the pool may be off or the **filtration system** might not be working properly. Report this situation immediately. Sometimes this problem can take several days to correct. If there is **debris** in the water, on the surface, or in the gutters, clean it out or report this to maintenance.

Water temperature. Warmer water is more enjoyable and less hazardous to patrons, since the body loses heat to the surrounding water. While cool water can make swimming refreshing, if the water is too cold, patrons might develop **hypothermia.**

Check that the water temperature is within the range for the population using the pool. Recreational pools usually have temperatures between 82-86 degrees F (27 to 30 degrees C). Temperature ranges for competitive swimming usually fall between 78-82 degrees F, while special populations and therapy pools fall between 86-90 degrees F (30-32 degrees C). If your facility has a spa, many state and local laws require that water temperatures do not exceed 104 degrees F.

Area 3: recreational equipment. The third area you inspect is the facility's recreational equipment, including diving boards and platforms, starting blocks, play structures, and water slides.

Diving boards and platforms. Check the steps or stairs to the diving board or platform to make sure they are not slippery and are firmly secured. Check that the rails along the sides of the steps and **diving mounts** are secure.

figure 6-6 *The main drain must be clearly visible from the deck.*

figure 6-7 *Two safety rails run from the rear of the mount to at least 1 foot beyond the edge of the pool.*

All diving mounts ideally have two safety rails from the rear of the mount to at least 1 foot beyond the edge of the pool (Fig. 6-7). State codes, however, may determine whether these features are required.

Inspect the diving board for algae or bare spots. You may be able to clean the board, or the facility may have to have it resurfaced. Inspect the entire diving apparatus for loose bolts, rust, cracks at stress points, and signs of warping.

The **fulcrum** under the center of the board lets the board bend and spring. If the fulcrum is movable, be sure it is locked in the forward position during recreational swim times (Fig. 6-8). Only trained divers should adjust a movable fulcrum for their strength, weight, and timing.

Starting blocks. Starting blocks for competitive swimming are permanent or removable. During recreational swims, removable starting blocks should be kept in a storage area.

If your facility has fixed starting blocks, make sure that "No Diving" signs and cones are on all blocks during recreational swims to prevent patrons from using the blocks (Fig. 6-9). Some facilities have covers for start-

figure 6-8 *A fulcrum needs to be locked in the forward position during recreational swims.*

figure 6-9 *Starting blocks must be marked during recreational swims so that patrons do not use them.*

Multi-Attraction Aquatic Facilities

Growth of multi-attraction aquatic facilities is a recent trend in aquatic recreation. Many park and recreation departments, communities, and private pool owners are adding play structures, inflatable play equipment, water slides, and activity pools. These provide a greater variety of aquatic activities for patrons. Often the idea is to turn a pool into a miniature waterpark for the whole family. Parents often choose these facilities for birthday parties and family outings. Facility owners realize that people want to get the most entertainment for their money, so they provide more options for their customers. Parents want their children to be safe while they have fun. Because of the variety of attractions in multi-attraction aquatic facilities, lifeguards should have additional training on the use and care of this equipment and for differences in surveillance that are needed to keep patrons safe.

ing blocks, which discourage their use. Be sure such covers are in place except when the starting blocks are to be used. Starting blocks are to be used only under an instructor's or coach's supervision.

Play structures. As patrons seek more variety at aquatic facilities, play structures are becoming more common. At some newer pools, play structures are part of the pool's design. At older pools, permanent play structures are being added—sometimes replacing other equipment, like diving boards. At all types of pools, removable play structures permit different activities during the day.

Permanent play structures include regular or drop-off slides, rope swings, sprays, fountains, and moving water (Fig. 6-10). Removable features include large floating toys, inflatable play structures, and water basketball and volleyball (Fig. 6-11).

Some pools allow patrons to bring toys and flotation devices to use. Be sure any toys brought into the water are clean and soft. Nonswimmers using flotation devices must be directly supervised by a parent or guardian. Do not let anyone use a flotation device as a safety device unless it is a Coast Guard–approved life jacket.

If your facility has such entertainment features, take precautions in addition to the basic principles of patron surveillance. Your careful observation helps ensure the safety of patrons and helps keep the play structure in good condition. Be alert for these potential problems:

figure 6-10 *Permanent play structures.*

figure 6-11 *Removable play structures.*

- The added excitement of play structures may lead nonswimmers or weak swimmers to become careless. They might try things they would not otherwise do, or they might enter deep water without meaning to.
- Swimmers can be surprised by the fall from a drop-off slide or rope swing, especially if they do not realize the slide or swing is over deep water. Watch that they return to the surface after dropping into the water.
- Sprays and fountains are usually in shallow water. Excited children may run and fall and be injured. A very young child who falls might not be able to get back up.
- Moving water can surprise people. They might lose their balance and be unable to stand up again.
- Patrons may climb onto floating toys and jump back into the water. They may not notice what is around them and jump onto other swimmers.
- Patrons may throw balls and other toys and hit unsuspecting swimmers, resulting in injury.

Some play structures require their own lifeguards; others can be monitored by lifeguards surveying a larger area. The surveillance depends on the location of the feature, the number of patrons in the facility and the number of patrons using the structures, the age and skills of those using the structures, the activity and excitement level, and the lifeguard's ability to see all around the structure (Fig. 6-12). Take the following precautions:

figure 6-12 *A lifeguard must be able to see around all play structures.*

- Don't let a play structure become overcrowded. Be prepared to restrict the number of patrons who use it at one time. You can form groups to use the structure or have a waiting line. If necessary, group users by age for safety.
- Keep activities involving balls away from other activities. Keep incompatible activities away from each other. For example, an aqua fitness class or preschool swim program should not be next to a water basketball or water polo game.

Always follow manufacturer's recommendations and facility policy for play structures. Check permanent play structures thoroughly at least once a day. Check removable play structures before they are set up for use. Use the guidelines supplied by the manufacturer.

Check all nonmoving parts of permanent play structures. Ladders, frames, and platforms should not be loose or wobbly. Check that all moving parts move properly. Joints should move freely and not stick or bind but should not be loose. All joints should be smooth, including joints on railings.

Check that water depth is proper for the type of play structure, the activity, and the age or skill level of users. The play structure should be far enough away from the side of the pool and other structures.

Check that removable play structures are **tethered** properly. Attachment points must be securely anchored. Check that hooks and connections are in good condition and there are no sharp edges. Check that tethers (ropes) are not worn or frayed, especially on inflatable slides.

Check all seams. On floating foam play structures, seams should cover all hard surfaces and have no gaps. On inflatable structures, seams should not leak.

Check that inflatable play structures have the correct air pressure. Do not allow anyone to climb on inflatable play structures on dry land.

When storing a removable structure, be sure it is clean and dry. This protects it and prolongs its life.

figure 6-13 *Check a water slide for any cracks or sharp edges.*

Water slides. Joints on water slides should not have gaps, cracks, or sharp edges. This is especially important on fiberglass slides, where cracks and sharp edges can cause severe cuts (Fig. 6-13). Be sure water keeps the surface of the slide wet to avoid rub burns. For small slides in shallow water, be sure landing pads in the pool under the slides are in good condition and securely fastened. Be sure removable slides are placed over water that is deep enough so that patrons do not hit the bottom of the pool.

Area 4: chemical storage areas. Check the filtration and **chlorination systems** and areas that are used to store chemicals and maintenance equipment. Do not enter such areas unless you have the special training required. However, you can make sure the doors are locked and that the area seems secure by observing it from the outside. Report any suspicious odors immediately.

Area 5: showers, locker rooms, and restrooms. Check to make sure areas are clean and hazard free.

table 6-1 *Sample Facility Safety Checklist*

	Yes	No	Action Taken	Date of Safety Check	Action Needed
Deck **Safety equipment in good repair**					
Rescue tubes and straps in good repair					
Backboards with head immobilizers and straps readily accessible					
First aid station clean; first aid equipment and supplies accessible and well stocked					
Telephones working properly					
Deck not slippery and in good repair					
Deck clear of patrons' belongings					
All equipment used by patrons stored properly if not in use					
Lifeguard stands clean and in good repair					
Clear of standing water					
Clear of glass objects					

table 6-1 *Sample Facility Safety Checklist—cont'd*

	Yes	No	Action Taken	Date of Safety Check	Action Needed
Pool					
Ladders secured properly					
Ladder handles clean and rust free					
Steps not slippery and in good repair					
Ramp not slippery and in good repair					
Drain covers secured properly					
Drain covers clean					
Suction at drains not excessive					
Lifelines and buoys in order					
Water clarity satisfactory					
Water color satisfactory					
Pool free of debris					
Gutters clean					
Water temperature in pool satisfactory					
Water temperature in spa satisfactory					
Recreational Equipment and Play Structures					
Ladders to diving boards not slippery and in good repair					
Rails at diving boards clean and in good repair					
Diving boards clean and not slippery					
Diving apparatus in good repair					
Movable fulcrums locked in forward position					
Removable starting blocks stored properly					
Access to permanent starting blocks restricted					
Play structures clean, in good repair, and not slippery					
Nonmoving parts on play structures secure					
Joints on play structures move freely					
Removable play structures placed at an appropriate distance from the deck and from other structures					
Removable play structures tethered properly: attachment points secure, hooks and connections in good condition with no sharp edges, tethers not worn or frayed					
Seams on play structures have no gaps or leaks					
Inflatable play structures have the correct air pressure					
"Flow-through" inflatable play structures have pump attached securely, located in a safe place, and plugged into the appropriate electrical circuit					

Continued.

table 6-1 *Sample Facility Safety Checklist—cont'd*

	Yes	No	Action Taken	Date of Safety Check	Action Needed
Recreational Equipment and Play Structures—cont'd					
Removable play structures stored properly					
Water slides smooth and in good repair					
Water flows properly on slides					
Landing pads under slides in good condition, securely fastened, and with no gaps to cause tripping					
Removable slides placed over water that is deep enough					
Equipment such as kickboards stored properly when not in use					
Chemical Storage Area					
Chemicals stored properly					
Door labeled properly					
Signs legible and in good condition					
Doors locked					
No suspicious odors					
Showers, Locker Rooms, and Rest Rooms					
All areas clean and free of algae					
Floors clean and not slippery					
Showers in good repair (no drips)					
Liquid soap available					
Drains clean					
Wastebaskets empty					
Drinking fountains and sinks clean and in good working order					
Signs in good repair and properly displayed					
Walls clean and free of markings					
Toilets and urinals clean					
Mirrors clean and unbroken					
No unpleasant odors					
Toilet tissue available					
Paper towels available					
Doors and windows working properly (including locks)					
No broken pins on locker keys					
All articles removed from lockers daily					
Collapsible shower seats in upright position					
Locker benches clean					
Clear of glass objects					

table 6-2 *Incident Chart*

#	Date	Time	Location	Type of Incident	Cause	Injured Area	Bather Load	Lifeguards on Duty	Water Conditions	Comments
1	5/30/93	1:45 pm	Diving Well	Near Drowning	Poor Ability	N/A	150	2	Clear	
2	6/11/93	12:15 pm	6' Wall	Near Drowning	Misjudg. Depth	N/A	125	2	Clear	
3	6/18/93	10:30 am	Diving Well	Drowning	Unknown	N/A	75	1	Cloudy	
4	6/21/93	11:15 am	Men's Entrance	Fall	Slippery Deck	Right Elbow	25	1	N/A	
5	6/21/93	2:30 pm	Shall. End Deck	Fall	Running	Left Knee	175	2	N/A	
6	7/2/93	3:30 pm	3.5' Wall	Spinal Injury	Diving	Head & Neck	160	2	Clear	
7	7/2/93	7:00 pm	4' Area	Tired Swimmer	Exhaustion	N/A	15	1	Clear	
8	7/3/93	2:10 pm	Diving Well	Near Drowning	Poor Ability	N/A	190	2	Clear	
9	7/4/93	11:00 am	3.5' Wall	Distress. Swim.	Misjudg. Depth	N/A	100	1	Clear	
10	7/4/93	1:30 pm	Pump Room	Chemical Burn	Unlocked Door	Both Hands	135	2	N/A	
11	7/11/93	12:30 pm	Diving Well	Distress. Swim.	Poor Ability	N/A	125	2	Clear	
12	7/15/93	10:45 am	4' Wall	Spinal Injury	Diving	Head & Neck	15	1	Clear	
13	7/24/93	7:30 pm	3.5' Wall	Argument	Lap Swimming	N/A	30	1	Clear	
14	7/28/93	5:30 pm	Pool Center	Tired Swimmer	Exhaustion	N/A	90	1	Clear	
15	8/1/93	3:45 pm	Diving Well	Near Drowning	Poor Ability	N/A	160	2	Clear	
16	8/1/93	4:15 pm	Diving Well	Near Drowning	Poor Ability	N/A	160	2	Clear	
17	8/7/93	10:45 am	Men's Entrance	Fall	Slippery Deck	Left Arm	20	1	N/A	
18	8/7/93	11:15 am	Men's Entrance	Fall	Slippery Deck	Left Ankle	25	1	N/A	
19	8/15/93	11:45 am	Men's Entrance	Fight	Unknown	N/A	10	1	N/A	
20	8/30/93	10:45 am	3.5' Wall	Distress. Swim.	Misjudg. Depth	N/A	120	1	Clear	
21	9/2/93	11:45 am	Diving Well	Near Drowning	Poor Ability	N/A	110	1	Clear	
22	9/5/93	2:15 pm	3.5' Wall	Distress. Swim.	Misjudg. Depth	N/A	190	2	Clear	
23										
24										
25										

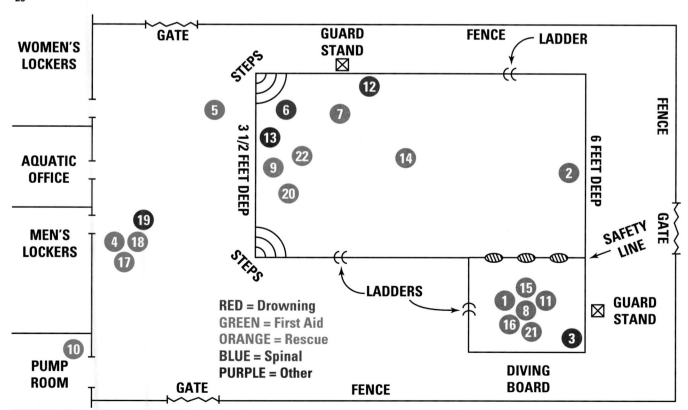

INCIDENT AND INJURY CHART

An incident and injury chart helps the facility management prevent injury. This is a diagram on which injuries at your facility are recorded. Table 6-2 shows examples of where and how injuries have happened and the type of injury. This information helps you and the management to eliminate or minimize any dangerous or potentially dangerous conditions.

An incident and injury chart usually shows all facility structures and equipment, such as lifeguard stands, lifelines, ladders, and diving boards along with fences and deck and grass areas. Any incident or injury that occurs is assigned a code and marked on the chart. Keeping track of all incidents and injuries, their frequency, and locations in this way helps management to identify what causes them. Then the head lifeguard or facility manager works to correct the condition by performing necessary maintenance, installing safety equipment, scheduling extra lifeguards, reassigning lifeguards for better supervision, or taking any other necessary steps.

You check showers, locker rooms, and rest rooms mostly for hazardous conditions like slippery floors and damaged equipment but also to look for health and sanitation reasons. Report hazards to the head lifeguard or facility manager immediately. Tell appropriate staff about maintenance needs.

WEATHER CONDITIONS

Weather can affect the safety of swimmers in outdoor and even indoor facilities. This section contains basic information about weather conditions. Since weather conditions vary greatly in different parts of the United States, you should know what conditions to look for at your facility and follow your facility's guidelines.

Some state weather bureaus and local television stations provide 24-hour telephone service for weather reports. The head lifeguard or facility manager may include these telephone numbers on the list of emergency telephone numbers at your facility. Local radio stations and some TV channels give weather reports throughout the day. In remote areas, you might get additional weather information from a CB radio and scanner.

Cloud formations

Certain cloud formations signal changes in the weather . Knowing these formations helps you anticipate likely changes in the weather. Following are some examples of cloud formations and the weather that usually goes along with them:

- High and hazy clouds usually form a halo around the sun or moon. These clouds indicate that a storm may arrive within hours (Fig. 6-14).
- Large clouds with cauliflower-like tops (known as thunderheads) signal an **imminent** thunderstorm. An active storm looks dark and heavy from below (Fig. 6-15).

figure 6-14 *Hazy clouds indicate a possible storm within hours.*

figure 6-15 *Clouds with cauliflower-like tops signal an imminent thunderstorm.*

- Rolling, dark clouds indicate that bad weather may arrive within minutes (Fig. 6-16).
- Fleecy white clouds indicate that good weather is ahead (Fig. 6-17).

Lightning

Lightning kills more people in this country than tornadoes, floods, or hurricanes. Thunderstorm activity in most areas is greatest during July and August. There are no set rules for when you should clear patrons from the water because of an impending storm. Since sound travels more slowly than light, a generally safe practice is to clear all patrons from the water at the first sound of thunder.

Once you become aware of a storm or other bad weather, be alert for thunder and lightning. Your facility may have guidelines for responding to thunder and lightning. The following procedures are recommended:

- When a thunderstorm threatens, clear the pool. If possible, get all patrons inside.
- Keep everyone away from windows inside. People can be injured by flying debris or glass if the window breaks.
- Do not let anyone take a shower during a thunderstorm. Water and metal can conduct the electricity of lightning.
- Do not use the telephone except for emergencies.

If there is not enough time to reach a safe building—

- Keep everyone away from structures in open areas, such as picnic shelters.
- Keep away from tall, isolated trees or objects that project above the landscape.
- Keep away from water and **grounded** objects, such as metal fences, tanks, rails, and pipes.

As a general rule, wait for 15 minutes after the thunder and lightning stop entirely before letting patrons return to the water. Continue to watch for another storm and monitor weather forecasts on the radio.

figure 6-16 *Rolling, dark clouds indicate approaching bad weather.*

figure 6-17 *Fleecy white clouds indicate good weather ahead.*

Heavy rain and hail

Heavy rain and hail can be dangerous. Rain is also a problem when it keeps you from seeing the bottom of the pool. In heavy rain or hail, clear patrons from the water and direct them to shelter.

Tornadoes

Monitor weather forecasts in areas prone to tornadoes. A **tornado watch** means that tornadoes are possible. A **tornado warning** means that a tornado has been sighted and that everyone should take shelter immediately. In this case, you and the patrons should—

- Stay away from all windows, doors, and outside walls.
- Go to the location specified in the facility's emergency action plan. This may be in the basement or an interior area of the lowest level of a building. Go to a designated shelter if time permits.

High wind

Wind may cause waves that reduce your ability to see patrons in the water. Wind also makes hypothermia more likely on cool days, especially for small children and the elderly. Remember to protect yourself from the effects of wind.

Fog

Fog can occur at any time of the day or night from weather conditions, such as a coming **cold front.** If the fog limits visibility, the head lifeguard or facility manager may have to close the facility.

Weather conditions and indoor facilities

Indoor facilities are safe from most weather problems but may still be affected by them. An indoor facility may or may not be grounded to protect patrons from lightning. Follow the procedures for severe weather described in the facility's operations manual.

Severe weather can cause a power failure. Every facility should have some type of portable or emergency lighting in case of a power failure. Keep everyone calm, and clear the pool and deck immediately. Inspect the pool to be sure everyone is out.

SUMMARY

To prevent injuries, an aquatic facility management tries to eliminate or reduce as many hazards as possible. You need to become very familiar with the features of the facility where you work. Frequent safety checks of all features help to control hazards. By combining facility surveillance with the other strategies of injury prevention, communication, and patron surveillance, you have a **comprehensive** approach for ensuring the safety of patrons at your facility.

STUDY QUESTIONS

Circle the letter of the correct answer or answers.
1. Which of the following areas have to be inspected for safety?
    a) Deck.
    b) Pool.
    c) Locker rooms.
    d) Recreational equipment.
    e) Chemical storage areas.
2. Which of the following are correct procedures to follow before or during a thunderstorm?
    a) No showers.
    b) Use the telephone only for emergencies.
    c) Clear the pool.
    d) Keep everyone away from windows.
    e) If there is not enough time to reach a safe building, stay near grounded objects.
3. After the last visible sign or sound of a thunderstorm, allow patrons to return to the water—
    a) Immediately.
    b) After waiting 15 minutes.
    c) After waiting 30 minutes.
    d) As soon as the air feels warm.
4. Heavy rain becomes a problem that requires clearing the pool when:
    a) The lifeguard stand gets wet.
    b) The deck becomes wet and slippery.
    c) You can no longer see the bottom of the pool.
    d) The sky turns dark.

5. If a tornado is expected, you should—
    a) Keep everyone away from all windows, doors, and outside walls.
    b) Send everyone home immediately.
    c) Go to the location specified in the emergency action plan for your facility.
    d) Go to a designated shelter if time permits.

Circle *True* or *False*.

6. If a pool drain's suction is too strong, the forces can trap and drown a child. True or False?
7. An incident and injury chart is a statement issued by a lifeguard after an incident or injury. True or False?
8. A tornado warning indicates that tornadoes are possible. True or False?

9. Match the following cloud formations with their probable weather conditions.
    ___ High and hazy clouds that may form a halo around the sun or moon.
    ___ Large clouds with cauliflower-like tops.
    ___ Rolling, dark clouds.
    ___ Fleecy white clouds.
    a) Good weather ahead.
    b) A storm may arrive within hours.
    c) Bad weather may arrive within minutes.
    d) Imminent thunderstorms.

See answers to study questions on p. 286.

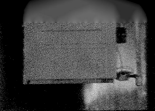

— POOL RULES —

• OBEY LIFEGUARD AT ALL TIMES
• NO RUNNING
• NO DIVING IN SHALLOW WATER
• NO ROUGH PLAY
• NO MORE THAN ONE PERSON ON THE
  DIVING BOARD AT ONE TIME
• STARTING BLOCKS USED ONLY BY
  COMPETITIVE SWIMMERS DURING
  PRACTICE AND MEETS

Objectives

After reading this chapter, you should be able to—

1. Explain what an emergency action plan is.
2. Describe the lifeguard's four basic responsibilities in an emergency.
3. Describe at least seven situations in which EMS should be contacted.
4. Describe the five steps involved in calling EMS.
5. Describe three types of communication often used at aquatic facilities.
6. Define the key terms for this chapter.

Key Terms

Emergency: A sudden, unexpected incident that demands immediate action.

Emergency action plan: A written plan detailing how facility staff are to respond in a specific type of emergency.

Emergency medical services (EMS) personnel: Trained and equipped community-based personnel dispatched through an emergency number to provide medical care for ill or injured people.

INTRODUCTION

It's late in the afternoon of your first day on the job. The pool is crowded. Your shift ends in about 5 minutes. As you scan the splashing, jumping, shifting crowd of children in your zone, you notice that something looks different—not quite right. Are you imagining something? Look closely. Yes, that child is in trouble. She needs help—now.

The difference between this—

SIX-YEAR-OLD DROWNS IN CROWDED POOL

and this— "You did a great job spotting that child and getting her out in time" lies in being prepared for emergencies.

A major part of your job is to be prepared for emergencies. An *emergency* is a sudden, unexpected incident that demands immediate action. In your entire career as a lifeguard, you may be lucky enough to encounter no emergency worse than a minor scrape or a simple assist from the water. But you can never relax or start thinking nothing serious ever happens. A child playing with his or her friends in the water can become a drowning victim right before your eyes. Unless you recognize what is happening and act appropriately, that child may not survive.

While in the water, people can have seizures, slip underwater, and suffocate. They can become ill from the heat or get chilled. They can find themselves in deep water and drown while struggling to reach safety. In or out of the water, people can have a heart attack or another sudden illness or an injury. They can suddenly pass out and submerge. They can fall on the deck or on a dock. They might dive into shallow water and strike their head on the bottom. The facility's electrical power might suddenly fail, or hazardous chemicals might spill. These are just a few of the possible emergencies in an aquatic facility.

To be able to handle emergencies, you must be prepared. This chapter explains various emergencies that can occur and prepares you to respond to them. Being prepared includes knowing your and other people's responsibilities for any emergency that might occur. Emergency response is a team effort. This chapter also discusses emergency action plans, how and when to call *EMS personnel,* and communication methods used in emergencies. The following chapters describe rescue skills, giving first aid in emergencies, and what needs to be done after an emergency has occurred.

RESPONDING TO EMERGENCIES

A lifeguard has four basic responsibilities in an emergency:

1 To keep all patrons safe by ensuring all zones stay covered at all times

2 To rescue and give first aid, including CPR, to a victim, or help another lifeguard doing so

3 To make sure EMS personnel are called when needed for the victim's condition

4 To ensure the victim gets the best possible care until EMS personnel arrive and to help these personnel as needed

Other staff at the facility may also have responsibilities in an emergency. They are part of the safety team. They may help clear the pool, control the crowd, or call EMS personnel. All staff follow the emergency action plan at the facility.

Emergency action plans

Emergency action plans detail how both staff and management are to respond in emergency situations. Without practical and well-rehearsed emergency action plans, staff would not be prepared for all emergencies that might occur. Fitness, rescue, first aid and CPR skills, and good intentions are not enough.

Facility management and head lifeguards usually develop the emergency action plans. Others outside the facility, such as police, EMS personnel, and the chemical supply company, may help develop some plans. Emergency action plans should be part of a facility's policies and procedures. You usually learn about them in your orientation to the facility.

Large facilities often have plans for many specific types of emergencies, such as a rescue or an evacuation of the facility. A small facility may have only a few plans that cover many situations.

Plans vary among different facilities also because of different rules and **ordinances** in different communities. For example, in some areas, **emergency medical technicians (EMTs)** are not allowed to enter the water to make a rescue. In others, only EMTs can put a spinal injury victim on a backboard and bring him or her out of the water.

At many facilities, you will practice your responsibilities in the emergency action plans during in-service training. All procedures should be practiced if possible at least twice a month to develop the needed teamwork. Before you begin your first shift as a lifeguard, you should know your facility's plan(s) and the assigned responsibilities for you and other staff for all emergencies. Ideally, your supervisor will have reviewed and practiced the plans with you. If your facility does not have an emergency action plan, suggest to management that a plan is needed and offer to help develop one.

General features of an emergency action plan.

Most plans have the following general features:

- Staff—What all staff should do in emergencies
- Emergency call—How and when to call EMS personnel and what information to give
- First aid—First aid procedures and designated area for giving first aid
- Communications—Systems and signals used at the facility
- Reports—Any reports a lifeguard must fill out after an emergency
- Working with the public after the emergency— Procedures for working with the public, the media, the local health department, and relatives of the victim. Lifeguards should know what to do or not do when questioned about an emergency and who in the facility is the designated **spokesperson** (see Chapter 12).

Emergency action plans or the facility's operations manual may also include the following information:

- A floor plan of the facility showing hazardous areas
- Equipment—What equipment is used, where it is kept, what is used to open the pool, and whom to tell about needed replacements or repairs

The lifeguard's responsibilities in an emergency.

In a facility with more than one lifeguard, your responsibilities depend on the area where the emergency occurs. When an emergency occurs in your area, you have to make a series of split-second decisions.

Your first step is to recognize that an emergency has occurred. You should always be aware of everything happening anywhere in your zone. Be ready to recognize if a person is drowning, ill, or injured—either in or out of the water.

Once you recognize an emergency, you signal other lifeguards and personnel. Your signal tells others that you are involved in an emergency and that someone has to cover your area of surveillance. If you are the only lifeguard, signal to patrons to leave the pool. Your facility's emergency action plan describes specific procedures for keeping all areas covered.

Backup coverage during zone surveillance.

When you leave your station for a rescue or to give first aid, your zone must be covered by other lifeguard(s). Backup coverage is planned for the facility depending on its size, shape, and staffing. Figure 7-1, *A* illustrates zone coverage when two lifeguards are on duty. In Figure 7-1, *B,* lifeguard X is the primary rescuer. Lifeguard X signals and leaves his or her assigned position and enters the water for a rescue (indicated by a solid line). The backup lifeguard (lifeguard Y) stands in the lifeguard chair (to improve visibility) and is responsible for scanning the whole pool.

Figure 7-2, *A* illustrates zone coverage when three lifeguards are on duty at the same type of pool. In Figure 7-2, *B,* lifeguard Y is the primary rescuer. He or she signals and enters the water (indicated by a solid line). The other two lifeguards (lifeguards X and Z) each stand in the lifeguard chairs and divide the responsibility for scanning the pool.

In Figure 7-2, *C,* lifeguard X is the primary rescuer. In this situation, lifeguard Y stands in the lifeguard chair and lifeguard Z moves to a new position on the deck (indicated by a dotted line). In this way, lifeguards Y and Z provide adequate coverage for the pool.

Checking the scene and assessing the victim.

Before you go into the water or take other action, make sure the scene is safe to enter. You have to decide within seconds. Always consider your safety and that of other patrons and lifeguards as well as the victim's safety.

figure 7-1 *A, Zone coverage for two lifeguards. B, Lifeguard X is the primary rescuer, and Lifeguard Y is responsible for scanning the whole pool.*

figure 7-2 *A, Zone coverage for three lifeguards. B, Lifeguard Y is the primary rescuer; Lifeguards X and Z both stand in lifeguard chairs and divide the responsibility for scanning the pool. C, Lifeguard X is the primary rescuer; Lifeguard Y stands in the lifeguard chair, and Lifeguard Z moves to a new position on the deck.*

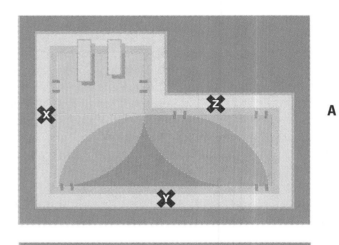

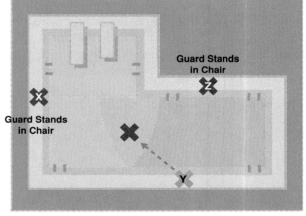

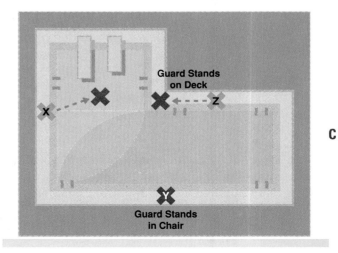

If conditions are unsafe, follow the emergency action plan for the situation.

Checking scene safety, for example, includes seeing whether the water is clear of swimmers in the area where you will enter the water. In another example, it may mean deciding whether you should approach the area of a chemical spill. The emergency action plan may state for you to have someone call a certain emergency number or contact a staff member with training to handle this type of emergency. You would also make sure patrons stay safe. In another example, when a person is in contact with an electrical source, the scene isn't safe until the power is turned off.

When you reach the victim, your next step depends on the victim's condition and location. Usually your goal is to get the victim at least to shallow water. If a victim is unconscious or was submerged, signal for EMS to be called. If the victim is conscious, bring him or her to shallow water or to the deck and then decide whether EMS personnel are needed. The decision whether to call EMS personnel usually depends on whether you believe the victim's condition is life-threatening.

To care for a victim before EMS personnel arrive, you and all lifeguards must know where special equipment, such as a resuscitation mask or a backboard, is kept. The emergency action plan should state who gets this equipment and how to get it to the victim.

If you decide the victim's condition is not life threatening, follow the facility's procedures and your first aid training (Fig. 7-3). You may decide the victim can go back in the water, you may tell the person not to go back in the water and recommend follow-up medical atten-

tion, or you may call EMS personnel. Procedures to follow after an emergency are described in Chapter 12.

The single-lifeguard facility. You may be a lifeguard at a smaller facility that has only one lifeguard on duty at a time, such as a swimming pool at an apartment complex, a small swim and racquet club, a hotel or motel, or a smaller private camp. One-lifeguard facilities involve different situations for supervision and emergency action plans. How is the facility supervised when the lifeguard takes a break? Who calls for help in an emergency? Who gets the first aid equipment? You need a clear understanding of these and other possible situations before beginning your job. Often another staff person, such as a cashier, is assigned to help the lifeguard in an emergency. This other person can help clear the pool, call EMS personnel, or help with a victim. If you know a reliable regular patron who is present when an emergency occurs, you might ask this person to help in some way.

Effective communication and patron education are especially important at a single-lifeguard facility. There should be signs posted stating that in an emergency all patrons must leave the pool when the lifeguard signals. The procedures for support personnel should be clear in the emergency action plans and rehearsed periodically, if possible. The system for communication with police, fire, and rescue personnel is important.

Following is a detailed emergency action plan for a single-lifeguard facility and flowcharts of single-lifeguard (Fig. 7-4), two-lifeguard (Fig. 7-5), and multi-lifeguard (Fig. 7-6) facilities follow the emergency action plan.

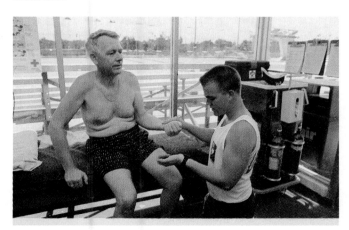

figure 7-3 *Lifeguard assessing a conscious victim's condition.*

Emergency action plan for a single-lifeguard facility

1 *Lifeguard recognizes that a person needs immediate help and acts.* If the lifeguard leaves a station, he or she first gives a prearranged signal, such as a whistle, to notify the patrons and any facility staff of an emergency and that patrons should leave the pool.

2 *Lifeguard contacts the victim and moves victim to safety.* In some cases, the lifeguard does not need to enter the water. He or she can contact the person from the deck. At other times, the lifeguard needs to enter the water. If available, designated safety team member supervises clearing of pool. The lifeguard enters the pool with a rescue tube and uses the appropriate rescue techniques to move the victim to safety.

figure 7-4 *Emergency action plan flowchart—single-lifeguard facility.*

figure 7-5 *Emergency action plan flowchart—two-lifeguard facility.*

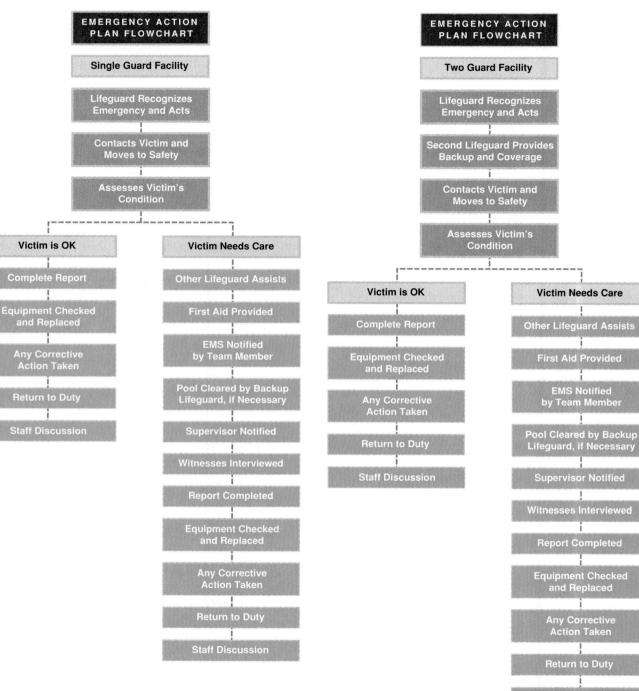

figure 7-6 *Emergency action plan flowchart—multi-lifeguard facility.*

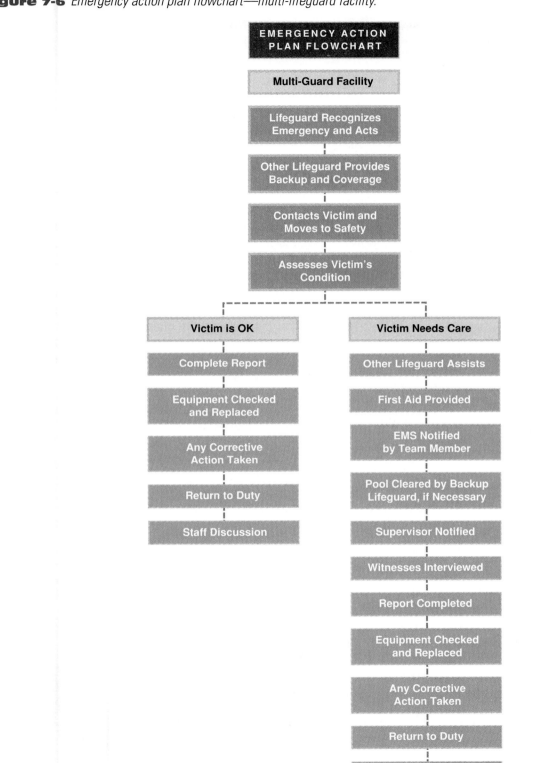

3 *The victim's condition is assessed.* If the lifeguard determines the victim is okay, then no further care is needed. If the victim is unconscious or not breathing, the lifeguard must provide first aid and see that EMS personnel are contacted. If a safety team member or bystander is present, he or she can call EMS.

4 *Chain of command notified.* If there is a serious injury or death, a designated person, such as the head lifeguard or the facility manager, notifies the appropriate supervisor(s) as soon as possible. The lifeguard who made the rescue must be available for questions and completion of a report. Supervisors will attempt to contact the victim's family.

5 *Witnesses interviewed.* As soon as possible, a designated person interviews witnesses to the incident. Interviews are conducted privately and documented in writing.

6 *Reports completed.* The lifeguard completes an incident report as soon as possible.

7 *Equipment checked.* The lifeguard checks any equipment used in the rescue and reports and replaces damaged or missing items. The pool is not reopened until all required equipment is in place.

8 *Corrective action taken.* Any conditions that contributed to the incident are corrected as soon as possible.

9 *Staff discussion.* If the incident involves a serious injury or death, a mental health professional may assist facility personnel.

Contacting EMS

Contacting EMS when needed is a vital part of all emergency action plans. You and other lifeguards, support staff, visiting coaches and instructors, and even patrons must be able to call EMS personnel immediately and give the right information to the dispatcher. Everyone in the facility should know where all telephones are located. Telephone signs should be posted where patrons can see them. Emergency numbers should be posted on all telephones along with the information the EMS dispatcher will want from the caller.

When to call EMS. EMS personnel should be called immediately whenever a victim —

- Is unconscious.
- Has a head injury.

- Has severe external bleeding or suspected internal bleeding.
- Has an obstructed airway (even if the victim recovers).
- Has a seizure in the water.
- Has critical burns.
- Has a suspected fracture.
- Has a suspected spinal injury.
- Has certain or suspected sudden illness as described in Chapter 10.

Any near-drowning victim or any victim who has received rescue breathing or CPR should be observed at a hospital regardless of how well he or she seems to have recovered. If a victim's condition is not life-threatening, the lifeguard caring for the victim can decide whether the problems warrant calling EMS personnel.

How to call EMS. Many areas have a 9-1-1 emergency telephone system for EMS. Some communities, however, have a local number to call in an emergency. Some facility phones require dialing 8 or 9 first to get an outside line. Knowing what number to call may mean the difference between life and death or permanent disability for the victim. The few minutes it could take to find the number to call could cost a life.

The number to call in an emergency should be posted by all telephones in the facility, along with instructions to dial 8 or 9 for an outside line if needed. You can call 9-1-1 on a pay phone without depositing any money, but in areas where the emergency number is not 9-1-1, coins should be kept near pay phones for emergency calls.

You or another lifeguard may make the call, or you may send someone else at the scene, such as support staff or a bystander, to call. If possible, send two people to ensure that the call is made correctly (Fig. 7-7). When

figure 7-7 *Calling for help can be the most important action to take to help the victim.*

anyone calls EMS in an emergency, he or she must give the **dispatcher** exact details. The facility should post the directions for what information to give and how to get to the facility from the nearest EMS location by the telephone. The caller only has to fill in the details.
To make the call—

1 **Call the emergency number.**

2 **Give the dispatcher the necessary information. Answer any questions he or she might ask. Most dispatchers will ask —**
   - **The exact location or address of the emergency. Include in your answer the name of the city or town, nearby landmarks, the street address or road name, the facility's name, and the location of the pool. You can give any posted directions for reaching the facility to the dispatcher.**
   - **The telephone number from which the call is being made.**
   - **The caller's name.**
   - **What happened—for example, a person had a seizure in the pool.**
   - **How many people are injured.**
   - **The condition of the victim—for example, not breathing.**
   - **What care is being given—for example, rescue breathing.**

3 **Be sure to describe who will meet the arriving EMS personnel and where they will be met—for example, person will be wearing red warm-up jacket with UMG on it and will be at the entrance on Fourth Street.**

4 **Do not hang up until the dispatcher hangs up. The dispatcher may tell you how to best care for the victim or may need more information.**

5 **Return and report to the lifeguard who is caring for the victim. If you are the lifeguard who is giving care, ask the caller(s) to report back to you and tell you what the dispatcher said.**

A lifeguard, staff member, or volunteer bystander should be in the right place to meet EMS when they arrive and guide them to the scene of the emergency. Once EMS is on the scene, continue to control the crowd and give any other help EMS personnel may need.

Appendix C is a form with instructions for emergency telephone calls. The page can be photocopied and posted next to telephones in the facility.

Communication

When you recognize an emergency is occurring, you need to communicate the situation to your safety team. You communicate with other lifeguards and staff with specific signals.

Every facility has a communication system that all staff must use. Systems vary depending on the type of facility and the number of staff. The signals used also vary among facilities, although certain signals are common. Signals must be simple, clear, and easily understood. Methods of communication include —

- **The whistle** (Fig. 7-8) . Use the whistle sparingly and only when needed. The following are examples of whistle signals:
  - **To get the attention of a swimmer**—One short blast.
  - **To get the attention of another staff member**— Two short blasts.
  - **To activate the emergency action plan** —Three short blasts.
  - **To clear the water**—One long blast

figure 7-8 *Use a whistle to get the attention of staff members and patrons.*

figure 7-9 *Point directly to a patron to gain his or her attention.*

figure 7-10 *Let swimmers know that they need to stop or stay where they are by holding your arm straight and your palms facing the individuals.*

- **Hand signals.** Hand signals are often used along with or immediately after whistle signals to communicate further messages. Hold the following hand signals for 5 seconds or until you see that the person received the signal.
  - **To gain attention**—Point directly to individual (Fig. 7-9).
  - **Stop or stay where you are**—Hold arm straight out, palm facing individual; arm is kept stationary (Fig. 7-10).
  - **Assistance is needed**—Hand with fist held high (Fig. 7-11).
  - **Cover my area**—Place hand on top of head and pat twice (Fig. 7-12).
  - **Situation is under control**—Place hand on top of head or show thumbs up or OK sign (Fig. 7-13, *A* and *B*).
- **Rescue equipment signals.** These signals are often used at a waterfront or waterpark, sometimes at a pool. Rescue equipment signals may be used in combination with hand or whistle signals. The following are examples of equipment signals:
  - **Assistance is needed**—Hold rescue tube vertically over head, and move it from side to side (Fig. 7-14).
  - **Situation is under control**—Hold rescue tube horizontally over the head (Fig. 7-15).

figure 7-11 *Holding your fist high in the air shows that assistance is needed.*

figure 7-12 *Placing your hand on top of your head and patting twice notifies other lifeguards to cover your area.*

figure 7-13 *A, Placing your hand on top of your head or B, giving the okay sign, is a way to signify that the situation is under control.*

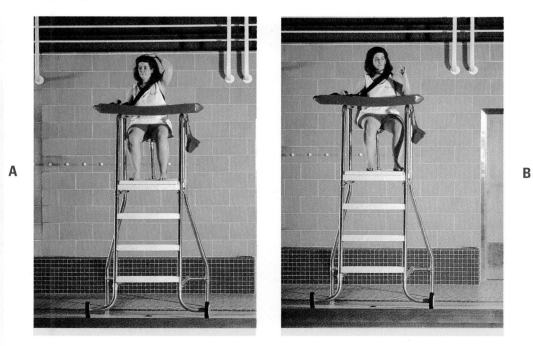

A

B

figure 7-14 *Holding a rescue tube vertically over your head shows that assistance is needed.*

Other means of communication include bull horns, public address systems, flags, electric buzzers, and telephones. Certain signals, such as flags and phones, are used at waterfronts or waterparks where distances between lifeguards may be greater than at pools (Fig. 7-16).

SUMMARY

As a lifeguard, you should be able to respond in all possible emergencies. Being able to rescue a victim and care for an injury or illness are as important as your efforts to prevent injuries. Use your knowledge, training, and experience to recognize an emergency, evaluate the situation, and respond to it safely and immediately. Your facility's emergency action plans serve as your guide.

figure 7-15 *By holding a rescue tube horizontally over your head, you show that the situation is under control.*

figure 7-16 *Lifeguards may use flag signals as a form of communication.*

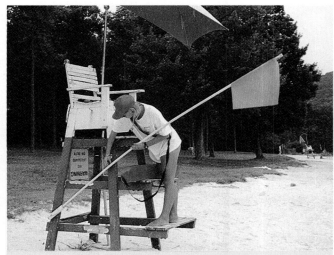

STUDY QUESTIONS

Circle the letter of the best answer or answers.

1. Which of the following is *not* one of the lifeguard's basic roles during an emergency?
   a) To make sure that the lifeguard's zones of responsibility are covered at all times
   b) To inspect all safety and rescue equipment on a daily basis and to repair or replace such equipment as needed
   c) To rescue or otherwise give first aid to a victim or to assist others in doing so
   d) To decide if the victim's condition requires calling EMS and to make sure the call is made
   e) To ensure the victim is given the best possible care until advanced medical help arrives

2. Before entering the scene of an emergency, check for safety. This may include—
   a) Checking to see if the area is cleared of swimmers.
   b) Deciding whether or not to approach the area of a chemical spill.
   c) Making sure the power is turned off if a person is in contact with a live source of electricity.
   d) Checking with the head lifeguard or facility manager to find out what to do next.

3. Under which of the following circumstances should EMS personnel be contacted immediately?
   a) If the victim is unconscious
   b) If the victim has a head injury
   c) If the victim has severe external bleeding or suspected internal bleeding
   d) If the victim complains of dizziness or shortness of breath
   e) If the victim has a seizure in the water
   f) If the victim has a front tooth knocked out
   g) If the victim has critical burns
   h) If the victim has a suspected spinal injury

4. Which of the following information should you be prepared to tell the EMS dispatcher?
   a) The telephone number for the facility
   b) How many people are injured
   c) The care being given
   d) The victim's condition
   e) Who caused the injury

5. Sequence the following steps to take when calling EMS for an emergency.
   ___ Describe the person who will meet EMS, and describe the location where they will be met.
   ___ Give the dispatcher the necessary information.
   ___ Return and report to the lifeguard who is caring for the victim.
   ___ Do not hang up until the dispatcher hangs up.
   ___ Call the emergency number.

6. Sequence the following steps a lifeguard should take when responding to an emergency.
   ___ Use a specific signal to alert other lifeguards and facility personnel so that your area of surveillance is covered.
   ___ Recognize that an emergency has occurred.
   ___ Contact the victim, and get him or her to safety.
   ___ Make sure the scene is safe to enter.
   ___ Signal for EMS to be called, if necessary.

Circle *True* or *False*.

7. If a victim recovers from an obstructed airway, EMS personnel do not need to be contacted. True or False?

8. The best and quickest way to activate the emergency action plan is to yell loudly for help. True or False?

See answers to study questions on page 286.

RESCUE SKILLS

8

After reading this chapter, you should be able to—

1. List the seven steps that are part of any rescue.
2. List three reasons for using rescue equipment when performing a rescue.
3. Explain when to use an extension assist from the deck.
4. Explain when to use a stride-jump entry and when to use a compact jump.
5. Explain the factors involved in deciding whether to move a victim from the water.
6. Explain the importance of follow-up care.
7. Define the key term for this chapter.

After reading this chapter and completing the appropriate course activities, you should be able to—

1. Demonstrate an extension assist from the deck.
2. Demonstrate two methods of entering the water.
3. Demonstrate two ways to approach a victim with rescue equipment.
4. Demonstrate the swimming extension rescue.
5. Demonstrate the active victim rear rescue.
6. Demonstrate the passive victim rear rescue.
7. Demonstrate the feet-first surface dive.
8. Demonstrate the submerged victim rescue.
9. Demonstrate the multiple-victim rescue.
10. Demonstrate how to remove a victim from the water using the two-lifeguard lift.

Rescue tube: A vinyl, foam-filled, floating support used in making rescues.

INTRODUCTION

As a lifeguard, you are expected to enter the water to make a rescue in an emergency. To do this properly, you must first assess that a person needs help and determine his or her condition and then *use an appropriate rescue skill for the situation*. Use the skills in this chapter in most aquatic environments, although you may have to modify some skills in a particular situation.

figure 8-1 *Activate the facility's emergency action plan once an emergency is identified.*

GENERAL RESCUE PROCEDURES

You use different rescue skills for someone who needs help in the water, depending on the situation. In all rescues, however, you must provide for your own safety, as well as the victim's. Always use rescue equipment to provide support and flotation for the victim so that he or she can breathe. Focus on the outcome of the rescue, not just the steps of the skill. Getting the victim safely out of the water is more important than performing each and every step perfectly.

In all rescue situations, follow these seven general procedures:

1. *Activate your facility's emergency action plan.* Once you recognize an emergency situation, alert other lifeguards and staff so that they can provide back-up coverage, give additional help, and call EMS personnel if necessary (Fig. 8-1).

2. *Enter the water.* Do this as quickly and safely as possible. Choose the best entry based on these factors:
   - Water depth
   - The height from which you make your entry
   - Facility design

3. *Approach the victim.* Swim to the victim to make contact and perform the rescue. Depending on the victim's location, you may slow your approach before making contact to get into a good swimming position to tow the victim to safety.

4. *Perform an appropriate rescue.* Before contacting the victim, determine the victim's condition: a distressed swimmer, active drowning victim, or passive drowning victim and whether he or she is at the surface or submerged. Then make contact and use the appropriate rescue skill for the situation.

5. *Move the victim to safety.* The type of kick you use depends on your strength, comfort, and ability.

6. *Remove the victim from the water.* If possible, get help for lifting the victim safely from the water.

7. *Provide emergency care as needed.* Depending on the victim's condition, you may have to clear the victim's airway or perform rescue breathing, CPR, or other first aid until EMS personnel arrive.

THE RESCUE TUBE

The *rescue tube* is a vinyl, foam-filled, floating support approximately 45 to 54 inches long. This is the most frequently used piece of equipment in lifeguarding today. It is most effective because it is easy to use and, depending on the size, can support three to five people. A tow line and shoulder strap are attached to the rescue tube. The total length of the tow line and shoulder strap varies from 4-6 feet (Fig. 8-2).

The rescue tube provides safety for both you and the victim, and it lets you perform rescues that would be difficult without it, such as a multiple-victim rescue. The rescue tube —

- Provides flotation for the victim and for you. A victim who can keep his or her mouth above water feels less anxiety and can more easily follow your directions.
- Reduces the energy needed to move the victim to safety.
- Reduces the chance of a victim grasping you during a rescue. Should a rescue not go as planned, you are protected by having the rescue tube between you and the victim.

Keep the strap of the rescue tube over your shoulder and head. Hold the rescue tube across your thighs when sitting in a lifeguard chair and across your stomach when standing. Hold the excess line in one hand to prevent getting the line caught in the lifeguard chair or other equipment when you enter the water. *Remember, always keep the rescue tube in a position for immediate response while on duty* (Fig. 8-3).

If your rescue tube slips out of position during a rescue, try to reposition it quickly. Make every effort to maintain control of the rescue tube you are using or to recover it if it slips away. Above all, always use your rescue equipment.

Extension assist from the deck

If a distressed swimmer is close to the side of the pool or dock, you can extend a rescue tube to him or her. This is the safest way to help a person in difficulty. Extending a rescue tube may not work with a drowning victim, since he or she might not be able to grasp it. In that case, you have to use a different rescue approach.

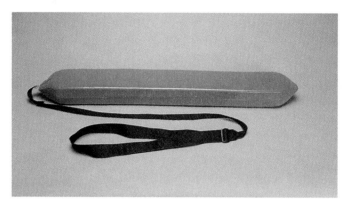

figure 8-2 *The rescue tube provides safety for both the lifeguard and the victim. A rescue tube consists of a tube, tow line, and shoulder strap.*

figure 8-3 *Keep the rescue tube in a position for immediate response.*

figure 8-4 *To assist a distressed swimmer close to the side of the pool or dock,* **A,** *extend rescue tube to the victim and* **B,** *pull the victim to safety.*

A

B

To perform an extension assist from the deck—

1 **Remove the rescue tube's shoulder strap from your shoulder.**

2 **Hold the shoulder strap in your hand, and extend the rescue tube to the victim. Talk to the victim to calm him or her, and give directions about what to do (Fig. 8-4, *A*).**

3 **When the victim grasps the rescue tube, slowly pull him or her to safety (Fig. 8-4, *B*).**

ENTRIES

When you recognize an emergency in the water, you often have to enter the water for a rescue. Following are two safe ways to enter the water for a rescue.

Stride jump

Use the stride jump with a rescue tube only in water at least 5 feet deep and only from a height of 3 feet or less above the water. To perform the stride-jump entry —

1 **Squeeze the rescue tube high against your chest with the ends under your armpits. Hold the excess line in one hand to avoid entanglement while you jump into the water (Fig. 8-5, *A*).**

2 **Leap into the water with one leg forward and the other leg back. Lean slightly forward. Keep your chest forward of your hips as you enter the water (Fig. 8-5, *B*).**

3 **As you enter the water, squeeze or scissor your legs together for upward thrust. The buoyancy of the rescue tube and your kick help bring you to the surface (Fig. 8-5, *C* and *D*).**

4 **When you surface, focus on the victim and begin your approach (Fig. 8-5, *E*).**

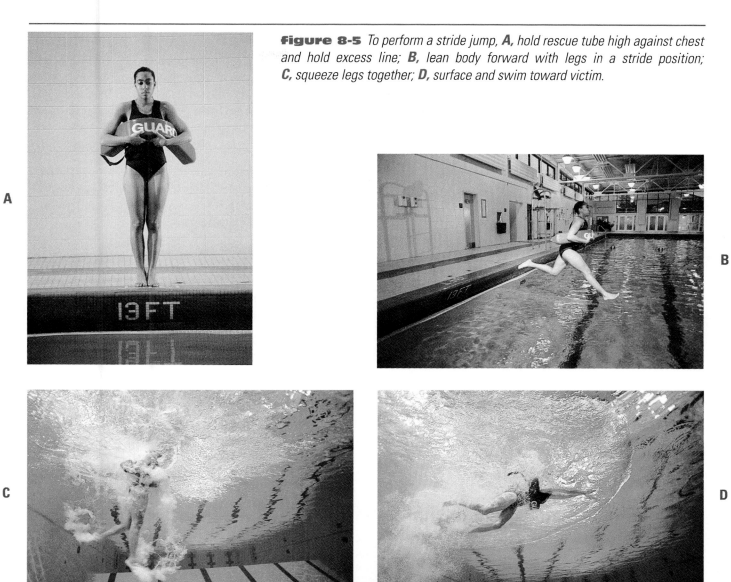

figure 8-5 *To perform a stride jump, **A,** hold rescue tube high against chest and hold excess line; **B,** lean body forward with legs in a stride position; **C,** squeeze legs together; **D,** surface and swim toward victim.*

figure 8-6 *To perform a compact jump,* **A,** *hold rescue tube high against chest and hold excess line;* **B,** *jump away from the lifeguard chair, keeping the knees bent and feet flat;* **C,** *surface and swim toward victim.*

Compact jump

Use the compact jump to enter the water from a height greater than 3 feet, such as from a lifeguard stand. Jump from this height only into water at least 5 feet deep. Use the compact jump also from the deck into water less than 5 feet deep. To perform the compact jump —

1 Squeeze the rescue tube high against your chest with the ends under your armpits. Hold the excess line in one hand to keep it from getting caught in the lifeguard chair or other equipment (Fig. 8-6, *A*).

2 Jump out and away from the lifeguard chair or pool deck. Keep your knees bent and your feet together and flat to absorb the shock if you strike the bottom (Fig. 8-6, *B*). Do not point your toes or enter with straight or stiff legs.

3 The buoyancy of the rescue tube helps bring you back to the surface.

4 When you surface, focus on the victim and begin your approach (Fig. 8-6, *C*).

A

B

C

APPROACHING THE VICTIM

The most effective swimming stroke for reaching a nearby victim is a modified crawl or breast-stroke (Fig. 8-7, *A* and *B*). Keep the rescue tube under your armpits or **torso**, and swim toward the victim with your head up. Keep the rescue tube in control at all times. If it slips out from under your arms or if you have a great distance to swim to the victim, let the rescue tube trail behind you (Fig. 8-8).

When you get close to the victim, slow your approach. This puts you in a good swimming position before you make contact with the victim and prepares you to support the victim with your rescue tube.

1　When you are about 6 feet from the victim, slow your approach (Fig. 8-9, *A*).

2　If the rescue tube was trailing behind you, bring it forward now and squeeze it high against your chest with the ends under your armpits.

3　Kick toward the victim and initiate the rescue (Fig. 8-9, *B*).

figure 8-7 *A, Modified crawl stroke with rescue tube. B, Modified breaststroke with rescue tube.*

figure 8-9 *To prepare to make contact with the victim, A, Slow down your approach. B, Kick toward the victim.*

A

A

B

figure 8-8 *Let the rescue tube trail behind if it slips out or the distance to the victim is great.*

B

Kicks Used In Lifeguarding

Scissors Kick

The scissors kick is a powerful kick and is easy to learn. Perform it as follows:

1. Recover your legs by flexing your hips and knees and drawing your heels slowly toward your buttocks. Keep your knees close together in this movement (A-1).

2. To prepare for the kick, flex your top ankle and point the toes of your bottom foot. Move the top leg forward and the bottom leg back. Your top leg is almost straight and the bottom leg extends the thigh slightly to the rear of the trunk, with that knee flexed (A-2).

3. Without pausing, press your top leg backward while extending the bottom leg forward until both legs are fully extended and together. Be sure to push the water with the bottom of your top foot and the top of your bottom foot. As you move your top foot backward, move that ankle from a flexed position to a toes-pointed position to press the sole of your foot as hard as possible against the water (A-3).

A-1

A-2

A-3

Inverted Scissors Kick

The inverted scissors kick is identical to the scissors kick but reverses the top and bottom leg actions. The top leg moves toward the rear of the body, and the bottom leg moves toward the front of the body.

Elementary Backstroke Kick

If you have a stronger elementary backstroke kick than scissors kick, you can use this kick to move a victim to safety. Perform the elementary backstroke kick as follows —

1   Recover your legs by bending knees and bringing your heels up toward your buttocks (B-1).

2   Gradually move your knees and heels apart until your knees are hip-width apart and your feet are outside your knees (B-2).

3   Flex your ankles and rotate your feet outward to engage the water with the soles of your feet (B-3) .

4   With a continuous whipping action, press your feet backward until the feet and ankles touch (B-4).

B-1

B-2

B-3

B-4

Continued.

Kicks Used In Lifeguarding—cont'd

Rotary Kick (Eggbeater Kick)

This kick is excellent for moving a victim to safety. It uses a continuous rotary movement of the feet around the knees to generate downward force. When performed well, the rotary kick is the best supporting kick for rescues. Perform the rotary kick as follows—

1 From a vertical position, keep your hips flexed and your thighs comfortably forward (C-1).

2 Flex your knees so that your lower legs hang at an angle of nearly 90 degrees to your thighs (C-2).

3 Flex your ankles and rotate your feet outward to engage the water with the soles of your feet (C-3).

C-1

C-2

C-3

4   With knees slightly wider than hip-distance apart, rotate your lower legs at the knee, one leg at a time. Move the left leg clockwise and the right leg counterclockwise (C-4).

5   Make large circular movements with each foot and lower leg. As soon as one leg completes its circle, the other leg starts (C-5).

C-4

C-5

VICTIMS AT OR NEAR THE SURFACE

Often a victim is at the surface or within reach of a rescuer at the surface. When rescuing a distressed swimmer or an active drowning victim, your goal is to support the person on the rescue tube with his or her head above water. Use the following skills with active victims.

Swimming extension rescue

The swimming extension rescue is simple and can be used for a distressed swimmer. To perform this rescue—

1 Approach the victim from the front (Fig. 8-10, *A*).

2 Extend the end of the rescue tube to the victim. Tell the victim to grab and hold the rescue tube for support and to kick if he or she can (Fig. 8-10, *B*).

3 Move the victim to safety (Fig. 8-10, *C*).

figure 8-10 *Use the swimming extension rescue for a distressed swimmer. **A**, Approach the victim from the front. **B**, Extend the rescue tube to the victim. **C**, Move the victim to safety.*

A

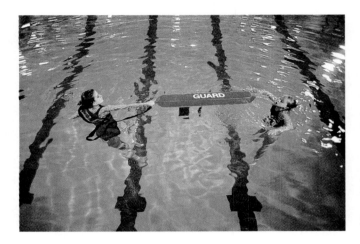

B

C

figure 8-11 *The active victim rear rescue.* **A,** *Approach the victim from the rear.* **B,** *Reach under the victim's armpits.* **C,** *Grasp the victim's shoulders.* **D,** *Lean back and pull the victim onto the rescue tube.*

A

B

Active victim rear rescue

The active victim rear rescue can be used for either a distressed swimmer or an active drowning victim. Approaching from the rear is safest for you. Keep your head to one side as you reach for and support the victim to prevent being hit by the victim's head if it comes back toward you.

 C

1 Approach the victim from the rear (Fig. 8-11, *A*).

2 Reach under the victim's armpits, and grasp his or her shoulders. Squeeze the rescue tube between your chest and the victim's back (Fig. 8-11, *B* and *C*).

3 Lean back and pull the victim onto the rescue tube. Use the rescue tube to support the victim with his or her face out of the water. Talk to the victim to calm him or her (Fig. 8-11, *D*).

4 Move him or her to safety.

 D

Passive victim rear rescue

Use the passive victim rear rescue when the victim seems unconscious and you do not suspect a spinal injury. If you suspect a spinal injury, use the techniques described in Chapter 11.

Because of differences in buoyancy, the victim's position may vary from nearly vertical to nearly horizontal. The objective of this rescue is to position the rescue tube under the victim's shoulders or back to support him or her face up. To perform a passive victim rear rescue—

1 Approach the victim from the rear.

2 Reach under the victim's armpits, and grasp his or her shoulders. Squeeze the rescue tube between your chest and the victim's back (Fig. 8-12, *A*).

3 Roll the victim over so that he or she is face up on top of the rescue tube (Fig. 8-12, *B*).

4 Move the victim to safety. If possible, use one hand to stroke. To do this, reach your right arm over the victim's right shoulder and grasp the rescue tube. Then use your left hand to stroke (Fig. 8-12, *C*). You can also reach with your left arm and stroke with your right hand.

figure 8-12 *The passive victim rear rescue.* **A,** *Reach under the victim's armpits and grasp the shoulders.* **B,** *Roll the victim over onto the rescue tube.* **C,** *If possible, use one hand to stroke when moving the victim to safety.*

A

B

C

SUBMERGED VICTIMS

Sometimes a victim is below the surface and beyond your reach. This may occur when a weak swimmer enters water over his or her head, such as by jumping or diving from a diving board or platform. A victim may also submerge after having a heart attack, stroke, or seizure or otherwise becoming unconscious in the water.

Feet-first surface dive

By surface diving, you can submerge to rescue or search for a submerged victim. To perform a feet-first surface dive—

1 When you are over the victim, let go of the rescue tube but keep strap around shoulders. From a vertical position, press downward with your hands and give a strong kick to rise out of the water (Fig. 8-13, *A*). Take a breath and let your body sink. Keep your legs straight and together with your toes pointed (Fig. 8-13, *B*).

2 When your downward momentum slows, turn your palms outward and sweep your hands and arms upward. Repeat this arm movement until you reach the desired depth (Fig. 8-13, *C*).

Depending on the depth of the victim, proceed with one of the following techniques:

- If the victim is not very deep, you can reach him or her without removing the strap. Proceed with your rescue.
- If the victim is a little deeper, you may have to remove the strap as you descend, but hold onto it so that you can use the rescue tube to help bring the victim to the surface.
- If the victim is deeper than the length of the tow line and strap, release the strap, secure the victim, and kick to the surface. When you return to the surface, place the rescue tube in position and proceed with your rescue.

A

B

C

figure 8-13 *Feet-first surface dive.* ***A,*** *Press downward with hands, and give a strong kick. Take a deep breath.* ***B,*** *Keep legs straight and toes pointed while letting your body sink.* ***C,*** *Turn palms outward, and sweep hands and arms upward.*

Submerged victim rescue

A submerged victim may either be passive or still active, but you use the same rescue skill in both cases. To perform a submerged victim rescue —

1 Do a feet-first surface dive, and position yourself behind the victim (Fig. 8-14, *A*).

2 Reach one arm under the victim's arm (right arm to right side or left arm to left side) and across the victim's chest. Hold firmly onto the victim's opposite side (Fig. 8-14, *B*).

3 When you have secured the victim, reach up with the other hand and grasp the towline, then pull it down and place it in the hand holding the victim. Keep pulling it in this way until you reach the surface. If possible, push off the bottom and kick to help you reach the surface (Fig. 8-14, *C*).

4 As you surface, position the rescue tube so that it is squeezed between your chest and the victim's back (Fig. 8-14, *D*).

5 Reach your free arm under the victim's armpit, and grasp his or her shoulder (right arm to right shoulder or left arm to left shoulder) (Fig. 8-14, *E*).

6 Move your other arm from across the victim's chest, and grasp his or her shoulder.

7 Support the victim in a face-up position on the rescue tube (Fig. 8-14, *F*).

8 Move the victim to safety.

If you had to release the strap of your rescue tube in order to reach the victim, you may come to the surface and find that the rescue tube is not within your reach. You may also find that the side of the pool or the dock is closer than the distance to the rescue tube. If either of these situations occurs, maintain your hold on the victim and move to safety.

figure 8-14 *Submerged victim rescue.* **A,** *Perform a feet-first surface dive.* **B,** *Position yourself behind the victim, reach one arm across the victim's chest, and hold firmly.* **C,** *Use your free hand to grasp the line of the rescue tube to pull it down.* **D,** *Place the tube between you and the victim as you surface.* **E,** *Reach your free arm under the victim's armpit, and grasp the shoulder.* **F,** *Support the victim on the rescue tube.*

A

B

C

F

Courtney Dunham

D

E

"A Real Grabber"

In rare situations, a rescuer may be grabbed by a victim. Regardless of the reason, the rescuer should maintain the use of the rescue tube as it will provide more than adequate flotation for both the rescuer and the victim.

If a rescuer is ever in a situation where he or she loses his or her equipment and is grabbed by a victim, the rescuer should take a quick breath, protect his or her airway by tucking the chin, and deliberately take the victim underwater. Commonly, taking the victim underwater releases the victim's grip on the rescuer because the victim is trying to maintain his or her ability to breathe.

The rescuer's ability to react properly in these situations will depend on the proficiency of his or her swimming skills and the ability to maintain a calm, cool head. This can only be achieved by understanding the principles of lifeguarding and by repeated practice of rescue skills in a variety of simulated situations.

MULTIPLE-VICTIM RESCUE

A rescue situation may involve two or more victims. Often a victim will clutch a nearby swimmer in an effort to stay at the surface. Several lifeguards should handle a multiple-victim situation if possible. For safety, the best arrangement is to have one lifeguard for each victim. Each lifeguard should have his or her own rescue tube.

Should a multiple-victim situation occur where water visibility is poor, at least one lifeguard should check the bottom for possible submerged victims while other lifeguards rescue victims at the surface. Ask the victims if anyone may still be underwater. Thoroughly search the area immediately after giving emergency care to the rescued victims.

If you are the only lifeguard in a situation where two victims are clutching each other—

1 Approach one victim from the rear (Fig. 8-15, *A*).

2 Grasp the victim by reaching under his or her armpits and grasping the shoulders (Fig. 8-15, *B*). Squeeze the rescue tube between your chest and the victim's back.

3 Begin kicking and lean back. This helps bring the faces of both victims out of the water. Remember to talk to the victims to calm them (Fig. 8-15, *C*).

4 Move the victims to safety.

If you cannot move through the water towing both victims, keep talking to them to calm them and continue to support them on the rescue tube. The buoyancy of the rescue tube should be enough to keep you and the victims afloat until help arrives. If the victims calm down, they may be able to help you kick to safety.

figure 8-15 *Multiple-victim rescue. A, Approach one victim from the rear. B, Reach under the victim's armpits and grasp the shoulders. C, Lean back and kick while moving both victims to safety.*

A

B

C

REMOVAL FROM THE WATER

Sometimes a victim is unconscious or too exhausted to climb out of the water, even on a ladder. Your decision whether to remove the victim from the water depends on the victim's condition, the length of time before you expect help to arrive, the size of the victim, and the availability of others to help you. If a victim needs rescue breathing or CPR, remove him or her from the water as soon as possible. In this process, maintain contact with the victim at all times. Lift with your legs and not your back. You can be injured by lifting improperly. The following skills can be performed in both deep and shallow water.

Two-lifeguard lift

Two lifeguards are needed to remove a victim from the water most safely. To perform the two-lifeguard lift—

1 Bring the victim to the side of the pool, and rotate him or her to face the deck (Fig. 8-16, *A*).

2 Support the victim with your knee. Reach under the victim's armpits, and grasp the edge of the deck (Fig. 8-16, *B*).

3 Place the victim's hands, one on top of the other, on deck or **overflow trough.** The second lifeguard then takes the hands and pulls the victim up slightly to keep the head above water. Be sure to support the victim's head so that it does not fall forward and strike the deck (Fig. 8-16, *C*).

4 Remove the tube and climb out of the water to help the second lifeguard.

5 Each lifeguard grasps one of the victim's wrists and upper arm (Fig. 8-16, *D*). Lift together until the victim's hips or thighs are at deck level (Fig. 8-16, *E*).

6 Step backward and lower the victim to the deck. Be sure to protect the victim's head from striking the deck (Fig. 8-16, *F*).

7 If necessary, pull the victim's legs out of the water, taking care not to twist the victim's back. Roll the victim onto his or her back (Fig. 8-16, *G*). Take care not to twist the victim's body as you roll it.

figure 8-16 *Two-lifeguard lift.* **A,** *Face the victim toward the deck.* **B,** *Support the victim with your knee, and reach under victim's armpits and grasp deck.*

A

B

figure 8-16—cont'd *C, The second lifeguard takes victim's hands. **D,** Each life-guard grasps a wrist and upper arm. **E,** At the same time, both lifeguards lift the victim out of the water. **F,** Lower the victim to a prone position, making sure to protect the head. **G,** Roll the victim over.*

E

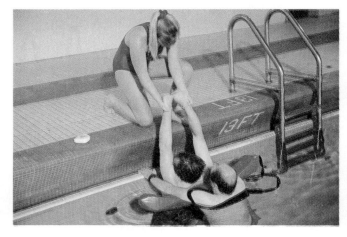

C

F

D

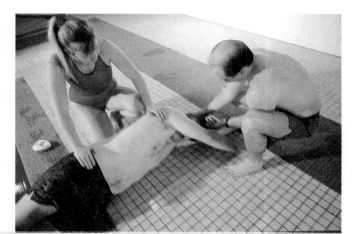

G

One-lifeguard lift

If no other lifeguard or bystander can help you remove a victim from the water, send someone to get help. If necessary, try to remove the victim by yourself, using the following modification of the two-lifeguard lift just described.

If the victim is too large or heavy for you to remove from the water by yourself, support him or her in the water until help arrives.

1 **Bring the victim to the side of the pool, and rotate him or her to face the deck.**

2 **Support the victim with your knee. Reach under the victim's armpits, and grasp the edge of the deck or overflow trough.**

3 **Place the victim's hands, one on top of the other, on the deck or overflow trough.**

4 **Hold the victim's hands on the deck or overflow trough with one hand. Remove the rescue tube, and climb out of the water (Fig. 8-17, A).**

5 **Grasp both of the victim's wrists. Using your legs, lift the victim until his or her hips or thighs are at deck level (Fig. 8-17, B).**

6 **Step back and lower the victim to the deck. Be sure to protect the victim's head from striking the deck (Fig. 8-17, C).**

7 **If necessary, pull the victim's legs out of the water, being careful not to twist the victim's back. Roll the victim onto his or her back. Keep the victim's body from twisting.**

figure 8-17 *One-lifeguard lift. **A,** The lifeguard holds victim's hand with one hand and uses the other to get out of the pool. **B,** Lift victim out of the water. **C,** Lay victim on the deck. Make sure to protect the head.*

A

B

PROVIDING EMERGENCY CARE

When you reach the victim and determine that he or she is unconscious, additional care is needed. The emergency does not end when you remove the victim from the water. Have someone call EMS personnel. Follow-up care is extremely important. If the victim is unconscious and not breathing, open the airway and check the mouth for any obvious obstruction, such as food or fluid. If the airway appears clear, attempt rescue breathing.

If the airway is obstructed, give abdominal thrusts (Heimlich maneuver) for children or adults to clear the airway. Once the airway is clear, provide rescue breathing or CPR as needed (Fig. 8-18).

If the victim is conscious but bleeding, control the bleeding. If the victim is cold, use dry towels or blankets to keep him or her warm. You will learn about first aid procedures for injuries and sudden illnesses in Chapters 9 and 10.

Follow-up care includes keeping the victim calm. Be reassuring and talk to the victim to let him or her know that everything is okay and that EMS personnel will be there soon. Giving first aid until EMS personnel arrive prevents further injury, disability, or even death.

figure 8-18 *Follow-up care is extremely important.*

SUMMARY

This chapter describes rescue skills for active and passive victims who may be on the surface or submerged. Your goal in a rescue is to get the victim safely out of the water. Stay focused on this outcome rather than worrying about performing each step perfectly. Although rescuing a victim safely is the goal, do not overlook your own safety. By using a rescue tube in a rescue situation, you can provide an extra measure of safety for yourself and the victim.

STUDY QUESTIONS

1. List the following steps that are part of any rescue in their proper sequence:
   ___ Approach the victim.
   ___ Move the victim to safety.
   ___ Activate your facility's emergency action plan.
   ___ Provide emergency care as needed.
   ___ Enter the water.
   ___ Remove the victim from the water.
   ___ Perform an appropriate rescue.

Circle the letter of the best answer or answers.

2. Which of the following statements are true regarding rescue tubes?
   a) Rescue tubes provide flotation for the victim and you.
   b) Rescue tubes reduce the energy you need to move the victim to safety.
   c) Rescue tubes help reduce the chances that a victim can grasp you during a rescue.
   d) Use a rescue tube only when the victim is heavier than you.

3. If a distressed swimmer is not far from the side of the pool, you can extend a rescue tube to him or her. This skill is called—
   a) A reaching assist.
   b) A swimming extension rescue.
   c) An extension assist from the deck.
   d) An active victim rescue.

4. The swimming extension rescue, the active victim rear rescue, and the passive victim rear rescue are all rescue skills used for—
   a) Multiple victims.
   b) Victims at or near the surface.
   c) Submerged victims.
   d) Spinal injury victims.

5. When a situation involves two or more victims, the victims may clutch each other in their efforts to stay at the surface. In a multiple-victim situation, the best safety arrangement is—
   a) Several lifeguards working together.
   b) One lifeguard working alone with a rescue tube.
   c) One lifeguard working alone with several rescue tubes.
   d) One lifeguard for each victim, with one rescue tube per lifeguard.

6. Sometimes a victim is unconscious or too exhausted to climb out of the pool, even when a ladder is available. You may have to remove the victim from the water. You should make your decision based on which of the following?
   a) The victim's condition
   b) The length of time before emergency personnel may arrive
   c) The size of the victim
   d) The help available to assist you
   e) If you are at the end of your lifeguarding shift

7. Follow-up care may include which of the following?
   a) CPR
   b) Rescue breathing
   c) First aid to control bleeding
   d) Blankets or dry towels to keep the victim warm
   e) Keeping the victim calm

Circle *True* or *False*.

8. The stride jump entry with a rescue tube is appropriate only from a height greater than 3 feet. True or False?

9. The compact jump can be used to jump from the deck into water that is less than 5 feet deep. True or False?

10. You use the same skill to rescue a submerged victim whether the victim is active or passive. True or False?

See answers to study questions on p. 286.

FIRST AID FOR INJURIES

9

Objectives

After reading this chapter, you should be able to—

1. Describe four types of open wounds.
2. Explain the uses of dressings and bandages.
3. Describe the care for closed wounds.
4. Describe the care for major and minor open wounds.
5. Describe the signs and symptoms of shock.
6. Describe how to care for an impaled object and a severed body part.
7. List the general care steps for burns.
8. Describe the burn injuries for which you would call EMS personnel.
9. Describe the care for chemical and electrical burns.
10. List five common signs and symptoms of musculoskeletal injuries.
11. List three signs and symptoms that would cause you to suspect a serious musculoskeletal injury.
12. Describe the general care for musculoskeletal injuries.
13. Explain when to immobilize an injured body part.
14. List six signs and symptoms of head injury.
15. Define the key terms for this chapter.

After reading this chapter and completing the appropriate course activities, you should be able to—

1. Demonstrate how to control bleeding.
2. Demonstrate how to effectively immobilize an injured body part.

Key Terms

Abdomen: The middle part of the trunk containing the stomach, liver, and other organs.

Abrasion: An open wound from which skin is rubbed or scraped away.

Avulsion: an open wound from which soft tissue is partially or completely torn away.

Bone: A dense, hard tissue that forms the skeleton.

Chest: The upper part of the trunk, containing the heart, major blood vessels, and lungs.

Dislocation: The displacement of a bone from its normal position at a joint.

Fracture: A chip, crack, or complete break in a bone.

Immobilize: Use a splint or other method to keep an injured body part from moving.

Impaled object: An object that remains in an open wound.

Joint: A structure where two or more bones are joined.

Laceration: A cut.

Ligament: A tough, fibrous connective tissue that holds bones together at a joint.

Muscle: A tissue in the body that lengthens and shortens to create movement.

Musculoskeletal system: The body system made up of muscles, bones, ligaments, and tendons.

Pelvis: The lower part of the trunk containing the intestines, bladder, and reproductive organs.

Puncture: An open wound created when the skin is pierced by a pointed object.

Rib cage: The cage of bones formed by the 12 pairs of ribs, the breastbone, and the spine.

Shock: A life-threatening condition in which the circulatory system fails to deliver blood to all parts of the body.

Splint: A device used to immobilize an injured body part; applying such a device.

Sprain: The stretching and tearing of ligaments and other soft tissue structures at a joint.

Strain: The stretching and tearing of muscles and tendons.

Tendon: A fibrous band that attaches muscle to bone.

INTRODUCTION

People do not get hurt easily. The body resists being injured. Injuries still do happen, however, and a certain percentage of them happen at aquatic facilities.

There are possibilities for injury at aquatic facilities other than the obvious one of drowning. For example, patrons jump on, dive into, and otherwise collide with each other and with the sides of the pool, resulting in cuts and bruises. People can get scraped or even tear off a nail on a rough area on a slide or diving board. A finger or wrist can be bent back and sprained or even broken.

Injuries can also occur outside the pool. Pool decks are made of hard materials that are often wet and slippery—people slip and fall. People of any age can break a bone by falling, and a fall can tear tissues and move bones out of place. Think about what a locker room is like. The floor is hard, the room is full of metal lockers with sharp corners, there are hooks on the walls, and the floors are likely to be wet. Add a large number of people, all either trying to get dressed to go home or getting ready to swim and probably in a hurry, and throw in some kids running and climbing on the benches. It makes a great recipe for injury.

Every aquatic facility should have a first aid area or room where an injured person can be safely moved to receive care and to rest. First aid supplies should be kept in this area, and you should know where they are stored and what they consist of. Figure 9-1 shows the first aid supplies needed. Equipment may include a cot, blankets, towels, and pillows. In addition to the supplies mentioned for a first aid station, you should consider placing a few supplies in a fanny pack that you keep on the stand so that you have them readily available on the pool deck (Fig. 9-2).

SOFT TISSUE INJURIES

The **soft tissues** include the layers of skin, fat, and muscles (Fig. 9-3). The skin's outer layer, the **epidermis**, keeps out bacteria and other germs that can cause infection. The deeper layer, the **dermis**, contains the nerves, the sweat and oil glands, and the blood vessels. Below the dermis is a layer of fat and the muscles.

figure 9-1 *First aid supplies needed for a facility.*

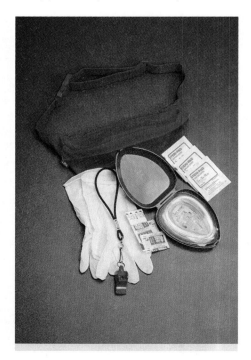

figure 9-2 *Keep a few supplies in a fanny pack for quick availability.*

Types of soft tissue injuries

An injury to the soft tissue is called a **wound**. Soft tissue injuries are typically classified as either **closed wounds** or **open wounds**. A wound is closed when the soft tissue damage is under the surface of the skin, as in a bruise. A wound is open if there is a break in the skin's surface, such as a cut. Open wounds usually bleed.

Burns are a special kind of soft tissue injury. A burn occurs when intense heat, certain chemicals, electricity, or radiation contacts the skin or other body tissues.

Closed wounds. The simplest closed wound is a bruise (Fig. 9-4, *A* and *B*). Bruises result when a blow to the body damages the soft tissue layers and blood vessels under the skin. At first, the area may only appear red. Over time, it may turn dark red or purple.

Violent forces can cause more severe soft tissue injuries that can result in heavy bleeding beneath the skin. Closed wounds that involve bones or muscles are discussed later in this chapter.

Signs and symptoms of serious internal bleeding include—

- Tender, swollen, bruised, or hard areas of the body, such as the abdomen.
- Rapid, weak pulse.
- Skin that feels cool or moist or looks pale or bluish.
- Vomiting or coughing up blood.
- Excessive thirst.
- Becoming confused, faint, drowsy, or unconscious.

figure 9-3 *The soft tissue includes the layers of skin, fat, and muscle.*

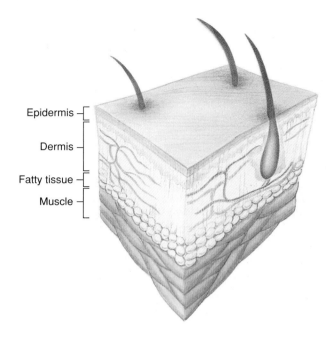

figure 9-4 *A* and *B,* The simplest closed wound is a bruise.

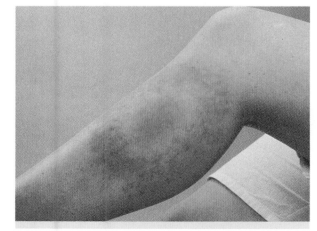

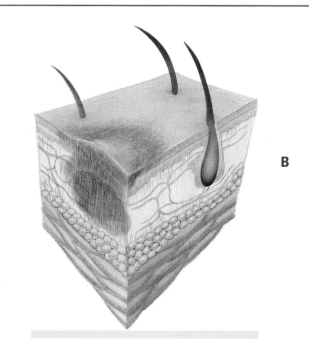

Open wounds. The break in the skin of an open wound can be as minor as a scrape or as severe as a deep cut or puncture. Bleeding occurs when a blood vessel is torn. Many severe wounds bleed heavily, but some do not. A minor wound may also bleed heavily, for example, a small cut to the scalp, but in most cases, the bleeding is easy to control.

There are four main types of open wounds:

• Abrasions
• Lacerations
• Avulsions
• Punctures

Abrasions. An *abrasion* is the most common type of open wound. Skin is rubbed or scraped away, as when a child falls on a pool deck or on a dock and scrapes his or her knee (Fig. 9-5, *A* and *B*). A friction burn that a person may get from going down a slide is an abrasion. An abrasion is usually painful. Bleeding is easily controlled and not severe. Because of the way the injury occurs, dirt may be ground into the skin, and infection can easily result if the wound is not cleaned.

Lacerations. A *laceration* is a cut (Fig. 9-6, *A* and *B*). A person can get a laceration from stepping on a sharp object, such as a piece of glass or metal. A laceration could also result from striking the diving board or the edge of the deck with the chin or lip, or by striking a chipped tile in the pool wall with the feet when doing a turn. Deep lacerations can damage both nerves and blood vessels. Lacerations may have smooth or jagged edges and usually bleed freely and sometimes heavily. If nerves are injured, a laceration may not be painful.

Avulsions. An *avulsion* is an injury in which part of the skin and sometimes other soft tissue is partially or completely torn away (Fig. 9-7, *A* and *B*). A partially avulsed piece of skin may remain attached but hangs like a flap. A violent force may completely tear away or sever an entire body part, such as a finger.

Slipping and falling down the ladder of a diving board could result in an avulsion. So could having a body part caught in a piece of machinery, such as the propeller of the motor on a boat.

An avulsion usually bleeds heavily. With a severed body part, however, bleeding is usually not as bad as you might expect. A surgeon can often successfully reattach a severed body part.

figure 9-5 *A* and *B,* Abrasions can be painful, but bleeding is easily controlled.

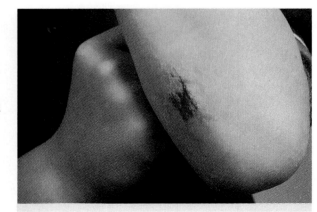

A

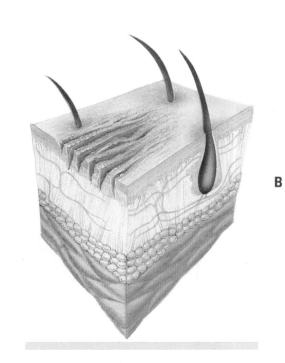

B

Punctures. When the skin is pierced with a pointed object, the wound is called a ***puncture*** (Fig. 9-8, *A* and *B*). An object that remains in the open wound is called an impaled object (Fig. 9-9, *A* and *B*). A splinter is a simple example of an impaled object. An object may also pass completely through a body part, making two open wounds—one at the entry point and one at the exit point.

Puncture wounds generally do not bleed heavily, but they can bleed severely internally if blood vessels or organs are damaged. They easily become infected, since objects that cause punctures often carry germs that cause infections deep into the body. The microorganism that causes tetanus, a severe infection, is particularly dangerous. Anyone whose skin is cut or punctured by a dirty object, such as a rusty nail or a piece of glass or wire, should check with his or her physician to learn if a tetanus immunization or a booster shot is needed.

---

figure 9-6 *A* and *B*, A laceration may have jagged or smooth edges.

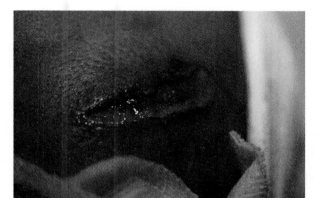

A

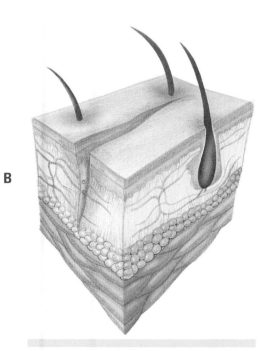

B

---

figure 9-7 *A* and *B*, In an avulsion, part of the skin and sometimes other soft tissue areas are torn away.

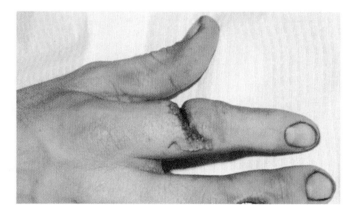

A

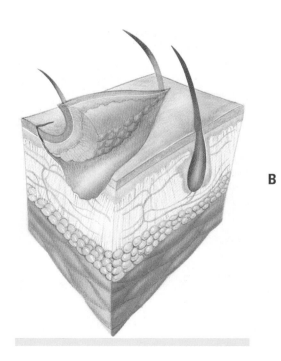

B

figure 9-8 *A* and *B,* A puncture wound results when skin is pierced by a pointed object.

A

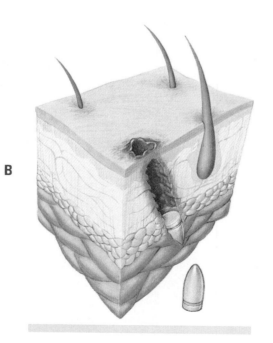

B

figure 9-9 *A* and *B,* An impaled object is an object that remains embedded in a wound.

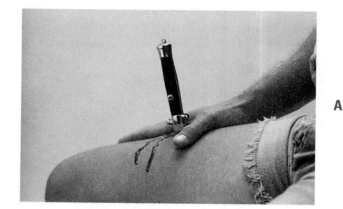

A

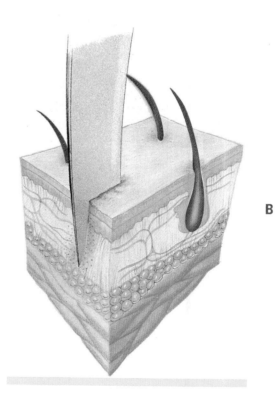

B

Infection

Preventing infection. When an injury breaks the skin, clean the area thoroughly. Pool water does not prevent a wound from becoming infected; neither does the water in lakes, rivers, bays, and oceans. For minor wounds, (those that do not bleed severely) wash the area with soap and water. Wear latex gloves while you are caring for the wound, and wash your hands thoroughly with soap and water when you are finished. Do not wash wounds that require medical attention, those with extensive tissue damage or bleeding, or deep or gaping wounds that require stitches. These wounds will be cleaned thoroughly in the medical facility. It is more important for you to control bleeding. (See Skill Summary, "Controlling Bleeding," on pages 166-167.)

Although the possibility that you will be caring for a patron's infected wound is slight, you should be able to recognize infection and know how to care for it. If the area around a wound becomes swollen and red, feels warm, or throbs with pain, the wound is very likely infected. Some wounds even develop a pus discharge. More serious infections may cause a person to develop a fever and feel ill. Red streaks may appear that progress from the wound in the direction of the heart.

To care for an infected wound, keep the area clean, soak it in warm water, and elevate the infected area. An antibiotic ointment may be applied. Change coverings over the wound daily. If red streaks or fever develop, the person should get medical help.

Dressings and bandages

All open wounds need some type of covering to help control bleeding and prevent infection. These coverings are commonly called dressings and bandages. The first aid kit at your facility should contain an assortment of them.

Dressings are pads placed directly on the wound. To minimize the chance of infection, dressings should be **sterile** (free from germs). Cotton gauze dressings commonly range from 2 to 4 inches square. Much larger dressings are used to cover very large wounds and multiple wounds in one body area (Fig. 9-10). Some dressings have surfaces that won't stick to the wound.

A **bandage** is any material used to wrap or cover any part of the body. Bandages are often used to hold dressings in place, to apply pressure to control bleeding, to protect a wound from dirt and infection, and to provide support to an injured part of the body (Fig. 9-11). A bandage applied snugly to create pressure on a wound or injury is called a **pressure bandage**.

A common type of bandage is a commercially made adhesive compress, such as a Band-Aid, which can be applied directly to small open wounds. Also available is the bandage compress, a thick gauze dressing attached to a gauze bandage. This bandage can be tied or taped in place. Because it is specially designed to help control severe bleeding, the bandage compress usually comes in a sterile package.

The roller bandage is usually made of gauze or gauze-like material. Roller bandages are available in assorted widths from ½ to 6 inches. A roller bandage is generally wrapped around the injured body part, over a dressing,

figure 9-10 *Dressings come in various sizes.*

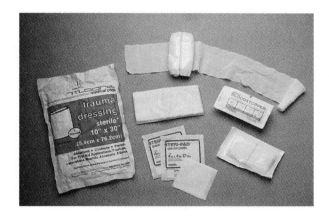

figure 9-11 *Different types of bandages are used to hold dressings in place, apply pressure to a wound, protect the wound from infection, and provide support to an injured area.*

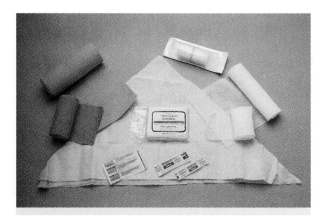

using overlapping turns until the dressing is completely covered. It can be tied or taped in place. A roller bandage may be folded to use as a dressing or compress. Roller bandages can also be used to help immobilize an injured limb.

Elastic roller bandages are designed to keep continuous pressure on a body part. When properly applied, they can effectively control swelling or support an injured limb. Elastic bandages are available in 2-, 3-, 4-, and 6-inch widths.

Another useful bandage is the triangular bandage. Folded, it can hold a dressing or splint in place on most parts of the body (Fig. 9-12).

Applying a bandage. The following are general guidelines for applying a roller bandage:

- If possible, elevate the injured body part above the level of the heart.
- Secure the end of the bandage in place. Wrap the bandage around the body part until the dressing is completely covered and the bandage extends several inches beyond the dressing. Tie or tape the bandage in place (Fig. 9-13, *A-C*).
- Do not cover fingers or toes, if possible. If the fingers or toes feel cold to the touch or begin to turn pale or blue, the bandage is too tight and should be loosened slightly (Fig. 9-13, *D*).
- If blood soaks through the bandage, apply additional dressings and another bandage. *Do not* remove the blood-soaked ones.

Elastic bandages can restrict blood flow if not applied properly. Restricted blood flow is painful and can cause tissue damage if not corrected. Elastic bandages are frequently used in athletic environments and should be applied only by people who are trained in their use. The first step in using an elastic bandage is to select the correct size. You would use a narrow bandage to wrap a wrist or hand and a medium width for an arm or ankle. A wide bandage would be used to wrap a leg. Always check the circulation of the limb beyond the bandage by looking for changes in skin color and temperature. Figure 9-14, *A-D* on page 136 shows the proper way to put on an elastic bandage.

Caring for wounds

Closed wounds. Most closed wounds do not require special medical care. You can use direct pressure on the area to decrease bleeding under the skin. Elevating the injured part helps reduce swelling. Applying cold can help control both swelling and pain. Always place a gauze pad, towel, or other cloth between the ice or cold pack and the skin.

Some closed wounds, however, can be serious. If a person complains of severe pain or cannot move a body part without pain or if you think the force that caused the injury was great enough to cause serious damage, call EMS personnel immediately. While you are waiting for EMS personnel to arrive, help the victim rest in the most comfortable position. Keep the victim from getting chilled or overheated. Reassure and comfort the victim.

figure 9-12 *A triangular bandage can be folded to hold a dressing in place.*

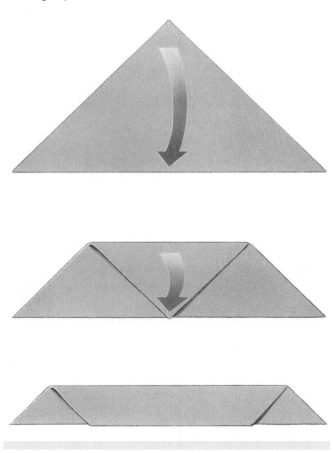

figure 9-13 *A, A roller bandage. **B,** Overlapping turns of a bandage cover the dressing completely. **C,** Tie or tape the bandage in place. **D,** Check the fingers for circulation to ensure the bandage is not too tight.*

A

B

C

D

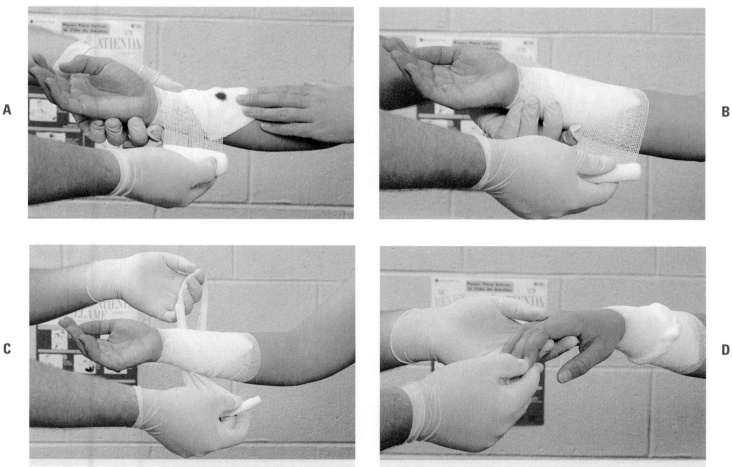

figure 9-14 A, *Start the elastic bandage at the point farthest from the heart.*
B, *Secure the end of the bandage in place.* ***C,*** *Wrap the bandage using overlapping turns.*
D, *Tape the end of the bandage in place.*

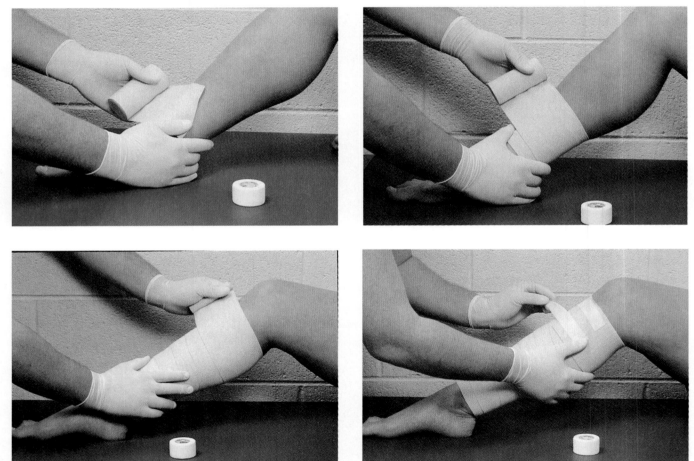

A

B

C

D

Minor open wounds. A minor wound, such as an abrasion, has slight damage and minimal bleeding. To care for a minor wound, follow these general guidelines:

1 **Wear latex gloves to reduce the risk of disease transmission.**

2 **Wash the wound thoroughly with soap and water.**

3 **Place a sterile dressing over the wound.**

4 **Apply direct pressure to control any bleeding.**

5 **Once bleeding is controlled, remove the dressing. An antibiotic ointment can be applied if available.**

6 **Apply a new sterile dressing.**

7 **Hold the dressing in place with a bandage or tape.**

8 **Wash your hands immediately after completing care.**

Major open wounds. A major open wound has severe bleeding, deep destruction of tissue, or a deeply embedded impaled object. To care for a major open wound, follow these general guidelines:

1 **Activate the emergency action plan.**

2 **Have someone call EMS personnel.**

3 **Put on latex gloves.**

4 **Do not waste time trying to wash the wound.**

5 **Quickly control bleeding using pressure and elevation. Apply direct pressure by placing a sterile dressing over the wound. If nothing sterile is available, use any clean piece of material, such as a towel, T-shirt, sock, disposable latex gloves, or plastic wrap. If no pad or cloth is immediately available, have the injured person use his or her hand or use your gloved hand. Elevate the wound above heart level.**

6 **Apply a bandage over any dressings to maintain pressure on the wound.**

7 **If bleeding is still not controlled, use a pressure point. A pressure point is a place on the body where you can squeeze the artery against the bone underneath. This can slow or stop the flow of blood to the wound.**

8 **Wash your hands immediately after completing care.**

Shock

Any severe bleeding, whether you can see it or not, can lead to a life-threatening condition called shock. *Shock* is a condition in which the circulatory system fails to deliver blood to all parts of the body. When the body's organs do not receive blood, they fail to function properly. The body responds by attempting to maintain adequate blood flow. This triggers a series of responses that produce the specific signs and symptoms of shock. Any significant fluid loss in the body, such as from severe diarrhea, persistent vomiting, or heat-related illness, can also bring on shock because it affects the heart.

When shock occurs, the body attempts to send blood to the most important parts, such as the brain, heart, lungs, and kidneys. It reduces blood flow to less important parts, such as the arms, legs, and skin. This is why the skin of a person in shock appears pale and feels cool. In the later stages of shock, the skin, especially on the lips and around the eyes, may appear blue.

Shock: The Domino Effect

Any serious injury or illness will trigger a series of responses in the body that acts like a chain of falling dominoes. This condition is known as shock.

Shock is the body's natural attempt to keep oxygen-rich blood flowing to the most important organs, such as the brain, heart, and lungs. Without oxygen, these organs will fail to function properly. When the oxygen-deprived tissues of the arms and legs begin to die, the body sends blood back to them and away from the vital organs. As the brain is affected, the person becomes restless, drowsy, and eventually unconscious. As the heart is affected, it beats irregularly, resulting in an irregular pulse. The heart's rhythm becomes chaotic and the heart fails to pump blood. There is no longer a pulse. When the heart stops, breathing stops. This chain of falling dominoes eventually results in death.

Signs and symptoms of shock. Although you may not always be able to determine the cause, you should be able to recognize the following signs and symptoms of shock:

• Restlessness or irritability (Often the first indication that the body is experiencing a significant problem)
• Altered consciousness
• Pale or ashen, cool, moist skin (The word **ashen** describes a grayish color that corresponds to pale in people with darker skin)
• Rapid breathing
• Rapid pulse

Caring for shock. To care for shock, take the following simple steps:

• Control any external bleeding.
• Call your emergency number immediately. Shock cannot be managed effectively by first aid alone. A victim of shock requires advanced medical care as soon as possible.
• Have the victim lie down. This is often the most comfortable position. Helping the victim rest comfortably is important because pain can cause shock to progress faster.
• Elevate the legs about 12 inches unless you suspect head, neck, or back injuries or possible broken bones involving the hips or legs. If you are unsure of the victim's condition, leave him or her lying flat.
• Help the victim maintain normal body temperature. If the victim is cool, cover him or her to avoid chilling. Dry the victim if necessary.
• Try to reassure the victim.
• Do not give the victim anything to eat or drink, even though he or she is likely to be thirsty.

Special situations

Severed body parts. If the victim has an avulsion in which a body part has been completely severed, try to retrieve the severed body part. Wrap the part in sterile gauze if possible or in any clean material, such as a washcloth. Place the wrapped part in a plastic bag. If possible, keep the part cool by placing the bag on ice (Fig. 9-15). Make sure the part is transported to the medical facility with the victim.

Impaled objects. If the victim has an *impaled object* deeply embedded in the wound, follow these additional guidelines:

1 *Do not* remove the object.

2 Use bulky dressings to stabilize it. Any movement of the object can result in further tissue damage (Fig. 9-16).

3 Control bleeding by bandaging the dressings in place around the object (Fig. 9-17).

If the object is only a splinter in the skin, it can be removed with tweezers; then the skin should be washed and covered to keep it clean.

figure 9-15 *Wrap a severed body part in sterile gauze, put it in a plastic bag, and put the bag on ice.*

figure 9-16 *Stabilize an impaled object with bulky dressings.*

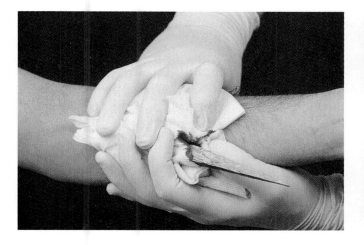

figure 9-17 *Bandage the dressings in place around the object.*

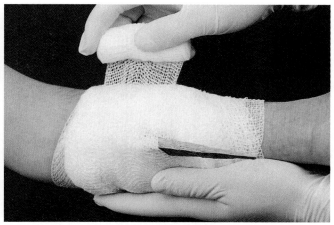

Fishhooks. At waterfront areas, people often go fishing. You may have to give first aid to a person who has a fishhook caught in his or her skin. If it is deeply embedded, do not try to remove it. Treat it like an impaled object. The person needs to see a physician. If the fishhook is not embedded but has cut the skin, care for it as for any minor open wound. The victim should check with his or her physician about the need for a tetanus booster shot.

Injuries to the head and face. A person can injure his or her head at an aquatic facility in many ways. For example, a person can misjudge a dive or jump and hit the diving board, a gutter, a ladder, or the bottom. Someone may hit his or her head on the side while going down a slide. In a race, a swimmer can hit the back wall while doing a turn. In a wave pool, a person can be thrown into the side or into another person by the force of a wave. Anyone who has fallen and hit his or her head may have injured it.

Scalp injuries. Scalp injuries can be minor or severe. They generally bleed heavily, but you can usually control the bleeding easily with direct pressure. If the victim suffered a severe blow to the head, be careful to apply pressure gently at first because of the possibility of skull fracture. If you feel a depression, a spongy area, or bone fragments, do not put direct pressure on the wound. Call EMS personnel. Attempt to control bleeding with pressure on the area around the wound (Fig. 9-18). Carefully part the hair around the injured area with your gloved

figure 9-18 *To avoid putting pressure on a deep scalp wound, apply pressure around the wound.*

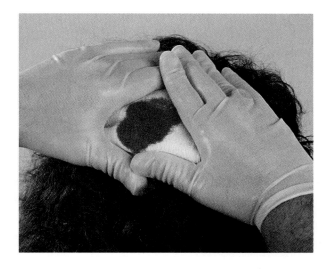

fingers because the victim's hair may hide part of the wound. If you are unsure about the extent of a scalp injury, call EMS personnel.

If the victim has an open wound and no indication of fracture, control the bleeding by applying several dressings and securing them with a bandage (Fig. 9-19, *A* and *B*).

Nose injuries. Nose injuries are usually caused by a fall or from bumping into someone or something, such as the side of a pool. The result is often a nosebleed. High blood pressure can also cause nosebleeds. In most

figure 9-19 *Apply pressure to control bleeding from a scalp wound. **A,** Hold several dressings against the wound with your hand. **B,** Then secure the dressings with a bandage.*

A

B

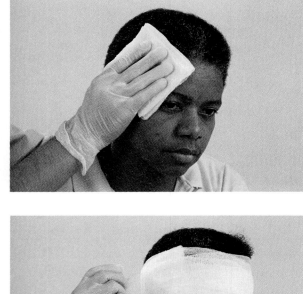

figure 9-20 *When flushing an eye with water, be sure to flush the affected eye from the nose outward to prevent washing anything into the unaffected eye.*

cases, you can control a nosebleed by having the victim sit with the head slightly forward and pinch the nostrils together for a few minutes. Other methods of controlling a nosebleed include applying an ice pack to the bridge of the nose or putting pressure on the upper lip just beneath the nose.

Eye injuries. Objects that get in the eye, such as sand, pieces of dirt, or slivers of wood or metal, are irritating to the eye, and some of them can cause damage. The victim is often in severe pain and may have difficulty opening the eye because light further irritates it.

First try to remove the object(s) by having the victim blink several times. The eye immediately produces tears in an attempt to wash the object out. If this fails, the eye can be flushed with water. If the object remains, the victim should receive professional medical attention. Never try to remove an object imbedded in the eye.

Flush the eye with water also if the victim gets any chemical, such as **granular chlorine**, in his or her eye. Have someone call EMS personnel. The eye should be flushed continually until EMS personnel arrive (Fig. 9-20). You can use water from a tap, hose, or shower. Even sunscreen or sunblock contains chemicals that can irritate the eyes. If a person gets sunblock or sunscreen in the eye, flush the eye immediately with water. If the victim is still in pain and finds it difficult to use the eye, advise the victim to seek medical help.

Anyone at an aquatic facility who works with chemicals is supposed to wear protective equipment, such as glasses or a mask, to prevent eye injury while handling those chemicals (Fig. 9-21). A list of safety rules should be posted by management in any areas of chemical use. Chemical burns and their care are discussed on page 145.

figure 9-21 *Wear a mask when handling chemicals.*

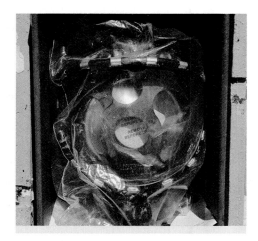

Mouth injuries. Mouth injuries are common in aquatic facilities. Your primary concern for injury to the mouth is to make sure the victim is able to breathe. Injuries to the mouth may cause breathing problems if blood, knocked-out teeth, or dentures block the airway. If someone is bleeding from the mouth and you do not suspect a serious head or spine injury, place the person in a seated position with the head tilted slightly forward to allow any blood to drain from the mouth.

For injuries that penetrate the lip, place a rolled dressing between the lip and the gum. You can place another dressing on the outer surface of the lip. If the tongue or lip is cut and bleeding, apply a dressing and direct pressure. Applying cold to a cut lip or tongue can help reduce swelling and ease pain. If an injury penetrates the cheek, place a dressing inside the mouth against the wound and apply a pressure bandage (Fig. 9-22, *A* and *B*).

For a broken tooth, there isn't much you can do. The person needs to see a dentist. If the injury knocked out one or more of the person's teeth, control the bleeding and save any teeth so that they can be reinserted. To control the bleeding, roll a sterile dressing and insert it into the space left by the missing tooth. Have the victim bite down to maintain pressure (Fig. 9-23).

The sooner the tooth is replanted, the better the chance it will survive. The knocked-out tooth must be handled carefully. Pick the tooth up by the chewing edge, not the root. Do not rub or handle the root of the tooth. If possible, place the tooth back in its socket in its normal position. Have the victim bite down gently or hold the tooth in position with a sterile gauze pad, a tissue, or a clean cloth. The victim should see a dentist immediately.

If you are unable to put the tooth back in its socket, preserve the tooth by putting it in a closed container of cool, fresh milk to accompany the victim to the dentist. If milk isn't available, use tap water.

Burns

If an aquatic facility seems an unlikely place for burns to occur, think again. At waterfronts, people build fires and cook. Pipes carry hot water to showers, and temperature controls can fail to work. Pool water is purified by caustic chemicals, which can burn the skin and lungs. Electricity powers underwater vacuum cleaners and equipment for swim meets and special events. Any time electrical cords and water are together, the possibility for injury exists. Outdoors in the summer, we have the sun.

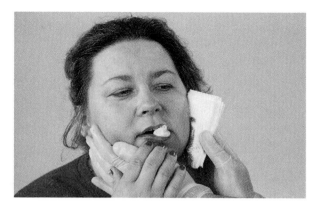

figure 9-22 *A, Control bleeding inside the cheek by placing a rolled dressing inside the mouth against the wound. B, Apply a pressure bandage.*

A

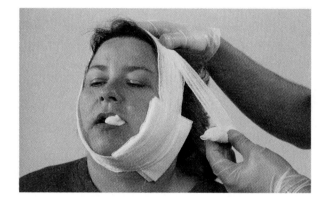

B

figure 9-23 *If a tooth is knocked out, place a sterile dressing in the place left by the tooth. Tell the victim to bite down.*

The majority of burns are caused by heat, but certain chemicals, electricity, and forms of radiation from the sun and other sources can also cause burns. Burns can break the skin, causing infection and fluid loss, and damage the body's ability to control its temperature. Deep burns can injure underlying tissue. Deep burns can also damage the victim's ability to breathe.

The severity of a burn depends on—

* The temperature or strength of whatever caused the burn.
* The length of exposure to the burn source.
* The location of the burn.
* The size of the area the burn covers.
* The victim's age and medical condition.

In general, people over age 60 have thinner skin and often burn more severely. Children under age 5 also may burn more severely.

Types of burns. The deeper the burn, the more severe it is. Generally, there are three classifications:

* **Superficial burns**, also called first-degree burns, are the least severe. They only damage or destroy the first layer of skin (Fig. 9-24, *A* and *B*). The skin is red or darker and dry, and the burn is usually painful. The area may swell. Most sunburns are superficial burns.
* **Partial-thickness burns**, also called second-degree burns, involve both layers of skin (Fig. 9-25, *A* and *B*). They are red and also have blisters that may open and weep clear fluid. The burned skin may look blotchy. These burns are usually painful and often swell. They are sometimes critical.
* **Full-thickness burns**, also called third-degree burns, destroy both layers of skin, as well as any or all of the fat, muscles, and blood vessels beneath (Fig. 9-26, *A* and *B*). They can even destroy bones. These burns look brown or blackish, and the tissues underneath may look white. These burns may be either extremely painful or surprisingly pain free if the burn destroyed the nerve endings. Because these burns are open, the body loses fluid, and shock is likely to occur. The body is also highly prone to infection. These burns are always critical.

figure 9-24 *A* and *B*, *A superficial burn.*

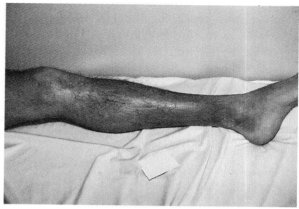

Alan Dimick, M.D., Professor of Surgery; Director UAB Burn Center

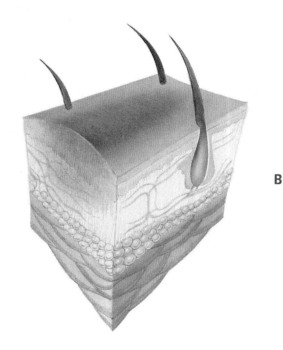

Critical burns need immediate medical attention. They can be life threatening. It isn't always easy to tell how severe a burn is right after it happened. Call EMS personnel immediately if —

* The person is having trouble breathing or has burns on more than one part of the body.
* The victim has burns on the head, chest, neck, back, both hands, both feet, or genitals.

figure 9-25 *A and B, A partial-thickness burn.*

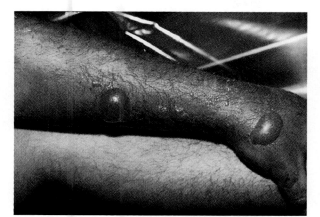

A

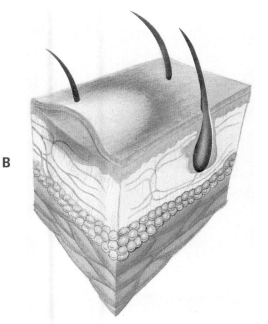

B

Alan Dimick, M.D., Professor of
Surgery; Director UAB Burn Center

figure 9-26 *A and B, A full-thickness burn.*

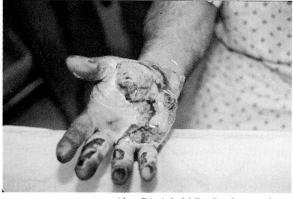

A

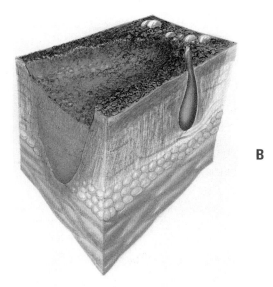

B

Alan Dimick, M.D., Professor of
Surgery; Director UAB Burn Center

- The burns are caused by chemicals, explosion, or electricity.
- A child or elderly person has any burn other than a very minor one.

Burns caused by flames usually need medical attention, especially if the victim is a child or an elderly person. Burns caused by hot liquid or vapor, such as scalding water from a shower or steam from a broken pipe, or by burning clothing are also serious, since the clothing keeps the heat in contact with the skin. Some fabrics even melt and stick to the skin. All these burns may look minor at first, but they can continue to get worse.

The scene of a burn injury. Most burn injuries, with the exception of sunburn, are unlikely to occur around the pool, where you are already on the scene. They are more likely to happen in other areas of the facility.

Burns from using charcoal lighter fluid or outdoor cooking equipment unsafely occur in picnic areas around pools and at waterfronts.

As you approach a burn victim, wherever he or she may be, make sure the scene is safe. Look for fire, smoke, steam, downed electrical wires, and any indications of chemicals. If the scene is unsafe, call your emergency number and wait for fire or EMS personnel to arrive.

Caring for burns. If the scene is safe, approach the victim and check for life-threatening problems. Call EMS personnel if the victim's condition is life-threatening. Pay close attention to the victim's airway. Note burns around the mouth, nose, or the rest of the face that may signal that air passages or lungs have been burned (Fig. 9-27). If you suspect a burned airway or burned lungs, continually monitor breathing. Air passages may swell, impairing or stopping breathing.

As you check the victim, look for additional burn injuries. Look also for other injuries, especially if there was an explosion or electric shock. If the victim is burned, follow these four basic care steps (Fig. 9-28, A-C):

1 Cool the burned area. (Do not cool a burn caused by electricity.)
2 Cover the burned area.
3 Prevent infection.
4 Minimize shock.

figure 9-27 *Burns or soot on the face may signal that air passages or lungs have been burned.*

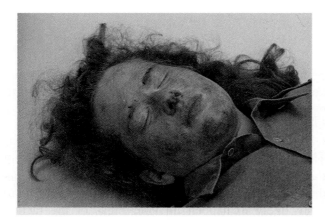

figure 9-28 *A, Cool burned areas with large amounts of cool water. B, Remove any clothing covering the burned area. C, Cover burns loosely with dry sterile dressings.*

A

B

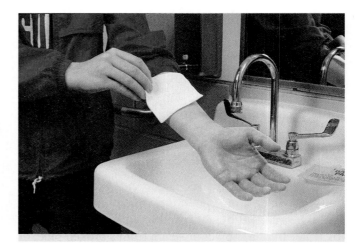

C

For small superficial burns not severe enough to need medical attention, care for the burned area as an open wound after cooling. Wash the area with soap and water, and keep the area clean.

Even after the source of heat has been removed, soft tissue can continue to burn. For a more severe burn, cool any burned areas immediately with large amounts of cool water. Do not use ice or ice water except on small superficial burns. Ice causes critical loss of body heat. Use whatever is available — water from a shower, a tap, or a hose. You can use pool water if nothing else is available. You can apply soaked towels, sheets, or other wet cloths to a burned face or other area that you can't put directly into water. Be sure to keep these compresses cool by adding more water. Otherwise, they will quickly absorb the heat from the skin's surface.

Cool the burned area for several minutes. If pain continues or if the edges of the burned area are still warm to the touch when the area is removed from the water, continue cooling.

Cover the burned area to help keep out air and dirt and help reduce pain. Use dry, sterile dressings if possible, and loosely bandage them in place. The bandage should not put pressure on the burn surface. If the burn covers a large area of the body, cover it with clean, dry sheets or other cloth.

Covering the burn also helps prevent infection. Do not break blisters. Unbroken skin also helps prevent infection. Do not put ointments, butter, oil, or other commercial or home remedies on blisters or burns. Oils and ointments seal in heat and do not relieve pain well. Other home remedies can cause infection.

Full-thickness burns and large partial-thickness burns can cause shock as a result of pain and loss of body fluids. Lay the victim down unless he or she is having difficulty breathing. Elevate burned areas above the level of the heart, if possible. Burn victims have a tendency to chill. Help the victim maintain body temperature by protecting him or her from drafts.

Chemical burns. Common chemicals used at aquatic facilities, such as chlorine compounds, dry acid (dry sulphuric acid), and muriatic acid, can cause severe burns if they contact the skin or eyes. So can cleaning solutions, such as bleach, drain cleaners, and toilet bowl cleaners; paint strippers; and lawn and garden chemicals. Chlorine gas can cause burns when it combines with perspiration on the skin. A bathing suit or SCBA (self-contained breathing apparatus) does not provide protection.

Chlorine and the following chemicals containing chlorine can quickly injure the skin.

- Calcium hypochlorite (granulated or powdered form)
- Lithium hypochlorite (powdered or granulated)
- Sodium hypochlorite (liquid)
- Chlorinated cyanurates (in granulated or tablet form)
- Bromine

Other chemicals include dry acid, also called pH decreaser, and muriatic acid.

As with heat burns, the stronger the chemical and the longer the contact, the more severe the burn. The chemical will continue to burn as long as it is on the skin. You must remove the chemical from the body as quickly as possible and call EMS personnel.

Flush the burn with large amounts of cool, running water (Fig. 9-29). Continue flushing until EMS personnel arrive. Do not use a forceful flow of water from a hose; the force may further damage burned skin. You can adjust the nozzle of most hoses to give a finer spray that is strong enough to remove the chemical. Have the victim remove any clothing with the chemical on it, if possible. Take steps to minimize shock. Do not forget the eyes. If an eye is burned by a chemical, flush the

figure 9-29 *Flush a chemical burn with cool running water.*

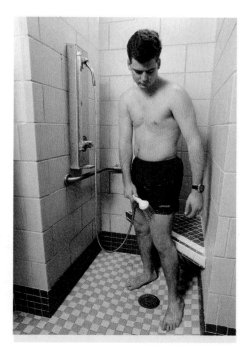

figure 9-30 *Continuously flush an eye that has been burned by a chemical with cool water.*

affected eye from the nose outward, to avoid washing the chemical into the unaffected eye, until EMS personnel arrive (Fig. 9-30).

Electrical burns. Contact with an electrical source can conduct electricity through the body. At an aquatic facility, the possibility of electrical fixtures and wires coming into contact with water exists with underwater lights, tape recorders, VCRs, portable stereos, automatic-timing devices, pace clocks, pool vacuum cleaners, and many other appliances that have wires stretched across pool decks or are used near spas. If electrical safety systems, such as **ground-fault interrupters (GFIs),** fail or if items cease to be **grounded** because of corrosion or some other problem, electrical injury can occur. Worn electrical wires, defective apparatus, and unprotected electrical outlets are possible sources of danger.

The severity of an electrical burn depends on the type and amount of contact, the current's path through the body, and how long the contact lasted. Electrical burns are often deep. The victim may have two wounds, one where the current entered the body and one where it exited. Although these wounds may look superficial, the tissues below may be severely damaged (Fig. 9-31).

Electrical injuries cause problems besides burns. Electricity can make the heart beat erratically or even stop. Respiratory arrest may occur. Because a powerful electric shock can cause strong muscular contractions or can throw the victim to the ground, the victim may have a fracture or a spinal injury. Suspect a possible electrical injury if you hear a sudden loud pop or bang or see an unexpected flash.

The signs of electrical injury include—

- Unconsciousness.
- Dazed, confused behavior.
- Obvious burns on the skin surface.
- Breathing difficulty.
- Weak, irregular, or absent pulse.
- Burns where the current entered and where it exited, often on the hand or foot.

Never approach a victim of an electrical injury until you are sure the power is turned off. If a power line is down, *wait for the fire department and the power company.*

To care for a victim of an electrical injury, have someone call EMS personnel immediately. The victim may have breathing difficulties or be in cardiac arrest. Give care for any life-threatening conditions.

figure 9-31 *An electrical burn may severely damage underlying tissues.*

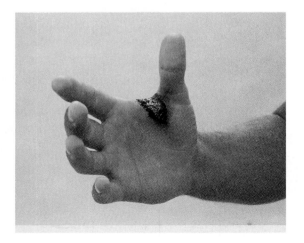

Within Striking Distance

In medieval times, people believed that ringing church bells would get rid of lightning during thunderstorms. It was an unfortunate superstition for bell ringers. In 33 years, lightning struck 386 church steeples and 103 bell ringers died.[1]

Church bell ringers have dropped off the list of people most likely to be struck during a thunderstorm, but lightning strikes remain very dangerous. Lightning causes more deaths each year in the United States than any other weather hazard, including blizzards, hurricanes, floods, tornadoes, earthquakes, and volcanic eruptions. The National Weather Service estimates that lightning kills nearly 100 people every year and injures about 300 others. Lightning occurs when particles of water, ice, and air moving inside storm clouds lose electrons. Eventually, the cloud becomes divided into layers of positive and negative particles. Most electrical current remains inside the cloud. Sometimes, however, the negative charge flashes toward the ground, which has a positive charge. An electrical current snakes back and forth between the cloud and the ground many times in the seconds that we see a flash. Anything tall—a tower, a tree, or a person—becomes a path for the electrical current.

Traveling at speeds up to 300 miles per second, a lightning strike can hurl a person through the air. It can burn clothes off and can sometimes cause the heart to stop beating. The most severe lightning strikes carry up to 50 million volts of electricity, enough to serve 13,000 homes. Lightning can "flash" over a person's body, or it can travel through blood vessels and nerves to reach the ground.

Besides burns, lightning can also cause nervous system damage, broken bones, and loss of hearing or eyesight. Victims sometimes act confused and suffer memory loss. They may describe what happened as getting hit on the head or hearing an explosion.

Use common sense during thunderstorms. If you see a storm approaching in the distance, don't wait until you are soaked to seek shelter. If a thunderstorm threatens, the National Weather Service advises you to—

- Go inside a large building or home.
- Go inside a car and roll up the windows.
- Stop swimming or boating as soon as you see or hear a storm, since water conducts electricity.
- Stay away from the telephone, except in an emergency.
- Stay away from telephone poles and tall trees if you are caught outside.
- Stay off hilltops; try to crouch down in a ravine or valley.
- Stay away from farm equipment and small metal vehicles, such as motorcycles, bicycles, and golf carts.
- Avoid wire fences, clotheslines, metal pipes and rails, and other conductors.
- Stay several yards apart if you are in a group.

1. Kessler, Edwin, *The Thunderstorm in Human Affairs,* Norman, OK; University of Oklahoma, 1983.
2. Randall, Teri. *The Chicago Tribune,* Section 2D. August 13, 1989, p. 1.

Look for two burn sites. Do not cool the burn. Cover any burn injuries with a dry, sterile dressing, and give care for shock.

With a victim of lightning, look for life-threatening conditions, such as respiratory or cardiac arrest. The victim may also have broken bones, including injury to the spine, so do not move him or her. Any burns are a lesser problem.

Radiation burns. Radiation from the sun and other sources can cause painful burns that may blister. Sunburn is usually mild but can be painful. Blisters may involve more than one layer of skin. Care for sunburn as you would any other burn. Cool the burn, and protect the burned area from further damage by staying out of the sun. People are rarely exposed to other types of radiation unless working in special settings, such as certain medical, industrial, or research settings. When they do, they are trained to prevent exposure and how to respond if it happens.

Too Much of a Good Thing

Contrary to some beliefs, tan is not in. Although brief exposure to the sun causes your skin to produce the vitamin D necessary for the healthy formation of bones, long exposure can cause problems, such as sunburn, skin cancer, and early aging—a classic case of too much of a good thing being bad.

There are two kinds of ultraviolet (UV) light rays to be concerned about. Ultraviolet beta rays (UVB) are the burn-producing rays that more commonly cause skin cancer. These are the rays that damage the skin's surface and cause you to blister and peel. The other rays, ultraviolet alpha rays (UVA), have been heralded by tanning salons as "safe rays." Tanning salons claim to use lights that emit only UVA rays. Although UVA rays may not appear as harmful as UVB rays to the skin's surface, they more readily penetrate the deeper layers of the skin. This increases the risk of skin cancer, skin aging, eye damage, and changes that may alter the skin's ability to fight disease.

How do you get enough sun without getting too much? First avoid exposure to the sun between 10:00 a.m. and 2:00 p.m. UV rays are most harmful during this period. Second, wear proper clothing. Third, if you are going to be exposed to the sun, protect your skin and eyes.

Commercial sunscreens come in various strengths. The American Academy of Dermatology recommends year-round sun protection including use of a high Sun Protection Factor (SPF) sunscreen for everyone, but particularly for people who are fairskinned and sunburn easily. The Food and Drug Administration (FDA) has evaluated SPF readings and recognizes values between 2 and 15. It has not been determined whether sunscreens with ratings over 15 offer additional protection.

You should apply sunscreen 15 to 30 minutes before exposure to the sun and reapply it often (every 60 to 90 minutes). Swimmers should use sunscreens labeled as water-resistant and reapply them as described on the label.

Your best bet is to use a sunscreen that claims to protect against both UVB and UVA rays. Carefully check the label to determine the protection a product offers. Some products offer protection against only UVB rays.

It is equally important to protect your eyes from sun damage. Sunglasses are a sunscreen for your eyes and provide important protection from UV rays. Be sure to wear sunglasses that are labeled with their UV-absorbing ability. Ophthalmologists recommend sunglasses that have a UV absorption of at least 90 percent.

The next time the sun beckons, put on some sunscreen and your sunglasses, go outside, and have a great time.

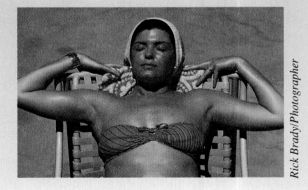

Rick Brady/Photographer

MUSCULOSKELETAL INJURIES

The *musculoskeletal system* is made up of muscles and bones that form the skeleton and the tendons and ligaments that connect them. They all work together to allow the body to move. Movement, however, can play a part in musculoskeletal injuries. When people are active as they are at aquatic facilities, diving, going down slides, jumping, kicking, moving their arms and legs strenuously, there is the possibility of injury.

The skeleton

The skeleton is formed by over 200 bones of various sizes and shapes (Fig. 9-32). The skeleton protects certain vital organs and other soft tissues, such as the brain, the heart and lungs, and the spinal cord. Two or more bones come together to form joints, which are held together by fibrous bands called *ligaments.*

Bones. *Bones* are hard, dense tissues. Because bones have a rich supply of blood and nerves, bone injuries can bleed and are usually painful. The bleeding can become life-threatening if not properly cared for. Bones heal by

figure 9-32 *Over 200 bones in various sizes and shapes form the skeleton.*

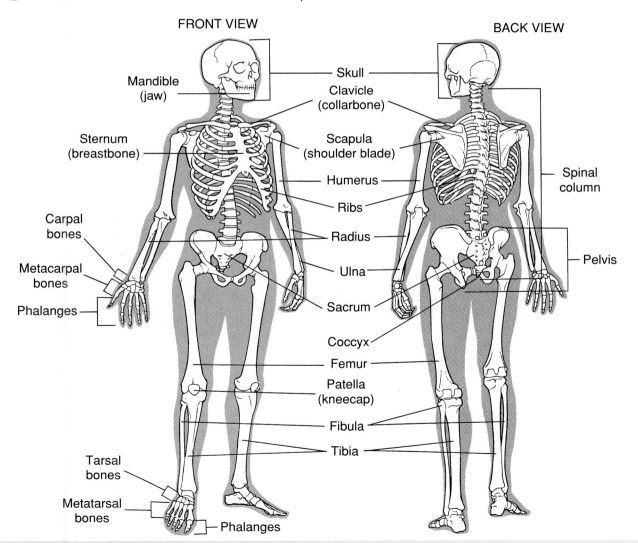

FRONT VIEW

BACK VIEW

Mandible (jaw)

Sternum (breastbone)

Carpal bones

Metacarpal bones

Phalanges

Skull

Clavicle (collarbone)

Scapula (shoulder blade)

Humerus

Ribs

Radius

Ulna

Sacrum

Coccyx

Femur

Patella (kneecap)

Fibula

Tibia

Spinal column

Pelvis

Tarsal bones

Metatarsal bones

Phalanges

figure 9-33 *A typical joint consists of two or more bones held together by ligaments.*

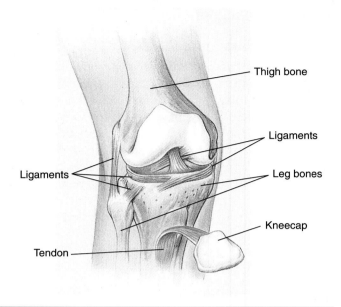

Thigh bone

Ligaments

Ligaments

Leg bones

Kneecap

Tendon

figure 9-34 *The body has over 600 muscles.*

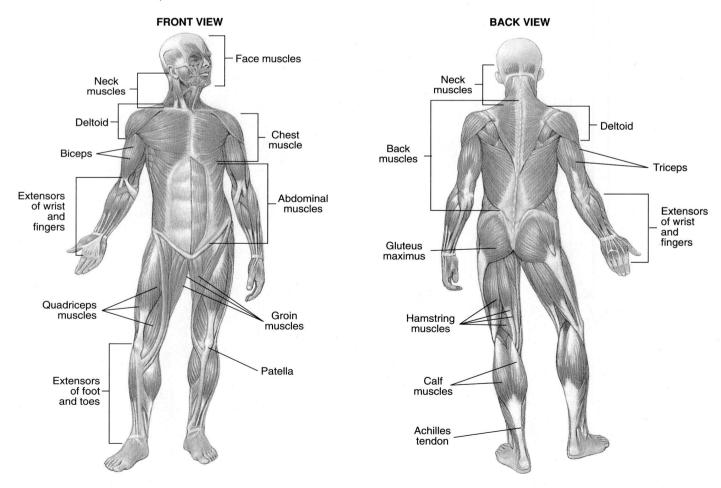

FRONT VIEW

Face muscles

Neck muscles

Deltoid

Biceps

Extensors of wrist and fingers

Chest muscle

Abdominal muscles

Quadriceps muscles

Groin muscles

Patella

Extensors of foot and toes

BACK VIEW

Neck muscles

Deltoid

Back muscles

Triceps

Extensors of wrist and fingers

Gluteus maximus

Hamstring muscles

Calf muscles

Achilles tendon

forming new bone cells. Bone is the only body tissue that can regenerate in this way.

Bones weaken with age. Bones in young children are more flexible than adults' bones, so they are less likely to break. In contrast, elderly people have more brittle bones that sometimes break surprisingly easily. A fall that might not damage a child could result in a fracture in an elderly person.

Joints. A *joint* is formed by the ends of two or more bones coming together at one place. Most joints allow the body to move at that spot. However, the bone ends at some joints are fused together, which restricts motion.

Joints are held together by tough, fibrous connective tissues called ligaments (Fig. 9-33). All joints have a normal range of movement, an area in which they can move about freely without stress or strain. When a joint is forced beyond its normal range of motion, ligaments stretch and tear.

Muscles. The body has over 600 muscles (Fig. 9-34). Most are attached to both ends of bones by strong, cord-like tissues called *tendons.*

Unlike the other soft tissues, *muscles* are able to contract (shorten) and relax (lengthen), which causes all body movement. The brain directs muscle movement through the **spinal cord,** a pathway of nerves in the spine. When the muscles contract, they pull the ends of the bones closer together, causing motion at the joint.

Motion is usually caused by a group of muscles close together pulling at the same time. For instance, the "hamstrings" are a group of muscles at the back of the thigh. When the hamstrings contract, the leg bends at the knee. Injuries to the brain, the spinal cord, or the nerves can affect muscle control. A loss of muscle control or a permanent loss of feeling and movement is called **paralysis.**

Muscle cramps. Cramps are common when a person's muscles become tired or cold from swimming or other activity. A muscle contracts suddenly, usually in the arm, foot, or calf. Advise a person with a cramp to stop the activity or change his or her swimming stroke. Explain that changing the position of the muscle and massaging it often relieves the cramp. Tell a person who has a leg cramp in deep water to swim to the side or get out of the water. Once the person has reached safety, you can tell him or her to extend the leg, flex the ankle, and massage the cramp.

A cramp in the abdominal muscles, sometimes mistakenly called a stomach cramp, is rare. It can happen,

however, when a person is tired and cold. Advise a person with a mild cramp to get out of the water. Help the person if necessary. Someone with severe cramps in deep water must be helped to safety immediately.

Types of musculoskeletal injuries

The four basic types of musculoskeletal injuries are fracture, dislocation, sprain, and strain.

Fracture. A *fracture* is a chip, a crack, or a complete break in a bone (Fig. 9-35). A fracture at an aquatic facility may be caused by a fall, jump, or dive in which a person strikes the pool deck or the edge or bottom of the pool or a hard object under water. Tumbling down a slide at a multi-attraction facility can result in a fracture. A person who falls when running or even from a standing position can crack, chip, or break a bone. Extremely strong twisting forces and muscle contractions, such as from a powerful electrical shock, can also cause a fracture.

figure 9-35 *Fractures include chipped or cracked bones or bones broken all the way through.*

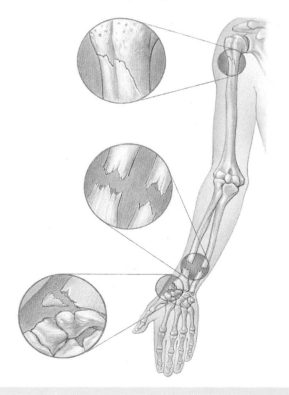

figure 9-36 *A dislocation is a displacement or separation of a bone from its normal position at a joint.*

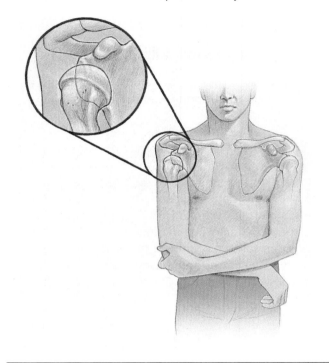

figure 9-37 *A sprain results when bones that form a joint are forced beyond their normal range of motion, causing ligaments to stretch and tear.*

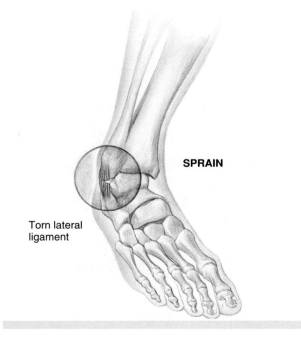

SPRAIN

Torn lateral ligament

Fractures are classified as open or closed. Closed fractures leave the skin unbroken and are more common than open fractures. An open fracture involves an open wound. Open fractures often occur when an arm or a leg is sharply bent, causing bones to break and bone ends to tear the skin and surrounding soft tissues or when an object penetrates the skin with violent force and breaks the bone.

Bone ends do not have to be visible for a fracture to be classified as open. Open fractures are more serious than closed fractures because of the risks of infection and severe blood loss. Although fractures are rarely immediately life-threatening, any fracture involving a large bone can cause severe shock because bones and soft tissue may bleed heavily.

Fractures are not always obvious unless there is an open wound with protruding bone ends or a body part that looks very unnatural or out of shape. The way in which the injury occurred, such as a fall from a height, can often suggest a possible fracture.

Dislocation. A *dislocation* is a displacement or separation of a bone from its normal position at a joint (Fig. 9-36). Dislocations are usually caused by a violent force that tears the ligaments that hold the bone in place. A fall can cause a dislocation. Dislocations are generally more obvious than fractures because the displaced bone end often causes a **deformity**— an abnormal lump, ridge, or hollow area.

Sprain. A *sprain* is the tearing of ligaments and other tissues at a joint. A sprain usually results when the bones that form a joint are suddenly and violently forced beyond their normal range of motion (Fig. 9-37). This can happen in a hard fall, especially one in which a body part, such as an ankle, is twisted. Forcing a joint beyond its range of motion can even dislocate or fracture the bones. Severe sprains or strains that involve a fracture usually cause pain when the joint is moved.

Strains. A *strain* is a stretching and tearing of muscles or tendons. It is sometimes called a muscle pull or tear. Because tendons are tougher and stronger than muscles, tears usually occur in the muscle itself or where the muscle attaches to the tendon. Strains are often the result of lifting something too heavy or working a muscle too hard. They can also result from sudden or awkward movement, such as an incorrectly performed dive.

General signs and symptoms of musculoskeletal injuries

Because they appear to be similar, it may be difficult for you to determine exactly what type of injury has occurred. Look and listen for clues that may indicate a musculoskeletal injury.

Five common signs and symptoms of musculoskeletal injuries are—

- Pain— The area is painful to the touch.
- Swelling—Swelling may appear rapidly, gradually, or not at all.
- Deformity—You may notice abnormal lumps, ridges, hollows, bends, and angles in the injured area. Comparing the injured part to the uninjured part may help you detect deformity.
- Discolored skin— At first the skin may look red, then it begins to look bruised.
- Inability to use or move the affected part—The victim may tell you that it hurts too much to move the injured part or he or she is unable to move it.

Signs and symptoms of serious musculoskeletal injuries. It isn't always easy to tell how serious an injury to a muscle, bone, or joint is. Sometimes only an X-ray film can show the extent of an injury. Suspect a serious injury if the victim shows the general signs and symptoms of musculoskeletal injury plus the following:

- The victim felt bones grating or felt or heard a snap or pop at the time of injury.
- Numbness, tingling, or change of color in a hand, foot, fingers, or toes, indicating loss of circulation.
- Cause of the injury suggests the injury may be severe.

Care for musculoskeletal injuries

You don't need to know whether the injury is a sprain, strain, dislocation, or fracture to care for it. Proper care includes making the victim more comfortable. You can apply ice to reduce pain and swelling and have the victim rest in a comfortable position (Fig. 9-38). You can elevate the injured part on pillows or folded towels or a folded blanket, but be careful not to move the victim in any way that causes pain. If the victim says that moving

it hurts, stop. The injury may be serious. If you suspect a serious musculoskeletal injury, call EMS personnel and **_immobilize_** the injured part (keep it from moving).

Call EMS personnel if —

- The injury involves the head, neck, or back.
- You suspect a fracture or dislocation.
- The victim has difficulty breathing.
- The victim is unable to move or to use the injured part.
- You suspect or see more than one injured body part.

Immobilize the injured part if you must move the victim. Immobilizing the injured part reduces pain; prevents further damage, such as a closed fracture becoming an open fracture; reduces the risk of severe bleeding; and reduces the possibility of loss of circulation to the injured part.

There are several ways to immobilize an injured body part. One method is to apply a **_splint_**. Don't apply a splint, however, unless you can do so without hurting the victim. A splint is a device that holds an injured part in place. An effective splint must extend above and below the injury site (Fig. 9-39, _A_ and _B_)

---

figure 9-38 _To care for musculoskeletal injuries, you can apply ice and have the victim rest in a comfortable position._

figure 9-39 *A, To immobilize a bone, splint the joints above and below the fracture. **B**, To immobilize a joint, a splint must extend to the bones above and below the injured joint.*

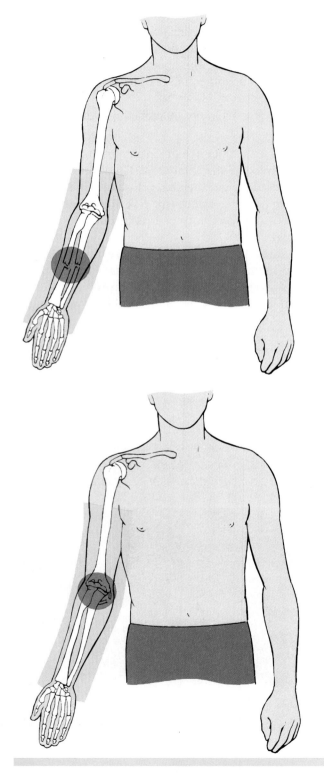

A

B

Follow these guidelines when splinting:

- Immobilize an injury in the position you find it.
- Immobilize the injured area and the joints above and below the injury site.
- Check the fingers or toes to make sure the splint is not too tight. The fingers and toes will turn blue or become cold or numb if their circulation is lessened or cut off. After you have splinted the injury, apply ice and raise the injured part.

Types of splints. There are three types of splints—soft splints, rigid splints, and **anatomic splints.** Soft splints include folded blankets, towels, pillows, and a sling or cravat (Fig. 9-40). A sling is a triangular bandage tied to support an arm, wrist, or hand (Fig. 9-41). A cravat is a folded triangular bandage used to hold dressings or splints in place. A wad of cloth and bandages can serve as an effective splint for small body parts, such as the hand or fingers.

Rigid splints include boards, metal strips, folded magazines or newspapers, and heavy cardboard (Fig. 9-42). The backboard, a piece of equipment that all facilities should have available, serves as a splint in cases of suspected spinal injury in the pool. Chapter 11 tells how a backboard is used. The ground can also serve as a splint. If a person with an injured leg or back is stretched out on a hard surface, such as the ground or a pool deck, that surface serves as a splint.

figure 9-40 *Soft splints include folded blankets, towels, pillows, and a triangular bandage tied as a sling or folded as a cravat.*

Anatomic splints refer to the use of the body as a splint. You may not ordinarily think of the body as a splint, but it works very well. For example, an arm can be splinted to the chest. An injured leg can be splinted to the uninjured leg (Fig. 9-43).

You may not have commercial splints immediately available. If they are available, however, you should learn to use them in your in-service training. Commercial splints include padded board splints, air splints, and specially designed flexible splints (Fig. 9-44).

To splint an injured body part—

1 Support the injured part. If possible, have another lifeguard or a bystander help you.

2 Check fingers or toes for feeling, warmth, and color.

3 Cover any open wounds with a dressing and bandage to help control bleeding and prevent infection.

4 If using a rigid splint, pad the splint so that it is shaped to the injured part. This will help prevent further injury.

5 Secure the splint in place with folded triangular bandages (cravats), roller bandages, or other wide strips of cloth.

6 Check fingers or toes to ensure the splint is not too tight, and loosen it if necessary.

7 Elevate the splinted part, if possible.

figure 9-42 *Rigid splints include boards, metal strips, and folded cardboard or plastic.*

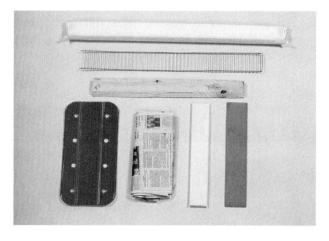

figure 9-43 *An injured leg can be splinted to the uninjured leg.*

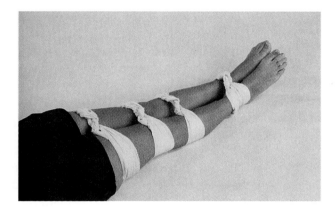

figure 9-41 *A triangular bandage tied as a sling can support an injured arm.*

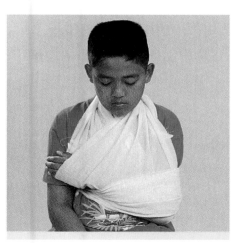

figure 9-44 *Commercial splints.*

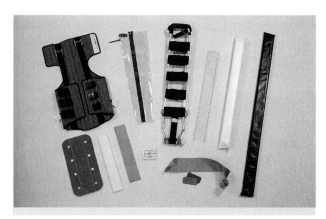

After the injury has been immobilized, recheck the victim's breathing. Help the victim rest in the most comfortable position, apply ice or a cold pack, maintain normal body temperature, and reassure him or her. Continue to monitor the victim's level of consciousness, breathing, and skin color until EMS personnel arrive. Be alert for signs, such as shock, that may indicate the victim's condition is worsening.

SPECIAL SITUATIONS

Injuries to the head

Injuries to the head often damage both bone and soft tissue, including brain tissue. A force strong enough to damage the head can also damage the neck and spine. Injuries to the spine are discussed in detail in the next chapter. It is usually difficult to determine the extent of damage in head injuries. In most cases, the only way to find out is by having X-ray films taken. Since you cannot know how severe a head injury is, always care for such an injury as if it is serious.

An injury to the head can cause bleeding inside the skull. The blood can build up and cause pressure that can cause further damage (Fig. 9-45). The first and most important sign of brain injury is a change in the victim's level of consciousness. He or she may be dizzy or confused or become unconscious.

Causes of head injury. The cause of the injury can help you determine whether a head injury may have occurred. Strong forces are likely to cause severe injury to the head and to the neck and spine as well. A diver who hits his or her head on the bottom or side of a swimming pool, a person who faints and falls on a pool deck, a person who collapses and falls in a locker room, or a person who hits the head on an underwater object may have a head injury.

Consider the possibility that a person has a head injury in several situations. These include—

• A person who has fallen from a height greater than his or her height.
• Any diving incident.
• Any incident involving a lightning strike.
• A person found unconscious for unknown reasons.
• A person who has been injured by a force to the head, such as from a car or other vehicle, or by striking the head while moving at high speed, for example on a speed slide.
• A person with an injury that penetrates the head, such as a gunshot wound.
• A motor vehicle crash involving a driver or passengers not wearing safety belts.
• A person thrown from a motor vehicle.
• A person who has received an injury in which the person's helmet is broken, including a bicycle, motorcycle, football, or industrial helmet.

Signs and symptoms of head injuries. Certain signs and symptoms indicate a head injury. They may be obvious at first or may develop later. These signs and symptoms include—

• Changes in the level of consciousness.
• Severe pain or pressure in the head.
• Tingling or loss of sensation in the hands or feet.
• Partial or complete loss of movement of any body part.
• Unusual bumps or depressions on the head.
• Blood or other fluids in the ears or nose.
• Heavy external bleeding of the head.
• Seizures.

figure 9-45 *Injuries to the head can rupture blood vessels in the brain. Pressure builds within the skull as blood accumulates, causing brain injury.*

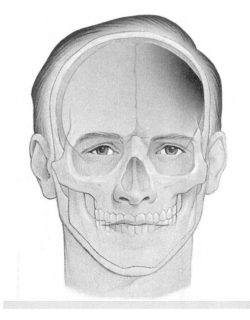

- **Impaired** (damaged or made worse) breathing or vision as a result of injury.
- Nausea or vomiting.
- Persistent headache.
- Loss of balance.
- Bruising of the head, especially around the eyes and behind the ears.

These signs alone do not always suggest a serious head injury, but they may when combined with the cause of the injury. Regardless of the situation, always call EMS personnel when you suspect a serious head injury or if a person is unconscious.

General care for head injuries. Head injuries at an aquatic facility are as likely to occur in the pool as out of the water. Any head injury caused by striking the head on the bottom can also involve the neck and spine.

Head injuries can become life-threatening emergencies. A serious head injury can cause a victim to stop breathing. A person who has suffered a head injury while in the water and loses consciousness, even for an instant, could become a drowning victim within seconds. For a head injury that occurs out of the water, such as from a fall, or clearly involves only the head, always give the following care while waiting for EMS personnel to arrive:

- Minimize movement of the victim's head and body.
- Maintain an open airway.
- Monitor consciousness and breathing.
- Control any external bleeding.
- Maintain normal body temperature.

You will learn about providing care for head injuries in the water in Chapter 11.

Concussion. Any significant force to the head can cause a **concussion.** A concussion is a temporary impairment of brain function. It usually does not result in permanent physical damage to the brain. In most cases, the victim loses consciousness for only an instant and may say that he or she "blacked out" or "saw stars." A concussion sometimes results in a loss of consciousness for longer periods of time. Other times, a victim may be confused or have memory loss. Be aware that a person in a pool who received a blow severe enough to cause a concussion could lose consciousness temporarily and submerge. Anyone suspected of having a concussion in or out of the water should be examined by a physician.

Injuries to the chest, abdomen, and pelvis

Most injuries to the chest, abdomen, and pelvis are only minor cuts, scratches, and bruises. Sometimes more serious injuries can occur, such as those resulting from motor vehicle crashes, falls, and stab and bullet wounds. These injuries can cause severe bleeding or make breathing difficult. The chest and abdomen hold many organs important to life, and injury to these areas can also cause a serious injury to the spine. Care for any life-threatening conditions first, then give any additional care that is needed.

General care for injuries to the chest, abdomen, and pelvis includes—

- Calling EMS personnel immediately.
- Monitoring breathing and pulse.
- Controlling bleeding.
- Minimizing shock.
- Limiting movement.

The chest. The *chest* is the upper part of the **trunk,** formed by the ribs, breastbone, and spine. It contains the heart, lungs, and muscles that control breathing. A puncture wound to the chest can range from minor to life threatening.

General signs and symptoms of chest injury include—

- Difficulty breathing.
- Severe pain at the site of the injury.
- Flushed, pale, or bluish discoloration of the skin.
- Obvious deformity, such as caused by a fracture.
- Coughing up blood.

Rib fracture. The *rib cage* is the cage of bones formed by the 12 pairs of ribs, the breastbone, and the spine (Fig. 9-46). Rib fractures are usually caused by direct force to the chest (Fig. 9-47). Ribs can be broken by falling. Although painful, a simple rib fracture is rarely life threatening. A victim with a fractured rib generally remains calm and breathes shallowly because normal or deep breathing is painful. The victim will usually attempt to ease the pain by supporting the injured area with a hand or arm.

If you suspect a fractured rib, have the victim rest in a position that makes breathing easier. Binding the victim's arm to the chest on the injured side helps support the injured area and make breathing more comfortable.

figure 9-46 *The rib cage surrounds and protects several vital organs.*

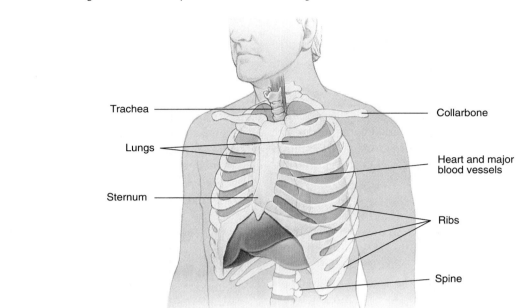

figure 9-47 *Forceful blows to the chest can fracture the ribs.*

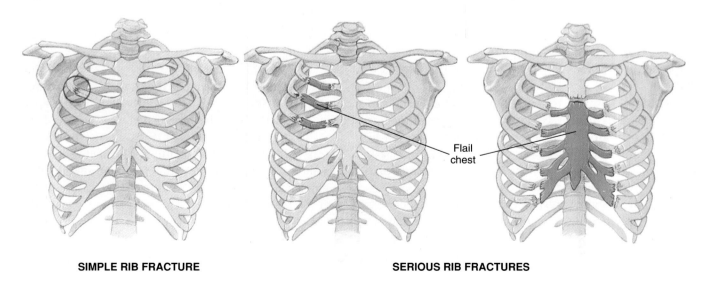

SIMPLE RIB FRACTURE   SERIOUS RIB FRACTURES

figure 9-48 *For fractured ribs, support and immobilize the injured area.*

You can use an object, such as a pillow or rolled blanket, to support and immobilize the area (Fig. 9-48). Monitor breathing and pulse carefully, and take steps to minimize shock.

Sucking chest wound. A forceful blow to the chest may penetrate the rib cage. This allows air to pass freely in and out through the wound. With each breath the victim takes, you may hear a sucking sound coming from the wound. This is the main sign of a sucking chest wound. The penetrating object can also injure organs and tissues inside the chest, including the lungs, heart, or major arteries or veins.

Call EMS personnel immediately. Without care, the victim's condition will quickly get worse. One or both lungs will fail to work properly, and breathing will become difficult. Your primary concern is the victim's breathing problem.

To care for a sucking chest wound, cover the wound with a dressing that does not allow air to pass through it. A plastic bag, a plastic or latex glove, or a piece of aluminum foil folded several times and placed over the wound will work if a special sterile dressing is not available. Tape the dressing in place except for one corner that should stay loose. If none of the materials are available, use a folded cloth. Give any other necessary care.

The abdomen. The *abdomen* is the middle part of the trunk containing the stomach, liver, and other organs.

Because the abdomen is not protected by bones, it is easily injured. A forceful blow to the abdomen or a fall from a height can cause severe bleeding inside the body. The signs and symptoms of serious abdominal injury include—

- Severe pain.
- Bruising.
- External bleeding.
- Nausea.
- Vomiting (sometimes vomit containing blood).
- Weakness.
- Thirst.
- Pain, tenderness, or a tight feeling in the abdomen.
- Organs possibly protruding from the abdomen.

If you suspect severe internal bleeding, keep the victim lying flat and watch for signs of internal bleeding. Bending the victim's knees and hips slightly may make the victim more comfortable. A folded blanket or pillow can be placed under the knees to support the legs in this position. If movement of the legs causes pain, leave the victim lying flat.

Sometimes a severe or penetrating blow to the abdomen can cause organs to be exposed or protrude. In this case, carefully position the victim on his or her back. Do not apply any pressure to the organs, and do not attempt to push the organs back inside. Remove any clothing from around the wound, and apply moist, sterile dressings or a clean cloth loosely over the wound. Use warm tap water to moisten the dressings (Fig. 9-49, A-C). Cover with plastic wrap.

The pelvis. The *pelvis* is the lower part of the trunk containing the intestines, bladder, and reproductive organs. Injuries to the pelvis may include fractures to the pelvic bone and damage to structures within. Fractured bones may puncture or lacerate internal structures, or they can be injured by forceful blows.

Signs and symptoms of injury to the pelvis are the same as those for an abdominal injury. Certain pelvic injuries may cause loss of sensation in the legs or inability to move them. This may indicate a lower spine injury.

Care for pelvic injuries is the same as that for abdominal injuries. Do not move the victim unless necessary. If possible, try to keep the victim lying flat. If not, help him or her become comfortable. Control any external bleeding, and cover any protruding organs. If you suspect a spinal injury, minimize movement of the victim. Always call EMS personnel, and take steps to minimize shock.

figure 9-49 *A, Carefully remove clothing from around the wound. **B,** Cover the wound with a large, moist sterile dressing and cover the dressing with plastic wrap. **C,** Place a blanket or folded towel over the dressings to keep the organs warm.*

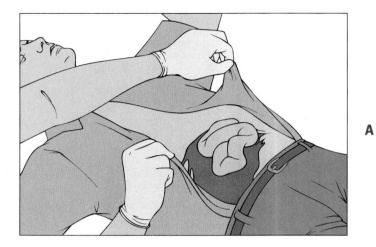

A

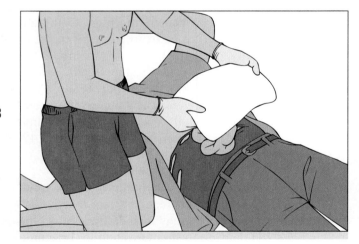

B

C

MOVING A VICTIM

Usually when you give first aid, you will not have to move the victim immediately except in the case of a victim who is drowning. When a victim is injured out of the water, in many cases, you will care for that victim where you find him or her. If the victim's injury is minor, he or she will probably be able to go to the first aid area. Moving a victim needlessly, however, can lead to further injury. For example, if the victim has a closed fracture of the leg, movement could result in the end of the bone tearing the skin. Soft tissue damage, damage to nerves, blood loss, and infection all could result unnecessarily.

You should move a victim in cases of immediate danger, such as fire, lack of oxygen, risk of drowning, risk of explosion, risk of gas formation or a chemical leak, or a collapsing structure.

Before you act, consider the following limitations to ensure moving one or more victims quickly and safely:

- Dangerous conditions at the scene
- The size of the victim
- Your physical ability
- Whether others can help you
- The victim's condition

Considering these limitations will help you decide how to proceed. For example, if a person has been overcome by chlorine fumes, you do not enter the scene unless you have been trained to do so and have the proper equipment. The same holds true for an electrical emergency. If the victim is still in contact with the source of the electricity, you cannot attempt to move that person until the power is turned off. If you become injured, you may be unable to move the person and will only risk making the situation worse. If you become part of the problem, EMS personnel will have one more person to rescue.

To protect yourself and the victim, follow these guidelines when moving a victim:

- Only attempt to move a person you are sure you can comfortably handle.
- Bend your body at the knees and hips.
- Lift with your legs, not your back.
- Walk carefully using short steps.

- When possible, move forward rather than backward.
- Always look where you are going.
- Support the victim's head and spine.
- Avoid bending or twisting a victim with possible head or spine injury.

Emergency moves

There are many different ways to move a person to safety. There is *no one best way for all situations*. As long as you can move a person to safety without injuring yourself or causing further injury to the victim, the move is successful. Three common types of emergency moves are the—

- Walking assist.
- Two-person seat carry.
- Clothes drag.

All of these emergency moves can be done by one or two people and without any equipment.

Walking assist. The most basic emergency move is the walking assist. Either one or two rescuers can use this method with a conscious victim. To do a walking assist, place the victim's arm across your shoulders and hold it in place with one hand. Support the victim with your other hand around the victim's waist (Fig. 9-50, *A*). In this way, your body acts as a "crutch," supporting the victim's weight while you both walk. A second rescuer, if present, can support the victim in the same way from the other side (Fig. 9-50, *B*).

Two-person seat carry. The two-person seat carry requires a second rescuer. Put one arm under the victim's thighs and the other across the victim's back (Fig. 9-51, *A*). Interlock your arms with those of the second rescuer under the victim's legs and across the victim's back (Fig. 9-51, *B*). Lift the victim in the "seat" formed by the rescuers' arms (Fig. 9-51, *C*). Use this move for a victim who is conscious but cannot walk unless you suspect spinal injury.

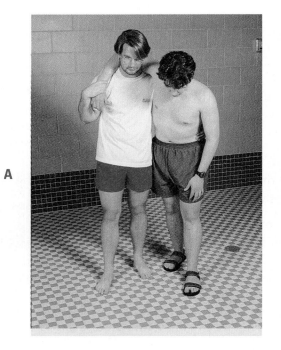

A

figure 9-50 *A,The most basic emergency move is the walking assist. B, A second rescuer can support the victim from the other side.*

B

figure 9-51 *A, For the two-person seat carry, put one arm under the victim's thighs and the other arm across the victim's back. B, Rescuers interlock their arms under the victim's legs and across the victim's back. C, The rescuers lift the victim in a seat formed by the rescuers' arms.*

A

B

C

Clothes drag. You might use this move if a clothed person fell into the water or suddenly became unconscious. You can use the clothes drag to move a person suspected of having a head or spine injury because it helps keep the head and neck stabilized. Gather the victim's clothing until tight from behind the victim's neck. Using the clothing, pull the victim to safety. During the move, the victim's head is cradled by both the clothing and the rescuer's hands (Fig. 9-52). This emergency move is exhausting and may cause back strain for the rescuer, even when done properly. This move is to be used only if you are alone and the victim can't walk with assistance.

SUMMARY

Drowning is not the only injury you may encounter in an aquatic setting. People can be injured in many ways, and part of your job is to be able to give effective, appropriate care to an injured person. The purpose of the information and skills presented in this chapter is to help you feel confident in your ability to make informed decisions and give the best possible care.

figure 9-52 *The clothes drag is most appropriate for moving a person suspected of having a head or spine injury.*

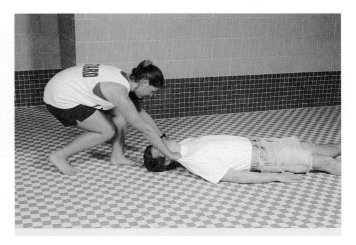

STUDY QUESTIONS

Circle the letter of the best answer or answers.

1. If nerves are injured, a laceration may—
   a) Be very painful.
   b) Be painless.
   c) Bleed heavily.
   d) Bleed lightly.

2. A bandage applied snugly to create pressure on a wound or injury is called a—
   a) Pressure bandage.
   b) Elastic roller bandage.
   c) Triangular bandage.
   d) Bandage compress.

3. If the fingers or toes below a bandage feel cold to the touch, you should—
   a) Cover them with the bandage.
   b) Tighten the bandage.
   c) Loosen the bandage.
   d) Remove the bandage.

4. Use a pressure point to control bleeding—
   a) Immediately.
   b) By placing a sterile dressing over the wound.
   c) Before elevating the wound above the heart.
   d) By squeezing the artery against the bone beneath it.

5. When caring for a shock victim, you should not—
   a) Have the victim lie down.
   b) Elevate the victim's legs.
   c) Cover the victim to prevent chilling.
   d) Give the victim anything to eat or drink.

6. Once you have wrapped a severed body part and placed it in a plastic bag, you should—
   a) Keep it warm by holding it next to your skin.
   b) Keep it cool by placing the bag on ice.
   c) Put the bag in the freezer.
   d) Put ice in the bag.

7. Primary concern for an injury to the mouth is—
   a) Swelling.
   b) Infection.
   c) Ability to breathe.
   d) Lost or broken teeth.

8. The following burn injuries always require immediate medical attention:
   a) Full-thickness burns
   b) Partial-thickness burns
   c) Superficial burns
   d) Sunburn

9. Cool burned areas immediately with:
   a) Cool water.
   b) Ice water.
   c) Pain relief spray.
   d) Burn ointment.

10. The signs of electrical injury include—
    a) Unconsciousness.
    b) Breathing difficulty.
    c) Strong, regular pulse.
    d) Dazed, confused behavior.

11. Which of the following is a sign or symptom of a musculoskeletal injury?
    a) Pain at the injury site
    b) Numbness or tingling in a hand or foot
    c) Discolored skin
    d) Feeling weak and faint
12. Call EMS personnel for which of the following conditions?
    a) The injury involves the head, neck, or back.
    b) You suspect a fracture or dislocation.
    c) The victim has difficulty breathing.
    d) The victim is unable to move.
13. Which of the following signs and symptoms indicate a serious head injury?
    a) Severe pain or pressure in the head
    b) Tingling or loss of sensation in the hands and feet
    c) Partial or complete loss of movement
    d) Unusual bumps or depressions on the head
14. If you suspect an injury to the chest, abdomen, or pelvis, you should—
    a) Move the victim to a quiet spot.
    b) Call EMS personnel immediately.
    c) Minimize shock.
    d) Perform CPR.
15. The most appropriate method of moving a person with a suspected head or spine injury is the—
    a) Walking assist.
    b) Two-person seat carry.
    c) Clothes drag.
    d) a and c.
16. The sequence of the following basic care steps for burns is—
    ___ Minimize shock.
    ___ Cover the burned area.
    ___ Cool the burned area (unless caused by electricity).

17. Match the type of splint with the material used. (There is more than one example for each type of splint.)

Material Used	Type of Splint
___ Boards	1) Soft splints
___ Towels	2) Rigid splints
___ Folded magazines	3) Anatomic splints
___ Uninjured leg	
___ Pillows	
___ Chest	

Circle *True* or *False*.
18. After you have splinted an injured body part, the victim can be left alone until EMS personnel arrive. True or False?
19. Abrasions usually bleed severely. True or False?

Fill in the blank with the correct answer.
20. An injury to the soft tissues is called a wound. The three types of soft tissue injuries are typically classified as _____ wounds, _____ wounds, and _____.
21. An object that remains in an open wound, a splinter, for example, is called an _____.

See answers to study questions on p. 286.

SKILL SUMMARY: CONTROLLING BLEEDING

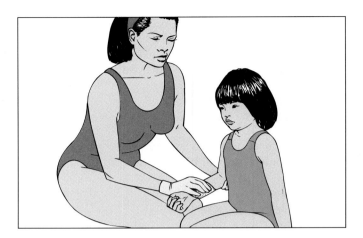

Cover wound with dressing and press firmly against the wound with hand.

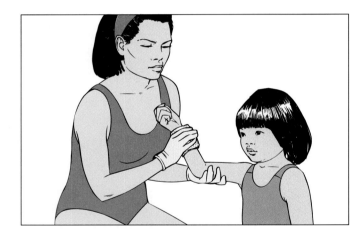

Elevate arm above the level of the heart.

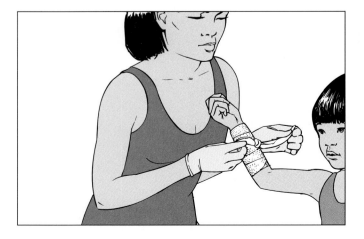

Cover dressings with a roller bandage.

Apply additional dressings.

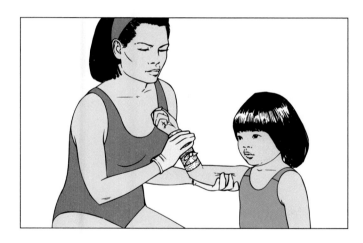

Squeeze the artery against the bone.

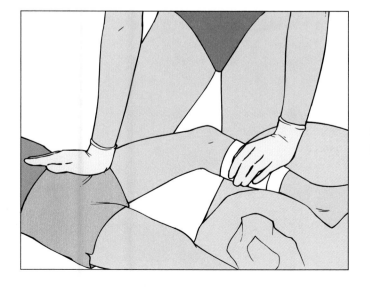

If bleeding is from the leg, press with the heel of your hand where the leg bends at the hip.

SKILL SUMMARY: APPLYING AN ANATOMIC SPLINT

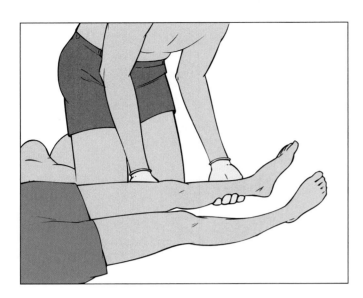

Support the injured area above and below the site of the injury.

Check for feeling, warmth, and color.

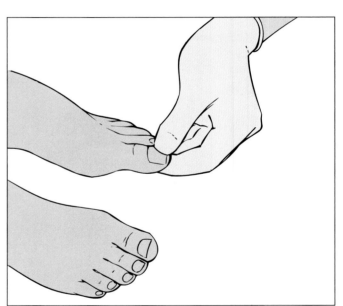

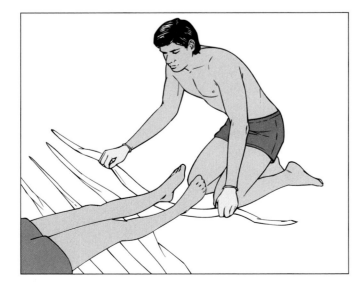

Place several folded triangular bandages above and below the injured area.

Place uninjured area next to injured area.

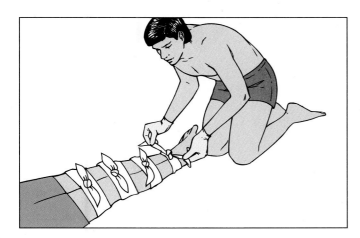

Tie triangular bandages securely.

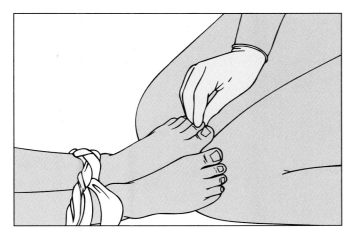

Recheck for feeling, warmth, and color.

SKILL SUMMARY: APPLYING A SOFT SPLINT

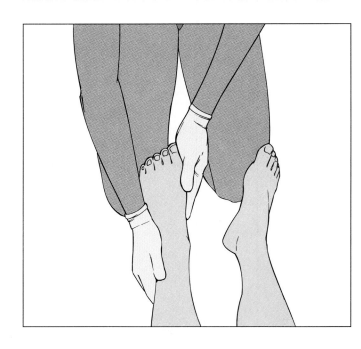

Support the injured area above and below the site of the injury.

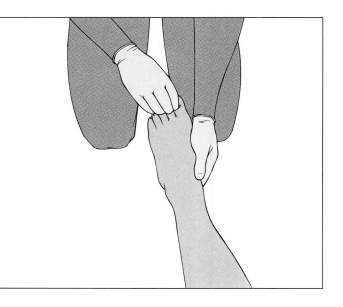

Check for feeling, warmth, and color.

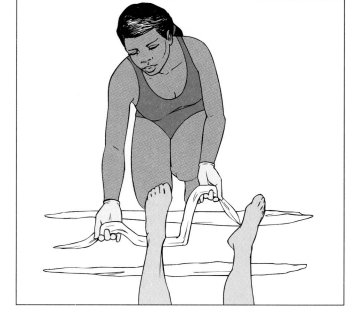

Place several folded triangular bandages above and below the injured area.

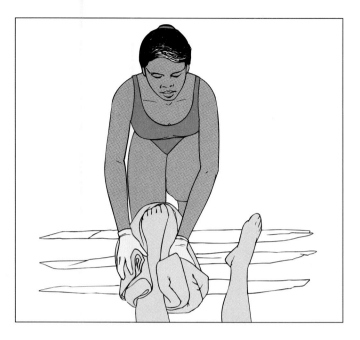

Gently wrap a soft object (a folded blanket or a pillow) around the injured area.

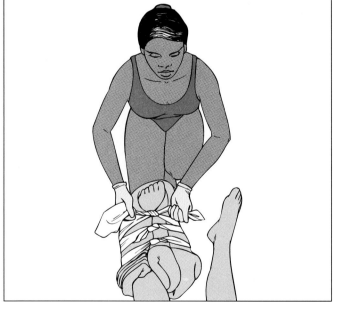

Tie triangular bandages securely.

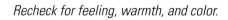

Recheck for feeling, warmth, and color.

SKILL SUMMARY: APPLYING A SLING

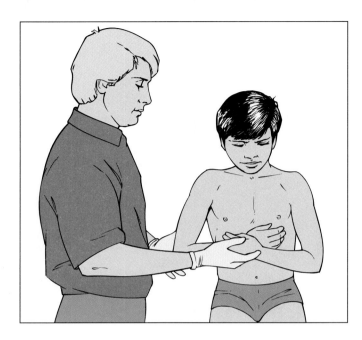

Support the injured area above and below the site of the injury.

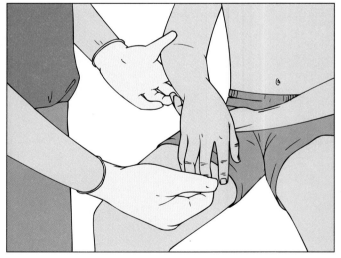

Check for feeling, warmth, and color.

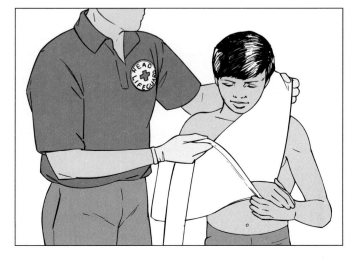

Place triangular bandage under the injured arm and over the uninjured shoulder to form a sling.

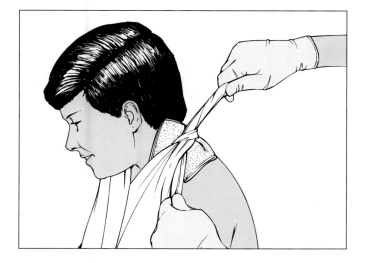

Tie the ends of the sling at the side of the neck.

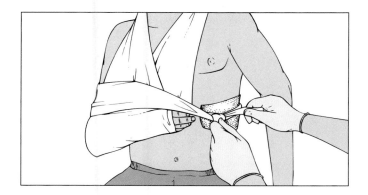

Bind the injured area to the chest with folded triangular bandage.

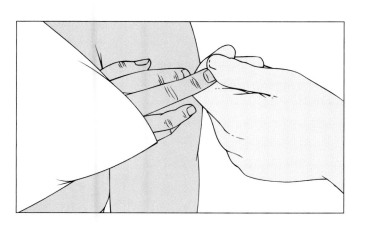

Recheck for feeling, warmth, and color.

SKILL SUMMARY: APPLYING A RIGID SPLINT

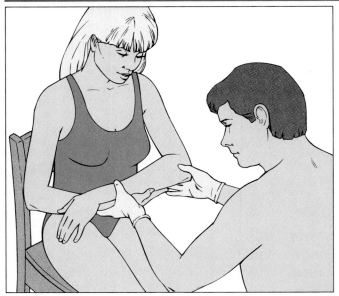

Support the injured area above and below the site of the injury.

Check for feeling, warmth, and color.

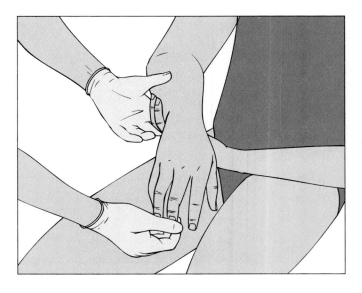

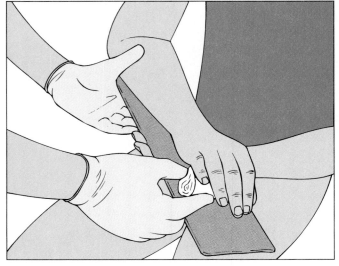

Place the rigid splint (board) under the injured area and the joints above and below the injured area.

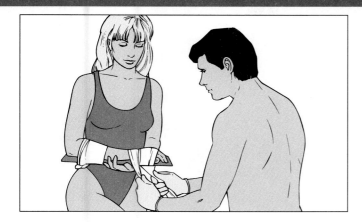

Tie several folded triangular bandages above and below the injured area.

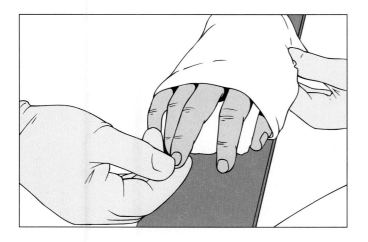

Recheck for feeling, warmth, and color.

After reading this chapter, you should be able to—

1. Identify at least eight general signs and symptoms of sudden illness.
2. List at least six basic principles of care for any sudden illness.
3. Describe the care for a person who you suspect is having a diabetic emergency.
4. List at least seven instances when you should call EMS personnel for a person having a seizure.
5. Describe the care for a seizure victim.
6. Describe the care for a stroke victim.
7. Describe the general care for a suspected poisoning emergency.
8. List four signs and symptoms that would lead you to suspect a heat-related illness.
9. Describe how to care for a person you suspect is suffering from heat-related illness.
10. List three signs and symptoms that would lead you to suspect hypothermia.
11. Describe how to care for a person you suspect is suffering from hypothermia.
12. Define the key terms for this chapter.

Key Terms

Absorbed poison: A poison that enters the body through the skin.

Anaphylaxis (an ah fi LAK sis): A severe allergic reaction; a form of shock.

Diabetes (di ah BE tes): A condition in which a person's body does not produce enough of the hormone insulin, causing too much sugar in the blood.

Diabetic: A person with diabetes.

Diabetic emergency: A situation in which a person becomes ill because of an imbalance of insulin and sugar in the body.

Epilepsy (EP i lep see): A chronic condition characterized by seizures that vary in type and duration; can usually be controlled by medication.

Fainting: A temporary loss of consciousness.

Frostbite: The freezing of body parts exposed to the cold.

Heat cramps: Painful muscle spasms following exercise or work in warm or moderate temperatures, usually involving the calf and abdominal muscles.

Heat exhaustion: A form of shock, often resulting from strenuous work or exercise in a hot environment.

Heat stroke: A life-threatening condition that develops when the effect of heat causes the body to become unable to cool itself, causing body systems to begin to fail.

Hypothermia: A life-threatening condition in which the body is unable to maintain warmth and the entire body cools.

Inhaled poison: A poison that a person breathes into the lungs.

Injected poison: A poison that enters the body through a bite, sting, or hypodermic needle.

Insulin (IN su lin): A hormone that enables the body to use sugar for energy; frequently used to treat diabetes.

Poison: Any substance that causes injury, illness, or death when introduced into the body.

Poison Control Center (PCC): A specialized kind of health center that provides information in cases of poisoning or suspected poisoning emergencies.

Seizure (SE zhur): A disorder in the brain's electrical activity, marked by loss of consciousness and often uncontrollable muscle movement.

Stroke: A disruption of blood flow to a part of the brain, causing permanent damage.

INTRODUCTION

Certain illnesses occur suddenly. Often there are no warnings to alert you that a person has become ill. At other times, the person may look ill, feel ill, or say that he or she feels that something is wrong. The signs and symptoms of sudden illness are often unclear. You may find it difficult to determine whether the victim's condition is an emergency and whether to call EMS personnel.

People can get sick without warning at an aquatic facility just as they can anywhere else. A person may complain of suddenly feeling dizzy or weak. He or she may turn pale or **ashen,** feel nauseated, or even become unconscious. If a person looks and feels ill, there is a problem.

Sudden illness can occur to anyone in the facility — young or old, fit or out of shape, active or quiet, male or female. It can occur anywhere in the facility — in the water, in the locker room, on the deck, in a picnic area, on a float, on a slide.

Signs and symptoms of sudden illness include —

- Feeling lightheaded, dizzy, confused, or weak.
- Changes in skin color (pale, ashen, or flushed).
- Sweating.
- Slurred speech.
- Nausea or vomiting.
- Diarrhea.
- Difficulty seeing.
- Severe headache.
- Persistent pressure or pain.
- Breathing difficulty.
- Seizure.
- Paralysis.
- Changes in consciousness.

You don't need to know the exact cause to provide appropriate care for the victim. Knowing and following some basic principles of care are all you need to care for a victim of sudden illness.

If the problem is not resolved quickly and easily or if you think the person may be severely ill, always call your local emergency number for help. Should a person become suddenly ill while in the water, it is unlikely you will be able to tell the cause. Your main concern is to get that person out of the water as quickly and safely as possible and to find out if there are any life-threatening conditions.

The following are the basic principles of care for any sudden illness:

- Care for any life-threatening conditions first.
- Call EMS personnel if the victim has any life-threatening conditions or if you have any doubts about the seriousness of the victim's condition.
- Help the victim rest comfortably.
- Keep the victim from getting chilled or overheated.
- Reassure the victim.
- Watch for changes in consciousness and breathing.
- Do not give the victim anything to eat or drink unless the victim is fully conscious.
- If the victim vomits, place the victim on one side.

SPECIFIC SUDDEN ILLNESSES

Fainting

One of the most common sudden illnesses is *fainting.* The victim suddenly loses consciousness. Fainting can be caused by heat; pain; an emotional shock; a specific medical condition, such as heart disease; standing for long periods of time; or **overexertion.** Some people, such as pregnant women or the elderly, may faint when suddenly changing positions, such as moving from sitting or lying to standing up.

---

figure 10-1 *To care for fainting, place the victim on the back and elevate the feet.*

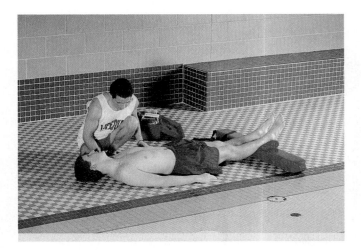

Signs and symptoms of fainting. Fainting may occur with or without warning. Often, the victim may initially feel lightheaded or dizzy and have pale, cool, moist skin. The person may feel nauseated and complain of numbness or tingling in the fingers and toes. You may not be present to see or hear these warnings when a person suddenly faints, but always ask anyone near or with the person if the person complained of feeling ill or dizzy or looked unusual in any way before fainting.

Care for fainting. Usually, a person who faints regains consciousness within a minute. Fainting itself does not usually harm the person, but injury may occur from falling. If you can reach the person as he or she starts to collapse, lower him or her to the deck or ground and position the person on the back. If possible, elevate the person's legs 8 to 12 inches (Fig. 10-1). Loosen any restrictive clothing. Check the airway, breathing, and circulation. Do not give the person anything to eat or drink. Also, do not splash water on the person's face. This does little to stimulate the person, and the person could inhale the water. If the person vomits, place the person on one side. Since you will not be able to determine whether the fainting is linked to a more serious condition, *you should call EMS personnel in all cases of fainting.*

Diabetic emergencies

The condition in which the pancreas, an organ in the body, does not produce enough of the hormone ***insulin*** is called ***diabetes.*** The person with this condition is a ***diabetic.*** There are between 11 and 12 million diabetics in the United States. Insulin is needed to take sugar into the body cells, which need sugar as a source of energy. When there is not sufficient insulin in the body, too much sugar remains in the blood. When the amount of sugar and the amount of insulin in the body are not in proper balance, illness results (Fig. 10-2).

There are two major types of diabetes. Type I, insulin-dependent diabetes, occurs when the body produces little or no insulin. This type of diabetes usually begins in childhood. Insulin-dependent diabetics have to inject insulin into their bodies daily (Fig. 10-3).

Type II, noninsulin-dependent diabetes, occurs when the body produces insulin but not enough of it. This condition usually occurs in older adults.

Anyone with diabetes must carefully monitor his or her diet and exercise. Insulin-dependent diabetics must also regulate their use of insulin. When the insulin level

figure 10-2 *The hormone insulin is needed to take sugar from the blood into the body cells.*

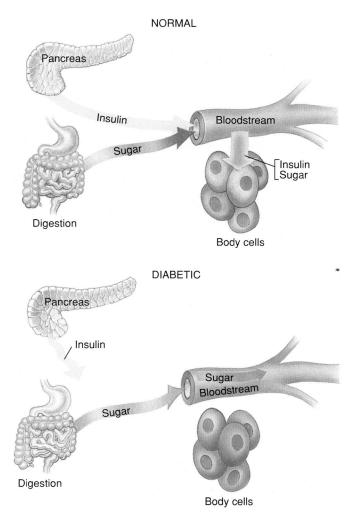

NORMAL

DIABETIC

figure 10-3 *Insulin-dependent diabetics inject insulin to regulate the amount in the body.*

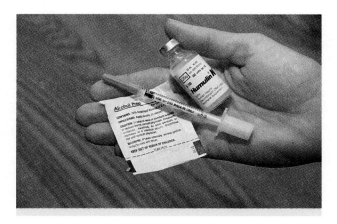

in the body is too high, the person has a low sugar level. Too low a sugar level can rapidly make a person ill with a condition called **insulin reaction.** Children with diabetes, for example, may become so involved in playing and having fun at an aquatic facility that they forget to eat enough to counteract the extra amount of exercise they are getting. The sugar level in their blood becomes too low. If, on the other hand, the sugar remains too high and the insulin too low, the victim can become seriously ill with a condition called **diabetic coma.** This occurs when diabetics fail to take their insulin. Both these conditions are *diabetic emergencies.*

Signs and symptoms of diabetic emergencies.

The signs and symptoms of diabetic coma and insulin reaction differ somewhat, but the major signs and symptoms are similar. These include—

• Changes in the level of consciousness, including dizziness, drowsiness, and confusion.
• Rapid breathing.
• Rapid pulse.
• Feeling and looking ill.

It is not important for you to decide whether a person is having an insulin reaction or is in diabetic coma. The basic care for both conditions is the same.

Care for diabetic emergencies.

First, care for any life-threatening conditions. If the victim is conscious, ask if he or she is a diabetic. Look for a **medical alert tag** (Fig. 10-4). Some diabetics wear a medical alert bracelet identifying them as diabetic. If you find one or if the person tells you that he or she is a diabetic and exhibits the signs and symptoms, then suspect a diabetic emergency.

If the conscious victim can take food or fluids, give him or her sugar. Most candy, fruit juices, and nondiet soft drinks have enough sugar to be effective (Fig. 10-5). Common table sugar, either dry or dissolved in a glass of water, also works well. If the person's problem is low sugar, the sugar you give will help quickly. If the person already has too much sugar, the excess sugar will do no further harm. Often diabetics know if they are having an insulin reaction and will ask for something with sugar in it. They may carry a source of sugar for such occasions. If the person is conscious but does not feel better within approximately 5 minutes after taking sugar, call EMS personnel immediately.

If the person is unconscious, do not give anything by mouth. Call EMS personnel immediately, monitor breathing and pulse, and keep the victim from getting chilled or overheated.

figure 10-4 *Medical alert tags can provide important medical information about the victim.*

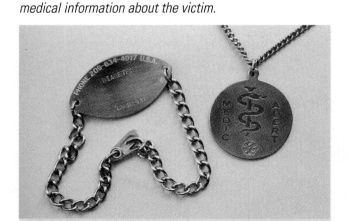

figure 10-5 *If a victim of a diabetic emergency is conscious, give him or her food or fluids containing sugar.*

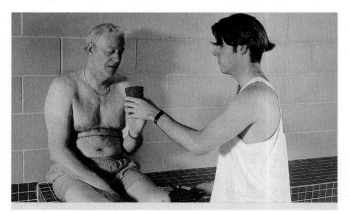

Seizures

Seizures are a loss of body control as a result of disruption to the electrical activity of the brain. Causes of seizures include sudden illness, extreme heat, an injury to the brain, and *epilepsy,* a **chronic** (long lasting or recurring) condition that affects about 2 million Americans. Epilepsy is usually controlled with medication, but some people with epilepsy continue to have seizures from time to time.

Seizures can be brought on by flickering lights (such as sunlight on water) and by being startled by a sudden unexpected touch (such as when playing and diving into cold water). They can also be caused by hyperventilating (breathing more rapidly then normal) and by neglecting to take prescribed antiseizure medication.

Children with seizure disorders are at a much higher risk of drowning than children without seizure disorders. They need close and uninterrupted supervision. Unfortunately, you may not be aware that a particular child in the facility has a seizure disorder and therefore may not provide this supervision. If you are told about such a child, however, ensure the child is constantly supervised by a parent or another responsible adult. If no such person is available, tell your supervisor about the situation at once.

Signs and symptoms of seizures. Seizures range from mild blackouts that others may mistake for daydreaming to **convulsions** (sudden, uncontrolled muscular contractions) lasting several minutes.

Signals of seizures. Before a seizure occurs, the person may experience an **aura**. An aura is an unusual sensation or feeling such as a visual hallucination; a strange sound, taste, or smell; or an urgent need to get to safety. If the person recognizes the aura, he or she may have time to tell bystanders and sit down before the seizure occurs.

Care for seizures. Although it may be frightening to see someone having a seizure, you can easily help care for the person. Remember that he or she cannot control the seizure and the violent muscular contractions that may occur. Don't try to stop the seizure. Don't hold or restrain the person unless he or she is in the water and needs support to keep water from entering the mouth and nose until you can remove the person from the water.

If you know the person has periodic seizures or others with the person tell you so, you do not need to call EMS personnel immediately. The person will usually recover from a seizure in a few minutes. However, EMS personnel should always be called if—

- The seizure lasts more than a few minutes.
- The person has repeated seizures.
- The person appears to be injured.
- You are uncertain about the cause of the seizure.
- The person is pregnant.
- The person is a known diabetic.
- The person is an infant or child.
- The seizure takes place in water.
- The person fails to regain consciousness after the seizure.

Out of the water. With a person who has a seizure, your objectives are to protect the person from injury and make sure the airway is open. If a person has a seizure out of the water, first move nearby objects that might cause injury. Protect the person's head by placing folded clothing or a towel beneath it. If there is saliva, blood, or vomit in the person's mouth, position him or her on one side so that the fluid drains from the mouth (Fig. 10-6).

Don't try to place anything between the person's teeth. People having seizures rarely bite their tongues or cheeks hard enough to cause significant bleeding; however, some blood may be present.

---

figure 10-6 *Position the victim on one side if there is saliva, blood, or vomit in the victim's mouth.*

When the seizure is over, the person will be drowsy and **disoriented.** Check to see if he or she was injured during the seizure. Be reassuring and comforting. If the seizure occurred in public, the person may be embarrassed and self-conscious. Ask bystanders not to crowd around the victim, who will be tired and want to rest. Stay with the person until he or she is fully conscious and aware of the surroundings.

In the water. If a person has a seizure in the water and has submerged, that person has very likely inhaled or swallowed water. Get that person out of the water as soon as possible. If the person is having convulsions, and other lifeguards are available, get someone to help you. If the person has not submerged, support him or her with the head above water until the convulsions stop and then remove the person from the water.

The person may also be unconscious. Have someone call EMS personnel at once. Place the victim lying down on the deck, and give the same care as for a person who has had a seizure out of the water. Check the victim's breathing, and give rescue breathing if necessary.

Stroke

A *stroke* is a disruption of blood flow to a part of the brain that is serious enough to damage brain tissue (Fig. 10-7). Most commonly, a stroke is caused by a blood clot in the arteries that supply blood to the brain. Another common cause is bleeding from a ruptured artery in the brain.

Signs and symptoms of stroke. As with other sudden illnesses, the primary signals of stroke are looking or feeling ill or behaving abnormally. Other signals of stroke include sudden weakness of muscles and numbness in the face, arm, or leg. Usually, this occurs only on one side of the body. The victim may have difficulty talking or understanding speech. Vision may be blurred or dimmed; the pupils of the eyes may be of unequal size. The victim may also experience a sudden, severe headache; dizziness, confusion or changes in mood; or ringing in the ears. The victim may become unconscious or lose bowel or bladder control.

These signs and symptoms will most likely be apparent to you only if the victim is out of the water. If the victim is in the water, you will probably be able to tell only that the person is distressed or drowning and must be removed from the water as soon as possible.

Care for stroke. If the victim is unconscious, make sure he or she has an open airway and care for any life-threatening conditions. Have someone call EMS personnel immediately. If there is fluid or vomit in the victim's mouth, position him or her on one side to allow any fluids to drain from the mouth. You may have to use a finger sweep to remove some of the material from the mouth. Stay with the victim, and monitor his or her breathing and pulse.

If the victim is conscious and you see signs of a stroke, call EMS personnel. A stroke can make the victim fearful and anxious. Offer comfort and reassurance. Often he or she does not understand what has happened. Have the victim rest in a comfortable position. Do not give him or her anything to eat or drink. If the victim is drooling or having difficulty swallowing, place him or her on one side to help drain any fluids or vomit from the mouth.

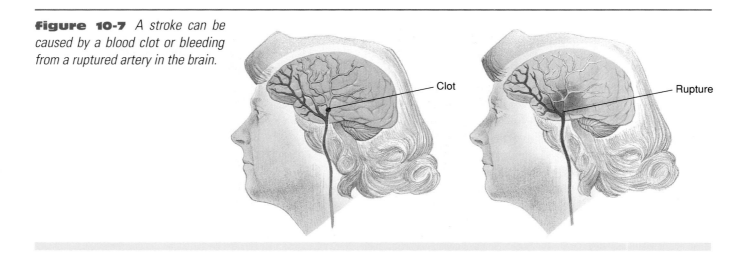

figure 10-7 *A stroke can be caused by a blood clot or bleeding from a ruptured artery in the brain.*

Clot

Rupture

POISONING, BITES, AND STINGS

How poisons enter the body

Poison is any substance that causes injury, illness, or death when introduced into the body. Poison can be swallowed, inhaled, or absorbed through the skin. It can also be injected through the skin by a bite, sting, or hypodermic needle (Fig. 10-8). Poisons a person can swallow include foods, such as certain mushrooms and shellfish; excess amounts of alcohol or medications, such as aspirin; illegal drugs; cleaning products and pesticides; and certain plants.

Poisoning can also occur when a person inhales poisonous fumes. At a pool facility, the main concern would be the presence of chlorine gas or gases formed by chlorine mixing with other chemicals such as acid or ammonia. Other gases and fumes include carbon monoxide from an engine, carbon dioxide from sewers, and fumes from household and industrial products, such as glues and cleaners.

An *absorbed poison* enters the body through the skin. Absorbed poisons come from plants such as poison ivy, poison oak, and poison sumac, as well as from fertilizers and pesticides used in lawn and plant care.

Injected poisons enter the body through bites or stings of insects, spiders, scorpions, ticks, animals, and snakes, or as drugs or medications injected with a hypodermic needle.

figure 10-8 *A poison can enter the body by being swallowed, inhaled, absorbed through the skin, or injected.*

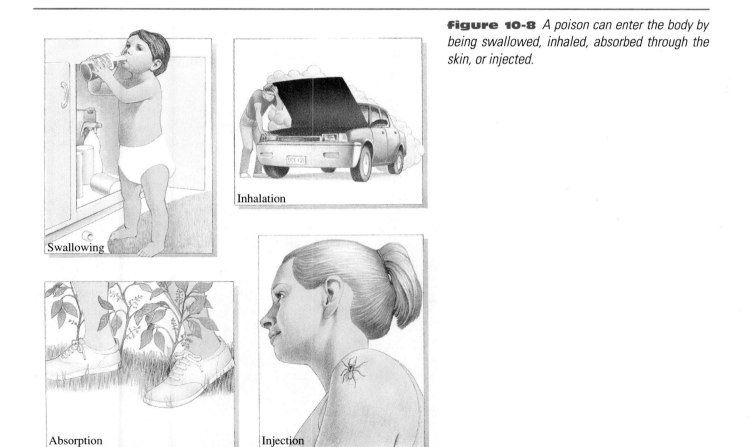

Swallowing

Inhalation

Absorption

Injection

Signs and symptoms of poisoning

The most important thing is to *recognize that a poisoning may have occurred.* As with other serious emergencies, evaluate the condition of the victim and ask for information from the victim or bystanders. If you then have even a slight suspicion that the victim has been poisoned, call EMS personnel immediately.

The general signs and symptoms of poisoning are the same as for other sudden illnesses. They include nausea, vomiting, diarrhea, chest or abdominal pain, breathing difficulty, sweating, loss of consciousness, and seizures. Other signs of poisoning are burn injuries around the lips or tongue or on the skin. Look also for any drug paraphernalia or empty containers. Note any suspicious odors. Chlorine gas, for example, has an easily recognizable, characteristic odor—like very strong household bleach.

If you suspect a poisoning, try to get answers to the following questions:

- What type of poison was it?
- How much was taken?
- When was it taken or when was the victim exposed to it?

This information will be useful to EMS personnel when they arrive.

Care for poisoning

Follow these general principles for any poisoning emergency:

1 Make sure it is safe to approach and to gather clues about what happened.

2 Remove the victim from the source of the poison, if necessary.

3 Assess the victim's airway, breathing, and circulation.

4 Care for any life-threatening conditions.

5 If the victim is conscious, gather additional information from him or her.

6 Look for any containers, and take them to the telephone.

7 Call your local Poison Control Center or emergency number according to the procedures at your facility. A *Poison Control Center (PCC)* is a specialized health center that provides information in cases of poisoning or suspected poisoning. The number of the PCC should be posted with other emergency numbers at facility telephones.

8 Follow the directions of the PCC or the EMS dispatcher.

9 Do not give the victim anything to drink or eat unless advised by medical professionals. If the poison is unknown and the victim vomits, save some of the vomit. If the victim goes to a hospital, the hospital may want to analyze it to identify the poison.

Swallowed poisons. Besides following these general principles for any poisoning, you may also need to provide additional care for specific types of poisons. Usually, if the person has swallowed a poison in the last 30 minutes, the stomach should be emptied, although with some poison, vomiting should not be **induced.** At many aquatic facilities, EMS personnel would arrive in time to deal with the situation. At facilities in more remote areas or at a greater than usual distance from immediate advanced medical care, such as some summer camps, a nearby or resident medical professional would use medication to induce vomiting if recommended or would give other appropriate care.

Inhaled poisons. Poisonous fumes come from a variety of sources. They may have an odor or be odor free. One commonly *inhaled poison* is **carbon monoxide (CO).** It is present in car exhaust and can be produced by defective cooking equipment, fires, and charcoal grills. A pale or bluish skin color that indicates a lack of oxygen may be a sign of carbon monoxide poisoning.

All victims of inhaled poison need oxygen as soon as possible. First, however, check to determine if it is safe for you to help. If you can remove the person from the source of the poison without endangering your life, then do so. You can help a conscious victim by just getting him or her to fresh air and then calling EMS personnel. Remove an unconscious victim from the area of the poison, maintain an open airway, give rescue breathing and CPR if necessary, and call EMS personnel.

Chlorine gas is highly **toxic.** If your facility keeps a supply of chlorine gas, all staff must be trained to recognize and test for its presence and to perform specific emergency procedures for dealing with it. Procedures should be written in the facility's policies and procedures manual or in a specific emergency action plan. Many facilities use only liquid or solid forms of chlorine, but chlorine gas can also easily be generated by mixing these forms with small amounts of water or with other chemicals used in cleaning pools. Gas can also be produced by an equipment failure.

Since chlorine gas is heavier than air and is attracted to water, emergency procedures must include a system for clearing the pool and evacuating the area until it is safe to return. Because it is heavier than air, chlorine gas also collects in other low areas, such as a pump/filter room that may be below pool level at a facility. The areas at your facility that would be especially dangerous in a chlorine gas emergency should be identified to you by facility management. The immediate care for chlorine gas inhalation is the same as for other inhaled poisons.

Absorbed poisons. People often contact poisonous substances that can be absorbed into the body. Millions of people each year suffer from contact with poisonous plants, such as poison sumac, poison oak, and poison ivy (Fig. 10-9, *A-C*). Other poisons absorbed through the skin include dry and wet chemicals, such as chemicals containing chlorine used at aquatic facilities and chemicals used in yard and garden maintenance.

Chemicals. If poisons such as dry or wet chemicals, including chlorine, chemicals containing chlorine, or chlorine gas, contact the skin, flush the affected area continuously with large amounts of water (Fig. 10-10). Chlorine gas is extremely irritating to the skin and eyes. Call EMS personnel immediately. Continue to flush the area until EMS personnel arrive. If a chemical gets in the eyes, flush the eyes with cool, clean running water until EMS personnel arrive.

If running water is not available, brush off dry chemicals, such as calcium hypochlorite, with your gloved hand (Fig. 10-11). Take care not to come in contact with the chemical yourself or to brush it into the eyes of the victim or any bystanders. Dry chemicals are activated by contact with water. If continuous running water is available, however, it will flush the chemical from the skin before activating it. Running water reduces the threat to you and quickly and easily removes the chemical from the victim.

Poison Control Centers

To help people deal with poisonings, a network of Poison Control Centers (PCCs) exists throughout the United States. Many centers are in the emergency departments of large hospitals. Medical professionals in these centers have access to information about virtually all poisonous substances. They will tell you how to counteract a poison if you can identify it. The number of the closest PCC should be posted by the facility telephone(s). You can get the telephone number from the telephone directory, a local doctor or hospital, or your local EMS system.

Your facility may have established procedures to follow in cases of suspected poisoning and have made them part of an emergency action plan. If so, you will follow them in a poisoning emergency. However, since many poisonings can be cared for without the help of EMS professionals, PCCs help prevent overburdening of the EMS system. If your facility does not have such procedures, if you know a victim has been poisoned and the victim is conscious, call your local or regional PCC first. The center will tell you what care to give and whether EMS personnel are needed. If the victim is unconscious or if you do not know your PCC telephone number, call your local emergency number. Often the dispatcher will link you with the PCC. The dispatcher may also monitor your talk with the PCC and send an ambulance if needed.

Post the number of the closest PCC by the telephones in the facility.

figure 10-9 *Annually, millions of people suffer from contact with poisonous plants whose poisons are absorbed into the body:* **A,** *Poison sumac.* **B,** *Poison oak.* **C,** *Poison ivy.*

A

John Shaw/Tom Stack and Associates

B

Walt Anderson/Tom Stack and Associates

C

John Shaw/Tom Stack and Associates

figure 10-10 *Whenever chemical poisons come in contact with the skin, flush the affected area continuously with large amounts of water.*

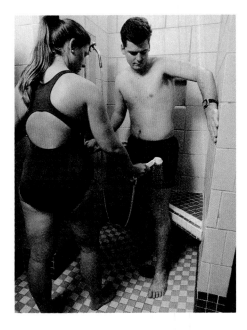

figure 10-11 *If running water is not available, brush off dry chemicals with a gloved hand.*

Poisonous plants. As a lifeguard, you are most likely to deal with the results of contact with poisonous plants if you work at a summer camp or an open-water facility, such as a park. These plants, especially poison ivy or poison oak, are probably growing nearby. The best defense against them is to know what they look like and avoid them. If you know that someone has just contacted a poisonous plant, immediately wash the affected area thoroughly with soap and water. If a rash or weeping blisters have begun to develop, apply a paste of baking soda and water to the area, and suggest to the person that he or she apply more several times a day and that lotions, such as Calamine® or Caladryl®, may help soothe the area. **Antihistamines,** such as Benadryl®, may also help dry up the blisters. If the condition spreads to large areas of the body or to the face, the person should see a doctor.

Alcohol and Other Drugs

There are many different types of drugs. Some are legal, some are not. Sometimes misusing or abusing them causes the user to behave strangely, dangerously, or unpleasantly. Alcohol is a drug that, when misused or abused, can have an unfavorable effect on the user's behavior. How to act toward people who behave in a troublesome way at your facility is discussed in Chapter 2.

Sometimes alcohol or another drug can have the effect of poison and make the user ill. When a person suddenly has the signs and symptoms of poisoning or illness, your immediate concern is not whether alcohol or some other drug might be causing these signs and symptoms. Your first concern is to recognize that a person is ill and to give the appropriate care. If you can positively identify alcohol or another drug as the cause, that information should be passed on to EMS personnel. Beware of making assumptions. A person who is stumbling, disoriented, or whose breath smells like alcohol may not be drunk. The signs and symptoms of a person who is ill from alcohol or another drug are in many ways similar to the signs and symptoms of other sudden illnesses. They include —

- Moist or flushed skin or sweating.
- Chills.
- Nausea and vomiting.
- Headache.
- Dizziness, changes in consciousness, drowsiness, or confusion.
- Rapid pulse and breathing.
- Slow pulse and breathing.
- Chest pain.
- Restlessness, irritability, and excitement.
- Generally looking and feeling ill.

A certain group of drugs called hallucinogens can produce sudden mood changes, and the victim may claim to see or hear something that is not present or be especially anxious or frightened.

Care for illness related to alcohol or another drug follows the same general principles as care for any sudden illness. You don't need to know the cause, such as a specific drug, to provide care. Any information you can learn from the scene, bystanders, the victim's family and friends, or the victim about what caused the problem may prove to be useful information for advanced medical personnel. Since abuse or misuse of alcohol or other drugs is a form of poisoning, give the same care as you would for any poisoning:

- Make sure it is safe to help the person.
- Care for any life-threatening conditions.
- Call the local PCC or your local emergency telephone number, and follow their directions.
- Question the victim or bystanders to try to find out what and how much was taken, and when it was taken.
- Calm and reassure the victim.
- Keep the victim from getting chilled or overheated.
- If the victim becomes violent or threatening, report it to your supervisor immediately and/or follow the emergency action plan in your facility.

Injected poisons

Insects. Many stinging insects, such as bees and hornets, are found around some outdoor aquatic facilities. Although insect stings are painful, they are rarely fatal. Fewer than 100 reported deaths from insect stings occur each year. Some people, however, have a severe allergic reaction to an insect sting that can result in a life-threatening respiratory emergency.

Care for insect stings. To care for an insect sting, examine the sting site to see if the stinger is in the skin. If it is, scrape the stinger away from the skin with your fingernail or a plastic card, such as a credit card (Fig. 10-12). Often the venom sac will still be attached to the stinger. Do not remove the stinger with tweezers, since putting pressure on the venom sac can cause further poisoning.

Wash the site with soap and water. Cover it to keep it clean. Apply ice or a cold pack to the area to reduce the pain and swelling. Do not put the pack or ice on the victim's bare skin. Observe the victim for signs of a severe allergic reaction. This reaction is also called ***anaphylaxis.***

Signs and symptoms of anaphylaxis. In an anaphylactic reaction, the skin or the area of the body where the sting occurred usually swells and turns red (Fig. 10-13). Other signs and symptoms include hives, itching, rash, weakness, nausea, vomiting, dizziness, and breathing difficulty that includes coughing and wheezing. The throat and tongue may swell and block the airway.

Care for anaphylaxis. If a person begins to develop any of these signs or symptoms after an insect bite or sting, observe that person carefully. If the person has any breathing difficulty or says that his or her throat is closing, call EMS personnel at once. Help the person into the most comfortable position for breathing. Monitor breathing and pulse, and reassure the person. People who know they are allergic to certain insect stings may carry a kit with them in case they are stung and have an allergic reaction. Some facilities in remote areas, such as parks and summer camps, keep such a kit as part of their first aid supplies (Fig. 10-14). The kit contains a single dose of a medication that can be injected into the body to counteract the allergic reaction.

figure 10-12 *If someone is stung by an insect, remove the stinger. Scrape it away from the skin with your fingernail or a plastic card, such as a credit card.*

figure 10-13 *In anaphylaxis, the skin usually swells and turns red.*

figure 10-14 *The contents of an anaphylaxis kit.*

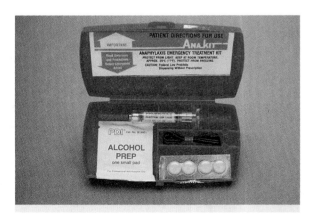

Spiders and scorpions. Few spiders in the United States have venom that causes death. However, the bites of the black widow and brown recluse spiders can be fatal. These spiders live in most parts of the United States. You can identify them by the unique designs on their bodies (Fig. 10-15, *A* and *B*). The black widow spider is black with a reddish hourglass shape on its underbody. The brown recluse spider is light brown with a darker brown, violin-shaped marking on the top of its body.

Both spiders prefer dark, out-of-the-way places where they are seldom disturbed. People reaching into piles of wood, brush, and rocks can be bitten on their hands and arms. If you are doing facility maintenance, picking up trash piles along a fence, or doing any landscape or gardening work at a facility, keep an eye out for black widow spiders. Often, the victim will not know that he or she has been bitten until signs and symptoms develop.

Scorpions live in dry regions of the southwestern United States and Mexico. As with spiders, only a few species of scorpions are fatally poisonous (Fig. 10-16). Scorpions live under rocks and logs and under the bark of certain trees and are most active at night.

Signs and symptoms of spider bites and scorpion stings. Signs and symptoms of spider bites and scorpion stings include—

- Nausea and vomiting.
- Difficulty breathing or swallowing.
- Sweating and salivating profusely.
- Irregular heart rhythms that can lead to cardiac arrest.
- Severe pain in the sting or bite area.
- Swelling on or around the site.
- A mark indicating a possible bite or sting.

Care for spider bites and scorpion stings. If you or the victim recognize a spider that bit as either a black widow or brown recluse, or if the victim has the signs and symptoms, call EMS personnel. The victim must go to a medical facility as soon as possible. Professionals will clean the wound and give medication to reduce the pain and inflammation. An **antivenin,** a material used to counteract the poisonous effects of snake, spider, or insect venom, is available for black widow bites.

figure 10-15 *A, The black widow spider and B, the brown recluse spider have characteristic markings.*

A

Rod Planck/Tom Stack and Associates

B

Ann Moreton/Tom Stack and Associates

figure 10-16 *The bite of only a few species of scorpions found in the United States can be fatal.*

Rod Planck/Tom Stack and Associates

Ticks

Some ticks carry Lyme disease; other ticks carry Rocky Mountain Fever. Both diseases can make people seriously ill. Lyme disease can cause arthritis, memory loss, numbness, high fever, and problems with sight and hearing.

The tick that carries Lyme disease is very small, often no larger than a poppy seed or the head of a pin. Other ticks are larger and easier to see, but they also tend to bite in areas such as behind the ears, in the hair, or in other areas where they are not easily noticed. A tick that has bitten someone should be removed as quickly as possible to minimize the risk of getting a disease.

If you find a tick, grasp the tick with fine-tipped tweezers as close to the skin as possible and pull slowly. If you do not have tweezers, use a glove, plastic wrap, or a piece of paper to protect your fingers. Wash your hands immediately. Do not try to burn a tick off.

Once the tick is removed, wash the area immediately with soap and water. If an antiseptic or antibiotic ointment is available, apply it to the wound to prevent infection.

Remove a tick by pulling steadily and firmly with fine-tipped tweezers.

In the event of a scorpion sting, call EMS personnel. The victim may need to go to a medical facility to receive an antivenin. While waiting for EMS personnel, wash the wound and apply a cold pack to the site.

Marine life. If you are lifeguarding at salt-water areas, you may encounter certain kinds of jellyfish or other marine life that give painful stings. A victim may become ill or even develop an allergic reaction (Fig. 10-17, *A-C*). If the victim was stung by a jellyfish, sea anemone, or Portuguese man of war, soak the affected area in household vinegar as soon as possible. You may use baking soda or rubbing alcohol as an alternative. Do *not* rub the area or apply ammonia. For a sting from a sting ray, sea urchin, or spring fish, flush the wound with tap water or ocean water. Immobilize the injured area and soak it in nonscalding hot water, as hot as the victim can stand, for about 30 minuutes. If hot water is not available, you can pack the area in hot sand. Observe the victim for signs or symptoms of allergic reaction, and call EMS personnel if they appear. Your facility management should inform you about any specific marine life to be aware of.

Snakes. Snakebites kill very few people in the United States. Of the 8000 people bitten annually, fewer than 12 die. Rattlesnakes account for most snakebites and nearly all deaths from snakebites. Figure 10-18, *A-D* shows the four kinds of poisonous snakes found in the United States. Most deaths occur because the victim has an allergic reaction, is in poor health, or because much time passes before the victim receives medical care. In most cases, the victim can reach professional medical care within 30 minutes. Often, care can be reached much faster, since most snakebites occur near the home.

At many pool facilities, you are unlikely to find a snake in the facility. Occasionally, in rural areas, a snake may find its way into a pool. Someone who had been bitten in a picnic or recreation area at or near a facility, however, might come to you as the nearest source of first aid. People at open-water facilities should be warned to look out for and avoid snakes in or around the water. Both copperheads and water moccasins can swim, and snakes sometimes crawl under or into boats pulled up on the shore.

figure 10-17 *The painful sting of some marine animals can cause serious problems:*
A, *Sting ray.* ***B***, *Jellyfish.* ***C***, *Sea anemone.*

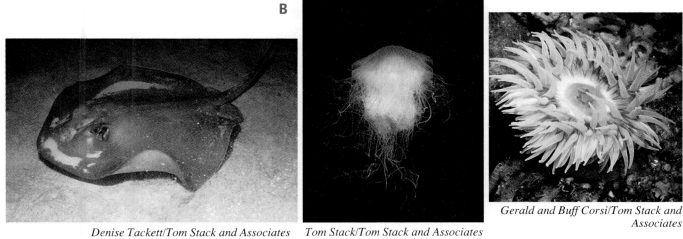

Denise Tackett/Tom Stack and Associates   *Tom Stack/Tom Stack and Associates*   *Gerald and Buff Corsi/Tom Stack and Associates*

figure 10-18 *There are four kinds of poisonous snakes found in the United States:*
A, *Rattlesnake.* ***B***, *Copperhead.* ***C***, *Water moccasin.* ***D***, *Coral snake.*

John Shaw/Tom Stack and Associates

David M. Dennis/Tom Stack and Associates

John Cancalosi/Tom Stack and Associates

David M. Dennis/Tom Stack and Associates

Care for snakebite. To care for someone bitten by a snake, wash the wound and immobilize the injured area, keeping it lower than the heart, if possible. Call EMS personnel. Do *not* apply ice to a snakebite. Do *not* apply a **tourniquet.** Do *not* use electric shock. If for any reason the victim has to be taken to a medical facility, the victim should be carried to a vehicle or should walk very slowly. If your facility is in a location where it is impossible for the victim to get professional medical care within 30 minutes, your facility should have a snakebite kit in its first aid supplies and people on staff trained in its use.

Animals. The bite of a domestic or wild animal can cause both infection and soft tissue injury. The most serious possible result of a bite is rabies. **Rabies** is a disease transmitted through the saliva of rabid animals, such as skunks, bats, raccoons, cats, dogs, cattle, and foxes.

Animals with rabies may act in unusual ways. For example, animals usually active at night, such as raccoons, may be active in the daytime. A wild animal that usually tries to avoid humans may not run away when you approach. Rabid animals may drool, appear partially paralyzed, or act irritable, aggressive, or strangely quiet. Advise patrons at your facility not to pet or feed stray domestic animals, wild animals, or touch the body of any dead animal.

If not treated, rabies is fatal. Anyone bitten by an animal suspected to have rabies must get medical attention. To prevent rabies from developing, the victim receives a series of vaccine injections to build up immunity.

Care for animal bites. If someone is bitten by a wild or domestic animal, try to get the person away from the animal without endangering yourself. Do not try to stop, hold, or capture the animal. If the wound is minor, wash it with soap and water. Then control any bleeding, and apply an antibiotic ointment and a dressing. If the wound is bleeding seriously, control the bleeding first. Do not clean the wound. The wound will be properly cleaned at a medical facility. Call EMS personnel.

If you can, try to remember what the animal looked like. When you call EMS, the dispatcher will get the proper authorities, such as animal control, to the scene.

HEAT AND COLD EXPOSURE

Exposure to extreme heat and cold can make a person ill, but a person can develop a heat- or cold-related illness even if temperatures are not extreme. The likelihood of illness also depends on factors such as physical activity, clothing, wind, humidity, working and living conditions, and a person's age and state of health.

Once the signs and symptoms of a heat- or cold-related illness begin to appear, the victim's condition can quickly get worse. A heat- or cold-related illness can be fatal. If you see any of the signs and symptoms of sudden illness and the victim has been exposed to extremes of heat or cold, suspect a heat- or cold-related illness.

People usually try to get out of extremes of heat and cold before they get ill, but some people cannot or do not. Athletes and people who work outdoors often keep working even after they begin to feel ill. People who are enjoying themselves, such as children and adults at aquatic facilities, may be unwilling to admit that they are not feeling well and should stop what they are doing. Sometimes people stand in lines for a long time in the heat waiting to get into a facility. A lifeguard on the stand may be unwilling to recognize or to admit to having too much sun or may forget to drink fluids and use shade.

Heat-related emergencies

Heat cramps. Heat cramps, heat exhaustion, and heat stroke are conditions caused by overexposure to heat. Heat cramps are the least severe and are often the first signs that the body is being overcome by heat.

Heat cramps are painful muscle spasms. They usually occur in the legs and abdomen. Heat cramps may be a warning of a possible heat-related emergency.

Care for heat cramps. To care for heat cramps, have the victim rest in a cool place. Give him or her cool water or a commercial sports drink. Usually, rest and fluids are all the person needs to recover. If the cramp is in a leg or arm, lightly stretch the muscle and gently massage the area (Fig. 10-19). The victim should not take salt tablets or drink salt water. They can make the situation worse.

When the cramps stop, if there are no other signals of illness, the person can usually resume activity again. He or she should continue to drink plenty of fluids. Tell the person and any people who are with him or her how to recognize the signs of heat-related illness and to stop any activity and tell a lifeguard if they occur.

Heat exhaustion. *Heat exhaustion* is a more severe condition than heat cramps. It typically occurs after long periods of strenuous exercise or work in a hot environment. Heat exhaustion can also be brought on by sitting in the sun for a long time. Signs and symptoms of heat exhaustion include—

• Normal or below normal body temperature.
• Cool, moist, pale, or red skin.
• Headache.
• Nausea.
• Dizziness and weakness.
• Exhaustion.

Heat stroke. *Heat stroke* is the least common but most severe heat emergency. It most often occurs when people ignore the signs and symptoms of heat exhaustion. Heat stroke develops when the body systems are overwhelmed by heat and begin to stop functioning. Heat stroke is a serious medical emergency. The signs and symptoms of heat stroke include red, hot, dry skin; changes in consciousness; rapid, weak pulse; and rapid, shallow breathing.

Care for heat exhaustion and heat stroke. When you recognize heat-related illness in its early stages, you can usually reverse it. Follow these general care steps immediately:

1 **Get the victim out of the heat.**
2 **Cool the body with cool, wet cloths, such as towels, and loosen tight clothing (Fig. 10-20).**
3 **If the victim is conscious, give him or her cool water.**
4 **Minimize shock.**
5 **Call EMS personnel immediately.**

Do not let the victim drink too rapidly. Give about one glass (4 ounces) of water every 15 minutes. Let the victim rest in a comfortable position, and watch for changes in his or her condition. The victim should not resume normal activity the same day.

If the victim refuses water, vomits, or has changes in consciousness, he or she is getting worse. If the victim vomits, stop giving fluids and position the victim on one side. Watch for signs of breathing problems. Keep the victim lying down, and continue to cool the body any way you can. If you have ice packs or cold packs, place them on the victim's ankles, in the armpits, and on the groin and the neck to cool the large blood vessels. Be sure to put a cloth or dressing between the victim's skin and the ice or cold pack. Do not put ice or a cold pack directly on the skin. Do *not* apply rubbing alcohol. It closes the pores in the skin and prevents heat loss. Be prepared to give rescue breathing or CPR, if necessary, while waiting for EMS personnel to arrive.

figure 10-19 *If the cramp is in the leg, lightly stretch the muscle and massage the area.*

figure 10-20 *Cool the victim's body by placing cool, wet towels on the skin, and give him cool water.*

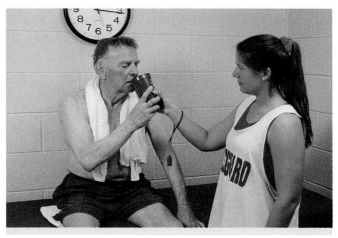

Cold-related emergencies

Hypothermia. *Hypothermia* is a general body cooling that develops when the body can no longer generate sufficient heat to maintain normal body temperature. There are several situations in which a lifeguard may encounter hypothermia.

The air temperature does not have to be below freezing for a person to develop hypothermia. Water temperature does not have to be below 70 degrees F (36 degrees C), especially to affect a child. Wind and humidity also affect the body's ability to control its temperature.

Anyone remaining in cold water or wet clothing for a long time may also easily develop hypothermia. Early or late in the season at many open-water facilities, the water is colder than in the middle of the season. Any swimmer—a patron or a lifeguard in preseason training—can become chilled without realizing it. Children under 12 are especially vulnerable to cold water (Fig. 10-21). Other factors that can affect the body's ability to keep warm are medical conditions, such as infection, diabetic emergency, and stroke, and drinking alcohol.

The signs and symptoms of hypothermia include—

- Shivering (may be absent in later stages).
- Slow, irregular pulse.
- Numbness.
- Glassy stare.
- Apathy and decreasing levels of consciousness.

Care for hypothermia. Hypothermia is a medical emergency. Care for any life-threatening problems. Call EMS personnel. Remove any wet clothing, and dry the victim.

Warm the body gradually by wrapping the victim in blankets or putting on dry clothing and moving him or her to a warm environment (Fig. 10-22). Apply other sources of heat (chemical heat packs, hot water bottles, or heating pads) if they are available, to the trunk of the person's body. Keep a barrier, such as a blanket, towel, or clothing, between the heat source and the victim to avoid burning him or her. If the victim is alert, you can give him or her warm liquids to drink but nothing containing caffeine. *Do not* warm the victim too quickly, such as by immersing the victim in warm water or putting the victim in a warm shower. Rapid rewarming and rough handling can cause dangerous heart problems. Handle the victim very gently.

In cases of severe hypothermia, the victim may be unconscious. Breathing may have slowed or stopped. The pulse may be slow and irregular. The body may feel stiff

figure 10-21 *Children under 12 are especially vulnerable to cold water.*

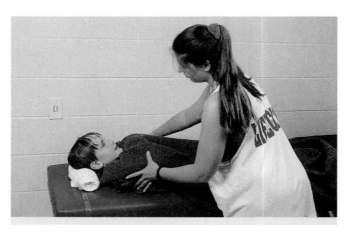

figure 10-22 *Rewarm a hypothermia victim by wrapping him in blankets.*

as the muscles become rigid. Monitor vital signs, give rescue breathing if necessary, and continue to warm the victim until EMS personnel arrive. Be prepared to start CPR.

Frostbite. *Frostbite* is the freezing of body parts exposed to the cold. Although in your job as a lifeguard you are unlikely to encounter frostbite, knowing what its signs and symptoms are and how to care for it could prove useful in other circumstances.

Frostbite occurs depending on the air temperature, length of exposure, and the wind speed. Water in and between the body's cells freezes and swells. The ice crystals and swelling damage or destroy the cells. Frostbite can cause the loss of fingers, hands, arms, toes, feet, and legs.

The signs and symptoms of frostbite include—

- Lack of feeling in the affected area.
- Skin that appears waxy.
- Skin that is cold to the touch.
- Skin that is discolored (flushed, white, yellow, or blue).

Care for frostbite. When caring for frostbite, handle the affected area gently. Never rub an affected area. Rubbing causes further damage because of the sharp ice crystals in the skin. Warm the area gently by soaking the affected part in water no warmer than 100 degrees F to 105 degrees F (39-41 degrees C) (Fig. 10-23, *A*). Use a thermometer to check the water temperature, if possible. If not, test the water temperature yourself. If the temperature is uncomfortable to your touch, the water is too warm. Do not let the affected part touch the bottom or sides of the container. Keep the frostbitten part in the water until it appears red and feels warm. Bandage the area with a dry, sterile dressing. If fingers or toes are frostbitten, place cotton or gauze between them (Fig. 10-23, *B*). Avoid breaking any blisters. Get professional medical attention as soon as possible.

CARING FOR CHILDREN AND OLDER ADULTS

Children

Many aquatic facilities have a regulation that children under a certain age or sometimes a certain height must be accompanied by a parent or other responsible adult. However, in the event of injury or sudden illness, you may still be responsible for giving care.

Caring for an ill or injured child is not always easy, especially if it is a child you don't know. Children have unique needs and require special care and attention.

figure 10-23 A, *Warm the frostbitten area gently by soaking the area in water. Do not allow the frostbitten area to touch the container.* **B,** *After rewarming, bandage the area with a dry, sterile dressing. If fingers or toes are frostbitten, place gauze between them.*

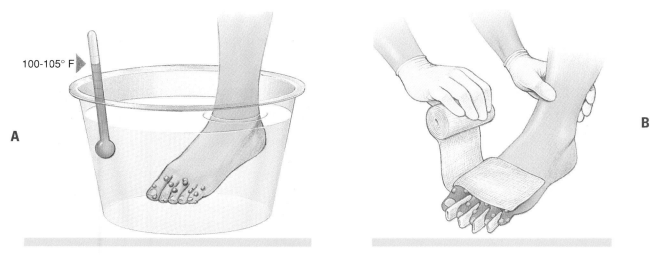

Some children do not readily accept strangers. This can make it difficult to accurately check a child's condition. Young children can be especially difficult to check, since they often aren't able to tell you what is wrong.

It is important to try to imagine how a young child with a serious illness or injury feels. One of that child's primary emotions is fear. The child is afraid of the unknown. He or she is afraid of being touched by strangers and of being separated from his or her parents or other familiar caretaker. Recognizing these fears can help you make the child feel less anxious and panicked.

Children up to 1 year of age are commonly referred to as infants. Infants less than 6 months of age are relatively easy to approach. Your presence will generally not bother them. Older infants, however, will often be afraid of strangers. They may cry and cling to a parent or caretaker.

Toddlers, children 1 and 2 years old, are frequently uncooperative. A toddler typically fears being separated from the parents or caretaker, so it is often best to check a toddler in a parent's or caretaker's lap.

Children ages 3, 4, and 5 are generally referred to as preschoolers. Children in this age group are usually easy to check if you use their natural curiosity. Allow them to inspect items such as bandages.

School-age children are those between 6 and 12 years old. Some facilities allow children as young as 6 to come to the facility unaccompanied by an older person or in the care of an older child. Fortunately, school-age children are generally cooperative and can provide information about what happened. You can usually talk with them readily. Children in this age group are becoming conscious of their bodies. Respect their modesty.

Adolescents are between the ages of 13 and 18. They are typically more like an adult than a child. Direct your questions to them rather than to a parent or guardian. However, allow input from a parent or guardian who is present. Occasionally, in the presence of a parent, guardian, or even friends, it may not be possible to get an accurate idea of what happened or what is wrong. Adolescents often respond better to a caregiver of the same sex.

Older adults

Older adults are generally considered those over 65 years of age. They are quickly becoming the fastest growing population group in the United States. Because water exercise, such as swimming and aquatic aerobics, has become very popular with older adults and is often recommended for them by medical professionals, you will continue to see them in increasing numbers at aquatic facilities.

Aging is a different process with different people. Some age faster, some slower; some stay in relatively good health both mentally and physically; others do not. Changes, however, occur with age. Reflexes become slower, hearing and eyesight may fail, and arthritis and numbness due to blood vessel problems can develop. Such changes place the elderly at increased risk of injury from falls. Falls frequently result in fractures because the bones become weaker and more brittle with age.

An elderly person is also at greater risk for serious head injury. This is mainly because as we age the size of the brain decreases, creating more space between the surface of the brain and the inside of the skull. This space allows more movement of the brain within the skull, which can increase the likelihood of serious head injury. You should always suspect a head injury as a possible cause of unusual behavior in an elderly person, especially if the victim has had a fall or a blow to the head.

The elderly are also susceptible to stroke and other problems of the nervous system. Some elderly people become confused as they grow older. If you are giving care to an elderly person who seems confused, try to find out if the confusion is the result of an immediate injury or a condition the person already has. To speak to a confused elderly person, get at eye level where he or she can see and hear you more clearly. Sometimes, confusion is the result of decreased hearing or sight. Listen carefully and speak clearly. Don't talk down to an elderly person. Keep in mind that the person may have special problems and concerns.

When you are giving care to any person, regardless of his or her age, remember that the person is in some way hurt, frightened, or otherwise upset. Your job is to give the best care you can. Doing so requires you to respond not only to the physical problem but also to the person's state of mind and special needs, as well as you are able to determine them.

SUMMARY

You may recognize that a patron has become suddenly ill and needs immediate care. Remember that it is not important that you know exactly what has caused the person to become ill. Follow the basic principles of care for any sudden illness, and consider the environmental conditions and any specific circumstances that you should report to EMS personnel if they are present.

STUDY QUESTIONS

Circle the letter of the correct answer or answers.

1. Signs and symptoms of sudden illness include—
   a) Changes in skin color.
   b) Slurred speech.
   c) Dizziness and weakness.
   d) Nausea or vomiting.

2. You should always call EMS personnel for a person having a seizure if—
   a) The person is pregnant.
   b) The person is a known epileptic and recovers in a few minutes.
   c) The person is a known diabetic.
   d) The person is an infant or child.

3. Signs and symptoms of stroke include—
   a) Sudden weakness of muscles and numbness in face, arm, or leg.
   b) Reddened skin.
   c) Sudden, severe headache.
   d) Abdominal cramps.

4. If you know a person has swallowed poison, you should—
   a) Have the person lie down.
   b) Call the local Poison Control Center.
   c) Induce vomiting.
   d) Give the person something to drink.

5. To remove a stinger from the site of an insect bite, you should—
   a) Scrape it away from the skin with your fingernail or with a plastic card.
   b) Remove it with tweezers.
   c) Pinch it between your fingers.
   d) Wipe it away with a clean cloth.

6. For a black widow or brown recluse spider bite—
   a) Apply baking soda.
   b) Call EMS personnel.
   c) Wait to see if the area swells and turns red.
   d) Apply rubbing alcohol.

7. In the event of a jellyfish sting, immediately soak the affected area in—
   a) Fresh water.
   b) Hot water.
   c) Household vinegar.
   d) Carbonated water.

8. Proper care for a snakebite includes—
   a) Applying ice.
   b) Applying a tourniquet.
   c) Giving the victim an electric shock.
   d) Washing and immobilizing the injured area, keeping it lower than the heart.

9. With heat-related illnesses, call EMS personnel immediately if the victim—
   a) Has cool, moist, pale or red skin.
   b) Refuses water.
   c) Vomits.
   d) Undergoes changes in consciousness.

10. While waiting for EMS personnel to arrive, care for victims of severe heat-related illness by—
    a) Having the victim walk around to cool off.
    b) Cooling the victim's body with wet sheets or ice packs.
    c) Giving rescue breathing or CPR if needed.
    d) Applying rubbing alcohol.

11. Signs of hypothermia include—
    a) Numbness.   c) Glassy stare
    b) Nausea.   d) Increased heart rate.

Circle *True* or *False*.

12. If you suspect someone is having a diabetic emergency, under no circumstances allow that person to have sugar. True or False?

13. When caring for frostbite, warm the area as quickly as possible. True or False?

14. If a person has been poisoned, general care includes induced vomiting. True or False?

15. All victims of absorbed poison need oxygen as soon as possible. True or False?

16. Always try to capture the animal involved when a person has been bitten so that it can be checked for rabies. True or False?

17. If a victim is suffering from hypothermia, you should not warm the body too quickly. True or False?

18. Rate the following from least severe (1) to most severe (3).
    ____ Heat exhaustion.
    ____ Heat stroke.
    ____ Heat cramps.

Fill in the blank with the correct answer.

19. A boy has been stung by a bee. He develops hives, vomits, and the site of the sting is red and swollen. The boy is probably suffering from an _____ reaction.

See answers to study questions on p. 287.

SPINAL INJURY MANAGEMENT

11

NO DIVING
4 FT 1.21 M

Objectives

After reading this chapter, you should be able to—

1. List three situations in which an aquatic-related spinal injury is possible.
2. List at least five physical indications of a possible spinal injury.
3. List the seven general guidelines for caring for a possible spinal injury.
4. Define the key terms for this chapter.

After reading this chapter and completing the appropriate course activities, you should be able to—

1. Demonstrate two ways to stabilize a victim's head and neck.
2. Demonstrate how to immobilize a victim on a backboard.
3. Make appropriate decisions about care when given an example of an emergency involving a possible injury to the spine.

Key Terms

Backboard: A standard piece of rescue equipment at all aquatic facilities used to maintain in-line stabilization while immobilizing and transporting a victim with a suspected spinal injury.

In-line stabilization: A technique used to minimize movement of a victim's head and neck.

Spinal column: The linked bones (vertebrae) from the base of the skull to the tip of tailbone (coccyx).

Spinal cord: A bundle of nerves extending from the base of the skull to the lower back and protected by the spinal column.

Vertebrae: The 33 bones of the spinal column.

INTRODUCTION

You are on the lifeguard chair when you see an adult male dive into a shallow area of the pool. The victim seems to be struggling and cannot lift his head out of the water. He is face down, just below the surface, in about 4 feet of water. Would you recognize this situation as a possible spinal injury? Are you ready to respond appropriately?

Every year, nearly 2 million Americans have a head injury or spinal injury serious enough to need medical care. Thirteen percent of these injuries occur during sports and recreation, most from headfirst entries into shallow water (Fig. 11-1).

Spinal injury rarely occurs during supervised diving into deep water. Most injuries result from unsupervised activity. In pools, these injuries often occur at the shallow end, in a corner, or where the bottom slopes from shallow water to deep water. They also occur when individuals strike floating objects, such as inner tubes, while diving.

At waterfront facilities, such as lakes, rivers, or oceans, spinal injuries typically occur in areas where depths change with tides or currents. At beaches, these injuries occur mainly when someone runs and plunges headfirst into shallow water or a breaking wave, causing his or her head to hit the bottom. These injuries also result from collisions with underwater hazards, such as rocks, tree stumps, and sandbars.

In addition to those individuals who die each year from spinal injuries, many more become permanently disabled. Survivors can have a wide range of physical and mental impairments, including paralysis and speech and memory problems.

In this chapter, you will learn how to recognize a possible spinal injury and give care to prevent further injury.

figure 11-1 *Sports-related injuries account for 13 percent of all spinal injuries.*

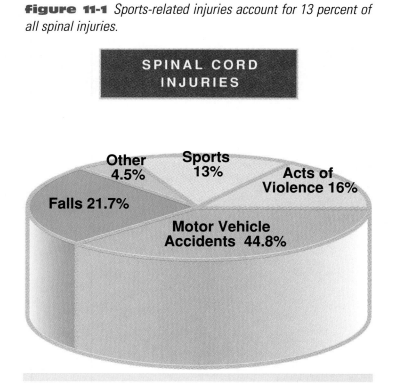

Spinal Cord Injuries: The Facts and Figures, 1993, University of Alabama, Birmingham, Spinal Cord Injury Care Systems, part of the National S.C.I. Data Base

It Only Takes A Second

Every year, about 1000 people suffer permanent spinal cord damage from diving mishaps. Statisticians describe the typical victim with grim accuracy. He is a single, white male between the ages of 15 and 30, an active person who loves sports and the outdoors.

Bill Brooks fits this description. This 29-year-old from Davidsonville, Maryland, tried to dive through an inner tube into a pool, but his neck hit the tube. As he floated in the water, he was aware of everything, yet powerless to move.

At the hospital, doctors told Brooks he was a "C5" quadriplegic, which described the cervical vertebra damaged. In college, Brooks had played baseball and after college, slow-pitch softball. In one moment's action, Brooks had lost control of his legs, chest, and arms. He lost the ability to dress himself, feed himself, go to the bathroom by himself, or even hold a softball in his hand.

Months of rehabilitation have improved Brooks' life. Although his right hand remains paralyzed, he can grasp a telephone and control a computer mouse with his left hand. With the computer mouse, he is learning to design the sprinkler systems he once installed as the foreman for a sprinkler company. Brooks is learning to survive with his injury, but since spinal nerves will never regenerate, he has little hope that he will ever walk again.

Many states and private organizations have started education and prevention programs to lower the high number of diving injuries. The American Red Cross offers the following tips to prevent head and spine injuries:

- Check for adequate water depth. When you first enter the water, enter feet first.
- Never dive into an above-ground pool.
- Only trained swimmers should use starting blocks and only under the supervision of a qualified coach.
- Never drink alcohol and dive.
- Never dive into water where you cannot see the bottom. Objects, such as logs or pilings, may be hidden below the surface.
- Running into the water and then diving headfirst into the waves is dangerous.
- If you are bodysurfing, always keep your arms in front of you to protect your head and neck.

Lifeguards and EMTs with victim on backboard.

ANATOMY AND FUNCTION OF THE SPINE

The spine is a flexible column that supports the head and trunk and protects the spinal cord. The *spinal column* extends from the base of the skull to the tip of the tailbone. It is made of small bones called *vertebrae.* The vertebrae are separated by cushions of cartilage, called disks. This cartilage acts as a shock absorber when you walk, run, or jump. The *spinal cord,* a bundle of nerves extending from the skull to the lower back, runs through openings inside the vertebrae. Nerves reach the body through openings on the sides of the vertebrae (Fig. 11-2, *A*).

The spine is divided into five regions: cervical (neck), thoracic (midback), lumbar (lower back), sacrum, and coccyx (small triangular bone at the bottom of the spine). Although injuries can occur anywhere along the spine, most aquatic injuries damage the cervical region. A serious injury is likely to cause temporary or permanent paralysis, even death. The extent of paralysis depends on which area of the spinal cord is damaged (Fig. 11-2, *B*).

RECOGNIZING SPINAL INJURY

When considering whether the person may have a spinal injury, first think about what caused the injury. Look at the scene and think about the forces involved in the injury. Strong forces are likely to cause severe injury. For example, a person who dives into shallow water and strikes his or her head on the bottom may suffer serious injury.

Always consider the possibility of a spinal injury in certain situations that you see or that bystanders tell you about. They include —

• An injury involving a diving board, water slide, or an individual entering water from a height, such as a bank or a cliff.
• A headfirst entry into shallow water.
• A fall from a height greater than the victim's height.

In addition to these situations, certain physical signs and symptoms indicate possible spinal injury. These include —

• Neck or back pain.
• Loss of body movement below the injury site.
• Tingling or loss of sensation in the arms or legs and hands or feet.
• Bumps or depressions on the head, neck, or back.
• Altered consciousness.
• Bruising of the head, neck, or back.
• Impaired breathing.
• Loss of balance.
• Fluid or blood in the ears.
• Seizures.

These signs and symptoms alone do not always mean the victim has a spinal injury. If the victim is in the water, you may not be able to recognize these signs and symptoms at all. Usually you decide to care for the victim as if there is a spinal injury based on what you see or are told.

CARING FOR SPINAL INJURY

Caring for a spinal injury is similar to caring for other serious bone or muscle injuries. You must **stabilize** and **immobilize** the area. Because movement can cause more damage, keep the victim as still as possible until medical help arrives. If you are unsure whether the victim has a serious injury, always give care as if the spine is injured. The specific care you give depends on several factors:

• The victim's condition, including whether he or she is breathing and has a pulse
• The location of the victim (deep or shallow water, at the surface of the water, under water, or out of the water)
• Availability of other personnel to assist, such as other lifeguards, bystanders, fire fighters, police, or rescue squad personnel
• Procedures used at your facility
• The temperature of the water or air

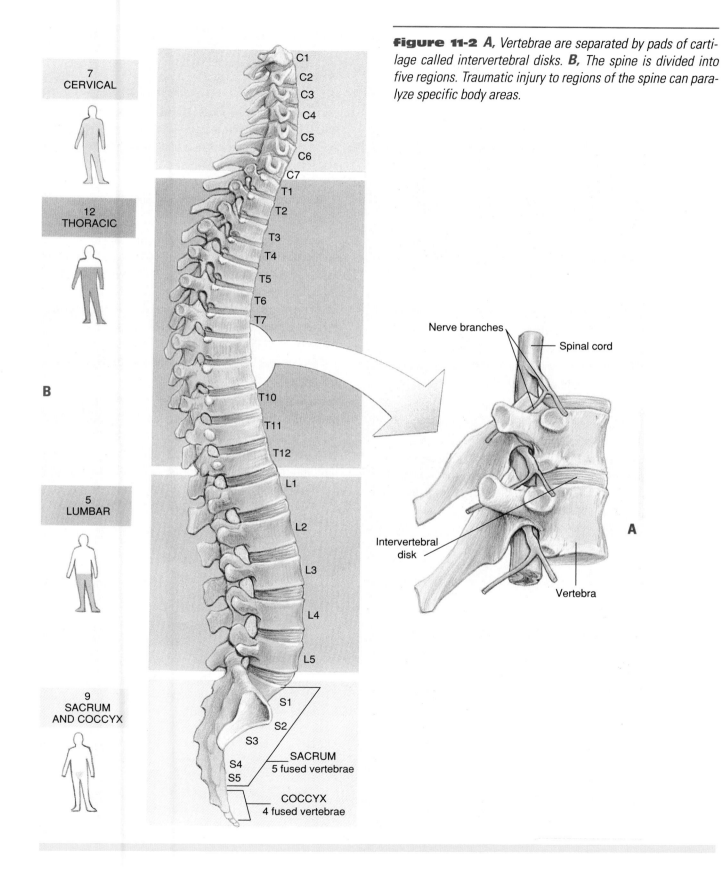

figure 11-2 *A, Vertebrae are separated by pads of cartilage called intervertebral disks.* ***B,*** *The spine is divided into five regions. Traumatic injury to regions of the spine can paralyze specific body areas.*

7
CERVICAL

12
THORACIC

B

5
LUMBAR

9
SACRUM
AND COCCYX

C1
C2
C3
C4
C5
C6
C7
T1
T2
T3
T4
T5
T6
T7
T10
T11
T12
L1
L2
L3
L4
L5
S1
S2
S3
S4
S5
SACRUM
5 fused vertebrae
COCCYX
4 fused vertebrae

Nerve branches
Spinal cord
Intervertebral
disk
Vertebra
A

General guidelines for care

Follow these guidelines if you suspect a spinal injury:

1 **Activate your facility's emergency action plan.** This alerts other staff to the emergency. Others can call for an ambulance and help you as needed.

2 **Minimize movement of the victim's head or spine.** Hold the victim's head in line with the body. This is called *in-line stabilization.* Support the head in a straight line with the body. Do not pull on the victim's head. If the victim is in the water, use your hands and arms to gently place the head in the proper position. Two techniques for in-line stabilization are described later (Fig. 11-3, *A* and *B*).

3 **Position the victim face up at the surface of the water.** You may have to bring a submerged victim to the surface and rotate him or her face up. Keep the victim's face out of the water so that he or she can breathe. Keep maintaining in-line stabilization.

4 **Check for consciousness and breathing.** A victim who can talk is conscious and breathing. If the victim is not breathing, start rescue breathing as soon as possible. Because it is difficult to stabilize the spine and perform rescue breathing in the water, even with an additional rescuer, remove the victim from the water as soon as possible.

5 **Move the victim to shallow water whenever possible.** It is much easier to care for the victim in shallow water. If you cannot move a victim to shallow water (for example, in a deep-water pool), support the victim and yourself with the rescue tube (Fig. 11-4). Whenever possible, seek the help of other rescuers for deep-water spinal injuries.

6 **Immobilize the victim on a backboard.** Securing the victim to a *backboard* fully immobilizes the victim's head, neck, and body and lets you remove the victim from the water. With at least one additional rescuer, secure the victim to the backboard to help prevent further injury when removing the victim from the water (Fig. 11-5). Always secure the victim's body to the backboard first and then the head, using a **head immobilizer.**

7 **Remove the victim from the water.** With the help of at least one other lifeguard, lift the victim from the water (Fig. 11-6). Once the victim is out of the water, give care to minimize shock. Keep the victim lying flat, and help maintain normal body temperature. You might have to dry off the victim and cover him or her with a blanket. If the victim vomits, tilt the backboard on its side.

figure 11-3 *A, Head splint. **B,** Head and chin support.*

A
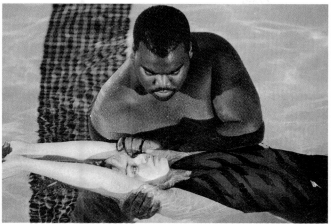

B

figure 11-4 *In deep water, use a rescue tube to support you and the victim.*

figure 11-5 *Secure the victim to the backboard to help prevent further injury when removing him or her from the water.*

figure 11-6 *With the help of at least one other lifeguard, lift the victim from the water.*

Specific rescue techniques

Two specific techniques are used in the water to minimize movement of the victim's head and neck: the head splint and head and chin support. Use your hands and arms to support the victim securely. Be familiar with both techniques, even though you use only one in any given emergency.

Head splint. The head splint technique is used only for a victim face down at or near the surface of the water. You can use this technique in shallow or deep water. In deep water, use the technique while the rescue tube provides buoyancy for both you and the victim.

To perform the head splint technique —

1 Approach the victim from the side.

2 Gently move the victim's arms up alongside the head. Do this by grasping the victim's arms midway between the shoulder and elbow. Grasp the victim's right arm with your right hand and the victim's left arm with your left hand.

3 Squeeze the victim's arms against his or her head to help keep the head in line with the body (Fig. 11-7, *A*).

4 With your body at about shoulder depth in the water, glide the victim slowly forward.

5 Continue moving slowly, and rotate the victim toward you until he or she is face up. Do this by pushing the arm of the victim closer to you under water while pulling the victim's other arm across the surface (Fig. 11-7, *B*).

6 Position the victim's head in the crook of your arm, with the head in line with the body (Fig. 11-7, *C*).

7 Maintain this position in the water until help arrives.

Head and chin support. The second technique for stabilization is the head and chin support. You can use it for a victim found either face up or face down. Use it also to remove a victim with possible spinal injury from the bottom of a pool. The head and chin support has two limitations. First, it is difficult to perform while using the rescue tube to assist a face-down victim in deep water. Second, do not use it for a victim face down in

figure 11-7 *A, Grasp the victim's arms midway between shoulder and elbow, squeezing victim's arms against the victim's head. B, Rotate the victim by pushing the closer arm under water, pulling the other arm across the surface. C, Position the victim face up with head in crook of the arm and in line with the body.*

A

B

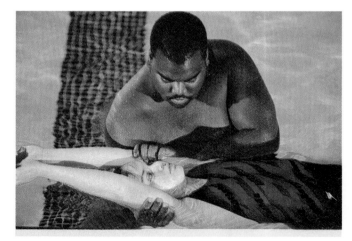

C

water less than 3 feet deep. This is because the technique used to turn the victim face up requires you to submerge and roll under the victim while maintaining in-line stabilization. It is difficult to perform this skill in water less than 3 feet deep without the risk of injury to yourself or further injury to the victim.

To perform the head and chin support —

1   **Approach the victim from the side.**

2   **With your body at about shoulder depth in the water, place one forearm along the length of the victim's breastbone and the other forearm along the victim's spine.**

3   **Use your hands to gently position the victim's head in line with the body. Hold the victim's lower jaw with one hand and the back of the head with the other (Fig. 11-8, *A* and *B*).**

4   **Squeeze your forearms together, clamping the victim's chest and back. Continue to support the victim's head.**

5   **If the victim is face down, you must turn him or her face up. Using the head and chin support to stabilize the spine, begin moving the victim forward. Rotate the victim toward you while you start to submerge (Fig. 11-8, *C*). Roll under the victim while turning the victim over (Fig. 11-8, *D*). Do this slowly to avoid twisting the victim's body. The victim is face up when you surface on the other side (Fig. 11-8, *E*).**

6   **Support the victim face up in the water until help arrives.**

 A

 B

 C

 D

 E

figure 11-8 *A, Place one hand on the victim's lower jaw and the forearm along the breastbone; place other hand on the back of victim's head and forearm along the middle of the spine. B, The hand is on the back of the head, and the forearm is along the spine. If the victim is face down, C, Rotate the victim toward you while you submerge. D, Roll under the victim while turning him or her over. E, Rotate to the other side, turning the victim face up.*

figure 11-9 *A, Bring the victim up at an angle using the head chin support. B, Rotate the victim faceup as you reach the surface.*

A

B

You may also use the head and chin support with a submerged victim found faceup, facedown, or on one side. Bring the victim to the surface at an angle. Rotate the victim face up, if necessary, as you move to the surface (Fig. 11-9, *A* and *B*).

Using a backboard

After stabilizing the victim's head and neck with one of these two techniques, fully immobilize the victim using a backboard. Backboards come in different shapes and sizes and with different characteristics, such as the construction material, the number and size of handholds, and the amount of buoyancy (Fig. 11-10).

At least two lifeguards are needed to secure a victim to a backboard, but it is easier with help from more lifeguards or bystanders, when available. These others can help hold the backboard under the victim, if necessary. In shallow water, immobilize the victim as follows:

figure 11-11 *A, The second lifeguard submerges the backboard next to the victim.*

figure 11-10 *Backboards.*

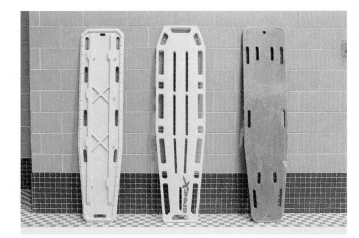

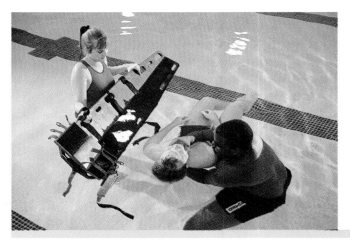

A

1   As the primary lifeguard brings the victim toward the side of the pool, a second lifeguard enters the water, submerges the backboard, and positions it under the victim so that it extends beyond the victim's head when it is raised (Fig. 11-11, *A* and *B*).

2   While the second lifeguard raises the backboard into place, the primary lifeguard carefully withdraws his arm from beneath the victim. If the primary lifeguard is using the head and chin support, he keeps his hand on the chin and places the other hand under the backboard (Fig. 11-11, *C*). If the primary lifeguard is using the head splint technique, he moves his arm that is under the victim towards the top of the victim's head while the second lifeguard holds the victim using the head and chin support (one hand on the chin and one hand on the board) (Fig. 11-11, *D*).

3   When the backboard is raised, the second lifeguard supports the backboard against her chest and shoulders and squeezes the sides of the backboard with her arms. The victim's head is supported by the second lifeguard placing both hands on the side of the head (Fig. 11-11, *E*). Other available lifeguards can help support the backboard at the sides.

figure 11-11, *B, The backboard is positioned under the victim.*

B

figure 11-11, *C, The primary lifeguard keeps one hand on the victim's chin and places the other hand under the backboard.*

D

figure 11-11, *D, The second lifeguard uses the head and chin support to hold the victim, one hand on the chin, one hand on the board.*

figure 11-11, *E, The second lifeguard supports the board against the chest and shoulders, and squeezes the sides of the backboard with the arms.*

C

E

Continued.

4 The primary lifeguard secures the victim to the backboard. At a minimum, he places straps across the victim's chest, hips, and thighs. He places the chest strap across the chest and under the arms. Positioning this strap under the armpits helps prevent the victim from sliding on the backboard during removal (Fig. 11-11, *F*). Using the strap, he secures the victim's hands along his or her sides (Fig. 11-11, *G*) or in front of the body (Fig. 11-11, *H*). He puts the third strap across the victim's thighs (Fig. 11-11, *I*).

figure 11-11, *F, Strap under the victim's armpits and across the chest to prevent sliding.*

figure 11-11, *H, Hip strap securing hands in front of the body.*

F

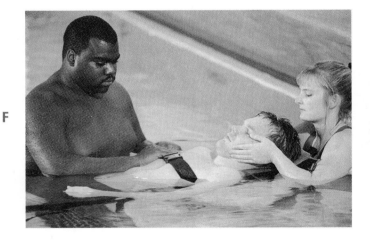

H

figure 11-11, *G, Hip strap securing the hands along the side.*

figure 11-11, *I, Strap on the thighs.*

G

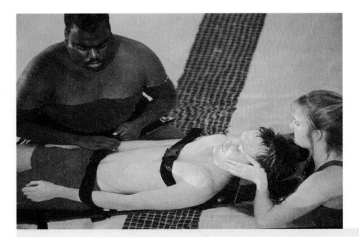

I

When using straps, be sure they do not go across the bottom of the backboard or over the "runners" on the bottom of some backboards. Such straps could snag on the edge of the deck while the backboard is slid onto the deck. One common method to prepare the straps is to place them over the top of the backboard (Fig. 11-11, *J*). Another method is to attach the straps to the backboard after the victim is on the board, such as with a one-piece **"spider strap"** system (Fig. 11-11, *K*).

5 Using a head immobilizer, the primary lifeguard secures the victim's head to the board. Then he secures a strap across the victim's forehead (Fig. 11-11, *L*).

You can place a victim on a backboard and secure a victim to a backboard in different ways. Just be sure that you safely immobilize the spine. Regardless of the strapping method, the victim's body should always be secured to the backboard before the head is secured. Whenever possible, follow the manufacturer's directions.

figure 11-11, *K, Spider strap system applied.*

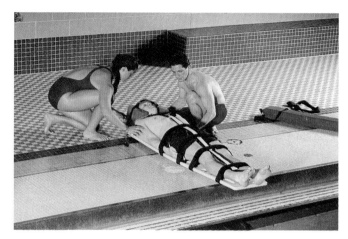

K

figure 11-11, *J, Straps placed on backboard.*

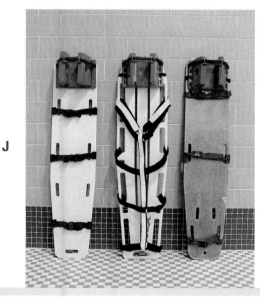

J

figure 11-11, *L, The head immobilizer secures the victim's head to the backboard with a strap across the victim's forehead.*

L

Removing the victim from the water

Once the victim is secured on the backboard, remove him or her from the water. The lifeguards work together in this process:

1 Position the backboard with the head end by the side of the pool and the foot end straight out into the pool.

2 With one lifeguard on each side, lift the head of the backboard slightly and place it on the edge of the gutter if possible (Fig. 11-12, **A**).

3 One lifeguard gets out of the pool and grasps the head of the backboard. The other lifeguard moves to the foot end of the backboard (Fig. 11-12, **B**). As the lifeguard on deck stands and steps backward and pulls the backboard, the lifeguard at the foot end pushes on the backboard (Fig. 11-12, **C**). Together they slide the backboard up over the edge of the deck out of and away from the water (Fig. 11-12, **D**). Any others helping should stay in the water at the sides of the backboard and help lift the backboard and the victim onto the deck.

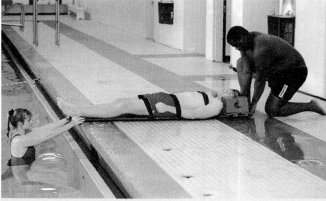

figure 11-12 **A,** Head of backboard placed on the edge of the gutter. **B,** One lifeguard gets out of the pool while the other lifeguard goes to the foot end of the backboard. **C,** The lifeguard on the deck stands up and steps backward, pulling the board. **D,** The backboard is slid onto the deck away from the water.

Cervical Collars

Cervical collars are devices put around the neck to help keep the head in line with the body and to limit movement. They come in a variety of shapes and sizes and in one- and two-piece models. Some are rigid, others soft. Rigid collars are most commonly used because they provide better support than soft collars. When applied properly, the rigid cervical collar restricts movement of the neck by approximately 30 percent. Since a cervical collar does not completely immobilize the victim's spine, do not release the head even when using one.

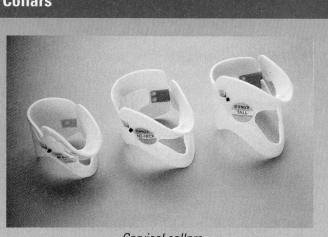

Cervical collars

Select a cervical collar that fits the victim properly. One method of sizing the cervical collar is to measure the length of the victim's neck using your fingers. Then find a collar with this length. Manufacturers also suggest how to properly size their collars for victims.

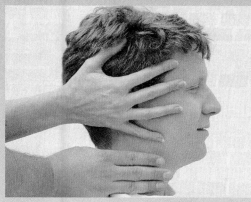

Sizing with fingers

When applying the collar, keep the victim's head in line with the body, with the chin resting in the collar's groove. The collar must not be so tight that it restricts breathing or so loose that it allows the chin to drop within the collar. Cervical collars are used commonly in EMS systems. In the water, where few rescuers have this special training, the use of the cervical collar is limited. If your facility uses cervical collars, in-service training with your local EMS agency is recommended.

Cervical collar applied to victim.

CARING FOR A VICTIM IN DEEP WATER

Fortunately, spinal injuries rarely occur in deep water. If one does occur, you can often move the victim to shallow water. This may mean removing a lane line or safety line separating shallow and deep water.

If someone has a spinal injury in deep water and cannot be moved to shallow water, such as in a separate diving well, use the rescue tube to help support you and the victim until additional help arrives (Fig. 11-13, *A* and *B*). Additional lifeguards arriving to assist with the backboard in deep water can use a platform attached to the deck, more rescue tubes, or even lifejackets to help support themselves and the victim.

To stabilize the victim's spine and secure the victim on the backboard in deep water, slightly modify the procedures you used in shallow water. Follow these steps:

1 The primary lifeguard minimizes movement of the victim's head and neck by using either the head splint technique or the head and chin support. If the victim is submerged, the primary lifeguard leaves the rescue tube on the surface and surface dives to the victim. He brings the victim to the surface using the head and chin support (Fig. 11-14, *A*). When a second lifeguard enters the water, he or she can retrieve the primary lifeguard's rescue tube and place it under his or her arms. The primary lifeguard uses the rescue tube to support himself and the victim (Fig. 11-14, *B*).

2 To immobilize the victim on a backboard, the primary lifeguard moves the victim toward a corner of the pool. The second lifeguard places the backboard under the victim while the primary lifeguard keeps the head in line with the body (Fig. 11-14, *C*).

3 The second lifeguard moves to the head of the backboard, rests the backboard on the rescue tube, and supports the victim's head (Fig. 11-14, *D*).

4 The primary lifeguard secures the victim to the backboard (Fig. 11-14, *E*).

5 They remove the victim from the water (Fig. 11-14, *F*).

---

figure 11-13 *A, The rescue tube gives support while the lifeguard uses the head splint.*
B, The rescue tube gives support while the lifeguard uses the head and chin support.

A
 B

figure 11-14 *A, Lifeguard in deep water using the head and chin support without the support of a rescue tube.* *B, The second lifeguard replaces the rescue tube by placing it under the first lifeguard's arms.* *C, Backboard being placed under the victim.* *D, The second lifeguard rests the backboard on the rescue tube while immobilizing the victim's head.* *E, Victim secured to backboard with straps and head immobilizer.* *F, Victim being removed from the water.*

figure 11-15 *A*, *The lifeguard minimizes movement to the victim's head by holding it in line with the body while the victim is standing.* *B*, *The lifeguard minimizes movement to the victim's head by holding it in line with the body while the victim is sitting.* *C*, *The lifeguard minimizes movement to the victim's head by holding it in line with the body while the victim is lying down.*

A
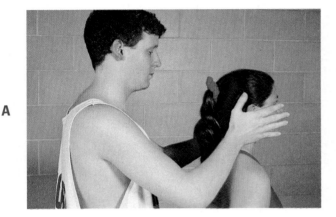

B
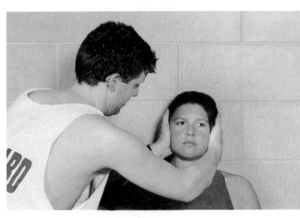

C
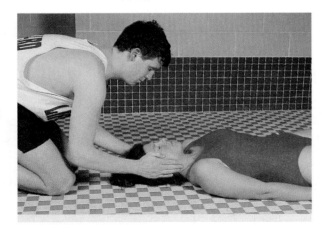

SPINAL INJURY ON LAND

If a victim has a possible spinal injury on land, follow the same general guidelines as in the water. Stabilize the victim's head by holding it in line with the body, regardless of whether the victim is standing, sitting, or lying down (Fig. 11-15, *A-C*). Keep the victim in this position until EMS personnel arrive and take over.

SUMMARY

An important part of lifeguarding is recognizing and caring for spinal injury. To judge whether an injury could be serious, consider both the cause and the physical signs and symptoms. If you suspect a spinal injury in the water, make sure someone calls EMS personnel while you care for the victim. Minimize movement with one of the two techniques for in-line stabilization. Secure the victim to a backboard to completely immobilize the spine.

STUDY QUESTIONS

Circle the letter of the best answer or answers.

1. In a pool, a spinal injury is most likely to occur—
   a) In the deep end.
   b) At the shallow end.
   c) Where the bottom slopes from shallow to deep water.
   d) When an individual strikes a floating object, such as an inner tube, while diving.

2. At a waterfront, a spinal injury is most likely to occur—
   a) When a swimmer runs into the water and plunges headfirst into breaking waves.
   b) When a swimmer collides with an underwater hazard, such as a sandbar.
   c) In an area where the water level almost never varies.
   d) When a swimmer plunges headfirst into shallow water.

3. The _____ consists of small bones called vertebrae with circular openings.
   a) Spinal cord
   b) Spinal column

4. Which of the following situations indicate a possible spinal injury?
   a) An injury related to a diving board
   b) A headfirst entry into shallow water
   c) A fall from a height greater than the victim's height
   d) A sudden cramp in deep water
   e) An injury related to entering the water from a cliff

5. Which of the following signs and symptoms indicate a possible spinal injury?
   a) Neck or back pain
   b) Loss of body movement below the injury site
   c) Impaired breathing
   d) Loss of balance
   e) Fluid or blood in the ears

6. A swimmer is injured while body surfing and complains of tingling and loss of sensation in both legs. You should—
   a) Massage the area vigorously.
   b) Keep the victim as still as possible until more advanced help arrives.
   c) Begin rescue breathing.
   d) Have the victim try to walk out of the water.

7. The specific care you provide a victim who may have suffered a spinal injury will depend on—
   a) Whether the victim is breathing and has a pulse.
   b) Whether the victim is an adult or a child.
   c) The location of the victim.
   d) Availability of others to assist.
   e) The temperature of the water or air.

8. The _____ is used only for a victim found facedown at or near the surface of the water.
   a) Head splint technique.
   b) Head and chin support.

9. Which of the following tips can help prevent head and spine injuries?
   a) When you enter the water for the first time, enter feet-first.
   b) For diving off a 1-meter diving board, the water should be at least 7 feet deep.
   c) Never dive into an above-ground pool.
   d) Never drink alcohol and dive.
   e) While bodysurfing, always keep your arms by your sides to improve your balance and increase your speed.

10. List the following guidelines for care in their proper sequence.
    ___ Check for consciousness and breathing.
    ___ Minimize movement of the victim's head or spine.
    ___ Position the victim faceup at the surface of the water.
    ___ Remove the victim from the water.
    ___ Activate your facility's emergency action plan.
    ___ Immobilize the victim on a backboard.
    ___ Move the victim to shallow water if possible.

See answers to study questions on p. 287.

AFTER AN EMERGENCY

12

DEBRIEFING
OF A
RESCUE
- THE REVIEW OF THE RESCUE
- HOW PEOPLE FEEL ABOUT
  WHAT HAPPENED.
- WHAT TO DO WITH YOUR
  EXCESS ADRENALINE
- IMPROVE EMERGENCY SYSTEM

Objectives

After reading this chapter, you should be able to—

1. Name six facility-related responsibilities of a lifeguard after an emergency.
2. Describe how to control a crowd that gathers around the victim of an emergency.
3. Explain how an incident or injury report may help prevent similar incidents in the future.
4. Explain how a lifeguard should respond to questions from the media and others not affiliated with the facility after an emergency.
5. List three purposes of a staff debriefing.
6. Explain what stress is, and list six negative effects of stress.
7. Describe at least six ways of coping with stress.
8. Explain the purpose of a critical incident stress debriefing.
9. Define the key terms for this chapter.

Key Terms

Critical incident: Any occurrence that causes an unusually strong emotional reaction that can affect a lifeguard's ability to function at a later date.

Critical incident stress: The stress a person feels after a highly stressful emergency.

Critical incident stress debriefing (CISD): A process by which professionals trained in dealing with the effects of stress help someone who has suffered stress.

Incident: An occurrence or event that interrupts normal procedure or causes a crisis.

Incident report: A report filed by a lifeguard involved in an emergency or other incident.

Media: Forms of mass communication, such as newspapers, television, radio, and magazines.

Stress: A physical, mental, or emotional state that causes tension, distress, or disruption in a person's mental or emotional balance.

INTRODUCTION

It happened about a month ago. It was a nice summer afternoon and the pool was crowded. As I scanned my zone, I spotted a man who was in real trouble. I signaled I was going in. I moved fast, but before I could reach him, he went under.

I brought him up right away, and another lifeguard and I got him out of the water. He wasn't breathing, and he was unconscious. I told another lifeguard to call EMS and gave the man a couple of breaths. He started to breathe on his own. Then he came to but he seemed very confused and wasn't sure what happened. We kept him lying down and kept checking his breathing. He seemed sort of sleepy.

People crowded around, some quiet and staring, some talking and offering advice. A couple of kids were crying. Someone asked how I could let this happen. I felt terrible. I'd gotten him out right away, but they made me feel as if I'd done something wrong.

The EMTs arrived right away, even though it seemed like forever. They told us we did a good job. It turned out the man had a seizure. They took him to the hospital, and I heard the next day he stayed overnight for evaluation. I felt good about rescuing him, but I just couldn't shake the feeling that what happened was my fault.

The next few days I began to have trouble sleeping and could not concentrate on my job. I felt nervous all the time. The pool manager had someone, a specialist, come talk to us about what happened. She told us it was normal to feel upset, and she explained about stress and what it can do to you. I felt better after I'd had this chance to talk about how I was feeling, and after a couple of weeks, I felt fine again.

Sometimes, despite all precautions, a serious *incident* such as an emergency still occurs. When this happens, you deal with the situation according to the facility's emergency action plan. You might recognize a person is in trouble, rescue him or her, and give follow-up care. Or you might call EMS or take over surveillance when another lifeguard is making a rescue. Regardless of how you are involved, certain things have to happen after an emergency. This chapter describes what you and others at the facility should begin to do as soon as a victim is brought to safety and is receiving care.

RESPONSIBILITIES RELATED TO THE FACILITY

You have two kinds of responsibilities after an emergency. You have facility responsibilities involving actions you take as a lifeguard. You also have responsibilities for taking care of yourself, as discussed later in this chapter.

Controlling bystanders

One of your responsibilities after an emergency may be controlling bystanders. You need to manage bystanders who gather around the victim. People who crowd around the scene of an emergency are usually not trying to cause trouble. Most are curious, and some may want to help. If you need immediate help, you can ask bystanders. They can do several things to help. First consider, however, whether they might get in your way as you care for the victim or make unthinking comments about the victim's condition that can frighten the person. Sometimes bystanders must be moved back to give the rescuers and the victim space.

At many facilities, when lifeguards are involved in immediate care, controlling bystanders is the job of other staff such as cashiers, maintenance personnel, swimming instructors, or locker room attendants.

Recruit any bystanders you need, and with a firm but calm tone direct others to back away. If a crowd forms and keeps getting too close, you can rope off the area if you have enough people to help and enough time to do it. Bystanders can help rope off the area, which also can keep them busy. Chairs can be positioned around the area with rope stretched between them.

Try to move the crowd as far away from the pool as you can. Patrons usually respond well when the pool must be cleared, but sometimes someone can get pushed in by mistake or a child may wander into the water.

If the facility has a public address system, the emergency action plan may designate someone to instruct the crowd to keep back. If you do not have such a system, keep your voice low but loud enough to be clearly heard. Do not yell at patrons. Repeat your command as often as necessary. Spread your arms and use forward hand motions along with your commands (Fig. 12-1). If anyone makes unpleasant remarks or yells at you, do not respond or react.

If EMS has been called, instruct the crowd to make room for EMS personnel to reach the scene and victim. If you can move the victim safely and without causing harm, move him or her to a first aid room or other area for privacy and comfort. (Chapter 9 discusses moving victims.)

Closing the pool

While care is being provided to the victim, patrons still on the deck are likely to be milling around and restless. Some may leave, but most are still there. Someone now must decide whether to close the pool after a significant incident. This decision depends on several factors: whether adequate lifeguards are still available, whether they are too upset or distracted to do a good job of surveillance, how much longer the facility would otherwise remain open, how many patrons remain, and whether all required equipment is in place. In some areas, regulations may require that the pool be closed and not reopened until after inspection by a local agency.

Usually a head lifeguard or facility manager makes the decision about closing the facility temporarily and when to reopen. That person has to decide if the lifeguards are ready to resume their responsibilities. As a lifeguard, you need to decide if you are up to the job. Tell your supervisor if you don't feel ready yet. If you made a rescue or cared for a victim, you may also be busy interviewing witnesses or filling out an incident report form.

If the facility is closed temporarily to get things in order, it should not be reopened until lifeguards take their stations. Lifeguards or support staff can then let patrons return to the pool in an orderly way. If the crowd is large and enough lifeguards are available, you may organize the return to the water by groups rather than all at once.

Filing a report

Once the victim has recovered or is receiving medical care, and EMS personnel and others no longer need your help, your role as a rescuer is over. Your role as a lifeguard in the incident is not. If you are the one who made the rescue or gave the initial care, you may need to be available for questions from supervisors. The facility may require statements from witnesses (Fig. 12-2). Getting a statement or the witnesses' names, addresses, and phone numbers may be your responsibility, although often this is the job of a head lifeguard or facility manager. Witnesses write their statements on separate forms that are dated. They record the incident in their own words. Lifeguards and other staff should not influence anything a witness says in this statement.

While the emergency is still fresh in your memory, you also file an *incident report* using the facility's form (Fig. 12-3). Some facilities have separate report forms for incidents, such as theft, vandalism, and disruptive events, and for injuries. Other facilities use only one report form for all types of incidents. Your report serves many purposes, which follow on p. 222.

figure 12-1 *After an incident, control any crowd that may gather.*

figure 12-2 *Have witnesses record in their own words what happened.*

- It is a record of what happened and what, if anything, facility management can do to prevent similar incidents. If several reports describe injuries in the same area of the facility, for instance, management may be alerted to a hazard in that area. The hazard may be eliminated or staff and patrons made aware of the problem. Management may use these reports to make a facility diagram showing where injuries have occurred, such as the one shown in Chapter 6.
- It may be required by a state or local government or agency.
- It serves as a legal document in case of a lawsuit. Therefore, an incident or injury report should contain only factual information, not any personal opinion or **hearsay.** The report should *not* say or suggest who was at fault, how the incident could have been prevented, or what should have occurred. Be careful to be accurate when filling out such a report. It may be used in a legal argument about whether staff acted correctly to prevent the incident. All lifeguards involved in the incident or injury should file individual reports.

Dealing with questions

Attorneys, *media* people such as local television or newspaper reporters, insurance company representatives, or people who are simply curious may ask you questions immediately after an emergency or some time later. *Do not give them any information.* Giving any information about a victim is a **breach of confidentiality.** Always respect the victim's privacy. Discussing any aspect of what happened could also lead to legal action. Only management or the facility's representatives should talk to the media or others about an incident.

If people ask you questions, say the facility's **spokesperson** will make a statement when appropriate. Make no statements yourself. The facility's procedures for dealing with questions from the media and others should be in the facility policies and procedures manual or emergency plan, including the designated spokesperson's name. That person is the only one permitted to speak to the public and others about the emergency. Do not discuss the emergency with anyone outside the facility except for trained emergency counselors.

If the area of the incident is visible from public property, you cannot stop someone from taking a picture from the public area. Anyone who asks to take a photo of the facility, however, must first get clearance from the facility management.

Checking equipment

If any equipment or first aid supplies were used or moved in the emergency, they must be replaced. As a lifeguard, you may be the one selected to check equipment and supplies and report anything missing to management or the head lifeguard. If the victim was put on a backboard, for example, EMS personnel will likely keep the victim on the backboard while transporting him or her to a hospital. If that happens, EMS personnel may be able to temporarily exchange backboards with your facility. Otherwise, if the facility is without a backboard, the facility may have to be closed.

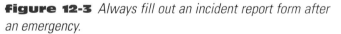

figure 12-3 *Always fill out an incident report form after an emergency.*

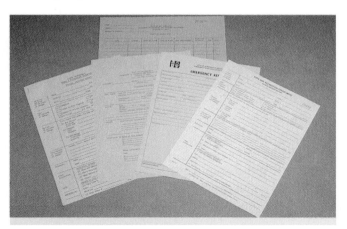

Sample Incident Report Form

Date of Report:	Date of Incident:	Time of Incident:	A.M. ☐ P.M. ☐

Facility Information

Facility: _____   Phone #: (   ) _____

Address: _____ City _____ State _____ Zip _____

Personal Data - Injured Party

Name: _____ Age: _____ Gender: Male ☐ Female ☐

Address: _____ City _____ State _____ Zip _____

Phone Number(s):   Home (   ) _____   Work (   ) _____

Family Contact (Name and Phone #): _____ (   ) _____

Incident Data

Location of Incident: _____
_____

Description of Incident: _____
_____
_____
_____

Was an injury sustained? Yes ☐ No ☐

If yes, Describe the type of injury sustained: _____
_____
_____
_____

Witnesses

1. Name: _____ Phone #: (   ) _____

    Address: _____ City _____ State _____ Zip _____

2. Name: _____ Phone #: (   ) _____

    Address: _____ City _____ State _____ Zip _____

Sample Incident Report Form

Incident Report Form - Page 2

Care Provided

Did victim refuse medical attention by staff?   Yes ❑ No ❑

Was care provided by facility staff?   Yes ❑ No ❑

Name of person that provided care: _____

Describe in detail care given: _____

_____

_____

_____

_____

_____

Was EMS called?   Yes ❑ No ❑   If yes, by whom?_____

Time EMS called: _____ A.M. ❑ P.M. ❑

Was the victim transported to an emergency facility?   Yes ❑ No ❑

If yes, where? _____   If no, person returned to activity?   Yes ❑ No ❑

Victim's signature (Parent's/Guardian's if victim is a minor): _____

Facility Data

Number of lifeguards on duty at time of incident: _____ Number of patrons in facility at time of incident: _____

Weather condition at time of incident: _____

Water condition at time of incident: _____

Deck condition at time of incident:_____

Name(s) of lifeguard(s) involved in incident: _____

_____

Report Prepared By:

Name (please print): _____   Position: _____

Signature: _____

You may need to replace bandages from your first aid kit (Fig. 12-4). Report damaged or missing equipment and items to the head lifeguard. At some facilities, you may replace used items such as first aid supplies yourself. Also report any equipment that does not work effectively or malfunctions, such as a rescue tube that broke during the rescue. All required equipment should be in place and functioning properly.

Participating in staff debriefing

At many facilities, staff directly or indirectly involved in an incident get together with management to discuss the situation afterward (Fig. 12-5). This debriefing is not intended to air emotions but to examine what happened, how the emergency action plan worked, and how to prevent similar incidents in the future. All staff compare notes, try to get a complete picture of what happened, and develop a thorough report. *The purpose is not to assign blame or to criticize.*

Facility management and lifeguards can later use such reports when preparing emergency plans and making changes to eliminate or minimize hazards. The head lifeguard or the facility manager should make sure this debriefing follows rules to meet its goals. Help keep the discussion on track by sticking to the point in your comments.

This meeting usually occurs after incident reports are filed, and often the entire safety team is involved. This debriefing does not, however, replace the critical incident stress debriefing discussed in the next section.

RESPONSIBILITY TO YOURSELF

You need to be aware of the physical and emotional effects an emergency can continue to have on you after the incident. These reactions can affect both your ability to do your job and how you live and feel. You have a responsibility to yourself to understand such consequences and do what is needed to cope with them.

Stress

In an emergency situation, your body reacts in several ways. Your muscles tense, your brain waves move rapidly, your heart rate and breathing rate increase, and your body produces **adrenaline** and other hormones. Fats and carbohydrates are quickly converted to energy. These are all natural responses to stress.

Stress is a physical, mental, or emotional state that causes tension, distress, or disruption in a person's mental or emotional balance. Stress can result even from positive things, such as from a challenge like performing in public or a welcome surprise. When stress becomes too great or is caused by something unpleasant, it has negative effects. It can cause sleeplessness, anxiety, depression, exhaustion, restlessness, nausea, nightmares, and other problems. Some effects may not occur right away but may appear days, weeks, or even months after the stressful event. Different people react to stress in dif-

figure 12-4 *Make certain that all first aid supplies are replaced.*

figure 12-5 *Management and staff work together at a staff debriefing after an incident.*

ferent ways, even from the same incident. You may not even recognize that you are suffering from stress or know its cause.

Critical incident stress. A *critical incident* is any occurrence that causes an unusually strong emotional reaction that overwhelms one's ability to cope and function, either during or after an incident. Common critical incidents a lifeguard can encounter include—

- A child's death.
- Any patron's death, especially after a prolonged rescue attempt.
- An event that threatens the rescuer, such as one that endangers the victim's or the rescuer's life or threatens someone important to the rescuer.
- The death of a co-worker on the job.
- Any powerful emotional event, especially one that attracts media coverage.

A rescue can be stressful for any lifeguard involved, especially if it involves severe injury or death. It is even more stressful if a lifeguard feels he or she did something wrong or failed to do something—even after doing exactly what he or she was trained to do.

The stress a person feels after such an emergency is called *critical incident stress.* This is a normal reaction to a stressful situation. People experiencing this stress need help to recognize it, understand it, and cope with it. If you do not identify and accept it, this stress can have serious long-term effects.

Critical incident stress debriefing. *Critical incident stress debriefing (CISD)* is the process by which professionals trained in dealing with the effects of stress help someone who has suffered stress. These are often mental health professionals. Their job is to help everyone involved in a stressful incident talk about what happened and express their feelings and reactions. They then help the people involved acknowledge their feelings, recognize them as normal, and learn ways to cope with them.

CISD may take place a few hours after the incident or 1 or more days later. Participating in this process does not mean you are weak in any way. It is extremely important to avoid the damaging effects of stress. These effects can disrupt your personal life and your effective-

ness on the job. The facility management should know how to contact a CISD team in your community. Police, fire, and EMS personnel usually know professionals trained to help with critical incident stress.

In addition to this professional help, you can help yourself. Table 12-1 provides eight ways to cope with stress.

---

table 12-1 *Coping With Stress*

- **In the first 24 hours after the incident, alternate physical exercise, such as swimming ¼ mile, with relaxation.**
- **Keep busy. Don't stop doing things you enjoy, and don't hesitate to take up new things.**
- **Don't withdraw, stop communicating, or avoid people. People do care.**
- **If you feel miserable, don't try to hide or suppress your feelings. Talk to someone.**
- **Remind yourself that your reaction is normal after a stressful incident. Do not think of yourself as going "crazy."**
- **Watch your diet. Cut down on sugar, fats, and caffeine while feeling the effects of stress.**
- **Avoid alcohol and drugs.**
- **Keep your life as normal as possible. Stick to your regular schedule, and eat regular meals.**

SUMMARY

No matter what its outcome, an emergency is confusing and upsetting. In an emergency, your skills, teamwork, in-service training, and practice of emergency action plans pay off. The events that take place after an emergency may make sense to you only after you have been through one. The incident may help you learn how to prevent a similar incident from happening in the future and better ways to respond if one does happen. You cannot always prevent emergencies from occurring, but you can learn from them.

STUDY QUESTIONS

Circle the letter of the best answer or answers.

1. After an incident, which of the following might be a responsibility of a lifeguard?
   a) Controlling bystanders.
   b) Deciding if you are able to return to work.
   c) Filing a report.
   d) Checking and reporting any missing items to the management.

2. Which of the following are acceptable steps in crowd control?
   a) Consider roping off the area.
   b) Yell at the patrons if necessary.
   c) Recruit any bystanders you may need.
   d) Direct those not helping you to back away from the victim.

3. An incident or injury report may help prevent similar incidents in the future by—
   a) Alerting management to a specific hazard in that area.
   b) Serving as a legal document in the case of litigation.
   c) Fulfilling a requirement of the state.
   d) Allowing management to create a diagram of the facility that shows where injuries have occurred.

4. When people not affiliated with your facility ask you questions about an incident, do not give them any information because—
   a) It's none of their business.
   b) To give them any information about the victim is a breach of confidentiality.
   c) To do so could be grounds for legal action.
   d) Only the facility management or representatives should make statements to others regarding an incident.

5. After an incident has occurred, if a facility was closed—
   a) It can reopen automatically.
   b) It should not be reopened until all required equipment is in place and functioning properly.
   c) Patrons must leave the facility.
   d) The facility stays closed for the rest of the day.

6. Which of the following are acceptable purposes for a staff debriefing?
   a) To compare notes.
   b) To get a well-rounded picture of what occurred.
   c) To prepare emergency plans and eliminate or minimize hazards.
   d) To assign blame or criticize.
   e) To generate material for a thorough report of the incident.

7. Negative stress can cause—
   a) Sleeplessness.
   b) Nausea.
   c) Happiness.
   d) Depression.
   e) Exhaustion.
   f) Anxiety.

8. Which of the following critical incidents might a lifeguard encounter?
   a) The death of a co-worker on the job.
   b) The death of a child.
   c) The death of any victim.
   d) An event that is particularly threatening to the rescuer.
   e) Green hair.

9. The purpose of a critical incident stress debriefing is to—
   a) Help all the people involved talk about what happened and express their feelings and reactions.
   b) Help those involved learn to acknowledge their feelings and recognize them as a normal result of the incident.
   c) Help all the people involved figure out what went wrong and who was responsible.
   d) Help those involved learn ways to cope with the feelings that result from the incident.

10. Helpful ways to cope with stress are to—
    a) Continue doing things you enjoy.
    b) Do physical exercise alternating with relaxation.
    c) Eat comfort foods, such as doughnuts and ice cream.
    d) Avoid being with people. No one wants to be around a stressed-out individual.
    e) Remind yourself you are having a normal reaction to a stressful incident. Do not label yourself "crazy."

Circle *True* or *False*.

11. Positive things can cause stress. True or False?

12. Critical incident stress is an abnormal reaction to a distressing situation. True or False?

References

Bruess, C.E., Richardson, G.E., and Laing, S.J. *Decisions for Health.* Dubuque, Iowa: William C. Brown Publishers, 1989.

Mitchell, Jeffery T. "Stress: The History, Status and Future of Critical Incident Stress Debriefings." *JEMS: Journal of Emergency Medical Services,* 13:47-52.

See answers to study questions on page 287.

WATERFRONT FACILITIES

13

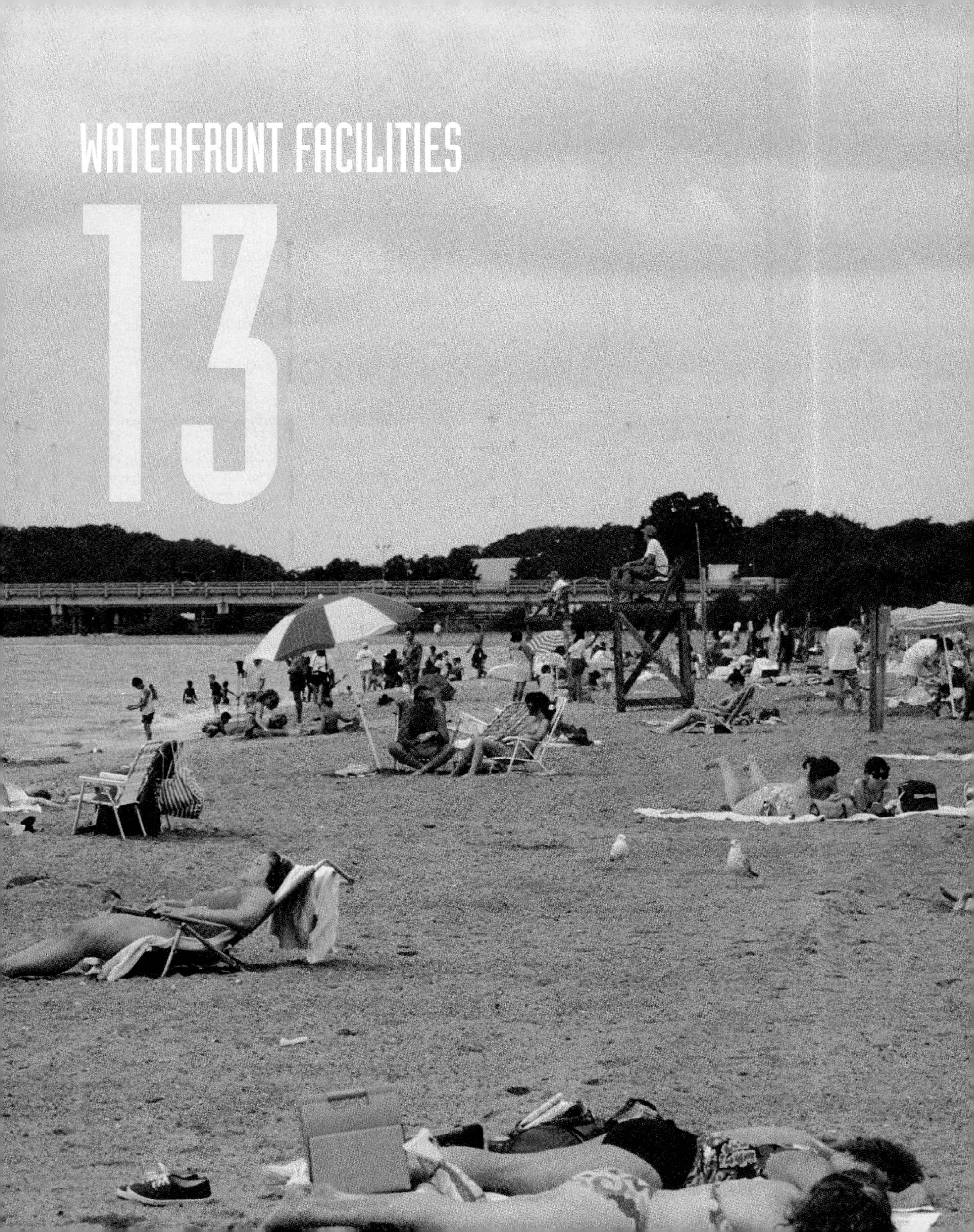

Objectives

After reading this chapter, you should be able to—

1. Describe different types, uses, and designs of waterfront facilities.
2. Describe two methods of zone coverage that may be used at a waterfront.
3. Describe environmental conditions that affect scanning at a waterfront.
4. List at least three potential hazards at a waterfront.
5. Discuss how and when to use rescue boards and rescue craft at waterfront facilities.
6. Describe how the buddy system and the buddy board are used to supervise swimmers at camp waterfronts.
7. Describe the appropriate rescue techniques and skills used in special rescue situations such as missing person procedures, search for a SCUBA diver, and cold water rescues.
8. Describe the sequence for a missing person procedure.
9. Define the key terms for this chapter.

After reading this chapter and completing the appropriate course activities, you should be able to—

1. Demonstrate the run-and-swim entry.
2. Demonstrate the walking assist and the beach drag.
3. Demonstrate how to perform a feet-first surface dive.
4. Demonstrate how to use a rescue board to rescue a distressed swimmer.
5. Demonstrate how to use a rescue board to rescue someone who cannot get onto the rescue board.
6. Demonstrate the proper use of mask and fins during a deep-water line search.

Key Terms

Bow: The front end of a boat or rescue board.

Contour map: A map or chart showing underwater characteristics and structures at a waterfront.

Crib: An enclosed area in a dock formation with walls extending down to the bottom of a lake.

Cross bearing: A technique for determining the place where a submerged victim was last seen; performed by two persons some distance apart pointing to the place such that the position is where the lines of their pointing cross.

Deep-water line search: An effective pattern for searching in water that is greater than chest deep.

Flat water: Water that has no wave action.

Gasp reflex: A sudden involuntary action to "catch one's breath."

Nonsurf open water: Bodies of water, such as lakes, ponds, rivers, bays, reservoirs, and sounds, that do not have waves like the ocean and are not enclosed as a swimming pool.

Personal water craft: A motorized vehicle, designed for one or two riders, that skims over the surface of the water.

Sighting: A technique for noting where a submerged victim was last seen, performed by imagining a line to the opposite shore and estimating the victim's position along that line. (See also cross bearing.)

Stern: The back end of a boat or rescue board.

Towline: A heavy piece of rope or cord attached to rescue equipment.

INTRODUCTION

The term *open water* refers to lakes, rivers, bays, **reservoirs,** canals, the ocean—any body of water not enclosed as a swimming pool is. Open-water areas have always been popular because of the many aquatic activities they offer.

For the purpose of this chapter, we will focus on waterfront facilities that are primarily **nonsurf open-water** areas, such as those found at resorts, national and state parks, summer camps, and campgrounds (Fig. 13-1). Each has its own characteristics, such as water quality, currents, and beach conditions. Because of these conditions, lifeguarding at waterfront areas is different from lifeguarding at pools. You therefore need additional knowledge and skills. Training in an open-water setting can help prepare you for the environment where you will be working.

You may be reading this chapter in preparation to work at a state park, camp, or private waterfront. Most of this chapter applies to any waterfront facility, with some material applying only to camps. This chapter does not, however, discuss lifeguarding in a situation with surf, conditions involving extreme wave action, or strong currents. Surf lifeguarding requires other specialized skills. Even a large open-water area might sometimes have wave conditions beyond your rescue abilities. If so, the head lifeguard or facility manager must decide whether to suspend swimming until conditions improve.

figure 13-1 *A waterfront.*

Because each facility has unique conditions, this chapter cannot cover every aspect of lifeguarding at every waterfront facility. You will receive in-service training for your specific facility. Once you are familiar with that waterfront facility and know your responsibilities on the lifeguarding team, you will be prepared to keep the facility safe and enjoyable for patrons.

Much of the information and skills you have learned in previous chapters also apply directly to waterfront settings. The importance of professionalism, teamwork, public relations, and many rescue skills is unchanged. If it has been a while since you read Chapters 1 through 12, you may want to review that material before continuing.

This chapter introduces you to other rescue equipment: the rescue board, rescue boat, and mask and fins. You will also learn new rescue skills. This chapter helps you apply skills learned in previous chapters to become an effective lifeguard in a waterfront setting.

INJURY PREVENTION

Chapters 4 through 6 describe three injury prevention strategies: communication, patron surveillance, and facility surveillance. You adjust these strategies as needed when lifeguarding at a waterfront facility. Most strategies for communication, for example, are similar, but patron and facility surveillance can be different at a waterfront facility.

Rules and regulations

At waterfront facilities, just as at pools, rules and regulations are important for everyone's safety. Chapter 4 discusses rules and regulations of typical aquatic facilities. Additional rules are developed for specific facilities. In your orientation and in-service training, you will review all the rules and can ask about any new rules you do not understand. Examples of rules that may be posted at waterfronts follow:

- Swim only when a lifeguard is on duty.
- Swim only in designated areas.
- Rough play is not allowed: no running, splashing, pushing, or dunking.
- No playing or swimming under docks, rafts, or platforms.
- No boats in the swimming area.
- Dive only in designated areas.

- No glass containers allowed on the beach.
- No alcohol or other drugs allowed.
- Floats, air mattresses, and tubes not allowed.
- No fishing near the swimming area.
- Keep away from lifeguard stand areas.

Remember what you read in Chapter 4 about enforcing rules in a fair and positive manner.

FACILITY SURVEILLANCE

When lifeguarding at a waterfront facility, you need to know what potential hazards might cause an injury. Hazards may include underwater obstructions, water quality, currents, weather conditions, and plants and animals in the water. The following sections describe hazards to watch for and how to adapt your facility surveillance. Some conditions may change daily or even more often and require several specific safety checks at the facility.

Facility characteristics

Each waterfront is unique, and conditions may change daily or more frequently with the wind, tides, and weather. You need to know the facility, its hazards, and potential changes in the environment to adapt to changing conditions. You must anticipate changes in the shoreline and underwater contours caused by **erosion,** currents, wind, debris, and waves. This is especially true at rivers, bays, inlets, and large lakes.

On some days the water may be totally calm, a condition known as *flat water*. Other days may have considerable wave action, especially in a bay or large lake. If the waves are high enough that you might lose sight of swimmers, you have to adjust your surveillance techniques, for example, by standing in your lifeguard stand or the facility manager may close the facility. Your facility orientation will tell you about changes at that facility.

Underwater characteristics. All facilities should have a map or chart (called a *contour map*) showing the physical characteristics and structures in and around the water (Fig. 13-2). The chart should show the water depth at different places, the slope of the bottom, holes, and drop-offs. It should also show all structures, docks, rafts, diving platforms, pilings, and lifeguard stands. Study this map well to know the area you are guarding and what hazards to be alert to.

Dock formations. A dock extends into the water and often designates areas for specific activities and different swimming abilities. Docks also give you greater access to swimmers. Docks have many shapes, and some include cribs. *Cribs* are enclosed areas with walls extending down to the bottom of the lake, designed for those who are not good swimmers. In some facilities, buoyed safety lines mark designated swimming areas.

Docks are designed for the specific needs of the facility. This is especially true for camps. A camp waterfront facility is usually designed with separate areas for different swimming levels and boating activities. Figure 13-3, *A-G,* shows common dock formations. Dock formations can be adapted for people with disabilities.

Be sure that floating docks and rafts are anchored securely. In your daily safety checks, make sure floating docks and rafts with a diving board are strongly anchored. Check the boundaries of the diving area for proper depth for safe diving and for objects that may

---

figure 13-2 *Contour map.*

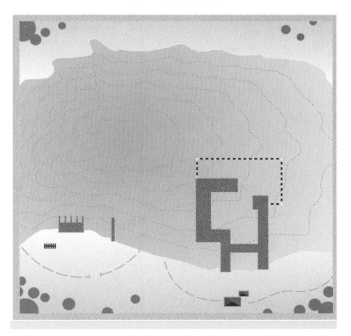

figure 13-3

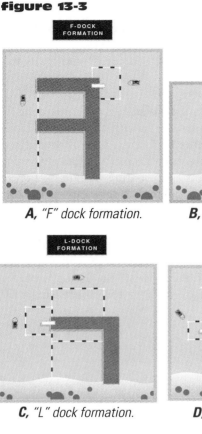

A, "F" dock formation.

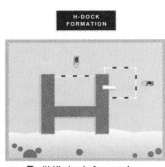

B, "H" dock formation.

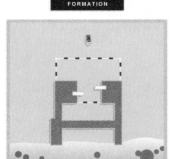

C, "L" dock formation.

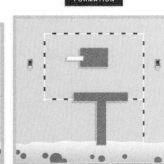

D, "A" dock formation.

E, Modified "H" dock formation   F, "T" dock formation.

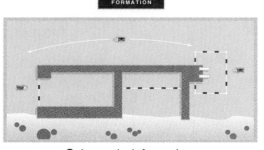

G, Large dock formation.

have floated in. Since some dock surfaces can become very hot from the sun, keep these areas wet to prevent burns to patrons' feet.

Changing water conditions. Both water depth and current can affect the safety of patrons. Heavy rainfall can make a river rise, and a long, dry period may make it too shallow for activities such as diving. When a dam releases water, the depth of the lake above the dam drops and the river below the dam rises. Water depth and the current, as well as debris and the cloudiness of the water, may affect the safety of people in the river.

Open-water facilities are not likely to have a **filter system** or any type of **purifying mechanism** for keeping the water clean. Debris, leaves, and dirt may be brought in by a current or blown in by the wind. Algae, pollen, leaves, and underwater plants may limit visibility. Swimmers can become entangled in underwater plants, which can become a serious hazard (Fig. 13-4). Check for any objects that may have washed into the area and for changed water and bottom conditions that may affect patron safety.

Water is usually colder early in the summer and after a rain. Alert swimmers to cold water, and watch for signs of hypothermia. Although surface water may be warm and comfortable, water at a depth of several feet can be much colder. This condition, known as a **thermocline,** can be a cold water hazard. At some open-water facilities, water temperatures are checked at various depths several times a day. Use this information to warn swimmers of hazards and to avoid personal risks during a rescue.

figure 13-4 *Underwater plant life can become a serious hazard at a waterfront.*

Safety checks

Although many facility characteristics seldom change, others change more often and require frequent safety checks. Follow the principles for safety checks described in Chapter 6. The head lifeguard or facility manager usually has developed a safety check form specific to the facility.

Inspecting the area. Before opening the area for the day, inspect the entire beach or shoreline area for sharp objects, broken glass, rocks, and litter. Carefully check the sand around the lifeguard towers for hidden objects that could injure you when you jump off the tower during a rescue. When checking docks, look for loose or rotting wood, protruding nails, and weak or frayed anchor lines. Go into the water.

Inspecting equipment. Make sure all safety equipment is in its proper location and in good working condition. Always inspect your rescue equipment carefully, and report any damaged or missing equipment to the head lifeguard or facility manager. Be sure to clean any suntan oils or lotions from rescue equipment.

PATRON SURVEILLANCE

Waterfront facilities often have many activities that appeal to the public. Swimming classes, recreational swimming, boating, sailing, canoeing, **SCUBA** diving, water skiing, and using personal water craft are just some of the activities found at waterfronts. (A *personal water craft* is a motorized vehicle, designed for one or two riders, that skims over the surface of the water.) The variety of these activities makes your surveillance more complicated. In addition to watching swimmers, you may have to warn people on boats, personal water craft, or water skis not to come too close to the swimming area.

Your facility may have different zones for boating, swimming, fishing, and other activities. The head lifeguard or facility manager usually sets zone coverage based on factors such as the following:

- Size and shape of the waterfront
- Size and shape of docks and rafts
- Number of people using the waterfront
- Types of activities that may take place
- Size of the lifeguarding staff

- Environmental conditions such as sun, currents, wind, and wave action
- History of injuries in the area (recorded on the incident chart)

Make sure you know the exact area you are assigned to cover. Talk to the head lifeguard or facility manager if you feel your zone is so large that your response time in an emergency would be too long. Figure 13-5, *A* and *B*, shows two possible zone coverage patterns at a waterfront.

figure 13-5 *A, Two-lifeguard zone coverage pattern at a waterfront. B, Three-lifeguard zone coverage pattern at a waterfront.*

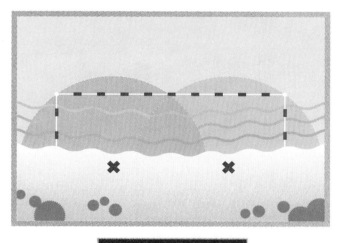

A

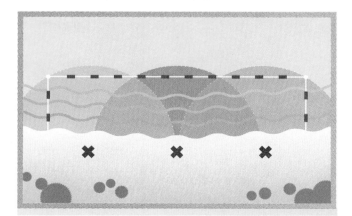

B

The location of your lifeguard station must enable you to see your entire area of responsibility. You may have to move your lifeguard stand or change your position during the day to adjust for changing sun, wind, or water conditions. Make sure you always have a clear view of the whole area and can see everyone in it (Fig. 13-6). If waves reduce your visibility, the facility manager may suspend swimming until conditions improve. Be sure to watch the lifelines at the far end of the swimming area when you scan. Distressed swimmers may rely on these for flotation when they become tired.

figure 13-6 *The lifeguard should have a clear view of the swimming area.*

figure 13-7 *Your facility may require a swim test be given to patrons before they are allowed to swim in a particular area.*

At some waterfronts, different swimming areas are marked by **buoyed lifelines** for various skill levels. Often there are zones for nonswimmers, beginners, intermediates, and swimmers. If you feel someone might not be safe in a marked area, you may give a polite caution or simple skill test before letting the person stay in that area (Fig. 13-7).

Supervision from rescue craft

In many facilities, rescue craft are used to improve the surveillance of swimmers as part of the safety program. Rescue craft typically patrol the outer edge of the swimming area. A craft may be assigned to a zone of coverage opposite a lifeguard position on land. This increases coverage of the swimming area and improves the response time to reach someone having trouble in the water (Fig. 13-8).

The type and size of rescue craft used depend on the area's size, water and wind conditions, and staffing. In small, calm areas, a flat-bottomed rowboat may work well. In rougher water a **v-hull** or **tri-hull** rowboat may be more stable and maneuverable. Powerboats, inflatable boats, and personal water craft also can be used as rescue craft (Fig. 13-9, *A* and *B*). You will learn about the facility's rescue craft in your orientation.

Be sure your rescue craft is properly equipped. Inspect your equipment at the start of each shift, and tell the head lifeguard or facility manager about any damaged or missing equipment. A rescue boat should have at least the following equipment:

- Extra oars or paddles
- Several life jackets
- Rescue tube
- Anchor and line
- First aid kit
- Bailer

Other equipment also may be included based on the facility's needs or state and federal regulations.

If you are stationed in a boat in an area with currents, you may have to row often to stay in proper position. In rough water or strong winds, this requires you to be in good physical condition for constant rowing. Some rescue craft have a special anchor with a quick release for immediate response. In some larger rescue craft, one lifeguard may row while a second watches the swimming area.

Make sure you are well trained in operating your facility's rescue craft before you use them for surveillance or to make a rescue. Be even more cautious with rescue craft with a motor. Take care to avoid injuring swimmers or damaging lifelines when you cross into the swimming area to make a rescue.

Patron surveillance at camps

Patron surveillance at camp waterfronts is similar to surveillance at other open-water facilities. Pay special attention to the characteristics of the waterfront and the ages and abilities of the swimmers. Classifying swimmers, using a buddy system, and using a buddy board can help your supervision.

Classification of swimmers. Patron surveillance at camps includes screening participants for all aquatic activities, including boating, to assess swimming skills and abilities. This screening is done at the beginning of the camp session to determine which activities individual campers can participate in. Groups for different activities are formed based on these abilities. In some camps the swimmers also wear color-coded swim caps or wrist bands to help you see that they stay in their designated areas (Fig. 13-10).

Buddy system. The buddy system for supervising swimmers is used in many camps. This involves pairing off campers with equal swimming ability. In situations with an uneven number in the group, have three campers

figure 13-9 *A, Rowboats, and B, inflatable power boats are two types of rescue crafts.*

A

B

figure 13-8 *A rescue craft located opposite a lifeguard station increases coverage of the swimming area.*

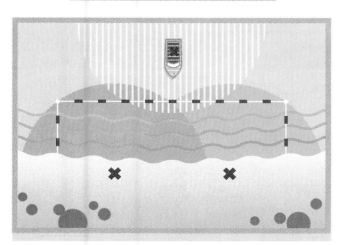

3 GUARD ZONE COVERAGE
WITH RESCUE CRAFT

form a triplet. The buddies must stay together in the assigned swimming area. If either buddy leaves the water for any reason, the other buddy also must leave.

A buddy check is a way to periodically make sure all swimmers are safe. There are two methods. In one a lifeguard gives a signal, such as a whistle blast. The buddies grasp each other's hands, raise their arms over their heads, and hold still until the lifeguards have counted the swimmers in each area (Fig. 13-11). In the other method, pairs of buddies are given numbers at the beginning of the swim period. A lifeguard gives a signal and then calls off numbers in sequence. The buddies respond when their buddy number is called.

Buddy boards. Along with the buddy system, some camps use buddy boards as a way to be sure buddies stay in their assigned area. Buddy boards are usually located at the entrance to the swimming area. Based on the initial screening, campers get colored tags with their names on them. The tags may also be labeled by swimming ability, such as "nonswimmer" or "beginner." The name tags are kept in the "out" section of the buddy board when the campers are not in the swimming area. Before entering the area, campers move their tags to the "in" section and are then paired up with a buddy (Fig. 13-12). A lifeguard or other staff stationed at the buddy board makes sure that the tags are placed correctly. When campers leave, the tags are put back in the "out" section (Fig. 13-13). Buddy boards may also be used for boating.

A tag found in the "in" section after the water is cleared indicates one of several possibilities:

- The camper forgot to move the tag from the "in" side of the buddy board to the "out" side before leaving the area.
- The tag was wrongly placed by another camper leaving the swim area.

figure 13-10 *At some camp settings, color-coded swim caps are used to identify campers of different swimming ability.*

figure 13-11 *During a buddy check, swimmers pair up with hands raised above their heads. Swimmers hold still until lifeguards count the pairs in their area.*

figure 13-12 *Campers move their tags to the "in" section and are paired up with a buddy.*

- A lifeguard or other staff stationed at the buddy board did not make sure the tag was placed correctly when the camper left the area.
- A tag has fallen off the buddy board and is not easily visible.
- A camper may be playing a joke.
- You have a missing person.

In any case, respond quickly and efficiently. Perform the buddy check one or even two more times. If you have any doubt at all about the whereabouts of the missing person, you must initiate your missing person procedure. (See p. 251.)

PREPARING FOR EMERGENCIES

Being prepared for an emergency means more than just knowing how to rescue a person. You must also know the communication system used at the facility and your specific role in the emergency action plan.

Communication

Chapter 7 described communication techniques. Good communication is also essential at waterfronts. Besides whistles, waterfront communication systems may include two-way radios, telephones, flags, megaphones, and signals with rescue equipment (Fig. 13-14, *A-C*).

figure 13-13 *When campers leave the area, all tags should be in the "out" section.*

figure 13-14 *Lifeguards use* ***A***, *two-way radios,* ***B***, *flags, and* ***C***, *rescue equipment to communicate at waterfronts.*

A

B

C

In your orientation to the facility, be sure you understand the methods of communication used there. When you do the first safety check each day, be sure the telephone is working. If it is a pay phone, make sure that change is available for using it.

Emergency action plan

Every facility should have its own emergency action plans for possible emergency situations. Table 13-1 is a sample emergency action plan for a waterfront. Emergency action plans at waterfronts and camps may include additional steps because of the environment, the weather, or the size of the waterfront and its surround-

---

table 13-1 *Emergency Action Plan for Waterfront Facilities*

In case of an emergency, you should be prepared to respond as follows:
1. **When you spot a patron who needs help, activate the facility's emergency action plan. By immediately blowing one long, loud whistle blast, you notify your safety team that there is an emergency. Once you have given the signal, members of the safety team can react to the situation.**
2. **Once you activate the emergency action plan, determine which method of rescue is needed. If you must enter the water to make a rescue, use the entry that is most appropriate for your location. For example, you may use a run-and-swim entry from the beach. If it isn't necessary to enter the water, use the appropriate equipment to help the victim. If the emergency is a missing person, follow the missing person procedure included in this chapter.**
3. **If you are not the lifeguard making the rescue, make sure the rescuing lifeguard's zone is covered. At waterfronts with large strips of beach, lifeguard stands may be positioned hundreds of yards away from each other, which makes backup coverage difficult. If you lifeguard at a waterfront that has docks and rafts, lifeguard stands are closer together, which makes backup coverage easier. Your facility should have a predetermined system for backup coverage based on the size of each lifeguard's zone coverage and the distance between lifeguard stands.**
4. **Once the situation is under control, the lifeguard and others involved in the rescue also complete and file an incident report as soon as time permits.**
5. **All equipment used in the rescue must be in good working condition and replaced in its original spot. Lifeguards return to duty, if able, and patrons are allowed back in the water if there are enough lifeguards to cover the area.**

ings. In rural areas, it may take longer for EMS personnel to respond than at an urban pool setting, and the waterfront's emergency action plan should take this into account.

In a park setting, other staff, such as rangers, security or maintenance personnel, and lookouts, may be included in the emergency action plan. At a camp, counselors and nurses may also have a role. All personnel should be properly trained and know their role in the emergency action plans. Although other people may assist, *you and the other lifeguards still have primary responsibility for managing the emergency.*

RESCUE SKILLS

You can use all rescue skills described in the earlier chapters at a waterfront along with new ones you will learn in this chapter. The American Red Cross recommends the use of a rescue tube rather than a rescue buoy. If your facility requires you to use a rescue buoy, however, you need to practice with that equipment in your in-service training. Since many waterfronts use rescue craft and rescue boards, this chapter includes techniques for that equipment also. Be sure to get the experience you need with all equipment used at your facility.

Entries

In most waterfront situations, you use the same entries as you learned in Chapter 8. The compact jump and stride jump are especially useful for entering the water from a dock.

Run-and-swim entry

When you enter from a gradually sloping shoreline, use the run-and-swim entry, following these guidelines:

1 While holding your tube in one hand and the strap over your shoulder, run into the water, lifting your legs to avoid falling (Fig. 13-15, *A*).

2 When you reach the point where you can no longer run, drop the tube to your side, lean forward, and start swimming. *Do not dive or plunge into the water because it may result in serious injury* (Fig. 13-15, *B* and *C*).

figure 13-15 *When performing a run-and-swim entry, A, run into the water, lifting your legs to avoid falling. B, When you can no longer run, lean forward. C, Start to swim.*

A

B

C

Swimming with a rescue tube

Depending how far you are from the victim, you can swim with your rescue tube two ways. Use the stroke that gets you there most quickly. For a shorter distance, you can swim with the tube under your armpits (Fig. 13-16, *A*). At a waterfront, there is often a great distance between you and the person needing assistance. If so, let the tube trail behind you as you swim (Fig. 13-16, *B*).

Removal from water

To remove someone from the water at a dock, use the same method you have learned for pools. However, with a sloping shoreline, you have two effective ways to help someone out of the water: the walking assist and the beach drag.

figure 13-16 *You can swim with the rescue tube either A, under your armpits or B, trailing behind you, depending on the distance you must swim to the victim.*

A

B

Rescue Buoy

Rescue buoys are often used as equipment at waterfronts and at surf beaches. Most rescue buoys are made of lightweight, hard, buoyant plastic. They vary in length from 25 to 34 inches. The shorter buoy weighs 3.5 pounds, and the longer one weighs 5 pounds. Molded handgrips along the sides let a victim keep a firm hold on the buoy. Some newer models of buoys are made of foam and covered with vinyl, similar to rescue tubes.

While swimming to the victim, allow the rescue buoy to trail behind you. Once you get close to the victim, reach back and grasp the buoy with one hand and extend the buoy to the victim. Carefully tow the victim back to safety.

The buoyancy of the rescue buoy, along with your reassuring talk, should comfort and calm the victim. If the victim begins to panic and move up the line, however, you can release the line and reassess your rescue options before approaching the victim again.

Walking assist. Use the walking assist to help a conscious victim walk out of shallow water. Follow these steps:

1 Place one of the victim's arms around your neck and across your shoulder.

2 Grasp the wrist of the arm that is across your shoulder, and wrap your free arm around the victim's back or waist to provide support.

3 Maintain a firm grasp, and help the victim walk out of the water (Fig. 13-17).

figure 13-17 *A lifeguard assisting a conscious victim from shallow water.*

Beach drag. On a sloping beach, the beach drag is a safe and easy way to remove an unconscious victim or a person who is very heavy and unable to walk from the water (Fig. 13-18, *A* and *B*). In that case, once you bring the victim to shallow water, call for assistance from another lifeguard if one is available. Then remove the strap of the rescue tube or position it at the victim's side. This helps keep it out of your way so you don't trip on it. Do not use this technique if you suspect the person has a spinal injury.

Follow these steps for the beach drag:

1 Stand behind the victim, and grasp him or her under the armpits, supporting the victim's head, when possible, with your forearms.

2 While walking backward, drag the victim toward the shore.

3 Remove the victim completely from the water or at least to a point where the head and shoulders are out of the water.

figure 13-18 *A* and *B, to remove an unconscious victim from the water, the beach drag may be performed by either one lifeguard or two.*

A

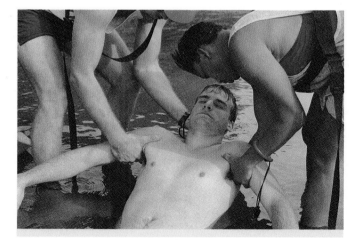

B

Surface diving

Surface diving enables you to submerge to moderate depths to search for a submerged victim. There are two kinds of surface dives: the feet-first surface dive and the headfirst surface dive.

Feet-first surface dive. To perform a feet-first surface dive during a *deep-water line search* (a searching pattern that is discussed later), follow this sequence:

---

figure 13-19 *When performing a feet-first surface dive, A, press downward with your hands, and execute a strong kick to raise your body out of the water. B, Keep your legs straight and together with toes pointed. C, Sweeping hands and arms upward, repeat until you reach desired depth. D, Tuck your body and roll to horizontal position. E, Swim under water.*

1 When the lead lifeguard (the lifeguard in the water leading the search) gives the command, position your body vertically, press downward with your hands, and kick strongly to raise your body out of the water (Fig. 13-19, *A*). Then take a breath, and allow your body to sink. Keep your legs straight and together with the toes pointed (Fig. 13-19, *B*).

2 As your downward momentum begins to slow, turn your palms outward and sweep your hands and arms upward. Repeat this arm movement until you reach the desired depth (Fig. 13-19, *C*).

3 Once you have reached the desired depth, tuck your body and roll to a horizontal position (Fig. 13-19, *D*). Then extend your arms and legs, and swim under water (Fig. 13-19, *E*).

A

B

C

D

E

Headfirst surface dive. To perform a headfirst surface dive during a line search, follow this sequence:

1 Once the lead lifeguard gives the command, take a breath, plunge one arm downward, and bend at the hips (Fig. 13-20, **A**). Tuck your chin to your chest.

2 Bring the other arm down to meet the extended arm (Fig. 13-20, **B**).

3 Lift your legs up in the air so that the weight of your legs aids the descent. Your body should be fully extended, streamlined, and almost vertical (Fig. 13-20, **C**).

4 The weight of your legs and forward momentum may take you deep enough without further movement. If necessary, kick and stroke your arms (pulling them back to the thighs) until you reach the desired depth (Fig. 13-20, **D**). Then level out and swim forward under water.

Spinal injury management

You may have to modify how you provide care for a person with a head or back injury if waves or currents are moving the water. In water with waves, move the victim to calmer water, if possible. A dock or raft may reduce the waves. If there is no barrier from the waves, have other rescuers form a "wall" with their bodies to block the waves.

In water with a current, point the victim's head up into the current once the victim is face up. The victim's body will become aligned with the current, minimizing the possibility of additional injury from the moving water. Your orientation and in-service training will cover the specific conditions at your facility and teach you how to adapt the spinal injury management procedures you learned in Chapter 11.

A

B

C

D

figure 13-20 *When performing a headfirst surface dive,* **A,** *plunge one arm downward and bend at the hips.* **B,** *Bring the other arm down to meet the extended one.* **C,** *Lift your legs up in the air so that the weight of your legs aids the descent.* **D,** *Once you are submerged, kick your legs and stroke your arms to reach desired depth.*

Using a rescue board

Some waterfronts use rescue boards as standard equipment. The rescue board is fast, stable, easy to use, and comes in various lengths and weights. Many waterfronts use rescue boards to patrol the outer boundaries of a swimming area. At others the rescue board may be ready for emergency use at the base of the lifeguard stand (Fig. 13-21).

If your facility uses a rescue board, learn how to quickly paddle and maneuver it in all weather conditions. Practice often to keep your skills sharp. Wind, currents, and waves can affect the handling of the rescue board. Make sure that the rescue board is cleaned of suntan lotion and body oils, which can make a board slippery and hard to manage.

Surfboards as Rescue Equipment

Surfboards are occasionally used at open-water facilities as rescue equipment, particularly at those facilities that occasionally have high waves. Surfboards that are used for this purpose are usually 10 to 12 feet long and 2 feet wide. This size tends to be the easiest for a lifeguard to handle because it is light, small, and easy to turn over. Weight and ease of handling are advantages the surfboard has over the rescue board. Both surfboards and rescue boards are more efficient than swimming when rescuing a distressed swimmer if you have a great distance to cover, since they require less time and energy to reach the victim. Always approach a victim from the side because the pointed end could harm the already distressed swimmer. When approaching the victim, it is recommended that you use a butterfly arm stroke when paddling and kneel rather than lie flat for better visibility.

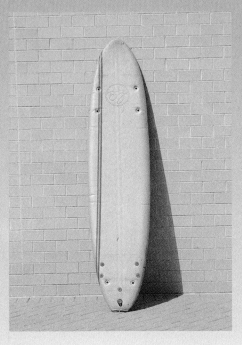

Launching a rescue board

1 When launching a rescue board, hold onto the sides about midboard as you enter the water (Fig. 13-22, *A*).

2 When you are about knee-deep, lay the rescue board on the water, and push it forward alongside you. Then climb on the rescue board just behind the middle and lie down (Fig. 13-22, *B*).

3 Paddle a few strokes, and bring yourself to a kneeling position so that you can paddle to the victim (Fig. 13-22, *C*). When patrolling with the rescue board, you may sit or kneel on it for better visibility.

figure 13-22 *When launching a rescue board, **A**, enter the water, pushing rescue board. **B**, Climb on the rescue board just behind the middle and lie down. **C**, Paddle a few strokes, and bring yourself to a kneeling position.*

A

B

C

figure 13-21 *Rescue boards are placed at the base of lifeguard stands for easy access in an emergency.*

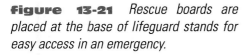

Approaching the victim. In calm waters, point the front end of the rescue board, the ***bow***, toward the victim. Then paddle with a butterfly arm stroke. Keep your head up, and try to keep the victim in sight (Fig. 13-23). In rough water or high winds, adjust your body position and your angle of approach as needed.

figure 13-23 *Paddle the rescue board with a butterfly arm stroke, keeping the victim in sight.*

Rescuing a distressed swimmer. When you use a rescue board to rescue a distressed swimmer—

1 Approach the victim from the side.

2 Grasp the victim's hand or wrist, and slide off the rescue board to the opposite side (Fig. 13-24, *A*).

3 Help the victim extend his or her arms across the rescue board, and encourage him or her to relax and be calm (Fig. 13-24, *B*).

4 Keep the rescue board as stable as possible, and assist the victim onto it (Fig. 13-24, *C*).

5 Have the victim lie on his or her stomach toward the bow (Fig. 13-24, *D*).

6 Kick to turn the bow of the rescue board toward shore. Then carefully climb onto the rescue board from the back, and lie between the victim's legs. Be careful not to tip the rescue board; keep your legs in the water for stability (Fig. 13-24, *E*).

7 Paddle the rescue board to shore (Fig. 13-24, *F*).

In your orientation and in-service training, practice using the rescue board with victims of various sizes. Adjust your position and the victim's to keep the bow of the rescue board clear of the water.

figure 13-24 *When rescuing a distressed swimmer with a rescue board: **A,** Grasp the victim's wrist, and slide off the rescue board to opposite side. **B,** Have the victim extend his or her arms across the rescue board. **C,** Assist the victim onto the rescue board. **D,** Have the victim lie on his or her stomach toward the bow. **E,** Climb on behind the victim and lie between the victim's legs. **F,** Paddle to shore.*

Rescuing someone who cannot get on the rescue board. When rescuing an unconscious victim or someone who cannot climb on a rescue board—

1 Approach the victim from the side, and position the rescue board so that the victim is slightly forward of the middle of the rescue board.

2 Grasp the victim's hand or wrist, then slide off the rescue board to the opposite side and flip the rescue board toward you (Fig. 13-25, *A* and *B*). At this point, you are holding the victim's arm across the rescue board, and the victim's chest is against the far edge of the rescue board.

3 Grasp the far edge of the rescue board with your other hand (Fig. 13-25, *C*).

4 Kneel on the edge of the rescue board, and use your body weight to flip the rescue board toward you (Fig. 13-25, *D*).

5 Rotate the victim so that he or she is lying lengthwise in the middle of the rescue board with his or her head toward the bow (Fig. 13-25, *E*).

6 Kick to turn the bow of the rescue board toward shore. Then carefully climb onto the rescue board from the back, and lie between the victim's legs. Be careful not to tip the rescue board; keep your legs in the water for stability (Fig. 13-25, *F*).

7 Paddle the rescue board to shore (Fig. 13-25, *G*).

If you are unable to get the victim onto the rescue board with this method, use the rescue board for flotation and keep the victim face up so that he or she can breathe. Call for help or proceed toward shore in whatever way you can.

---

figure 13-25 *When rescuing someone who cannot get on a rescue board, **A** and **B**, grasp the victim's wrist and slide off the rescue board opposite the victim as you flip the board toward you. **C**, Grasp the far edge of the rescue board with other hand.*

A

B

C

D

G

E

figure 13-25—cont'd *D, Kneel on the edge of the board, and flip it toward you. **E,** Rotate the victim lengthwise on the board. **F,** Climb on behind the victim, and lie between the victim's legs. **G,** Paddle to shore.*

F

Using water craft for a rescue

If your facility uses water craft for rescues, practice until you are skilled in managing them in all rescue situations and all weather conditions. Your facility must train you in the use of its water craft. Following are basic guidelines for using water craft.

Rescuing a distressed swimmer. To rescue a distressed swimmer when you are using a rescue craft—

- Extend an oar to the victim, and pull him or her to the *stern* of the craft (Fig. 13-26). The stern is the back end of the craft. It is the most stable area for a person to hold.
- If the victim cannot grasp or hold the oar or equipment, move the stern close to the victim. Then grasp the victim, and pull him or her to the stern (Fig. 13-27).
- Have the victim hang onto the stern as you move to safety.
- If you must bring the victim onto the craft, for example, if the water is very cold or the victim is fatigued, help the swimmer over the stern, being careful not to overturn the craft (Fig. 13-28).

When using motorized water craft, follow these principles:

1 Always approach the victim from downwind and downstream.

2 Shut off the engine when you are about three boat-lengths away from the victim, and coast or paddle to the victim.

3 Bring the victim on board before you restart the engine.

figure 13-26 *Extend an oar to the victim, and pull him or her to the stern of the craft.*

figure 13-27 *Grasp the victim, and pull him or her to the stern.*

figure 13-28 *Assist the victim onto the craft if necessary.*

SPECIAL SITUATIONS AND SKILLS

Sightings and cross bearings

When a drowning person submerges in open water, you must make sure that you are swimming in a straight line toward his or her last known position. Sighting and cross bearing are two techniques to help you keep track of where the person was last seen.

To take a *sighting*, note where the victim went under water. Line up this spot with a stationary object on the far shore, such as a tree, a building, or any identifiable part of the environment like a clearing or a field. Then note the victim's distance from the shore along that imaginary line (Fig. 13-29).

When another lifeguard is available, a *cross bearing* can be taken along the shore. Each lifeguard takes a sighting on the spot where the victim was last seen. If additional people are available, they can act as spotters from the shore. As the lifeguards swim to the victim they can periodically check the spotters on the shore for directions (Fig. 13-30). The spotter may communicate directions to the lifeguards by means of megaphones, whistles, or hand signals.

Missing person procedure

Every waterfront facility should have procedures for locating a missing person. All staff members should be thoroughly trained in these procedures. Time is a critical factor in a search for a missing person.

Often the "missing person" reported to you is a small child who has wandered off to the bathroom or the snack bar and cannot be found by the parent. Since you cannot know yet whether the person is or is not in the water, you must take every missing person report seriously.

The emergency action plan at your facility should have a procedure similar to the following guidelines for a missing person search.

Note: During all missing person procedures, one person must be in charge of the entire search to avoid confusion and wasted time. This may be the head lifeguard or facility manager.

figure 13-29 *Sighting a stationary object.*

SIGHTING

figure 13-30 *A cross bearing.*

CROSS BEARING

- Use a predetermined signal to alert all staff that a person is missing. Lifeguards clear the swimming areas and make sure all water areas are clear. Then the lifeguards quickly report to the location designated by the emergency action plan.
- All other staff, including those on break or assigned to other duties such as locker rooms or snack bar, also report to the designated location. The person who made the missing person report is brought to the same location to give a detailed description of the missing person and to wait there to identify him or her.
- If your facility has a public address system, make an announcement that describes the missing person. Ask patrons to stay calm, and ask for volunteers if needed. Tell the missing person to report to the main lifeguard area, since the person might not realize that he or she is "missing"!
- All lifeguards search the swimming area, starting where the missing person was last seen. Make sure to look under docks, piers, and rafts and in other potentially dangerous locations.
- Adult volunteers may help search shallow areas.
- Deeper areas should be searched by trained lifeguards.
- Other waterfront staff should check bathrooms, showers, locker rooms, and other areas.
- In a camp, staff should quickly check the missing person's cabin or tent and other camp areas. The entire camp staff is involved in the search for the missing person. A common practice is to move all campers to one central location to do an accurate count. Some camps do the count by section. While the camp is being searched, you and the other lifeguards continue to search the entire waterfront. The search continues until every person has been accounted for.
- At waterfront facilities such as state parks, staff may have to check other playgrounds, camp sites, and wooded areas. Park rangers, maintenance people, and volunteers may help. You and the other lifeguards must concentrate on the water areas.
- If the missing person is not found immediately, additional support may be needed from other emergency personnel, such as the local fire department, police, or search and rescue squad. Continue your search until they arrive on the scene to assist with the search.

Searching shallow-water areas. To search shallow-water areas with poor water clarity, have adult volunteers or non-lifeguarding staff members link arms or hold hands and form a line in the water (Fig. 13-31). The shortest person should be in the shallowest water, and the tallest person should be in water that is no more than chest deep. The whole line slowly moves across the area together. Start where the missing person was last seen. One lifeguard should be assigned to oversee this part of the search.

As the search line moves forward, the searchers gently sweep their feet across the bottom with each step. A typical search pattern for shallow water is shown in Figure 13-32. Searchers must not go deeper than chest-deep water. Only trained lifeguards should search deeper areas.

The deep-water line search. The *deep-water line search* is an effective pattern for searching in water that is greater than chest deep. Several lifeguards, wearing masks and fins, form a straight line, no more than an arm's length from each other. One lifeguard serves as a lookout standing above the water level (on a dock, raft, or water craft) with rescue equipment in case a searcher gets in trouble or the missing person is found. On command from the lead lifeguard, all searchers do the same surface dive (either feet first or headfirst) to the bottom and swim forward a set number of strokes—usually three. If the water is **murky,** the searchers search the bottom by sweeping their hands back and forth in front of them, making sure to cover the entire area (Fig. 13-33).

figure 13-31 *A shallow-water line search.*

Then the searchers return to the surface as straight up as possible. At the surface, the line backs up, the lead lifeguard checks to make sure all searchers are accounted for, reforms, and on command from the lead lifeguard, dives again. The searchers repeat this procedure until the entire swimming and diving area has been searched in one direction (Fig. 13-34). Make sure not to miss any areas on the bottom when you dive and resurface. The searchers then repeat the pattern at a 90 degree angle to the first search pattern. If the missing person is not found in the swimming and diving areas, expand the search to nearby areas. Consider the effects of any currents. Continue to search until the missing person is found or until emergency personnel arrive.

figure 13-32 *A shallow-water line search pattern.*

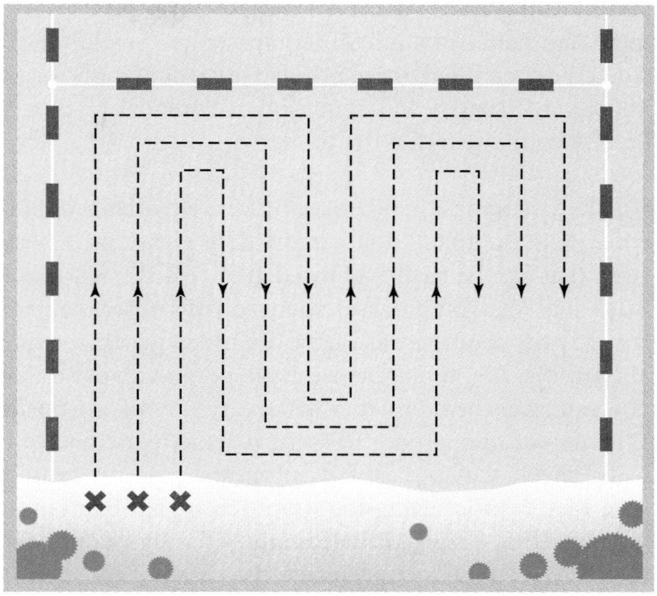

figure 13-33 *A deep-water line search.*

figure 13-34 *A deep-water line search pattern.*

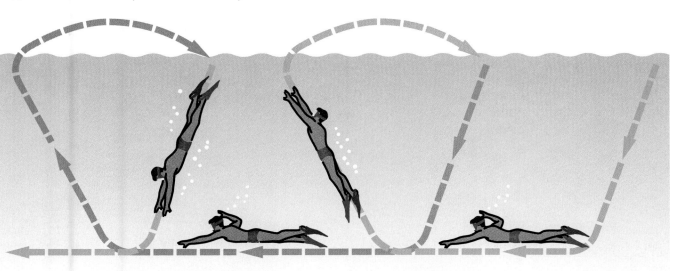

Mask and fins

Lifeguarding at a waterfront may require the use of a mask and fins. Although this equipment is typically considered recreational, these are also important tools for an underwater search for a missing swimmer. Use only quality equipment that fits properly.

Mask. Use a mask made of soft, flexible rubber or silicone, with nontinted, tempered safety glass and a head strap that can be easily adjusted (Fig. 13-35). Choose a mask that lets you block or squeeze your nose to equalize pressure. Some masks have a molded nosepiece that allows this. Some masks also have purge valves so that you can clear them of water without removing the mask. With any design, proper fit is the primary concern.

To check that a mask fits properly, place it against your face without using the strap. Keep your hair out of the way (Fig. 13-36). Inhale slightly through your nose to create a slight suction inside the mask. This suction should keep the mask in place without being held. A proper seal keeps water from leaking into your mask when you are using it.

Carefully adjust the strap so that the mask is comfortable on your face. If it is too tight, the mask may be distorted and not seal properly. Now, try your mask in the water. If it leaks a little, tighten the strap. If it continues to leak, check it again with suction—you might not have the right size.

A mask may fog during normal use. To prevent fogging, rub saliva on the inside of the face plate, and rinse the mask with water before you put it on. Commercial defoggers also can be used.

When you descend into deeper water, the increased pressure may cause discomfort, pain, and even injury if it is not equalized. Usually you feel the pressure in your ears first. You need to equalize pressure early and often. If you cannot equalize the pressure because of a head cold or sinus problem, return to the surface rather than risk an injury.

You can relieve ear pressure by placing your thumb and finger on the nosepiece of your mask, pinching your nose, and trying to exhale (Fig. 13-37). Repeat this if you still need to relieve ear pressure. If your ears hurt, do not attempt to go deeper until you successfully equalize the pressure.

As you descend, you will feel the mask squeezing your face because of the increased pressure. To relieve the squeezing, simply exhale a small amount of air through your nose into the mask.

figure 13-36 *Fitting the mask.*

figure 13-35 *Mask.*

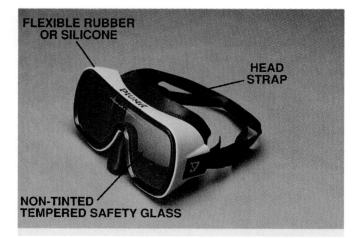

FLEXIBLE RUBBER OR SILICONE

HEAD STRAP

NON-TINTED TEMPERED SAFETY GLASS

Snorkel

A snorkel is a rubber or silicone tube that you place in your mouth so that you can breathe without having to lift, turn, or move your head. This allows you to keep a constant watch on the bottom when you are involved in a search operation.

When you use a snorkel, you should wear a mask. You may use a **keeper** to attach the snorkel to the side of your mask. With the mask on, adjust the snorkel so that the mouthpiece fits comfortably between your teeth and lips. Position the snorkel alongside your ear when you are facedown in the water.

First, practice breathing through the snorkel with your face out of the water. Breathing through your nose will fog the glass on your mask. Then practice with your face in the water. Finally, practice swimming on the surface while breathing through the snorkel. Be sure you are breathing comfortably through the snorkel before you try to clear the snorkel or practice surface dives.

When you descend, the snorkel fills with water. Waves or splashing can also let water into your snorkel. Clearing your snorkel is easy if you follow this sequence. Practice flooding and clearing your snorkel in shallow water. Take a deep breath and submerge enough to flood the snorkel. Stand up and forcefully exhale through the snorkel to blast the water out of it. You should be able to blast the water several feet into the air. Take your next breath carefully through the snorkel in case some water remains in it. Once the snorkel is clear, breathe normally.

Another way to clear a snorkel is the tilt method. As you near the surface, tilt your head back (look up) and exhale gently. Continue exhaling as you lower your head to a face-down position. The water clears the snorkel as you reach the surface. Take your first breath carefully in case water remains in the snorkel. Practice enough to become comfortable with flooding and clearing your snorkel. A search for a missing swimmer may involve continual surface dives and clearing the snorkel each time you return to the surface.

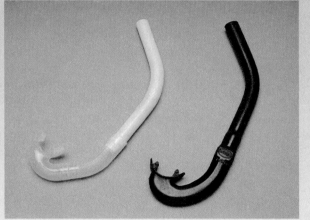

figure 13-37 *Equalizing ear pressure.*

Fins. The two basic types of fins are the full-foot or shoe-type fin and the open-heel type with a strap (Fig. 13-38). With either type, proper fit is important for comfort and efficient movement. The surface (blades) of fins comes in different sizes. Larger fins are faster but require more strength. Choose fins that match your ability.

Wetting your feet and the fins makes it easier to put them on. Be careful not to pull on the heels or straps of the fins because they can break or tear. Push your foot into the fin, then slide the heel or strap up over your heel.

Fins give you greater speed and let you cover greater distances with less effort. A modified flutter kick is usually best when wearing fins (Fig. 13-39). Use a kicking action that is deeper and slower, with a little more knee bend than your usual flutter kick.

The easiest way to swim under water with fins is to use your legs only. Keep your arms relaxed at your side. In unclear water, keep your arms out in front of you for protection.

Entering the water with mask and fins. Once you are proficient with mask and fins, you can learn how to enter the water safely wearing your equipment. Enter from a height of less than 3 feet, using a stride jump. Never attempt a headfirst entry with this equipment.

When doing a stride jump, put one hand over the mask to hold it in place. Keep your elbow close to your chest. Make sure no swimmers or other objects are below you. Step out with a long stride over the water, but do not lean forward (Fig. 13-40). As you enter the water, your fins will slow your downward motion. Swim with your arms at your side and your face in the water (Fig. 13-41).

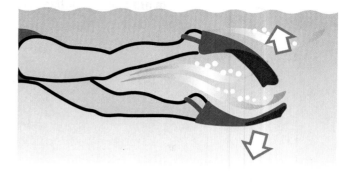

figure 13-39 *Modified flutter kick.*

figure 13-40 *Performing a stride jump when entering the water with mask and fins.*

figure 13-38 *Fins.*

figure 13-41 *Swimming while wearing mask and fins.*

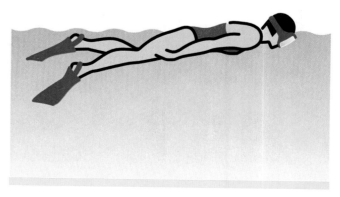

Searching for a missing SCUBA diver

All underwater searches for a SCUBA diver should be conducted by trained search and rescue SCUBA personnel. The emergency action plan for your facility may give you an assisting role, however, including one or more of these responsibilities:

1 Find out where the diver was last seen, or look for bubbles.

2 Check all out-of-water areas, including the parking lot or equipment storage area.

3 Use a sighting or cross bearing to keep track of the spot where bubbles were seen or where the diver was last seen.

Cold water rescue

A serious concern at many waterfront facilities is the sudden entry of someone into cold water. Cold water is defined as being 70 degrees F (21 degrees C) or colder, but as a general rule, if the water feels cold to someone, it is cold. Sudden entry into cold water usually occurs if a person accidentally falls in or intentionally enters the water without proper protection. A person may be swimming underwater and enter a *thermocline*. In any case, cold water can have a serious effect on the person and on the lifeguard making a rescue. The person can become unconscious and drown.

Sudden entry into cold water can cause the following reactions:

- A *gasp reflex*, a sudden involuntary action to "catch one's breath." If the person's face is under water, this reaction can cause water to be inhaled into the lungs.
- If the person's face is not under water, he or she may still begin to breathe rapidly. This can become hyperventilation, which can lead to unconsciousness.
- An increase in heart rate and changes in blood pressure can lead to a heart attack.
- If the person remains in the cold water, he or she may develop hypothermia, which can lead to unconsciousness.

Other effects of cold water. Not all of the effects of cold water are negative. Several factors actually increase a person's chances of survival in cold water, such as the body's response to cold water. In cold water, the body temperature begins to drop almost as soon as the person enters the water. Swallowing water accelerates this cooling. As the body's core temperature drops, body functions come almost to a standstill, so the person requires very little oxygen. Any oxygen left in the blood is diverted to the brain and heart to maintain minimal functioning of these vital organs. Because of this response, some people have been successfully resuscitated with little or no brain damage after being submerged in cold water for an extended period.

Other factors also may increase chance of survival:

- The victim's age — Children have survived cold water immersion more often than adults, possibly because a child's body cools more rapidly.
- **Laryngospasm** — Water taken in by the victim may go to the stomach rather than the lungs because a spasm of the vocal cord can close the airway.
- The water temperature — The colder the water, the faster the mechanism for protecting the brain and heart operates.
- Rapid recovery of the victim — The faster a lifeguard recovers a submerged victim, the greater the victim's chances of survival.

Rescues in cold water. As quickly as possible, you must locate and remove a victim in cold water. However, since cold water affects you the same as the victim, you should perform cold water rescues without entering the water, whenever possible. Extend the rescue tube if it will reach the victim.

If you must enter the water, do not attempt a rescue without assistance. Take your rescue tube with a towline attached to it. A *towline* is a heavy piece of rope or cord attached to rescue equipment. With it, you and the victim can be towed to safety. Whenever possible wear body protection, such as a wetsuit, to minimize the effects of the cold.

Once the victim has been removed from the water, assess his or her condition. Victims who have been submerged in cold water can be alive even though they have the following signs:

- Decreased or undetectable pulse rate.
- No detectable breathing.
- Bluish skin that is cold to the touch.
- Muscle rigidity.

Begin appropriate resuscitation techniques, such as rescue breathing and CPR. Give first aid for hypothermia as soon as possible. Call EMS immediately. The sooner the victim is transported to an emergency care facility and receives professional medical care, the better his or her chances of survival.

SUMMARY

Patrons use waterfront facilities for many activities. When you are guarding such areas, appropriately adapt your injury control strategies and rescue techniques for the specific conditions at the waterfront. You may use additional equipment when lifeguarding at such locations. The more you practice these techniques and use this equipment, the better prepared you will be to lifeguard at a waterfront facility.

STUDY QUESTIONS

1. List the three characteristics of open water that make lifeguarding at waterfront areas different from lifeguarding at pools.
2. List five potential hazards of lifeguarding at a waterfront.
3. List four factors that may determine your zone coverage.
4. List three types of rescue craft that can be used at waterfronts.
5. List at least five different types of equipment that should be in a properly equipped rescue boat.
6. When a drowning person disappears under water in an open-water area, you must make sure that you are swimming in a straight line toward the person. List the two techniques to help you do this.
7. List two pieces of equipment that would help you in an underwater search for a missing swimmer.

Fill in the blank with the correct answer.
8. Clearly define the boundaries of the diving area, and be sure there is sufficient _____ for safe diving.
9. Two water conditions that can affect the safety of swimmers at a waterfront are _____ and _____ .
10. _____ on a rescue board when paddling will give you better visibility.

Circle *True* or *False*.
11. A buddy check is a swim test that one camper gives to the other. True or False?
12. The beach drag is a safe, easy way to bring an unconscious victim out of the water. True or False?
13. In a deep-water line search, the searchers sweep their hands back and forth in front of them along the bottom, making sure to cover the entire area. True or False?

Circle the letter of the best answer or answers.
14. A chart showing contours and physical arrangements of a waterfront is called—
   a) An aquatic chart.
   b) A contour map.
   c) A waterfront guide.
   d) None of the above.
15. In many areas of the country, watch swimmers for signs of hypothermia—
   a) Before a rainstorm.
   b) Early in the season.
   c) Early in the morning.
   d) Late in the season.
16. If wave action reduces your visibility, you may have to—
   a) Ask for additional lifeguards.
   b) Move your lifeguard stand into the water.
   c) Post a sign warning swimmers of possible danger.
   d) Close the area until conditions improve.
17. The buddy system at camp waterfronts helps to ensure that—
   a) Each camper has a friend for the day.
   b) Each camper always wears a colored tag.
   c) No camper is alone in the water at any time.
   d) Campers teach each other to swim.
18. If you find a tag in the "in" section of a buddy board after the water is cleared, this could mean—
   a) The camper forgot to move the tag from the "in" side of the board to the "out" side of the board.
   b) The camper is swimming in another area, and there is nothing to worry about.
   c) The camper decided to go boating.
   d) The camper is probably at the snack bar or bathroom, and there is nothing to worry about.
19. Which of the following entries is particularly useful when entering the water from a shoreline?
   a) Compact jump
   b) Ease-in entry
   c) Run-and-swim entry
   d) Stride jump

20. When using a rescue board to rescue a distressed swimmer, approach the person from—
    a) Behind.
    b) The front.
    c) The side.
    d) Below.
21. To rescue a distressed swimmer when using a boat, carefully approach the person so that he or she can grasp the boat at the—
    a) Stern.
    b) Bow.
    c) Side.
    d) Gunwale.
22. When performing a missing person procedure, you may have to search the following:
    a) Playgrounds, camp sites, and wooded areas at waterfront facilities such as state parks.
    b) Bathrooms, showers, locker rooms, and parking lots.
    c) A camper's cabin or tent and other camp areas.
    d) All of the above.

23. When performing a shallow-water line search, searchers—
    a) Wear mask and fins.
    b) Search in water deeper than chest deep.
    c) Link arms and form a line.
    d) Perform surface dives.
24. Sudden immersion in cold water can cause the following reactions:
    a) Vertigo
    b) Gasp reflex
    c) Hyperventilation
    d) Hypertension
25. Which of the following factors does not help increase the chance for survival in cold water?
    a) Larger body size.
    b) Laryngospasm.
    c) Rapid recovery of the submerged victim.
    d) Colder water temperature.

See answers to study questions on p. 287.

WATERPARK FACILITIES
14

Objectives

After reading this chapter, you should be able to—

1. Explain the difference between a waterpark and other types of multi-attraction aquatic facilities.
2. Describe a winding river and the surveillance issues.
3. Explain safety considerations for dispatching riders at a waterslide, drop-off slide, speed slide, and free-fall slide.
4. Explain surveillance issues for a shallow catch pool, a deep catch pool, and a runout.
5. Explain surveillance issues for a wave pool.
6. Explain surveillance issues for deep- and shallow-water special attractions.
7. List the eight recommended rules for water slides.
8. Explain the safety rules for speed slides and free-fall slides.
9. Define the key terms for this chapter.

After reading this chapter and completing the appropriate course activities, you should be able to—

1. Demonstrate the compact jump from a height and the run-and-swim entry.
2. Demonstrate the walking assist, the front-and-back carry, and the beach drag.
3. Demonstrate a simple assist.
4. Demonstrate in-line stabilization techniques in a winding river, catch pool, and a speed slide.
5. Demonstrate backboarding techniques used at a speed slide.

Key Terms

Catch pool: A small pool at the bottom of a slide where patrons enter water deep enough to cushion their landing.

Dispatch: The method for informing patrons when it is safe to proceed on a ride.

Drop-off slide: A slide that ends with a drop of several feet into a catch pool.

Emergency stop button: A switch used at wave pools to stop the making of waves in an emergency.

Eddy: A condition in which water flows opposite the main current.

Flume: A trough-like structure in a water slide where water is forced through at greater speed.

Free-fall slide: A type of speed slide with a nearly vertical drop giving riders the sensation of falling.

Head wall: The wall at the back of a wave pool housing the mechanical system that creates the waves.

Hydraulic: A hydraulic is a strong force created by water flowing downward over an object and then reversing its flow.

Rapids ride: A rough-water attraction that simulates white water rafting.

Runout: The area at the end of a slide where water slows the speed of the riders.

Speed slide: A steep water slide on which patrons may reach speeds in excess of 35 mph.

Waterpark: An aquatic theme park that consists of a variety of attractions, such as a wave pool, speed slide, or winding river.

Wave pool: A pool that produces waves at various heights, intervals, and patterns.

Winding river: A shallow channel where water flows in a long circular or twisting path through a waterpark.

INTRODUCTION

Swimming pools aren't just swimming pools anymore. Attractions, such as activity pools, play structures, inflatable play equipment, and water slides, are increasingly popular. Facilities with these attractions in addition to a conventional pool are called **multi-attraction aquatic facilities.** *Waterparks* are aquatic theme parks with various attractions, from wave pools to speed slides to winding rivers.

In the last 20 years, the popularity of multi-attraction aquatic facilities has increased tremendously. Millions of people visit them every year. Many **metropolitan** areas have at least one waterpark; some cities have several. Because of their unique features and the large crowds they attract, lifeguards must know and be ready for the specific challenges these facilities present.

Much of what you have learned in previous chapters applies directly to this chapter. The importance of professionalism, teamwork, public relations, and many rescue skills are unchanged. If it has been a while since you read Chapters 1 through 12, you may want to review that material in your text before continuing.

This chapter discusses a variety of aquatic attractions. As with any training in lifeguarding, you must receive specific orientation and in-service training at the facility where you are a lifeguard.

INTERACTING WITH THE PUBLIC

Many factors make lifeguarding at a waterpark facility different from lifeguarding at a conventional pool. Some factors relate to the people who come to the facility. A significant issue is the number of guests who come to a waterpark during a day (Fig. 14-1). While patrons at a pool facility may number in the hundreds, daily attendance at a waterpark is often in the thousands. Rescues occur more often at a waterpark than at a pool.

A second issue involves patrons who have not been to a waterpark before. They are not familiar with the facility or with the mats, rafts, or tubes used on certain attractions. They might become frightened and need assurance. Most important, patrons might not be accustomed to moving water, wave action, currents, or the **turbulence** that sometimes occurs in certain attractions. You

should be ready to give additional assistance to patrons who are caught off balance by waves or water turbulence. In their excitement and eagerness to explore this new environment, guests often do not take the time to read signs or pay attention to the rules. You must be clear when you explain the rules and firm when you enforce them.

For large groups new to a facility, you can hold an orientation. When groups arrive from camps, church organizations, or recreation programs, have someone from your safety team discuss the rules and how to use the various attractions.

A third issue is that waterpark patrons may have only limited swimming ability. Many patrons assume that because they are not going "swimming," they don't need to know how to swim. Many patrons seem to think a waterpark is like an amusement park, only they get wet.

Waterparks may have U.S. Coast Guard–approved life jackets for weak swimmers. While this does not reduce your responsibility to be observant, it may cut down on the number of patrons who need to be rescued (Fig. 14-2). If you see a weak swimmer, suggest that he or she use a life jacket.

In many cases, these three issues are all present at the same time. Many near drownings at waterparks occur when large numbers of patrons, many of whom have little or no swimming ability and are not familiar with the attractions, enter the water for the first time that day.

Waterparks offer entertainment for the whole family.

figure 14-1 *Large numbers of people visit waterparks daily.*

This means that, besides watching out for children, you must also help parents understand the rules. Handle rule enforcement in a fair and friendly manner. You want the children to have fun, but first be concerned that they play safely. In addition, families often split up to go to different attractions. This means that children may roam around the waterpark without adult supervision. Watch for children who seem to be lost, and contact a supervisor to help locate the parents.

Keep an eye out for anyone who may need help. Some patrons may need support while they enter or exit an attraction. Others could have trouble regaining their balance if they fall off an inner tube or are hit by a wave. Some people might not ride all the way to the bottom of a slide. By being aware of such possibilities, you may prevent incidents from occurring.

As at any other aquatic facility, patrons in waterparks may have medical conditions that could lead to heart attacks, strokes, or seizures. The excitement and physical experience of aquatic attractions can lead to a medical incident. Because the patrons are strangers to you, you do not know their medical history. Watch for patrons wearing medical alert bracelets and necklaces.

Patrons who exhibit risky behavior on attractions or get into **confrontations** with other patrons or staff can cause serious problems for lifeguards. Sometimes this behavior is caused by misuse of alcohol or other drugs, which can impair a person's judgment and result in injury. The entire safety team should be alert for signs of belligerent or risky behavior and for obvious signs of misuse of alcohol or other drugs. Prohibit anyone who is behaving in a risky or threatening way from using the attraction. If a problem develops, contact your supervisor immediately.

Patrons come to waterparks to have a good time. In the process, they might ignore their own limitations, feel they know more about an attraction than they actually do, or simply get caught up in the excitement of the day. Set a positive tone in the way you assist them and by being clear and consistent in the way you enforce the rules.

figure 14-2 *Some waterparks provide life jackets for weak swimmers.*

Amusement Parks and Waterparks: A Combination of Fun

Today's society is looking for the most fun they can get for the least money. This certainly applies to commercial recreation facilities. Customers want an all-inclusive package of entertainment for the whole family at a reasonable cost. Many amusement parks are adding water attractions to offer more options to the customer, and in some cases, amusement parks and waterparks are being built together to appeal to all types of patrons. These all-inclusive parks offer a wide variety of activities from roller coasters to wave pools, kiddie rides to magic shows, food courts to video parlors, and miniature golf to concerts. As you can see, there is something for everyone.

Charles M. Neuman/Water Technology, Inc.

INJURY PREVENTION

Chapters 4 to 6 discuss injury prevention strategies for aquatic settings: communication, patron surveillance, and facility surveillance. You use the same strategies with minor modifications in a waterpark facility.

Rules and regulations

Signs give instructions and list rules that patrons must follow. If there are many signs posted, patrons might become confused or might not take the time to read the signs. Keep an eye out for those patrons who might not be paying attention to signs. Some aquatic facilities have **multilingual** signs and taped messages.

Waterpark facilities commonly require patrons to be a minimum height to use some attractions (Fig. 14-3). One common measure is that patrons must be at least 42 inches tall. This cutoff is usually based on manufacturer's recommendations that patrons be at least 6 inches taller than the depth of the catch pool. A *catch pool* is a small pool at the end of a slide where patrons enter water deep enough to cushion their landing. On the other hand, in some areas for small children, children over a certain height or age are not allowed to play in the area with the younger children.

A second type of warning sign gives the water depth in the catch pool of a given attraction. Some catch pools are shallow enough for patrons to stand up in them.

Others are very deep for the safety of patrons plunging into them. Guests may be caught off guard when they move from an attraction with a shallow catch pool to another with a deep catch pool.

A third sign found at many waterpark facilities warns that people with certain medical conditions could have a problem on some attractions. High blood pressure, a history of heart ailments, seizure disorders, and pregnancy could be affected either by the physical characteristics of an attraction or by the level of excitement that an attraction generates.

Safety checks

When you perform safety checks at any time of the day, follow the safety check form for your facility. Your safety check should include all areas open to the public. Take test rides on all attractions. When inspecting slides, look especially for rough spots in the **caulking** between sections of the slide (Fig. 14-4). If the joints are not smooth, riders may be injured while riding down the slide.

If possible, correct any unsafe conditions before the facility opens. If you cannot correct a problem yourself, contact your supervisor immediately. Any time a prob-

figure 14-4 *During daily safety checks, lifeguards should inspect all attractions and equipment.*

figure 14-3 *Many waterparks require patrons to be a minimum height to use some attractions.*

lem occurs during the day, contact the appropriate staff person immediately.

At some facilities, lifeguards check the equipment that patrons use, such as rafts, tubes, and sleds. Whether this is your responsibility or someone else's, stay alert all day for any equipment that seems to be damaged so that it can be repaired or replaced.

Check light signals, the public address system, telephones, and two-way radios daily. If you notice a problem with water quality, water levels, or water temperature, notify your supervisor.

Make sure all safety equipment is in its appropriate place. Rescue tubes must be in good condition and present at necessary stations. Make sure backboards with head immobilizers and straps are readily accessible (Fig. 14-5). Safety equipment should be put away when the facility is closed so that it is not damaged by weather or stolen. Make sure that the first aid station is clean, and check supplies daily.

Lifeguard rotation

Your day at a waterpark typically starts with safety and equipment checks. Be in your assigned position before the facility opens. During the day, you move from one

figure 14-5 *Backboards with a head immobilizer should be readily accessible in case of an emergency.*

station to another according to the schedule your supervisor prepares. You may rotate through different kinds of attractions and at different positions at the same attraction. This keeps you alert and your surveillance skills sharp.

Rotation is usually based on the locations of the stations, whether they are sitting or standing stations, whether they require the lifeguard to be in the water, and the number of patrons typically using the attractions. How long you stay at a station and how often you have breaks depends on the facility.

Weather

If you work at an outdoor facility, watch for heavy rain and thunderstorms. A lifeguard at the top of a slide tower has a good vantage point to track approaching storms. If you see a storm coming closer, tell your supervisor. Since it takes several minutes to clear patrons from all attractions, you may have to begin closing before the storm arrives. The supervisor may use the public address system to tell patrons the facility is closing and give instructions. Lightning often strikes tall metal structures, electrical wires, and moving water. Attractions, therefore, are prime targets for lightning. Follow the emergency action plan at your facility when severe weather threatens.

SURVEILLANCE

Chapter 5 discusses zone coverage and how to scan your area. You also learned how to recognize a person who needs help in the water. You can adapt the information and skills to the waterpark facility.

Follow three general principles for patron surveillance at all waterparks. First, watch patrons as they enter or exit an attraction. This includes setting proper intervals when you dispatch riders. *Dispatch* is the method of starting patrons safely on a ride.

Second, keep patrons in view as long as possible. On some attractions, this can be a problem. On long water slides, you might be able to see only the beginning or end of a ride. In other cases, caves, enclosed body tubes, bridges, buildings, and other structures may prohibit you from seeing the patron at all times.

Third, be aware of the added risk of play equipment. Structures that patrons sit on, climb on, or swim over or under can pose hazards. Carefully supervise such equipment. Patrons may also fall off mats, rafts, or tubes and be injured or pose a hazard to other patrons.

Winding rivers

A *winding river* is a shallow channel where water flows in a long circular or twisting path through a waterpark (Fig. 14-6). Water pumps maintain a steady current, and patrons float along slowly on inner tubes. Lifeguards may be stationed at entrances and exits and at sitting or walking positions with overlapping areas of responsibility (Fig. 14-7).

The facility sets guidelines for winding rivers, like other attractions, following the manufacturer's guidelines. Common rules and recommendations for winding rivers follow:

- Patrons should enter and exit the winding river only at designated locations. They should not jump or dive into the water.
- Patrons should stay in tubes at all times.
- Patrons may not be allowed to walk or swim in the winding river.
- Patrons should not stack up tubes.
- Only one patron is allowed per tube, except when an adult is holding a small child. *The child should be wearing a life jacket, in case the adult tips over.*

figure 14-6 *Winding river.*

figure 14-7 *Lifeguards may be stationed at entrances and exits and sitting or walking positions with overlapping areas of zone coverage at winding rivers.*

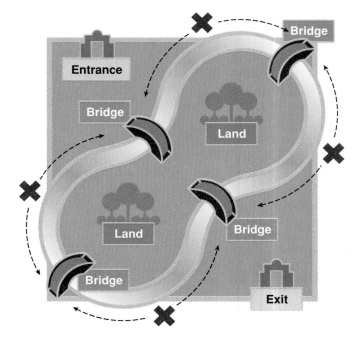

figure 14-8 *Water slide.*

Water slides

Water slides are long, winding slides, usually made of fiberglass or concrete (Fig. 14-8). Water is forced down the slide from the top into a catch pool. Some slides are enclosed in a tube, while others are open. There are many types of slides, but the lifeguarding principles are generally similar.

On some slides, patrons ride on an inner tube, raft, or mat; on other slides, no equipment is used. Do not let patrons stop or slow down on slides or form chains of riders. Usually only one person rides on an inner tube or a raft. Some parks let two or more people go down the slide together on a special tube or raft. On an inner tube or raft, the riding position is feet first in a sitting position (Fig. 14-9). If a mat or other equipment is not used, the riding position is face up and feet first.

You have several duties when stationed at the top of a slide. You may have to tell patrons how to ride down the slide, and you may have to help some patrons with their equipment. Make sure all patrons are tall enough to use the slide. You may have to measure patrons with a pole or stick to see if they are tall enough to stand in the catch pool. Some facilities use animal characters or lines on the wall as measuring devices.

Take care to dispatch riders at the right intervals to prevent one rider from catching up with the one ahead. Allow more time after lightweight riders and children, who go down the slide more slowly than larger riders. Every slide is unique, and each one should be tested to determine the safest dispatch time. Do not dispatch riders more quickly than the facility allows.

You may be stationed at the bottom of a slide in the catch pool. There you supervise riders on the slide and help them get out of the water. Watch for riders who may hit their head on the bottom of the catch pool.

A *hydraulic* is a strong force created by water flowing downward over an object and then reversing its flow. A hydraulic can be created by the water running off a water slide into the catch pool. Hydraulics produce a strong downward force that can knock a person off balance and can even hold a small or weak swimmer under water. Watch for this situation, and help the person stand up (Fig. 14-10).

In some situations, riders in the middle of a slide may need help. Riders may stop, slow down, or stand up on the slide. Such behavior may lead to an injury. Riders may also lose their mat, tube, or raft and have trouble getting down the slide. Riders may also hit their head on the side of the slide. When stationed at the top or the bottom of a slide, watch for these problems. At some

figure 14-9 *The riding position on water slides when using a inner tube or raft is feet first in a sitting position.*

figure 14-10 *Lifeguards stationed at bottom of slides should help patrons to their feet if they are caught off balance by turbulent water caused by hydraulics.*

figure 14-11 *Drop-off slides.*

Paula Panton/Water Safety Products

figure 14-12 *Speed slides.*

figure 14-13 *Runout at end of speed slide.*

very long slides, a lifeguard stationed in the middle of the slide watches and helps riders.

Common guidelines for water slides follow:

- No swimsuits or shorts with metal rivets, buttons, or fasteners on the water slides.
- Patrons must be a certain height to ride water slides.
- Eyeglasses or sunglasses are not advised on the slide.
- Sliding in a feet-first, face-up position only.
- No running, standing, kneeling, rotating, or tumbling on slides, and no stopping in *flumes* or tunnels.
- No diving into catch pools.
- Exit from the catch pool quickly.
- Do not cross in front of another slide when exiting from the catch pool.

Drop-off slides. A *drop-off slide* ends with a drop of several feet into the catch pool (Fig. 14-11). Patrons often need help in the water because they do not realize the catch pool is deep. Obviously, nonswimmers need help, but even good swimmers might be surprised when they enter water deeper than they expect.

When stationed at the top of a drop-off slide, make sure that riders are sitting or lying in a feet-first position. Be sure each rider has time to move out of the catch pool before dispatching the next. When stationed at the bottom, follow the same guidelines as with all water slides.

Speed slides. A *speed slide* is steep, and patrons may reach speeds over 35 mph (Fig. 14-12). Some speed slides have runouts to slow patrons to a safe stop. A *runout* is the area at the end of a slide where water slows the rider (Fig. 14-13). The water in a runout is several inches deep. Speed slides are usually straight, but some of them have small hills or rises. Only one person may go down the speed slide at a time. The recommended riding position is *feet first, lying on the back, with legs crossed at the ankles and arms crossed over the chest.* This riding position reduces the risk of injury and lets the rider reach a high speed.

When stationed at the top of a speed slide, do not dispatch a rider until the previous rider has left the runout or the catch pool and the lifeguard at the bottom has signaled for the next rider. If you can see the lifeguard at the bottom, a hand signal along with a whistle may be used. If the lifeguard at the top cannot see the lifeguard at the bottom, a mechanical signal often is used. A green flag indicates that the runout or catch pool is clear (Fig. 14-14).

When stationed at the bottom of a speed slide, you may have to help patrons out of the runout or catch pool because they may be disoriented or frightened from the ride.

Guidelines usually recommended by manufacturers of speed slides follow:

- Do not wear a life jacket because it may cause the rider to get caught or hung up.
- Eyeglasses, sunglasses, and goggles are not advised.
- Do not wear water shoes or sandals.

Free-fall slides. A *free-fall slide* is a speed slide with a nearly vertical drop that gives riders the sensation of falling. The free-fall slide is usually the tallest attraction at a waterpark. It is like a speed slide but has a steeper angle (Fig. 14-15). Because of the very high speed produced by such a slide, the ride lasts only a few seconds before the rider comes to rest in the runout.

Lifeguarding responsibilities at the top and bottom of a free-fall slide are like those for speed slides. At the top of a free-fall slide, give patrons specific directions:

- Riders in line must stand back away from the slide.
- Riders must wait for your signal to start. Signal only when you are sure the previous rider is out of the runout.
- Riders should lie flat, with ankles crossed and arms crossed over the chest.
- Riders must not sit up for any reason until they come to a complete stop.

Not following these directions can cause the following injuries:

- Friction burns on the legs and arms
- Bumps and bruises if the rider sits forward and then starts to roll down the slide
- Spinal injuries, broken bones, or sprains if the rider tumbles or twists down the slide

figure 14-14 *A green flag indicates to the lifeguard that the runout is clear.*

figure 14-15 *Free-fall slides.*

Paula Panton/Water Safety Products

Wave pools

A *wave pool* produces waves of various heights, intervals, and patterns. Wave pools are often the most popular attraction at a waterpark. They come in various sizes, shapes, and depths (Fig. 14-16). At one end is the *head wall,* a raised wall at the back of a wave pool that houses the mechanical system that creates the waves. The head wall may also be used as an observation deck where lifeguards have a better view of the wave pool (Fig. 14-17).

In some pools, waves are created by a system that blows air into chambers behind the head wall to make the waves. The air pressure on the water creates a wave that is pushed out through the bottom of the chamber into the pool (Fig. 14-18, *A* and *B*). In other pools, waves are generated by a system that uses mechanical paddles to press the water out into the pool (Fig. 14-19, *A* and *B*). The paddles are controlled by a computer and can be programmed to move at different times, creating different wave patterns at different heights. Still other pools create waves by releasing a large amount of water through chambers in the head wall (Fig. 14-20), producing a large breaking wave similar to ocean surf. Learn the patterns of waves at your facility and how they move through the pool.

A typical wave operation cycle is 10 minutes on and 10 minutes off, although times may vary. When the waves are on, stand to get a better view of the patrons (Fig. 14-21). When the waves are off, you can sit, but keep scanning your area. Rotation is often done at this time.

Lifeguards may be stationed at various places around or in a wave pool. The number of lifeguards depends on the size and shape of the pool and the number of people in the water (Fig. 14-22, *A* and *B*). More lifeguards may be assigned as the number of patrons increases.

Some lifeguard chairs have an *emergency stop button* (Fig. 14-23 on page 273) to stop the generation of waves in an emergency. Before entering the water to perform a rescue, you push this button. In some facilities, other lifeguards push their buttons if the first lifeguard's button does not stop the waves. The emergency action plan should also designate which lifeguard covers your zone while you are performing a rescue.

In wave pools, patrons often venture out to where the water breaks because it is exciting. However, weak swimmers can be knocked over by the waves or carried into deeper water. Most wave pool rescues take place where the waves break.

Let wave pool users enter the pool only at the shallow end. Do not let patrons dive into the waves. Keep the areas around ladders and pool railings clear of patrons so that others can exit from the pool quickly as needed.

Most waterparks rent or provide inner tubes or inflatable rafts for the wave pool. Keep a lookout for weak swimmers falling off their inner tube in deep water. A large number of inner tubes in the water makes it difficult to see all patrons and the bottom. In an extremely crowded pool, a swimmer who falls off an inner tube or inflatable raft may have trouble coming up for air if the inner tubes or rafts block the surface.

figure 14-16 *A wave pool.*

figure 14-17 *A head wall at a wave pool.*

figure 14-18 **A,** *A system that blows air pressure into chambers behind the head wall to create waves.* **B,** *Air pressure on the water creates a wave that is pushed out through the bottom of the chamber into the pool.*

A

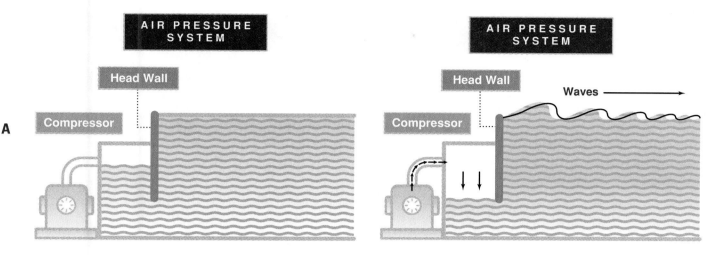

B

figure 14-19 **A,** *A system that uses mechanical paddles to press water out into the pool.* **B,** *Paddles are controlled by a computer and can be programmed to move at different times, creating different wave patterns at different heights.*

A

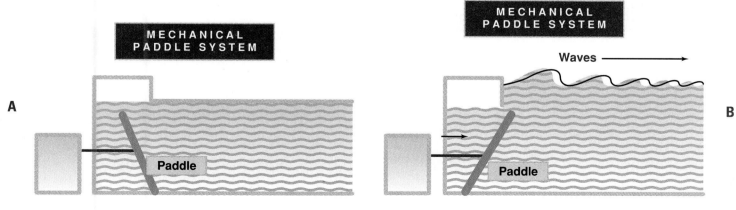

B

figure 14-20 *Large amounts of water are forced through chambers in the head wall and are released into the pool to create waves.*

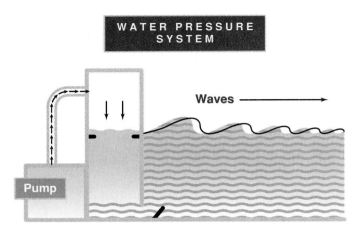

figure 14-21 *Lifeguards should stand while the wave cycle is on for a better view of their zone.*

figure 14-22 *Lifeguard coverage at a wave pool depends on the size and shape of the pool and the number of patrons in the pool.* **A,** *Four-lifeguard zone coverage.* **B,** *Eight-life-guard zone coverage.*

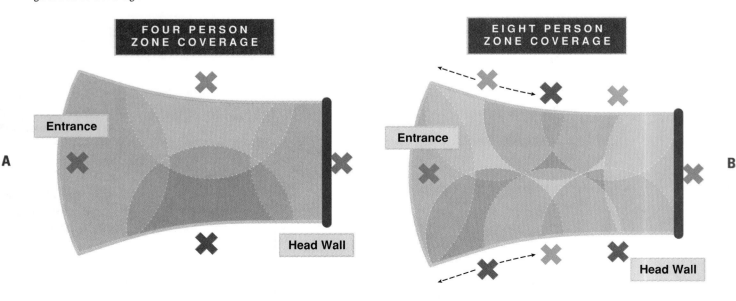

figure 14-23 *An emergency stop button at a wave pool.*

If a swimmer is hit unexpectedly by an inflatable raft, it could create problems. Swimmers may be knocked down by rafts and injured if they hit the cement bottom. A swimmer hit by a raft can quickly become distressed. Adapt your scanning technique for all these situations. Shift your position to eliminate blind spots, and give more attention to high-risk situations.

Some wave pools allow special activities like surfing at certain times. Anytime surfboards or **boogie boards** are allowed in the wave pool, nonsurfing patrons should stay out of the pool because of the hazards.

Kiddie areas

Many waterparks have shallow pools for small children. These areas may have play equipment like slides, swings, fountains, inflatable play equipment, and climbing structures (Fig. 14-24). Consistently enforce the rules at kiddie areas, such as height and age requirements. These rules help ensure the safety of the children. Older children often play more roughly, and they may be too large to play on some structures.

Lost children are a common problem. In an enclosed area, fewer children become lost. Encourage adults to supervise their children at all children's pools.

Another common problem in the kiddie area is children using the pool as a bathroom. Your facility should have a standard procedure for handling this situation, following local health department guidelines.

Children often do not realize the dangers of water and sun. If a child is getting sunburned, tell the child's adult guardian immediately.

figure 14-24 *Kiddie areas include many different types of play equipment for children.*

Special attractions

Some waterparks have deep-water pools that include activities such as specialty slides, diving platforms, cable swings, and hand-over-hand activities like ropes, nets, and rings (Fig. 14-25). These attractions have new surveillance challenges. Your attention may be divided between the water below and activities overhead. Patrons may experience injuries, such as becoming entangled in ropes, getting friction burns on the hands, and other problems. Your orientation and in-service training will include how to dispatch these attractions, the position you should guard from, and the age, height, and swimming ability a patron must have.

Many facilities have rope and cable swings above deep-water pools. Allow only one person to swing at a time. Do not allow horseplay on platforms. Be alert that

figure 14-25 *Some facilities have special attractions, such as specialty slides, diving platforms, cable swings, and hand-over-hand activities.*

figure 14-27 *On river rapid rides, lifeguards should be placed at various locations along the ride so that all parts of the ride are supervised.*

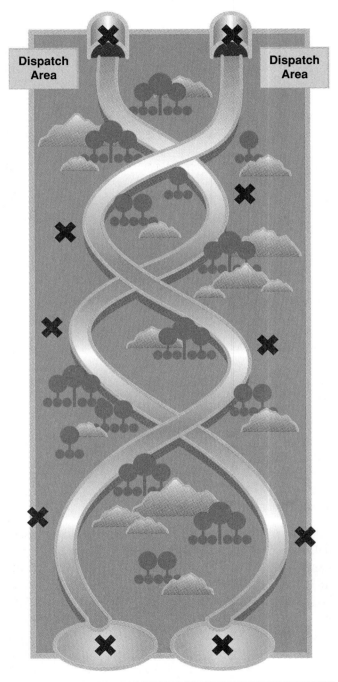

figure 14-26 *Some facilities have shallow water activities, such as lily pads where patrons walk from one floating structure to another.*

Paula Panton/Water Safety Products

patrons might not realize that the water depth varies at different attractions.

Shallow-water activities also are common, such as "lily pads"—flat, floating structures tethered to the bottom of the pool. Patrons try to walk from one lily pad to another, holding on to an overhead rope (Fig. 14-26).

You have already read about some other activities, such as play structures and shallow-water–activity pools. Review Chapter 5 on the surveillance techniques, lifeguard positioning, and guidelines for those attractions.

Some parks have a *rapids ride,* a rough-water attraction that simulates white-water rafting. Patrons ride in inner tubes or rafts in the same position as recommended for water slides. Lifeguards are typically positioned at the top, at the bottom, and at points between to supervise all parts of the ride (Fig. 14-27). Lifeguarding procedures are similar to those at water slides and winding rivers.

Another attraction is a slide on which the rider sits on a plastic sled. Some facilities have a height requirement for this attraction. The lifeguard at the top of the slide controls dispatch of sledders by means of a mechanical lift. Usually two side-by-side slides operate at the same time. The lifeguard at the bottom watches for sleds that may flip over or collide as they exit the slide. Lifeguards at the top and bottom use a signaling system to regulate dispatch. Lifeguarding procedures are similar to those at other slides.

PREPARING FOR EMERGENCIES

The entire staff at the facility may be part of the safety team. This includes **concessionaires,** equipment rental personnel, admissions personnel, security guards, maintenance personnel, and emergency medical personnel. In an emergency, these people may help control crowds, meet arriving EMS personnel, help clear attractions, make announcements on the public address system, and even help with first aid.

Depending on the facility's size, the training may vary for different employees. At a small facility, each staff member may be trained to perform multiple tasks. A large facility, however, may have many levels of training. Each staff person should know his or her role in the emergency action plans. A sample emergency action plan for a waterpark follows:

Sample *Emergency Action Plan*

In case of an emergency, you should be prepared to respond as follows:
- When you spot a patron who needs help, activate the facility's emergency action plan. By immediately blowing one long, loud whistle blast, you notify your safety team that there is an emergency. Once you have given the signal, members of the safety team can react to the situation.
- Once you activate the emergency action plan, stop the waves or slide dispatch. At a wave pool, hit your emergency stop button to be sure the waves are turned off. If you are on duty at the top of an attraction, do not dispatch any more riders. Communication between the top and bottom positions is vital. Use predetermined whistle signals, hand signals, flags, or lights, or a combination of these to indicate that there is an emergency.
- Determine which method of rescue is needed. If it is necessary to enter the water to make a rescue or an assist, use the entry most appropriate for the location you are lifeguarding. For example, you might use a compact jump from a head wall. If it isn't necessary to enter the water, use the appropriate equipment to help the victim.
- If you are not the lifeguard making the rescue, make sure the rescuing lifeguard's zone is covered. At a deep-water attraction, all lifeguards should stand in their lifeguard chairs and adjust zone coverage to compensate for the lifeguard who is making the rescue. At a shallow-water attraction, even though dispatch should be stopped, have a nearby lifeguard move to a place where he or she could cover his or her own zone along with the rescuing lifeguard's zone. A lifeguard who is nearby on a break may provide backup surveillance and take over the position of the rescuing lifeguard. If two lifeguards must enter the water to make rescues, other guards come in to cover their positions. At a single-guard attraction, the rescuing lifeguard's area should be covered by the lifeguard at the attraction closest to where the rescue is taking place.
- Once the situation is under control, the lifeguard who made the rescue also completes and files an incident report as soon as time permits. This report form should have a diagram of the pool or activity on the back so that the location of the incident can be marked for future study. All people involved must complete the appropriate reports.
- All equipment used in the rescue must be in good condition and replaced in its original spot. Lifeguards return to duty, if able, and patrons are allowed to participate in the activity again if there are enough guards to cover it.

Communication

Communication is essential to safety in a waterpark. Chapter 7 describes whistle signals and hand signals for communicating with other lifeguards. Some facilities use other signals, including a public address system, telephones, air horns, two-way radios, and electrical light systems (Fig. 14-28). A public address system is a good way to communicate with patrons and staff in an emergency. Often head lifeguards use two-way radios to communicate with supervisors and other staff.

RESCUE SKILLS

You can use all the rescue skills you learned in Chapters 8 and 11 at a waterpark facility. Additional skills for entering the water, assisting victims, and removing victims from the water are described here. You will also learn some modifications for spinal injury management.

Rescue equipment

The rescue tube is the most effective piece of lifeguarding equipment. At waterparks, however, you may not use a rescue tube at every station. At a shallow- or deep-water attraction or in or beside a catch pool, you keep a rescue tube with you (Fig. 14-29). At the top of a slide or at the bottom of a slide with a runout, you may not need a rescue tube to perform your job responsibilities.

Entries

Compact jump. Chapter 8 describes the compact jump for entering the water. You use this skill also at attractions with deep enough water. When entering from a height, such as a head wall or a lifeguard chair, use this entry for your own safety. At a wave pool, if waves are still forming, time your jump to land on the crest of a

figure 14-28 *Lifeguards communicate with each other by using telephones.*

figure 14-29 *The rescue tube is an essential piece of rescue equipment.*

wave, not in the trough. The water at the crest is deeper and better cushions your entry. To perform a compact jump—

1 Squeeze the rescue tube high against your chest with the ends under your armpits. Hold excess line in one hand to keep it from getting caught in the lifeguard chair or other equipment (Fig. 14-30).

2 Jump out and away from the wall or lifeguard chair, with your knees bent and your feet together and flat to absorb the shock if you strike the bottom. Do not point your toes or enter with straight or stiff legs.

3 The buoyancy of the rescue tube helps bring you back to the surface.

4 When you surface, focus on the victim and begin your approach.

figure 14-30 *When performing a compact jump, jump out and away from the wall with your knees bent and your feet together.*

Run-and-swim entry. To enter the water from a gradual slope, such as in a wave pool, use the run-and-swim entry. To perform this skill—

1 Hold the rescue tube in your hand and run into the water, lifting your legs to avoid falling (Fig. 14-31).

2 When you reach the point where you can no longer run, put the rescue tube across your chest, lean forward, and start swimming. *Do not dive or plunge into the water because this can result in serious injury.*

figure 14-31 *When performing a run-and-swim entry such as in a wave pool, run into the water, lean forward, placing the tube across your chest, and start to swim.*

Assists

Assists are the most common form of help you most often give to patrons. To perform an assist in any water attraction, first consider—

• The nature of the problem.
• The person's condition.
• The strategy that will be most effective.

Assists include—

• Supporting patrons who are entering and exiting an attraction.
• Helping patrons in or out of inner tubes or rafts.
• Helping a tired swimmer in deep water reach shallow water.
• Helping patrons who are stuck in a slide or who become frightened. (Sometimes you may have to climb up the slide to reach them or catch them when they come down.)

Talking to the person during the assist is calming and makes him or her more at ease. If you see that a rescue is needed rather than an assist, activate the emergency action plan. The plan should specify circumstances in which you must enter the water to make a rescue.

Simple assist. In some lifeguarding positions, you are stationed in the water, such as standing in a catch pool. A simple assist may be as easy as helping a person to his or her feet. You can do this in two ways:

1 Keeping your rescue tube between you and the person who needs help, reach across the tube and grasp the person at the armpit to help maintain his or her balance (Fig. 14-32, *A*).

2 If the person is under water, grasp him or her under the armpits with both hands and help the person stand up (Fig. 14-32, *B*).

Using a Second Lifeguard to Assist with a Rescue

When you are guarding at a wave pool or at a deep-water attraction, you may need extra assistance from another lifeguard when making a rescue. If the person who needs help seems to be violent or if he or she is considerably larger than you, signal for another lifeguard to assist you. Do not attempt the rescue alone.

The second lifeguard signals that he or she is entering the water then swims to the front of the victim while you remain in the back. At the count of three, the second lifeguard pushes his or her rescue tube into the victim's chest while you reach under the victim's armpits and grasp the second rescuer's rescue tube, squeezing the victim between the two rescue tubes. When the victim is under control, the second rescuer swims forward, pushing both the victim and you to the wall or to shallow water.

figure 14-32 A, *When helping a patron to his or her feet, a simple assist is easily done by reaching across the rescue tube and grasping him or her with one hand under the armpit.* **B,** *When helping a patron who has gone beneath the surface, a simple assist is easily done by reaching across the rescue tube and grasping him or her with both hands under the armpits.*

A

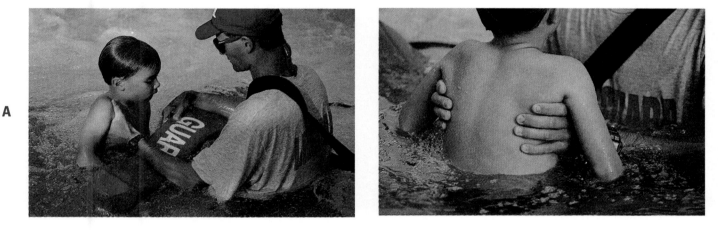

B

Removal from water

You have three easy techniques for helping someone out of shallow water: the walking assist, the front-and-back carry, and the beach drag.

Walking assist. Use the walking assist to help a conscious victim walk out of the water on a gradual slope, such as the entrance of a wave pool. To do this—

1 Place one of the victim's arms around your neck and across your shoulder.

2 Grasp the wrist of the arm that is across your shoulder, and wrap your free arm around the victim's back or waist to provide support.

3 Maintain a firm grasp and help the victim walk out of the water (Fig. 14-33).

figure 14-33 *Assisting a conscious victim from shallow water.*

Front-and-back carry. Use the front-and-back carry with a large victim who is unconscious or who cannot get out of the water without assistance. Do not use this technique if you suspect the victim has a spinal injury.

To do this—

1 Call a second lifeguard for assistance.

2 Get behind the victim, and reach under the armpits. Grasp the victim's wrists, your right hand on the right wrist and left hand on left wrist. Cross the victim's arms across his or her chest (Fig. 14-34, *A*).

3 The second rescuer stands between the victim's legs, facing the same direction as you and the victim. The second rescuer bends down and grasps the victim under the knees (Fig. 14-34, *B*).

4 On signal, the two rescuers lift the victim and carry him or her out of the water (Fig. 14-34, *C*).

Beach drag. The beach drag is a safe way to bring an unconscious victim or a person who is very heavy and unable to walk from the water. Do not use this technique if you suspect the person has a spinal injury. Once you bring the victim to shallow water, call for assistance from another lifeguard if available. Remove the strap of the rescue tube or put it on the victim's side to keep it out of your way so that you don't trip on it.

1 Stand behind the victim and grasp him or her under the armpits, supporting the victim's head when possible with your forearms.

2 While walking backward, drag the victim toward shallow water (Fig. 14-35, *A* and *B*).

3 Remove the victim completely from the water or at least to a point where the head and shoulders are out of the water.

A

B

figure 14-34 *When helping a victim who is unconscious get out of the water, the front-and-back carry is performed by* **A,** *grasping the victim's wrists and crossing them against the victim's chest.* **B,** *The second rescuer bends down and grasps the victim under the knees.* **C,** *Both rescuers lift the victim and carry him or her out of the water.*

C

figure 14-35 *A* and *B*, To remove an unconscious victim from the water, the beach drag may be performed by either one lifeguard or two.

figure 14-36 *A* and *B*, Once you have established in-line stabilization in a winding river, slowly turn the victim so that the current pulls his or her legs around to point downstream.

Spinal injury management

Use the same techniques for spinal injury management you learned in Chapter 11. In-line stabilization and backboarding are difficult to perform in certain waterpark attractions. Moving water, as in a winding river or a catch pool, and confined spaces like a speed slide can both present problems. In your orientation and in-service training, you should learn and practice in-line stabilization and backboarding procedures often in the attractions themselves.

Spinal injury management in winding rivers. Spinal injury is rare in winding rivers, but it can happen anytime. Rough horseplay in inner tubes or jumping or diving into the water could lead to a spinal injury. Your concern with moving water is that the current can pull or move the victim. The emergency action plan at your facility may include signaling to another lifeguard to turn off the flow of water if possible. Other lifeguards or patrons can help you keep objects and people from floating into you as you support the victim.

Another problem in a winding river is that the current could press sideways on the victim or force the victim into a wall, twisting his or her body. For this reason, keep the victim's head pointing upstream whenever possible. This position also reduces the splashing of water on the victim's face.

Once you have established in-line stabilization and the victim is face up, slowly turn the victim so that the current pulls his or her legs around to point downstream (Fig. 14-36, *A* and *B*). Once the victim is in this position, begin the backboarding procedure.

Spinal injury management in catch pools. The water in a catch pool moves with greater force than in a winding river. This force often creates an *eddy,* a condition in which water flows opposite the main current (Fig. 14-37). The surface of an eddy may be entirely still. As soon as you suspect a spinal injury in a catch pool, signal other lifeguards to stop dispatch. If possible, signal someone to stop the flow of water.

Once you establish in-line stabilization and the victim is face up, move the victim to a part of the catch pool where the water is calmest. When there is only one slide, the calmest area is usually at the center of the catch pool (Fig. 14-38, *A*). When several slides empty into the same catch pool, calmer water is usually between two slides (Fig. 14-38, *B*). Once the victim is in this position, begin the backboarding procedure.

Spinal injury management in a speed slide. With a spinal injury in a speed slide, the confined space causes an extra problem. A spinal injury can occur if the victim's body becomes twisted or turned the wrong way. The victim might strike his or her head on the side of the slide, or the victim might have sat up and tumbled down the slide. In any case, backboarding can be a challenge here.

figure 14-38 *Once you have established in-line stabilization in a catch pool, move the victim to the area that is the calmest.* ***A,*** *In catch pools with one slide the calmest area is in the center of the catch pool.* ***B,*** *In catch pools that have two slides, the calmest area is usually between the two slides.*

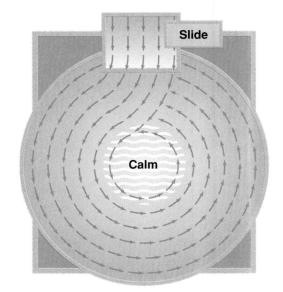

A

figure 14-37 *Water in a catch pool creates a force called an eddy, in which water flows opposite the main current.*

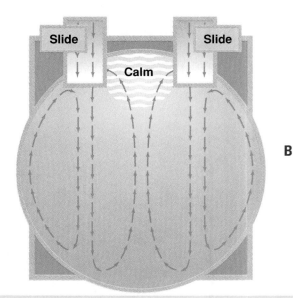

B

Because the water in the slide is only 2 or 3 inches deep, the water does not help support the victim. The following procedure requires several lifeguards:

1 **Immediately stop all dispatch.**

2 **Have someone turn off the water.**

3 **Approach and assess the victim's condition.**

4 **Apply in-line stabilization to the victim's head and neck (Fig. 14-39, *A*). You must maintain in-line stabilization the entire time.**

5 **Additional rescuers kneel along the outside of the slide. They place their hands beneath the victim with their arms and elbows inside the slide.**

6 **Lift the victim enough for the backboard to be slid under the victim (Fig. 14-39, *B*).**

7 **One more rescuer slides the backboard from the feet to the head underneath the victim, making sure that the straps are not caught under the backboard and that the backboard is centered under the victim (Fig. 14-39, *C*). Be careful to maintain in-line stabilization.**

8 **Lower the victim onto the backboard (Fig. 14-39, *D*).**

9 **Using straps and a head immobilizer, secure the victim to the backboard. Lift the backboard out of the slide, and move the victim to safety (Fig. 14-38, *E*). Move slowly and allow time for rescuers to step over the sides of the slide.**

figure 14-39 *When backboarding a victim in a speed slide, several rescuers are needed. The following procedures should be followed. **A,** A rescuer applies in-line stabilization to the head and neck inside the slide. **B,** Rescuers place their hands and elbows inside the slide to lift the victim so that the backboard may be slid in place. **C,** Slide the backboard from the feet to the head underneath the victim. **D,** Lower the victim onto the backboard. **E,** Once the straps and head immobilizer have been secured, lift the backboard out of the slide.*

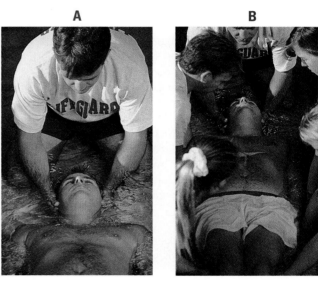

A   B

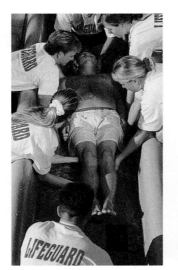

C   D   E

SUMMARY

Waterpark facilities are popular, and more are being built or expanded every year. Existing waterparks are installing new attractions to increase their appeal. You will use most of the skills you learned in earlier chapters in this environment, with some adaptations for the moving water and confined spaces. Your knowledge gained in this chapter helps prepare you for lifeguarding at waterpark facilities.

STUDY QUESTIONS

Short answer.

1. List the three factors that make lifeguarding at a waterpark different from lifeguarding at a conventional pool.

2. List three things you must consider when performing an assist at any type of water attraction.

3. When dealing with either confined conditions like those of a speed slide, or moving water like a winding river, what is the main concern in spinal injury management?

4. List the features that present additional difficulties with in-line stabilization and backboarding that a lifeguard would encounter at a waterpark.

Write the correct answer in each blank.

5. The primary goal of lifeguard rotation is to keep you _____ and _____.

Circle *True* or *False*.

6. Many guests at waterparks assume that, because they are not going "swimming," they do not need to know how to swim. True or False?

7. Dispatch is the technique of informing patrons when it is safe to proceed on a ride. True or False?

8. From a water level of zero, the front-and-back carry is used to help a conscious victim who is tired or distressed out of the water. True or False?

9. The walking assist is a quick and effective way to get an unconscious victim out of a wave pool. True or False?

10. Daily attendance at a waterpark often numbers in the thousands; thus, there are more rescues performed at a waterpark than at a pool. True or False?

Circle the letter of the best answer or answers.

11. If you recognize a weak swimmer, suggest that he or she—
    a) Should request a refund and go home.
    b) Should be especially careful when entering or leaving an attraction so as not to slip and fall.
    c) Only use the kiddie area.
    d) Use a life jacket.

12. When inspecting slides during a safety check, look especially for—
    a) Slick areas that could make the slide too fast, causing possible danger to patrons.
    b) A build-up of suntan lotions or oils, which could damage the slide's finish.
    c) Scratches in the concrete or other slide materials, which could breed bacteria.
    d) Rough spots in the caulking between sections of the slide, which could cause injuries.

13. During the day, be alert for any equipment that seems to be damaged so that—
    a) You can warn patrons about it.
    b) It won't ruin the fun of the attraction.
    c) It can be repaired or replaced with proper equipment.
    d) You don't have to close the attraction.

14. Check light signals, public address system, telephones, and walkie-talkies—
    a) Daily.
    b) Hourly.
    c) When problems arise.
    d) When the battery indicators show low levels.

15. The safety team at a large waterpark includes—
    a) Lifeguards and security guards.
    b) Food vendors and admissions personnel.
    c) Equipment rental and maintenance personnel.
    d) All of the above.

16. The most frequently used lifeguarding equipment at a waterpark is the—
    a) Rescue board.
    b) Rescue tube.
    c) Reaching pole.
    d) Ring buoy.

17. You can use the front-and-back carry if—
    a) The victim has a spinal injury.
    b) The victim is able to walk.
    c) A second lifeguard is available.
    d) You are strong enough to lift the victim by yourself.
    e) All of the above.

18. While making a rescue, if you are entering the water from a height such as a head wall or a guard chair, you must perform a—
    a) Compact jump.
    b) Stride jump.
    c) Run-and-swim.
    d) Ease in.

19. A zero-depth slope would be encountered in a—
    a) Winding river.
    b) Catch pool.
    c) Wave pool.
    d) Runout.

20. If you have brought a victim to shallow water and now need to perform a front-and-back carry, what is your next step?
    a) Get behind the victim, and grasp him or her under the armpits, placing the palms of your hands over the victim's ears and stabilizing the head.
    b) Call a second guard for assistance.
    c) The second rescuer stands facing the front of the victim straddling the victim's legs and grasps under the victim's knees.
    d) On the count of three, lift the victim and carry him or her out of the water. Remember to lift with your legs, not with your back.

21. For spinal injury management in a winding river, once the victim is in a face-up position, the victim's head should be—
    a) Pointing upstream.
    b) Pointing downstream.
    c) Pointing perpendicular to the current.
    d) Pointing diagonally to the current.

22. Which of the following is the first step in spinal injury management for a victim in a speed or free-fall slide once the water at the attraction has been turned off and all dispatch has been stopped?
    a) Lifeguard applies in-line stabilization to the victim's head and neck while the victim is still in the slide.
    b) Lifeguards place their hands beneath the victim with their arms and elbows inside the slide.
    c) Lifeguard rolls victim onto one side.
    d) Lifeguards place victim on backboard.

23. A patron's height is an important consideration in which of the following attractions?
    a) Winding rivers   c) Wave pools
    b) Drop-off slides   d) Speed slides

24. When patrons drop into the water from a drop-off slide, they frequently need assistance because—
    a) The height of the drop makes them dizzy.
    b) They become disoriented.
    c) They do not realize that the catch pool is deep.
    d) The water in the catch pool is moving.

25. The following guidelines are usually recommended by manufacturers of speed slides:
    a) Patrons are advised not to wear eyeglasses, sunglasses, and goggles.
    b) Life jackets must be worn by weak swimmers.
    c) T-shirts are recommended to prevent friction burns.
    d) Water shoes or thongs must be worn.

26. Which of the following are possible injuries a patron could sustain on a free-fall slide?
    a) Friction burns on the arms and legs
    b) Bumps, bruises, and broken bones
    c) Spinal injuries
    d) All of the above

27. The number of lifeguards around or in a wave pool depends on—
    a) The size of the pool.
    b) The shape of the pool.
    c) The number of patrons in the water.
    d) All of the above.

28. Most wave pool rescues occur—
    a) At the sides or wall.
    b) In the deep water.
    c) Where the waves break.
    d) At the entrance to the wave pool.

29. If a child seems to be getting sunburned—
    a) Notify the child's parents immediately.
    b) Take the child out of direct sun.
    c) Suggest the child get into the water.
    d) Put sunscreen on him or her.

30. When you spot a patron in trouble in the water, immediately—
    a) Blow two loud, short whistle blasts, and then react according to your training.
    b) Blow one long, loud whistle blast, and then react according to your training.
    c) Stop the waves or slide dispatch.
    d) Enter the water.

See answers to study questions on p. 287.

ANSWERS TO STUDY QUESTIONS

Chapter 1

1. d	9. a, c, d
2. a, b, c, e, f	10. b, c, d, e
3. a, b, d	11. a, d
4. a, b, d, e	12. a, b, c
5. a, b, d	13. a, b, c, e
6. a, c, d	14. d
7. c	15. False
8. c	16. False

Chapter 2

1. a, b, c, d	7. b
2. a, b, c	8. b, d, e
3. a, c, d	9. c
4. b, c, d	10. 4, 1, 7, 3, 6, 2, 5
5. b, d	11. False
6. a, b, c, e	12. False

Chapter 3

1. a, b, c, d, e	6. a
2. a, b, c	7. a, b, c, d
3. a, b, c	8. False
4. a, b, c, d	9. True
5. a, b, c, d, e	

Chapter 4

1. a, c, d	6. a, b, d
2. d	7. False
3. a, c, d, e	8. 3,
4. a, c, d	2,
5. b, a	4,
	1

Chapter 5

1. a, b, c, e	7. b
2. a, c, d, f	8. b
3. c	9. a, b, c
4. a, b, d, e	10. a, c, d, e
5. a, c	11. False
6. a, b, c, d, e, f	

Chapter 6

1. a, b, c, d, e	6. True
2. a, b, c, d	7. False
3. b	8. False
4. c	9. 1—b, 2—d, 3—c, 4—a
5. a, c, d	

Chapter 7

1. b	5. 3, 2, 5, 4, 1
2. a, b, c, d	6. 2, 1, 4, 3, 5
3. a, b, c, d, e, g, h	7. False
4. a, b, c, d	8. False

Chapter 8

1. 3, 5, 1, 7, 2, 6, 4	6. a, b, c, d
2. a, b, c	7. a, b, c, d, e
3. c	8. False
4. b	9. True
5. d	10. True

Chapter 9

1. b	14. b, c
2. a	15. c
3. c	16. Cool the burned area, Cover the burned area, Care for shock
4. d	
5. d	
6. b	17. 1—towels, pillows 2—folded magazines, boards 3—uninjured leg, chest
7. c	
8. a, b	
9. a	18. False
10. a, b, d	19. False
11. a, b, c	20. Open, closed, burns
12. a, b, c, d	21. Impaled object
13. a, b, c, d	

Chapter 10

1. a, b, c, d	11. a, c
2. a, c, d	12. False
3. a, c	13. False
4. b	14. False
5. a	15. False
6. b	16. False
7. c	17. True
8. d	18. Heat cramps, heat exhaustion, heat stroke
9. b, c, d	19. Allergic or anaphylactic
10. b, c	

Chapter 11

1. b, c, d	6. b
2. a, b, d	7. a, c, d, e
3. b	8. a
4. a, b, c, e	9. a, c, d
5. a, b, c, d, e	10. 4, 2, 3, 7, 1, 6, 5

Chapter 12

1. a, b, c, d	7. a, b, d, e, f
2. a, c, d	8. a, b, c, d
3. a, d	9. a, b, d
4. b, c, d	10. a, b, e
5. b	11. True
6. a, b, c, e,	12. False

Chapter 13

1. Water quality, currents, beach conditions.
2. Underwater hazards, water quality, how the water moves, weather conditions, plants and animals in the water.
3. Size and shape of the waterfront, size and shape of docks and rafts, number of people, types of activities, size of staff, environmental conditions, history of injuries in the area.
4. Power boats, inflatable boats, rowboats, and personal water craft.
5. Extra oars or paddles, several life jackets, rescue tube, reaching pole, anchor and line, first aid kit, bailer.
6. Sightings and cross bearings
7. Mask and fins
8. Water depth
9. Depth and current
10. Kneeling
11. False

12. True
13. True
14. b
15. b
16. d
17. c
18. a
19. c
20. c
21. a
22. d
23. c
24. b
25. a

Chapter 14

1. Very large number of patrons; patrons not accustomed to the attractions; patrons with little or no swimming ability.
2. The nature of the problem, the person's condition, the strategy that will be most effective.
3. Maintaining in-line stabilization.
4. Moving water, confined spaces.
5. Alert and your surveillance skills sharp
6. True
7. True
8. False
9. False
10. True
11. d
12. d
13. c
14. a
15. d
16. b
17. c
18. a
19. c
20. b
21. a
22. a
23. b, d
24. c
25. a
26. d
27. d
28. c
29. a
30. b

GLOSSARY

A

Abandonment Ending care of an ill or injured person without that person's consent or without ensuring that someone with equal or greater training will continue that care.

Abdomen The middle part of the trunk (torso) containing the stomach, liver, and other organs.

Abrasion An open wound in which skin is rubbed or scraped away.

Absorbed poison A poison that enters the body through the skin.

Accommodations Arrangements to help people with disabilities participate in programs and activities.

Active drowning victim A person exhibiting universal behavior that includes struggling at the surface for 20 to 60 seconds before submerging.

Adaptations Things or actions that change or are changed to become suitable for a new or special use or situation, such as a swimming stroke of a person with a disability.

Adrenaline A hormone produced by the body under certain circumstances that speeds up body functions by stimulating the heart and raising blood pressure and blood sugar levels.

Altered consciousness Changed awareness of one's existence, identity, and environment; often appears as confusion, drowsiness, or unconsciousness.

Americans With Disabilities Act (ADA) A federal regulation that requires people with disabilities to be given access to a wide range of opportunities and services.

Anaphylaxis (an ah fi LAK sis) A severe allergic reaction; a form of shock.

Anatomic splint A part of the body used to immobilize an injured body part.

Antihistamine A medication used to treat allergic reactions and cold symptoms.

Antivenin A material used to counteract the poisonous effects of snake, spider, scorpion, and insect venom.

Aquatic injury prevention Acting to prevent the factors that may cause physical harm to patrons at an aquatic facility.

Area of responsibility The zone or area for which a lifeguard conducts surveillance.

Ashen A grayish color that corresponds to pale in people with darker skin.

Assess To examine and evaluate a situation carefully.

Aura An unusual sensation or feeling, such as a visual hallucination; a strange sound, taste, or smell, or an urgent need to get to safety.

Avulsion An open wound in which soft tissue is partially or completely torn away.

B

Backboard A standard piece of rescue equipment at all aquatic facilities, used to maintain in-line stabilization while immobilizing and transporting a victim with a suspected spinal injury.

Balanced diet A selection of foods that provides all essential nutrients.

Bandage Any material used to wrap or cover an injured body part; often used to hold a dressing in place.

Bloodborne Pathogens Standard A federal regulation designed to protect employees from exposure to bodily fluids that might contain a disease-causing agent.

Bone A dense, hard tissue that forms the skeleton.

Boogie board A hard, formed composite board, generally 40 inches long and 30 inches wide, ridden on one's stomach in waves.

Bow   The front end of a boat or rescue board.

Breach of confidentiality   A violation of the legal principle of confidentiality; a violation of a person's privacy by giving out confidential information about that person.

Bulkhead   A movable wall placed in a swimming pool to separate activities or water of different depths.

Buoyancy   The upward force a fluid exerts on bodies in it.

Buoyed lifelines   A rope or line with buoyant floats, used to separate one area of water from another.

Burnout   Physical, mental, or emotional exhaustion; especially as a result of long-term stress.

Bystanders   People at the scene of an emergency who do not have a duty to provide care.

C

Carbon dioxide (CO_2)   A colorless, odorless gas, a waste product of the body, exhaled in respiration.

Carbon monoxide (CO)   A deadly, colorless, odorless gas.

Cartilage (KAR ti lij)   An elastic tissue in the body; in the joints, it acts as a shock absorber when a person is walking, running, or jumping.

Catch pool   A small pool at the bottom of a slide where patrons enter water deep enough to cushion their landing.

Caulking   The puttylike sealant or oakum that stops up the cracks or seams of a slide or pool tile.

Cerebral palsy   A central nervous system dysfunction in which a person has little or no control of the muscles.

Chain of command   The structure of employee and management positions in a facility or organization.

Chemical hazard   A harmful or potentially harmful substance in or around a facility.

Chest   The upper part of the trunk (torso), containing the heart, major blood vessels, and lungs.

Chlorination system   A system that regulates and dispenses the amount of chlorine used in a pool.

Chronic   Long-lasting or recurring.

Civil rights   Rights that belong to a person simply because he or she is a member of the general public.

Closed wound   An injury to the soft tissue in which the damage is under the surface of the skin.

Cold front   The forward edge of a cold air mass advancing under a warmer air mass.

Comprehensive   Large in scope and content.

Concessionaires   The personnel involved in running vending stands.

Concussion   A temporary impairment of brain function caused by any significant force to the head.

Cone   A device about 3 feet tall, shaped like an ice-cream cone, usually red or orange, placed on its circular base as a marker.

Confidentiality   Protecting a victim's privacy by not revealing any personal information you learn about the victim except to law enforcement personnel or EMS personnel caring for the victim.

Confrontation   A face-to-face disagreement or discussion.

Consent   Permission to provide care given by an ill or injured person to a rescuer.

Consequence   Something that logically follows from an action; a result.

Constricted   Compressed, squeezed.

Contour map   A map or chart showing underwater characteristics and structures at a waterfront.

Convulsions   Sudden, uncontrolled muscular contractions.

Crib   An enclosed area in a dock formation with walls extending down to the bottom of a lake.

Criteria   A standard, rule, or test on which a judgment or decision can be based.

Critical burns   Burns that need immediate attention; including all full-thickness burns and some partial-thickness burns.

Critical incident   Any situation that causes people to experience unusually strong emotional reactions that interfere with their ability to function.

Critical incident stress   The stress a person experiences during or after a highly stressful emergency.

Critical incident stress debriefing (CISD)   A process that brings the person or people who have suffered stress together with others who are trained to help them deal with its effects.

Crook of the arm   The inside part of the arm where it bends at the elbow.

Cross bearing   A technique for determining the place where a submerged victim was last seen, performed by two persons some distance apart, each pointing to the place such that the position is where the lines of their pointing cross.

Cultural diversity   Differences among groups of people related to cultural background and exemplified through customs, beliefs, and practices.

Customize   Adjust to suit a particular situation, group, or condition.

D

Daily log   A written journal kept by lifeguards, the head lifeguard, and management containing a daily account of safety precautions taken and meaningful events.

Debris   Bits and pieces of rubbish; litter.

Deep-water line search   An effective pattern for searching in water that is greater than chest deep.

Deformity   An abnormal lump, ridge, or hollow on the body.

Dehydrated   Having lost an abnormal amount of water from the body.

Dehydration   Excessive loss of water from the body or from a specific organ or other body part.

Dermis   The deeper layer of skin.

Diabetes (di ah BE tes)   A condition in which a person's body does not produce enough of the hormone insulin, causing too much sugar to be in the blood.

Diabetic   A person with diabetes.

Diabetic coma   A condition that occurs when diabetics fail to take their insulin.

Diabetic emergency   A situation in which a person becomes ill because of an imbalance of insulin and sugar in the body.

Disability   The loss, absence, or impairment of sensory, motor, or mental function.

Dispatcher   The person who answers the telephone when someone calls EMS; he or she has had special training in dealing with crises over the telephone.

Dislocation   The displacement of a bone from its normal position at a joint.

Disoriented   Being in state of confusion; not knowing place, identity, or what happened.

Dispatch   The method for informing patrons when it is safe to proceed on a ride.

Distressed swimmer   A person capable of staying afloat but likely to need assistance to get to safety.

Diving mount   The structures that support the diving board.

Diving well   A section of the pool beneath the diving board that is deeper than the rest of the pool.

Drain cover   A frame of metal bars placed over a drain so that large debris cannot enter.

Dressing   A pad placed on a wound to control bleeding and prevent infection.

Drop-off slide   A slide that ends with a drop of several feet into a catch pool.

Drug   Any substance other than food intended to affect the functions of the body.

Duty to act   A legal responsibility of certain people to provide a reasonable standard of emergency care; may be required by case law, statute, or job description.

E

Eddy   A condition in which water flows opposite the main current.

Emergency   A sudden, unexpected incident demanding immediate action.

Emergency action plan   A written plan detailing how facility staff are to respond in a specific type of emergency.

Emergency medical services personnel   Trained and equipped community-based personnel dispatched through an emergency number, usually 9-1-1, to provide medical care for ill or injured people.

Emergency medical services (EMS) system   A network of community resources and medical personnel that provides emergency care to victims of injury or sudden illness.

Emergency medical technician (EMT)   A person who has successfully completed a state-approved Emergency Medical Technician training program; paramedics are the highest level of EMTs.

Emergency stop button   A switch used at wave pools to stop the making of waves in an emergency.

Entanglement   Being tangled or twisted in or around an object.

Epidermis   The outer layer of skin.

Epilepsy (EP i lep se)   A chronic condition characterized by seizures that vary in type and duration; can usually be controlled by medication.

Equal Employment Opportunity Commission (EEOC)   A government agency that regulates how employees are recruited, hired, and treated.

Erosion   To wear away by the action of water, wind, or glacial ice.

Evacuation   Withdrawing from a dangerous or threatened area.

F

Facility surveillance   Checking the facility to help prevent injuries caused by avoidable hazards in the facility's environment.

Fainting   A temporary loss of consciousness.

Filter system   A system used to remove solid particles or impurities from water.

Filtration system   See Filter system.

Flat water   Water that has no wave action.

Flume   A structure in a water slide where water is forced through at greater speed.

Follow-up care   Additional care, such as first aid, provided by the lifeguard to a victim, once a rescue has been made.

Forearm   The upper extremity from the elbow to the wrist.

Fracture   A chip, crack, or complete break in bone tissue.

Free-fall slide   A type of speed slide with a nearly vertical drop, giving riders the sensation of falling.

Frontal vision   What you see when looking ahead or in front of you.

Frostbite   The freezing of body parts exposed to the cold.

Fulcrum   The part of the diving apparatus under the center of the board that lets the board bend and spring.

Full-thickness burn   A burn in which both layers of skin are destroyed as well as any or all of the fat, muscles, and blood vessels underneath. (Also called third degree burn.)

G

Gasp reflex A sudden uncontrollable attempt to "catch one's breath."

Geographic location The region or area in which a place exists.

Good Samaritan laws Laws that protect people who willingly give emergency care without accepting anything in return.

Granular chlorine Chlorine in the form of very fine grains or powder.

Ground fault interrupter (GFI) A device designed to eliminate the danger of electric shock or electrocution.

Grounded Allowing an object or structure to conduct electricity into the ground.

H

Hazard Communication Standard A federal regulation designed to protect employees from exposure to hazardous substances in the workplace.

Head immobilizer A device attached to a backboard, used to keep the victim's head from moving in a suspected spinal injury.

Head lifeguard A lifeguard who has a supervisory position in a facility's chain of command.

Head wall The wall at the back of a wave pool housing the mechanical system that creates the waves.

Hearing impairment Partial or total loss of hearing.

Hearsay Information based on the reports of others rather than personal knowledge.

Heat cramps Painful muscle spasms following exercise or work in warm or moderate temperatures, usually involving the calf and abdominal muscles.

Heat exhaustion A form of shock, often resulting from strenuous work or exercise in a hot environment.

Heat stroke A life-threatening condition that develops when the effects of heat cause the body to be unable to cool itself, causing body systems to fail.

Hydraulic A strong force created by water flowing downward over an object and then reversing its flow.

Hyperthermia A condition that occurs when a person's inner core temperature rises above its normal temperature of 98.6 degrees F (37 degrees C) to 102.6 degrees F (40 degrees C) or above.

Hyperventilation The act of taking deep breaths in rapid succession and forcefully exhaling.

Hypothermia A life-threatening condition in which the body is unable to maintain warmth and the entire body cools.

I

Imminent About to occur.

Immobilization The use of a splint or other method to keep an injured body part from moving.

Immobilize To use a splint or other method to keep an injured body part from moving.

Impaired Damaged, restricted, or made worse.

Impaled object An object that remains in an open wound.

Impending About to take place.

In-line stabilization A technique used to minimize movement of a victim's head and neck.

In-service training Regularly scheduled staff meetings and practice sessions that cover lifeguarding information and skills.

Incident An occurrence or event that interrupts normal procedure or brings about a crisis.

Incident report A report filed by a lifeguard who participated in an emergency or other incident.

Induced Brought about or produced.

Inflatable   That which can be filled and swelled up with air or a gas.

Inhaled poison   A poison that a person breathes into the lungs.

Injected poison   A poison that enters the body through a bite, sting, or hypodermic needle.

Injury   The physical harm from an external force on the body.

Instinctive drowning response   The four instinctive characteristics displayed by an active drowning victim. These involve breathing, arm and leg action, body position, and locomotion.

Insulin   A hormone that enables the body to use sugar for energy; frequently used to treat diabetes.

Insulin reaction   A condition that occurs when a diabetic has too much insulin and not enough sugar in the body.

Intrusion   When lifeguards are assigned to perform non-surveillance duties, thus leaving the pool without proper supervision.

J

Joint   A structure where two or more bones are joined.

K

Keeper   A device used to hold a snorkel onto a mask.

L

Laceration   A cut, usually from a sharp object; may have jagged or smooth edges.

Landmarks   An easily seen, identifying feature of a landscape.

Larynogospasm   A spasm of the vocal cords that closes the airway.

Larynx (LAR ingks)   A part of the airway connecting the back of the nose and throat with the trachea (windpipe); commonly called the voice box or vocal cords.

Lifeguard competitions   Events and contests designed to evaluate the skills and knowledge of individual lifeguards and teams of lifeguards.

Ligament   A tough, fibrous connective tissue that holds bones together at a joint.

Locomotion   The power of moving from place to place.

M

Mainstreaming   Including people with disabilities in the same programs and activities as the non-disabled.

Material Safety Data Sheet (MSDS)   A form that provides information about a hazardous substance.

Media   Forms of mass communication, such as newspapers, television, radio, and magazines.

Medical alert tag   A wrist bracelet or neck chain identifying the wearer as a medical risk, such as a diabetic.

Mental function   The brain's capacity to acquire and apply information.

Metabolism   The process by which cells convert nutrients to energy.

Metropolitan   Designating a population area consisting of a central city and smaller surrounding communities.

Mishaps   Unfortunate accidents.

Module   An educational unit that covers a subject or topic.

Multi-attraction aquatic facility   A facility that includes numerous water attractions, such as activity pools, play structures, inflatable play equipment, and water slides, as well as a conventional pool.

Multilingual   Able to speak several different languages.

Multiple sclerosis (MS)   A progressive disease characterized by patches of hardened tissue in the brain or spinal cord.

Murky Dark or cloudy.

Muscle Tissue in the body that lengthens and shortens to create movement.

Muscular dystrophy (MD) A hereditary disease characterized by progressive deterioration of muscles, leading to disability, deformity, and loss of strength.

Musculoskeletal system The body system made up of the muscles, bones, ligaments, and tendons.

N

Negligence The failure to provide the level of care a person of similar training would provide, thereby causing injury or damage to another.

Nonsurf open water Bodies of water, such as lakes, ponds, rivers, bays, reservoirs, and sounds, that do not have waves like the ocean and are not enclosed like a swimming pool.

Nutrients Substances that provide nourishment for growth and development, such as the minerals and vitamins that come from food.

Nutrition The process by which a living organism digests food and uses it for growth and replacement of tissues.

O

Occupational Safety and Health Administration (OSHA) A government agency that helps protect the health and safety of employees in the workplace.

Open wound An injury to soft tissue resulting in a break in the skin, such as a cut.

Ordinance A local government regulation.

Overexertion Too much tiring effort.

Overflow trough The gutter around the top edge of a pool; used to take water into the pool's filtration system and to remove oils and waste floating on the water surface.

Oxygen A tasteless, colorless, odorless gas necessary to sustain life.

P

Pancreas An organ in the body that produces the hormone insulin.

Paralysis A loss of muscle control; a permanent loss of feeling and movement.

Partial-thickness burn A burn that involves both layers of skin. (Also called second degree burn.)

Passive drowning victim An unconscious victim face-down, submerged or near the surface.

Pathogen (PATH o jen) A disease-causing agent; also called a microorganism or germ.

Patron surveillance Maintaining a close watch over the people using your facility.

Pelvis The lower part of the trunk (torso) containing the intestines, bladder, and reproductive organs.

Peripheral vision What you see at the edges of your field of vision.

Personal water craft A motorized vehicle designed for one or two riders that skims over the surface of the water.

Physical hazard A danger related to a physical feature; in an aquatic facility, a danger such as a broken ladder or a missing tile.

Pier A structure built out over the water and supported by pillars or piles; used as a landing place.

Poison Any substance that causes injury, illness, or death when introduced into the body.

Poison Control Center (PCC) A specialized kind of health center that provides information in cases of poisoning or suspected poisoning emergencies.

Policies and procedures manual A manual that provides detailed information about the daily and emergency operations of a facility.

Pressure bandage A bandage applied snugly over a dressing to help control bleeding.

Pressure point A place on the body where an artery can be pressed against the underlying bone to stop or slow bleeding.

Preventive lifeguarding The means of identifying and preventing a life-threatening emergency before it happens.

Professional rescuers Paid or volunteer personnel, including lifeguards, who have a legal duty to act in an emergency.

Public address system An electronic amplification system, used at an aquatic facility so that announcements can be easily heard by patrons.

Pull buoy Two connected styrofoam cylinders used by swimmers to keep the lower body afloat.

Puncture An open wound created when the skin is pierced by a pointed object.

Purifying mechanism See **Purifying system.**

Purifying system A system that cleans and recirculates water.

Q

Quadriplegic Someone who is completely paralyzed from the neck down.

R

Rabies A disease transmitted through the saliva of diseased animals such as skunks, raccoons, foxes, bats, dogs, cats, and cattle.

Rapids ride A rough-water attraction that simulates white-water rafting.

Record keeping Completing and maintaining documentation of incidents, operations, and personnel procedures.

Refusal of care The declining of care by a victim; the victim has the right to refuse the care of anyone who responds to an emergency.

Rehabilitation Restoring to a condition of health.

Rescue tube A vinyl, foam-filled, floating support used in making rescues.

Reservoir A natural or artificial lake or pond in which water is collected and stored for use.

Resuscitation mask A pliable, dome-shaped device that fits over a person's mouth and nose; used to assist with rescue breathing.

Rib cage The cage of bones formed by the 12 pairs of ribs, the breastbone, and the spine.

RID factor Three elements—recognition, intrusion, and distraction—related to drownings at guarded facilities.

Risk management Identifying and eliminating or minimizing dangerous conditions that can cause injuries and financial loss.

Runout The area at the end of a slide where water slows the speed of the riders.

S

Sacrum A triangular bone that forms the end of the pelvis in the back.

Safety check An inspection of the facility to find and eliminate or minimize hazards.

Safety check form A form on which lifeguards record safety inspections they make at the facility.

Safety team A network of people in the facility and EMS system who can respond to and assist a lifeguard in an emergency.

Scanning A visual technique used by lifeguards to properly observe and monitor patrons participating in water activities.

SCUBA Self-contained underwater breathing apparatus.

Seizure (SE zhur)   A disorder in the brain's electrical activity, marked by loss of consciousness and often uncontrollable muscle movement.

Sensory function   The ability to hear, see, touch, taste, and smell.

Shock   A life-threatening condition in which the circulatory system fails to deliver blood to all parts of the body, causing body organs to fail.

Sighting   A technique for noting where a submerged victim was last seen, performed by imagining a line to the opposite shore and estimating the victim's position along that line. (See also **cross bearing**.)

Soft tissues   Body structures, including the layers of skin, fat, and muscles.

Sound targets   Directional devices that use sound to indicate aspects of a facility, such as water depth and location of exits.

Spa   A small pool or tub in which people sit in rapidly circulating hot water.

Spasm   An involuntary and abnormal muscle contraction.

Speed slide   A steep water slide on which patrons may reach speeds in excess of 35 mph.

Spider strap system   An arrangement of straps for a backboard in which one long strap goes the length of the victim's body and attached straps cross the body horizontally.

Spinal column   The linked bones (vertebrae) from the base of the skull to the tip of tailbone (coccyx).

Spinal cord   A bundle of nerves extending from the base of the skull to the lower back and protected by the spinal column.

Splint   A device used to immobilize body parts; applying such a device.

Spokesperson   The person at the facility designated to speak on behalf of others.

Sprain   The stretching and tearing of ligaments and other soft tissue structures at a joint.

Stabilize   To make resistant to sudden change.

Standard of care   The minimal standard and quality of care expected of an emergency care provider.

Starting blocks   Platforms competitive swimmers dive from to start a race.

Statistician   A person who collects, organizes, and interprets numerical information.

Sterile   Free from germs.

Stern   The back end of a boat or rescue board.

Strain   The stretching and tearing of muscles and tendons.

Stress   Any influence, physical, mental, or emotional, that causes tension, distress, or disruption in a person's mental or emotional balance.

Stroke   A disruption of blood flow to a part of the brain, causing permanent damage.

Submerged   Under water, covered with water.

Sun poisoning   A severe reaction to ultraviolet radiation causing nausea, vomiting, headache, fever, and chills.

Sun protection factor (SPF)   The ability of a substance to prevent the sun's harmful rays from being absorbed into the skin; a concentration of sunscreen.

Superficial burn   A burn that involves only the top layer of skin.

Surveillance   A close watch kept over someone or something, such as patrons and the facility.

T

Tactile impairment   Partial or total loss of the sense of touch.

Tendon   A fibrous band that attaches muscle to bone.

Tethered   Fastened or confined.

Thermocline   A layer of water between the warmer, surface zone and the colder, deep-water zone in a body of water in which the temperature decreases rapidly with depth.

Tornado warning A warning issued by the National Weather Service notifying that a tornado has been sighted.

Tornado watch A warning issued by the National Weather Service notifying that tornados are possible.

Torso The human body excluding the head, arms, and legs.

Tourniquet A tight band placed around an arm or leg to constrict blood vessels to stop the flow of blood to a wound.

Towline A heavy piece of rope or cord attached to rescue equipment.

Toxic Harmful, deadly, or poisonous.

Tri-hull A boat with three separate V-shaped hulls.

Trunk The part of the body containing the chest, abdomen, and pelvis.

Turbulence Violent, irregular motion of water, air, or gas.

U

Ultraviolet (UV) light Light rays that can be harmful to the skin and eyes.

Universal response A reaction that everyone has in common.

V

V-hull A V-shaped deep, narrow hull designed on a boat, for use in rough water.

Vandalism An act of violence used to damage an object or a place.

Vertebrae The 33 bones of the spinal column.

Victim An injured or suddenly ill person; a drowning or near-drowning person.

Violence Physical force used to harm a person or damage an object or a place.

Vision impairment Partial or total loss of sight.

Visually impaired A person who is either blind or partially blind.

W

Waterpark An aquatic theme park that consists of a variety of attractions that may include a wave pool, speed slide, or winding river.

Wave pool A pool that produces waves at various heights, intervals, and patterns.

Winding river A shallow channel where water flows in a long circular or twisting path through a waterpark.

Wound Any injury to soft tissue.

Z

Zone A section or division of an area established for a specific purpose. (See also **area of responsibility.**)

APPENDIX A

Organizations that promote aquatics

American Alliance for Health, Physical Education, Recreation and Dance
1900 Association Drive
Reston, Virginia 22091
(703) 476-3400

American Camping Association
Bradford Woods
5000 State Road 67 N
Martinsville, Indiana 46151-7902
(317) 342-8456

American Canoe Association
8580 Cinderbed Road, Suite 1900
P.O. Box 1190
Newington, Virginia 22122-1190
(703) 737-8300

American National Red Cross
Health and Safety Services
8111 Gatehouse Road
Falls Church, VA 22042
(703) 206-7180

American Swimming Coaches Association
301 SE 20th St.
Fort Lauderdale, Florida 33316
(305) 462-6267

Boy Scouts of America
1352 Walnut Hill Lane
Irving, Texas 75038-3096
(214) 580-2000

The Canadian Red Cross Society
1800 Alta Vista Drive
Ottawa, Ontario
Canada K1G 4J5
(613) 739-3000

The Commodore Longfellow Society
2531 Stonington Road
Altanta, Georgia 30338

Council for National Cooperation in Aquatics
P.O. Box 26268
Indianapolis, Indiana 46226
(317) 546-5108

Jeff Ellis and Associates, Inc.
3506 Spruce Park Circle
Kingwood, Texas 77345
(713) 360-0606

Girl Scouts of America
420 Fifth Avenue
New York, New York 10018
(212) 852-5720

International Swim and Dive Federation
Avenue de Beaumont 9
Lausanne 1012
Switzerland

International Swimming Hall of Fame
1 Hall of Fame Drive
Fort Lauderdale, Florida 33316
(305) 462-6536

National Collegiate Athletic Association
6201 College Boulevard
Overland Park, Kansas 66211-2422
(913) 339-1906

National Federation of State High School Associations
11724 Plaza Circle
P.O. Box 20626
Kansas City, Missouri 64195
(719) 464-5400

National Junior College Athletic Association
1825 Austin Bluffs Parkway
P.O. Box 7303
Colorado Springs, Colorado 80933-7305
(719) 590-9788

National Intramural and Recreational Sports Association
850 SW 15th Street
Corvallis, Oregon 97333
(503) 737-2088

National Recreation and Park Association Aquatic Section
650 West Higgins Road
Hoffman Estates, Illinois 60195
(708) 843-7529

National Safety Council
1121 Spring Lake Drive
Itasca, IL 60143
1-800-621-7619

National Spa and Pool Institute
2111 Eisenhower Avenue
Alexandria, Virginia 22314
(703) 838-0083

National Swimming Pool Foundation
10803 Gulfdale, Suite 300
San Antonio, Texas 78216
(512) 525-1227

The Royal Life Saving Society Australia
P.O. Box 1567
North Sidney, NSW 2059
02-957-4799
FX 02-929-5726

The Royal Life Saving Society Canada
La Société Royale de Sauvetage Canada
287 McArthur Ave.
Ottawa, Ontario
Canada K1L 6P3
(613) 746-5694

The Royal Life Saving Society UK
Mountbatten House
Studley
Warwickshire
B80 7NN
0527 853943

Triathlon Federation/USA
3595 East Fountain Boulevard
Suite F-1
P.O. Box 15820
Colorado Springs, Colorado 80935-5820

United States Coast Guard
Commandant (G-NAB)
2100 Second Street, S.W.
Washington, D.C. 20593-0001
(202) 267-1060

United States Coast Guard Auxiliary
3131 North Abingdon Street
Arlington, Virginia 22207
(703) 538-4466

United States Diving, Inc.
Pan American Plaza
201 South Capitol Avenue, Suite 430
Indianapolis, Indiana 46225
(317) 237-5252

United States Lifesaving Association
425 East McFetridge Drive
Chicago, Illinois 60605
(312) 294-2332

United States Masters Swimming
2 Peter Avenue
Rutland, Massachusetts
(508) 886-6631

United States Power Squadron
P.O. Box 6568
Richmond, Virginia 23230
(804) 355-6588

United States Swimming, Inc.
1750 East Boulder Street
Colorado Springs, Colorado 80909
(719) 578-4578

United States Synchronized Swimming
Pan American Plaza
201 South Capitol Avenue
Suite 510
Indianapolis, Indiana 46225
(317) 237-5700

World Water Park Association
P.O. Box 14826
Lenexa, Kansas 66285-4826
(913) 599-0300

YMCA of the U.S.A.
101 North Wacker Drive
Chicago, Illinois 60606
1-800-872-9622

YWCA of the U.S.A.
726 Broadway
New York, New York 10003
(212) 614-2700

APPENDIX B

Orientation to the facility

At some facilities, one part of job training is an orientation to the facility. This might be as simple as having the head lifeguard or facility manager walk with you through the facility and point out its features. However, even if this is not a part of your formal training, you can orient yourself to a facility by noting its characteristics and potential hazards.

Some of these features might be very obvious; others might seem so obscure that they do not matter. The better you know your facility, however, the easier it is to anticipate risks to patrons and thus, to prevent injury. Such knowledge can also help keep you from being injured.

The following kinds of information can serve as background in your efforts at injury prevention.

- The water depth at all areas of the pool. Knowing the pool's dimensions helps you anticipate the kinds of activities that are safe in the various sections of the pool.
- The size and shape of the pool. This might affect the number of lifeguards required and the kinds of zones possible for patron surveillance.
- Whether there are lane lines and lifelines. Lane lines can affect the types of patron activity permissible at one time. Lane lines and lifelines might be used as boundaries for zone coverage.
- Whether there are any blind spots based on facility design. Blind spots can result from the layout of the facility, the improper location of lifeguard stands, or the position of the sun or indoor lighting in relation to the position of the lifeguards.
- Whether the lifeguard stands are movable. This provides more flexibility in dealing with blind spots.
- Whether overflow troughs pose a hazard to anyone jumping off them or climbing on them.
- Whether the overflow troughs are so high above the water that they cause difficulty when you try to remove a victim from the water.

- Whether an entrance is near the deep end of the pool. Nonswimmers or weak swimmers may jump or dive into water over their heads.
- Whether an entrance is near the shallow end of the pool. Swimmers may jump or dive into water that is too shallow.
- Where diving from the deck is permitted and where it is not.
- Whether the diving area is part of the pool. Patrons pursuing different activities might interfere with each other.
- If there is a diving board, the size of the area where patrons can enter the water safely. This can help you identify unsafe diving patterns.
- Whether diving boards have movable fulcrums and whether they can be locked. Restricting the spring in diving boards can help reduce diving injuries.
- Whether diving blocks are located over deep water and whether they have covers to prevent unauthorized use.
- Whether there is a separate wading pool or kiddie area.
- What play structures there are and whether they are permanent or removable.
- Whether the facility has a spa.
- What means patrons have for entering and exiting the pool (steps, ladders, ramps, equipment for people with disabilities).
- Whether flooring material is slippery when wet, or even when it is dry.
- The location of emergency exits, as well as the point of entry for EMS personnel.
- The location of the telephone and any other equipment used for communication.
- The location of emergency and first aid equipment.
- The location of the first aid station.
- The location of restricted areas, such as filtration equipment and chemical storage.

APPENDIX C

Instructions for emergency telephone calls

Emergency Telephone Numbers [Dial _____ for outside line]

EMS _____ Fire _____ Police _____

Poison Control Center _____

Number of this telephone _____

Other Important Telephone Numbers

Facility manager _____ Telephone number_____

Facility maintenance _____ Telephone number_____

Chemical company _____ Telephone number_____

Power company _____ Telephone number_____

Weather bureau _____ Telephone number_____

Name and address of medical facility with 24-hour emergency cardiac care:

_____

Information for Emergency Call

(Be prepared to give this information to the EMS dispatcher.)

1. Location _____

   Street address _____

   City or town _____

   Directions (cross streets, roads, landmarks, etc.) _____

   _____

2. Telephone number from which the call is being made   5. How many people are injured

3. Caller's name   6. Condition of victim(s)

4. What happened   7. Help (first aid) being given

Note: Do not hang up first. Let the EMS dispatcher hang up first.

REFERENCES

American Alliance for Health, Physical Education, Recreation and Dance. *Safety Aquatics.* Sports Safety Series, Monograph #5. American Alliance for Health, Physical Education, Recreation and Dance, 1977.

The American National Red Cross. *Adapted Aquatics: Swimming for Persons With Physical or Mental Impairments.* Washington, D.C.: The American National Red Cross, 1977.

_____. *Basic Water Safety.* Washington, D.C.: The American National Red Cross, 1988.

_____. *Community First Aid and Safety.* St. Louis: Mosby, 1993.

_____. *CPR for the Professional Rescuer.* St. Louis: Mosby, 1993.

_____. *Emergency Water Safety.* Washington, D.C.: The American National Red Cross, 1988.

_____. *Lifeguarding.* Washington, D.C.: The American National Red Cross, 1990.

_____. *Safety Training for Swim Coaches.* Washington, D.C.: The American National Red Cross, 1988.

_____. *Swimming and Diving.* St. Louis: Mosby, 1992.

Armbruster, D.A.; Allen, R.H.; and Billingsley, H.S. *Swimming and Diving.* 6th ed. St. Louis: The C.V. Mosby Company, 1973.

Association for the Advancement of Health Education. "Counting the Victims." HE-XTRA 18 (1993):8.

Baker, S.P.; O'Neill, B.; and Karpf, R.S. *The Injury Fact Book.* Lexington, Massachusetts: Lexington Books, D.C. Heath and Co., 1984.

Beringer, G.B., et al. "Submersion Accidents and Epilepsy." *American Journal of Diseases of Children* 137 (1983):604-605.

Bruess, C.E.; Richardson, G.E.; and Laing, S.J. *Decisions for Health.* Dubuque, Iowa: William C. Brown Publishers, 1989.

Brown, V.R. "Spa Associated Hazards—An Update and Summary." Washington, D.C.: U.S. Consumer Product Safety Commission, 1981.

Clayton, R.D., and Thomas, D.G. *Professional Aquatic Management.* 2nd ed. Champaign, Illinois: Human Kinetics, 1989.

Centers for Disease Control and Prevention. "Drownings at U.S. Army Corps of Engineers Recreation Facilities, 1986-1990." *Morbidity and Mortality Weekly Report* 41 (1992):331-333.

_____. "Drownings in a Private Lake—North Carolina, 1981-1990." *Morbidity and Mortality Weekly Report* 41 (1992):329-331.

_____. "Suction-Drain Injury in a Public Wading Pool—North Carolina, 1991." *Morbidity and Mortality Weekly Report* 41 (1992):333-335.

_____. *Suggested Health and Safety Guidelines for Recreational Water Slide Flumes.* Atlanta, Georgia: U.S. Department of Health and Human Services.

_____. *Swimming Pools—Safety and Disease Control Through Proper Design and Operation.* Atlanta, Georgia: United States Department of Health, Education, and Welfare, 1976.

Chow, J.M. "Make a Splash: Children's Pools Attract All Ages." *Aquatics International* (1993):27-32.

Committee on Trauma Research; Commission on Life Sciences; National Research Council; and the Institute of Medicine. *Injury in America.* Washington, D.C.: National Academy Press, 1985.

Consumer Guide with Chasnoff, I.J.; Ellis, J.W.; and Fainman, Z.S. *The New Illustrated Family Medical & Health Guide.* Lincolnwood, Illinois: Publications International, Ltd., 1988.

Cooper, K.H. *The Aerobics Program For Total Well-Being.* New York: Bantam Books, 1982.

Council for National Cooperation in Aquatics. *Lifeguard Training: Principles and Administration.* New York: Association Press, 1973.

Craig, A.B., Jr. "Underwater Swimming and Loss of Consciousness." *The Journal of the American Medical Association* 176 (1961):255-258.

Ebben, *A. Pool Lifeguarding.* Studley, Warwickshire, England: The Royal Life Saving Society UK, 1993.

————. "Scanning, Supervising and Observing." *Lifeguard* 1 (1992):22-23.

Ellis, et al. *National Pool and Waterpark Lifeguard Training Manual.* Alexandria, Virginia: National Recreation and Park Association, 1993 and 1991.

Fife, D.; Scipio, S.; and Crane, G. "Fatal and Nonfatal Immersion Injuries Among New Jersey Residents." *American Journal of Preventive Medicine* 7 (1991):189-193.

Gabriel, J.L., editor. *U.S. Diving Safety Manual.* Indianapolis: U.S. Diving Publications, 1990.

Gabrielsen, M.A. "Diving Injuries: Prevention of the Most Catastrophic Sport Related Injuries." Presented to the Council for National Cooperation in Aquatics. Indianapolis, 1981.

————. *Swimming Pools: A Guide to Their Planning, Design, and Operation.* Champaign, Illinois: Human Kinetics, 1987.

Getchell, B.; Pippin, R.; and Varnes, J. *Health.* Boston: Houghton Mifflin Co., 1989.

Hedberg, K., et al. "Drownings in Minnesota, 1980-85: A Population-Based Study." *American Journal of Public Health* 80 (1990):1071-1074.

Huint, R. *Lifeguarding in the Waterparks.* Montreal: AquaLude, Inc., 1990.

Johnson, R.L. *YMCA Pool Operations Manual.* Champaign, Illinois: Human Kinetics, 1989.

Kowalsky, L., editor. *Pool-Spa Operators Handbook.* San Antonio, Texas: National Swimming Pool Foundation, 1990.

Lierman, T.L., editor. *Building a Healthy America: Conquering Disease and Disability.* New York: Mary Ann Liebert, Inc., Publishers, 1987.

Litovitz, T.L.; Schmitz, B.S.; and Holm, K.C. "1988 Annual Report of the American Association of Poison Control Centers National Data Collection System." *American Journal of Emergency Medicine* 7 (1989):496.

Livingston, S.; Pauli, L.L.; and Pruce, I. "Epilepsy and Drowning in Childhood." *British Medical Journal* 2 (1977):515-516.

Maglischo, E.W. *Swimming Even Faster.* Mountain View, California: Mayfield Publishing Company, 1993.

————. *Swimming Faster.* Palo Alto, California: Mayfield Publishing Company, 1982.

Marion Laboratories. *Osteoporosis: Is It in Your Future?* Kansas City, Marion Laboratories, 1984.

Mitchell, J. T. "Stress: The History, Status and Future of Critical Incident Stress Debriefings." *JEMS: Journal of Emergency Medical Services* 13 (1988):47-52.

Mitchell, J. T. "Stress and the Emergency Reponder." *JEMS: Journal of Emergency Medical Services* 15 (1987):55-57.

Modell, J.H. "Drowning." *New England Journal of Medicine* 328 (1993):253-256.

Murphy, M.M. *On the Guard.* Champaign, Illinois: Human Kinetics, 1986.

National Committee for Injury Prevention and Control. *Injury Prevention: Meeting the Challenge.* New York: Oxford University Press as a supplement to the *American Journal of Preventive Medicine,* Volume 5, Number 3, 1989.

National Safety Council. *Accident Facts, 1992 Edition.* Itasca, Illinois: National Safety Council, 1992.

National Safety Council and Thygerson, A.L., editors. *First Aid Essentials.* Boston: Jones and Bartlett Publishers, 1989.

National Spa and Pool Institute. *American National Standard for Public Swimming Pools.* Alexandria, Virginia: National Spa and Pool Institute, 1991.

National Spinal Cord Injury Center. *Annual Report.* Birmingham, Alabama: A Spinal Cord Injury Data Base at the University of Alabama at Birmingham, 1990.

_____. *Spinal Cord Injury: The Facts and Figures.* A Spinal Cord Injury Data Base at the University of Alabama at Birmingham, 1986.

New York State Department of Public Health. *Drownings at Regulated Bathing Facilities in New York State, 1987-1990.* Albany, NY: New York State Department of Health, 1990.

_____. *Lightning Safety Tips.* Albany, NY: New York State Department of Health, 1984.

Payne, W.A., and Hahn, D.B. *Understanding Your Health.* St. Louis: Mosby-Year Book, Inc., 1989.

O'Connor, J. "A U.S. Accidental Drowning Study, 1980-1984." Thesis, University of Oregon, 1986.

O'Donohoe, N.V. "What Should the Child With Epilepsy Be Allowed to Do?" *Archives of Disease in Childhood* 58 (1983):934-937.

Orlowski, J.P.; Rothner, A.D.; and Lueders, H. "Submersion Accidents in Children With Epilepsy." *American Journal of Diseases of Children* 136 (1982):777-780.

Palm, J. *Alert: Aquatic Supervision in Action.* Toronto, Canada: The Royal Life Saving Society Canada, 1978.

Pearn, J. "Epilepsy and Drowning in Childhood." *British Medical Journal* 1 (1977):1510-1511.

Pearn, J.; Bart, R.; and Yamaoka, R. "Drowning Risks to Epileptic Children: A Study From Hawaii." *British Medical Journal* 2 (1978):1284-1285.

Pia, F. "Observations on the Drowning of Nonswimmers" *Journal of Physical Education* (July 1974): 164-167.

Pia, F. *On Drowning,* Water Safety Films, Inc. (1970).

Pia, F. "Reducing Swimming Related Drowning Fatalities" *Pennsylvania Recreation and Parks* (Spring 1991): 13-16.

Pia, F. "The RID Factor as a Cause of Drowning" *Parks and Recreation* (June 1984): 52-67.

Quan, L., and Gomez, A. "Swimming Pool Safety—An Effective Submersion Prevention Program." *Journal of Environmental Health* 52 (1990):344-346.

Rice, D.P.; MacKenzie, E.J.; et al. *Cost of Injury in the United States: a Report to Congress 1989.* San Francisco, California: Institute for Health and Aging, University of California, and Injury Prevention Center, The Johns Hopkins University, 1989.

Robertson, L.S. *Injury Epidemiology.* New York: Oxford University Press, 1992.

Royal Life Saving Society Canada. *Canadian Life Saving Manual.* Toronto, Canada: The Royal Life Saving Society Canada, 1973.

Strauss, R.H., editor. *Sports Medicine.* Philadelphia: W.B. Saunders Co., 1984.

Torney, J.A., and Clayton, R.D. *Aquatic Instruction, Coaching and Management.* Minneapolis: Burgess Publishing Co., 1970.

_____. *Aquatic Organization and Management.* Minneapolis, Minnesota: Burgess Publishing Co., 1981.

United States Lifesaving Association. *Lifesaving and Marine Safety.* Piscataway, New Jersey: New Century Publishers, Inc., 1981.

Wintemute, G.J., et al. "The Epidemiology of Drowning in Adulthood: Implications for Prevention." *American Journal of Preventive Medicine* 4 (1988):343-348.

World Waterpark Association. *Considerations for Operating Safety.* Lenexa, Kansas: World Waterpark Association, 1991.

_____. *The Aquatic Facility Operator Manual.* The National Recreation and Park Association, National Aquatic Section, 1992.

INDEX

MISSION OF THE AMERICAN RED CROSS

The American Red Cross, a humanitarian organization led by volunteers and guided by its Congressional Charter and the Fundamental Principles of the International Red Cross Movement, will provide relief to victims of disaster and help people prevent, prepare for, and respond to emergencies.

ABOUT THE AMERICAN RED CROSS

To support the mission of the American Red Cross, over 1.3 million paid and volunteer staff serve in some 1,600 chapters and blood centers throughout the United States and its territories and on military installations around the world. Supported by the resources of a national organization, they form the largest volunteer service and educational force in the nation. They serve families and communities through blood services, disaster relief and preparedness education, services to military family members in crisis, and health and safety education.

The American Red Cross provides consistent, reliable education and training in injury and illness prevention and emergency care, providing training to nearly 16 million people each year in first aid, CPR, swimming, water safety, and HIV/AIDS education.

All of these essential services are made possible by the voluntary services, blood and tissue donations, and financial support of the American people.

FUNDAMENTAL PRINCIPLES OF THE INTERNATIONAL RED CROSS AND RED CRESCENT MOVEMENT

HUMANITY

IMPARTIALITY

NEUTRALITY

INDEPENDENCE

VOLUNTARY SERVICE

UNITY

UNIVERSALITY